CICS Essentials

CICS Essentials

For Application Developers and Programmers

Joseph J. Le Bert

McGraw-Hill, Inc.
New York St. Louis San Francisco Auckland Bogotá
Caracas Lisbon London Madrid Mexico City Milan
Montreal New Delhi San Juan Singapore
Sydney Tokyo Toronto

Library of Congress Cataloging-in-Publication Data

Le Bert, Joseph J.
     CICS essentials for application developers and programmers / by
   Joseph J. Le Bert.

       p.   cm.
     Includes bibliographical references and index.
     ISBN 0-07-035869-9
     1. CICS   (Computer system)   I. Title.
   QA76.76.T45L39   1993b
   005.4'3—dc20   92-33854
                                                          CIP

6 7 8 9 10 11 12 13 14 BKMBKM 9 9 8 7

ISBN 0-07-035869-9

*The editor for this book was Carol J. Amato, the managing editor was
Lori Flaherty, the designer was Jaclyn J. Boone, and the production
supervisor was Katherine G. Brown. This book was set in Century
Schoolbook. It was composed by TAB Books.*

*For more information about other McGraw-Hill materials,
call 1-800-2-MCGRAW in the United States. In other
countries, call your nearest McGraw-Hill office.*

To my wife, Maryann, who encouraged me, and my children Joseph, Dorothy, and Jean, who inspired me.

Contents

Acknowledgments

CICS Essentials contains much information gathered through experience and contact with knowledgeable associates. I am grateful for the help obtained from the numerous proofreaders of my earlier books, *CICS Made Easy* and *CICS for Microcomputers*. I am especially grateful to Art Benson for sharing his experience in DB2 and SQL with me in making the chapter on those topics possible. I appreciate the constructive suggestions of my proofreaders and contributors, including Ralph Barone, Susan Jackson, Mike McNamara, Anthony Russoniello, and Ron Witt. I especially wish to thank Daniel Mok, who technically edited the manuscript and made numerous constructive suggestions regarding the new material. Concepts and examples of the use of transient data queues were obtained from associates Marisu Rodriguez and Andy Bologovsky.

I appreciate my daughter Dorothy's patience and accuracy in typing the entire manuscript with my numerous changes. Most of all, I want to thank my wife Maryann and children Joseph, Dorothy, and Jean for their patience and understanding for the countless times that I was home but not with them.

Finally, I would like to thank Jay Ranade, my series editor, who encouraged, supported, and assisted me in my efforts to write this updated text.

Introduction

CICS, like COBOL itself, continues to be enhanced internally and at the programmer interface level. It is still the online transaction processing software of choice for most large companies, and should maintain its leading role for the foreseeable future. Many enhancements have been made to CICS since my original book *CICS Made Easy* was published in 1986. All material in the original text is still applicable today, but much of it is obsolete. For instance, the RESP option eliminates the need to use the HANDLE CONDITION command. RESP is used in place of HANDLE CONDITION as appropriate in all program examples in this text.

Audience

Originally targeted to those new to CICS, this text has been enhanced so that it is also an excellent reference for experienced application developers and programmers. It should increase CICS knowledge and improve productivity for data processing consultants, application developers, project leaders, systems analysts, programmer analysts, and programmers. Technical writers, colleges, schools of continuing education, and commercial programming schools can also benefit. Owners of the first edition will want a copy of the revised edition to keep their reference current.

CICS Essentials should prove invaluable to data processing consultants and others who need to learn and review CICS using VSAM and different databases. VSAM file access, as well as the use of SQL with DB2 or CA-DATACOM/DB, IMS-DL/I using DL/I Calls and EXEC DLI commands, and native CA-DATACOM/DB are explained. All program examples in this book are converted from VSAM to various databases. VS COBOL II commands and concepts are explained and used to convert all programs presented in the book from OS/VS COBOL to VS COBOL II.

What You Need to Know

A knowledge of COBOL and of VSAM files enhances the understanding of all readers of this book. Nontechnical personnel can get a general understanding of how CICS functions by reading the earlier chapters of the text. A basic knowledge of databases is not necessary but would aid in understanding the use of CICS with the databases presented in later chapters of the book.

All material in this text has been rewritten and enhanced as appropriate. All CICS commands have been presented as relevant with syntax for move mode, locate mode, and for VS COBOL II.

Online systems, which send, receive, and process data via a terminal, are here to stay and will soon exceed the number of batch systems in many companies. CICS makes it easy for a programmer to code instructions that facilitate online functions. The more you learn about CICS, the better prepared you are to play a significant role in the transition from batch to online systems.

CICS Essentials illustrates techniques and concepts through numerous simple examples and programs. Designers and programmers using this text should become productive very quickly. The programs in the examples employ a simple structured programming style that eliminates most GO TOs without confusing you with numerous nested IF statements. The examples can serve as models for future programs and should result in increased programmer productivity.

Many CICS concepts and examples in the text are associated with COBOL commands and techniques with which you are familiar. The best way to learn anything is through examples and use; you will master these principles quite easily by using them when writing and testing your own programs.

Online systems have been around for many years. The importance of their use should continue to increase for the foreseeable future. Without knowledgeable and competent data processing personnel and users, this increase in the use of CICS will not occur smoothly. I hope this book will be successful in preparing you for the role you will play in putting your company online.

Joseph J. Le Bert

1

The User's View
of a CICS System

CICS (Customer Information Control System) is an IBM database/data-communication (DB/DC) system. CICS makes it easy to send, receive, and process data through interaction with a terminal that consists of a display unit or cathode-ray tube (CRT) and a keyboard. CICS runs on IBM and IBM-compatible mainframe and microcomputer systems and provides an interface between application programs and the computer's operating system. It functions like an online operating system. CICS application programmers use command-level COBOL to code easy-to-use instructions into their programs. These commands facilitate accessing and updating online database files, data entry, and display of data and other information on the display terminal. Users of CICS can transmit data from their terminals to the system where the data is processed and then sent back to the user.

Hands-on experience is important when learning a new system. Because a terminal is not available for a demonstration, this book uses pictures called *maps* on simulated 3270 terminal screens to illustrate CICS.

CICS, like most data processing, has its own jargon, which are explained as they arise. Familiarize yourself with your terminal keyboard; most are similar to typewriter keyboards, with some models containing additional keys that are used in combination with a primary key.

Terminal Keyboard Usage

The terminal keyboard keys referred to in this book are those found on a 3270 keyboard.

Attention IDentifier (AID) keys

- ENTER—This is the most commonly used key; it is usually pressed in order to effect the transfer of data from a terminal into a program. A program can test if this key or another key was pressed in order to control the flow of its logic.

- CLEAR—Use this key to terminate a session on the terminal. When the terminal operator is finished, the CLEAR key is pressed causing the program to display the message SESSION COMPLETED. This is a programmer-defined action, not a standard function.

- PFXX—Program function (PF) keys effect the transfer of data from a terminal into a program. They act as signals or switches set external to the program by keys on the terminal keyboard. PF keys can be used by a program to control the sequence of its logic. There are up to 24 PF keys, designated as PF1 through PF24.

- PAX—Program attention (PA) keys are similar to PF keys, but they do not cause the transfer of data from a terminal into a program as the ENTER and PF keys do. There are three PA keys: PA1, PA2, and PA3. Some systems use them as a signal to end a session or to transfer control to a previously displayed screen. Not all terminals are equipped with three PA keys.

Miscellaneous keys

- ALT—The ALTernate or shift key is used on some keyboards in conjunction with the CLEAR, PF, or PA keys in much the same fashion as the shift key is used on a typewriter.

- TAB—The TAB key is used to position the cursor to a specific location on the screen. It moves the cursor across the terminal screen in a left-to-right, top-to-bottom sequence, stopping at designated fields.

- EOF—The erase-to-End-of-Field (EOF) key erases data in a specific field on the screen, from the point of the cursor position to the end of the field.

Screen Format

Figure 1.1 shows the format used for all screen illustrations presented in this book. These displays consist of 24 lines and 80 columns. The screen is a grid in which line 1, column 1 represents screen position 1; line 1, column 2 position 2; line 2, column 1 position 81; line 3, column 1 position 161, etc. Screens for 3270 terminals contain a total of 1920 positions (24 lines by 80 columns). Screen position 1920 represents line 24, column 80.

```
1...5...10...15...20...25...30...35...40...45...50...55...60...65...70...75...80
```

Fig. 1.1 Screen layout for 3270 terminal.

Screen Classifications

Most examples are based on a simplified purchasing system. Menu programs are discussed as are vendor file inquiry and maintenance programs. Maintenance programs are presented for vendor file additions, changes, and deletions. A vendor file browse program illustrates how to scroll backward and forward through a file. You might encounter combined maintenance programs that perform all maintenance and inquiry functions.

Program maintenance is easier when there are individual maintenance programs, one for each function. This approach is employed in the program examples in this book. It is easier to restrict access to users, if required by your security system, when you have a separate program for each function. Your installation standards and system requirements will determine which approach you will take.

Screens used by CICS programs usually fall into one of our categories. They are discussed in more detail later in this chapter.

1. Menu or submenu screens are selection displays used to make a choice to initiate a desired function. Figure 1.2 is an example of a menu screen. A submenu, shown in Fig. 1.4, takes one of the functions shown on a menu and breaks it down into subfunctions.

2. Control screens are used by the user to enter a record key, which is used in inquiry and maintenance functions. The key entered on the control

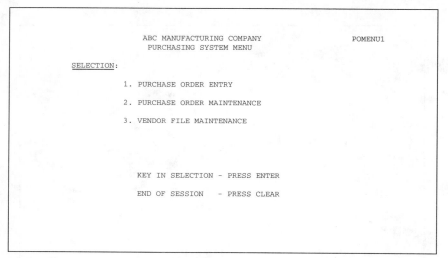

```
                    ABC MANUFACTURING COMPANY              POMENU1
                    PURCHASING SYSTEM MENU

        SELECTION:

              1. PURCHASE ORDER ENTRY

              2. PURCHASE ORDER MAINTENANCE

              3. VENDOR FILE MAINTENANCE




              KEY IN SELECTION - PRESS ENTER

              END OF SESSION   - PRESS CLEAR
```

Fig. 1.2 Purchasing system menu screen.

screen is used to format the detail screen, which is usually displayed next by the program. Figure 1.5 is an example of a control screen.

3. Detail screens are used to display or to facilitate the entry of data into a program during inquiry and maintenance functions. At the completion of the inquiry or maintenance function, control is passed back to the control screen. Figures 1.6 through 1.10 are typical detail screens.

4. Browse screens permit the terminal operator to view many occurrences of similar data, such as scrolling through a vendor file, as shown in Fig. 1.11.

The CICS program screens used in the examples in this chapter are not the only types of screens you will encounter. Some designers do not use control screens; they prefer to enter the key directly on the detail screen as is done on the browse screen in Fig. 1.11. Control screens are employed, for ease of understanding, in all other programs in this book. The method you employ in your design might be determined by standards in effect at your installation. CICS commands and concepts are basically the same regardless of the screen design you use.

Types of CICS Systems

Most companies have two types of CICS systems: a test system and a production system.

Test system

The test system is used to develop and enhance new and existing systems and programs. Test files might contain all of the records or only a subset of the records actually contained on the production system file, but they are representative of the production file. Do not rush programs through the test system without thoroughly testing them. It is difficult to explain to knowledgeable users why a program moved from the test system to the production system is not functioning properly.

Production system

Systems and programs that have been thoroughly tested and are error-free (hopefully) are put into the production system. This system is used for everyday online operations. Errors in design or programming not caught by the test system before programs are promoted to the production system can be a source of embarrassment to the data processing department.

Promotion from Test to Production

Moving or copying a program from the test to production system is often referred to as *promotion*. The interaction between the user and the system is the same for the test and production systems. Generally, users operate the test system until convinced that a program is error-free, then signs off on the program and authorizes its promotion to the production system. The program and map load modules, as appropriate, are then moved from the test to production load libraries. The program or map is also moved to the appropriate source program management library, which contains source code written by the programmer. This code is compiled to create an executable load module.

User Involvement

One major advantage of CICS is that users or user-interface personnel are required to get heavily involved in the development and testing of a system. High-quality work is essential, because, once a program is promoted, it might be accessed by users all across the country. The image of a system, or the reputation of data processing, is not enhanced if the system fails to function as expected.

Batch systems, in which all data is grouped and entered into an input file before a program is run, sometimes encounter an abnormal termination (ABEND). The error can be fixed and the program rerun without the user ever knowing a problem existed. Depending on the system, an ABEND of an online program could trigger calls from users all across the country. The frequently heard complaint, "There is never time to do it right the first time, but always time to correct it" should never be said of the work of the online designer/programmer.

Getting on the CICS System

The procedure for logging on to a CICS system is generally similar from one installation to another. Screens displayed by the system during the log-on/sign-on procedure are not shown here because they vary. To log on to the CICS system, the user may press the CLEAR key in order to clear the screen and set the cursor at position 1; key in TESTCICS, PRODCICS, or a similar entry; then press ENTER to get connected to the requested CICS system. An indicative message, such as TEST CICS SYSTEM, may be returned on the screen. Clear the screen and you are ready to sign on to CICS.

Key in a designated sign on transaction identifier in screen positions 1 through 4 and press ENTER; a screen is displayed requiring the entry of the user's name and password (assigned by each installation). Key in these entries and then press ENTER. The password is usually not displayed for security reasons.

If the name and password keyed in are valid entries, a message indicating that the sign-on is complete is displayed; otherwise, an error message is displayed. Error messages usually appear when the terminal operator keys in a name or password incorrectly. If this occurs, the user just clears the screen and restarts the sign on procedure.

Many installations have multi-session managers that enable you to sign on and then toggle between the test and production systems, as well as other applications, by pressing a designated program function key.

Initiating a CICS Transaction

After signing on and clearing the terminal's screen, you are ready to key in a TRANSaction IDentifier (TRANSID). The TRANSID is a key that searches a CICS table to determine which program to access. Some installations have several TRANSIDs a user can enter. Others have a general purpose menu from which applications are selected. A TRANSID is a one- to four-character code (usually four) that is keyed into screen positions 1 through 4 during a session in order to start a CICS transaction when an AID key, generally ENTER, is pressed. A *session*, which can consist of one or several programs being executed, is the period of time between signing on to the CICS system and the time a terminal operator signs off the CICS system.

Logging off CICS

When all CICS sessions are completed, a user is usually required to log off. This is accomplished by clearing the screen, keying in an appropriate sign off TRANSID, and pressing ENTER. The logging off procedure might be different if your installation uses a multi-session manager to perform its log on and log off.

Typical CICS Session

Sign on to CICS and clear the screen; you are now ready to start a session. Key in the TRANSID POMU and press ENTER; this TRANSID initiates the program, which displays the purchasing system menu map illustrated in Fig. 1.2. A map is a formatted screen identified in this book by the mapname in the upper-right corner of the screen (POMENU1 in Fig. 1.2). Maps are explained thoroughly in future chapters.

Purchasing System Menu

Menu programs have as their primary purpose the display of two or more options on a screen from which the one desired can be selected. Typically, a selection number or letter is keyed in and ENTER is pressed to start the program.

The purchasing system menu (Fig. 1.2) lists three selections, numbered 1, 2, and 3. The user should enter the selection number at the cursor, which is positioned to the right of SELECTION: (shown by an underscore in Fig. 1.2).

Erroneous menu entries

What would happen if the user:

- Entered a character other than a 1, 2, or 3?
- Pressed the CLEAR key?
- Pressed an invalid AID key, such as a PA or PF key?
- Pressed ENTER without keying in a selection?

The following list explains what would happen in each instance.

- Figure 1.3 illustrates what happens if a 4 or any other invalid character is entered. A programmer-defined message is displayed at the bottom of the screen, which is brighter than the rest of the screen's constants and data. Messages are usually displayed in a conversational fashion, notifying the operator of action taken or required. Generally, map line 24 is reserved for operator-notification messages. Some applications might require more than one message line at the bottom of a map, perhaps lines 23 and 24.

- For examples in this book, when the CLEAR key is pressed, the screen is cleared, then the message SESSION COMPLETED is displayed starting at position 1 of the screen.

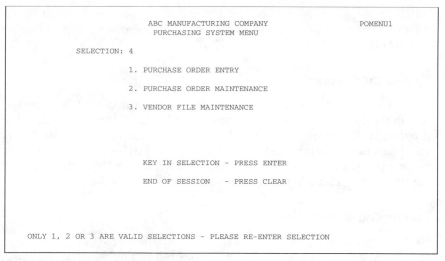

```
                    ABC MANUFACTURING COMPANY                 POMENU1
                    PURCHASING SYSTEM MENU

         SELECTION: 4

                 1. PURCHASE ORDER ENTRY

                 2. PURCHASE ORDER MAINTENANCE

                 3. VENDOR FILE MAINTENANCE




                    KEY IN SELECTION - PRESS ENTER

                    END OF SESSION   - PRESS CLEAR




      ONLY 1, 2 OR 3 ARE VALID SELECTIONS - PLEASE RE-ENTER SELECTION
```

Fig. 1.3 Invalid entry on menu screen.

- Pressing an invalid AID key would result in a programmer-defined high-lighted message being displayed at the bottom of the screen. The message displayed on line 24 of the menu screen in examples in this book is:

  ```
  ENTER AND CLEAR KEYS ARE ONLY VALID KEYS - PLEASE TRY AGAIN
  ```

- If ENTER is pressed without keying in a selection, the following high-lighted message appears on line 24 of the menu screen:

  ```
  NO SELECTION WAS MADE - PLEASE ENTER SELECTION CODE
  ```

Valid operator menu selection

Normally, the user makes a valid selection and presses ENTER, causing a transfer of control to the selected program. The system could be designed to display a default selection, perhaps a 1 next to SELECTION:. For our example, the user keys in a 3 next to SELECTION: and presses ENTER, causing the display shown in Fig. 1.4, the vendor file maintenance submenu screen.

If the user entered a 1 on this screen and pressed ENTER, the vendor file inquiry control screen shown in Fig. 1.5 would be displayed. The submenu shown in Fig. 1.4 could have been combined with the purchasing system menu shown in Fig. 1.2.

Generally, several options are available when designing a system. Sometimes a primary menu has so many entries that there is not adequate room to include submenu fields for all items.

The cursor in Fig. 1.5 is initially located at the first position of the vendor code entry field, ready for the terminal operator to key in a code. The user can key in, for example, X-9234-1, and press the ENTER key to display the vendor file inquiry detail screen shown in Fig. 1.6. The message section at the bottom of the control screen (see Fig. 1.5) can show, depending on the key pressed, the following messages:

```
INVALID KEY PRESSED - PLEASE TRY AGAIN


VENDOR CODE MUST BE ENTERED - PLEASE KEY IN


VENDOR CODE FORMAT MUST BE: A-9999-9 - PLEASE REENTER


VENDOR RECORD NOT ON FILE
```

Ending a Session

All programs in this book end a CICS session by having the user press the CLEAR key. The screen clears and the message SESSION COMPLETED is displayed starting in position 1 of the screen.

A session can be terminated by leaving a cleared screen, but this sometimes leaves the user wondering if the session was ended properly. Displaying SESSION COMPLETED leaves no doubt; it is more positive. Programs can be written to end a session based on any designated AID key being pressed.

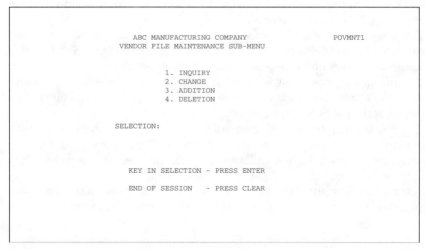

```
                 ABC MANUFACTURING COMPANY                 POVMNT1
                 VENDOR FILE MAINTENANCE SUB-MENU


                     1. INQUIRY
                     2. CHANGE
                     3. ADDITION
                     4. DELETION


           SELECTION:



              KEY IN SELECTION - PRESS ENTER

              END OF SESSION   - PRESS CLEAR
```

Fig. 1.4 Vendor file maintenance submenu screen.

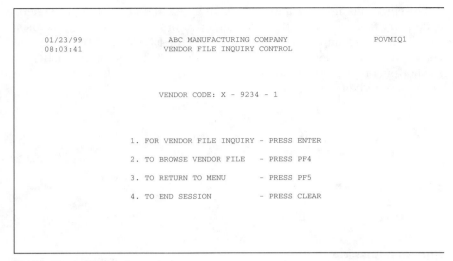

Fig. 1.5 Vendor file inquiry control screen.

Inquiry Function

An online inquiry function refers to the act of displaying an inquiry screen that shows data contained on one or several database records. If the user presses the ENTER key and the code entered in Fig. 1.5 is on the vendor file, the map named POVMIQ2 shown in Fig. 1.6 is displayed. The map shows all significant fields in the vendor master record for vendor code X-9234-1. Remember, I am using simplified examples—your vendor master record would most likely have additional or different fields.

The user can view all fields on the vendor file inquiry detail screen but cannot modify any fields on this screen. (Some systems have been designed to combine inquiry and changes.) The ability to view the current file status online has limited the number of batch reports needed by users. Batch reports reflect only the status of a file at some point in the past, while online inquiries reflect a file's current status.

The inquiry map in Fig. 1.6 prompts the user for the desired action with the instructions at the lower part of the screen. The only message likely to display would appear only if an invalid key was pressed. It might read: IN-VALID KEY PRESSED - PLEASE TRY AGAIN.

After an inquiry, the user can return to the inquiry control screen (map-name POVMIQ1, see Fig. 1.5) to enter another code. Depending upon the

AID key pressed, the program can also return to the vendor file maintenance submenu or end the session.

Maintenance Functions

File maintenance functions refer to the act of adding, changing, or deleting an individual record. Additions, changes, and deletions are maintenance functions that can be performed using an online system. Two types of online systems are:

1. *Online real-time system.* In a real-time system, the file being maintained is updated immediately when a change is entered by a user.

2. *Online data entry.* Data is entered online but does not immediately change the master file. Data might be written to an intermediate file and later processed by a different online transaction, or it might be run through a batch program in order to perform file updating.

All transactions in this book use a real-time system. This system allows the user to immediately see the results of any changes made to a file and to make corrections if required. Permitting users to make maintenance changes directly to a file or to enter transactions which later affect the data

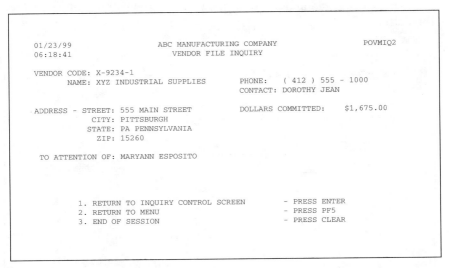

```
01/23/99                    ABC MANUFACTURING COMPANY                    POVMIQ2
06:18:41                       VENDOR FILE INQUIRY

VENDOR CODE: X-9234-1
       NAME: XYZ INDUSTRIAL SUPPLIES       PHONE:   ( 412 ) 555 - 1000
                                           CONTACT: DOROTHY JEAN

ADDRESS - STREET: 555 MAIN STREET          DOLLARS COMMITTED:    $1,675.00
           CITY: PITTSBURGH
          STATE: PA PENNSYLVANIA
            ZIP: 15260

TO ATTENTION OF: MARYANN ESPOSITO




       1. RETURN TO INQUIRY CONTROL SCREEN      - PRESS ENTER
       2. RETURN TO MENU                        - PRESS PF5
       3. END OF SESSION                        - PRESS CLEAR
```

Fig. 1.6 Vendor file inquiry detail screen.

in that file, places the responsibility for file integrity on the user. Systems might have many users entering data at various locations, and some files are constantly being added to, changed, and deleted from. Online systems are usually more accurate than batch systems for the following reasons:

- Transactions are usually entered by persons familiar with the input data, so there is less chance of interpretation errors.
- Data can be updated immediately in the desired files. It is not necessary to wait until later that evening or for several days.
- Data entry errors are often caught by the user and corrected immediately.
- Online systems can have many program edit checks built into them. For instance, if a vendor does not exist or is entered incorrectly, the system would detect the error and prompt the user to make a correction immediately.

Additions

Additions involve adding a new record to an existing file. On a vendor file addition control screen, similar to the inquiry control screen in Fig. 1.5, you could key in the vendor to be added and press ENTER to display the addition detail screen. The map in Fig. 1.7 displays, showing the fields with underlines, into which the user enters the required data. The underlines are not usually displayed and are only shown here to illustrate the fields and their size.

```
 01/23/99                ABC MANUFACTURING COMPANY              POVMAD2
 10:11:06                   VENDOR FILE ADDITION

VENDOR CODE: A-0100-1
      NAME: _____  PHONE:  (_____) ____ - ____
                                         CONTACT:  _____

ADDRESS - STREET: _____
          CITY: _____
          STATE: ____
           ZIP: _____

TO ATTENTION OF: _____




          1. ADDITIONS, KEY-IN REQUIRED DATA      - PRESS ENTER
          2. RETURN TO ADDITION CONTROL SCREEN    - PRESS PF3
          3. RETURN TO MENU                       - PRESS PF5
          4. END OF SESSION                       - PRESS CLEAR
```

Fig. 1.7 Vendor file additions detail screen.

The system assumes that all fields except CONTACT: and TO ATTEN-TION OF: require data to be entered. A program can edit each required field before it is entered into the file as an addition. Some fields need only to be checked for the presence of data. Other fields might be required to be numeric, have a valid state code, or perhaps contain a valid zip code.

Entering data on a screen. When a map such as that shown in Fig. 1.7 is displayed, the cursor is normally positioned at the first data entry field (NAME). Pressing the TAB key causes the cursor to move across the screen from left to right, top to bottom, stopping at the beginning of each data entry field. After the user tabs to the last field, pressing the TAB key again positions the cursor at the start of the first field to be entered.

Fields of fixed length, such as PHONE, STATE, and ZIP, when completely entered, cause the cursor to skip automatically to the next field. Remember the cursor moves left to right, top to bottom when you enter data (i.e., from NAME, to PHONE, to CONTACT, to STREET, to CITY, etc.).

Data-entry error indicators. A programmer has several methods to indicate data entry errors. Each of the following techniques displays an indicative message on line 24 of the screen and positions the cursor at the first field in error.

■ Display field identifiers are brighter than those of correctly entered fields. Field identifiers as used here refer to the descriptions preceding each data entry field, such as NAME, PHONE, and CONTACT (see Fig. 1.8).

■ Display the erroneous data field itself at a brighter intensity than correctly entered fields. The drawback is that if a user fails to key in an entry and that is the error, there is no data to highlight. Some users of this method move question marks or asterisks to a nonentry field.

■ Display one or more messages at the bottom of the screen without any highlighting of error fields or field identifiers. The drawback to this method is that when multiple errors occur, it is not always practical to display all error messages at once.

This book uses the first technique of brightening all erroneous field identifiers and positioning the cursor at the start of the first incorrect field. A highlighted message is displayed at the bottom of the screen, notifying the user to PLEASE CORRECT HIGHLIGHTED FIELDS.

Key in all required data on the screen (see Fig. 1.7), and following the instructions at the bottom of the map, press ENTER to record the addition. Assume three fields were entered incorrectly. The field identifiers of the three fields would be brightened and the message PLEASE CORRECT HIGH-LIGHTED FIELDS is displayed at the bottom of the screen as shown in Fig.

```
01/23/99                    ABC MANUFACTURING COMPANY                    POVMAD2
03:09:09                       VENDOR FILE ADDITION

VENDOR CODE: X-9234-1
        NAME: XYZ INDUSTRIAL SUPPLIES        PHONE:   ( 412 ) TTT - 1000
                                             CONTACT: DOROTHY JEAN

ADDRESS - STREET: 555 MAIN STREET
            CITY: PITTSBURGH
           STATE: 61
             ZIP: P5260

TO ATTENTION OF: MARYANN ESPOSITO




        1. ADDITIONS, KEY-IN REQUIRED DATA      - PRESS ENTER
        2. RETURN TO ADDITION CONTROL SCREEN    - PRESS PF3
        3. RETURN TO MENU                       - PRESS PF5
        4. END OF SESSION                       - PRESS CLEAR


   PLEASE CORRECT HIGHLIGHTED FIELDS
```

Fig. 1.8 Errors on vendor file additions detail screen.

1.8.

If only two of the three errors were corrected and you pressed ENTER again, only the field identifier of the one remaining incorrect item is highlighted. The two correct fields now have their field identifiers displayed at a normal intensity. The same notification message is displayed at the bottom of the screen.

When the final error is resolved and the operator presses ENTER, the record is added to the file and the addition control screen is displayed. The message displayed at the bottom of the control screen is RECORD SUC-CESSFULLY ADDED. The user can now perform an inquiry against the new record to see if it was added correctly. The change or delete function can be initiated if the addition was incorrect.

When entering data, an error sometimes cannot be resolved or it is decided not to add the record. If this occurs, the user has several options, as shown by the instructions at the bottom of the screen in Fig. 1.8:

- Return to the control screen.
- Return to the menu.
- End the session.

Changes

In data processing, there is only one thing that you can be sure of—changes! Change is a certainty; therefore, all systems, programs, files, etc., should be designed with built-in flexibility. The vendor file has an associated change function that enables a user to change any field in the record except for the vendor code and the dollars committed.

After adding a vendor record, you might realize that some of the data was entered incorrectly or that it requires a change. The vendor code would be entered on a control screen and ENTER pressed in order to display the change detail screen. The system then displays the change detail map shown in Fig. 1.9. The spaces before and after the area code field and other fields are actually occupied by screen attribute characters, which are discussed in chapters 2 and 6. The cursor is initially located at the first position of the vendor NAME field. Press TAB to position the cursor at the start of any field requiring a change, then enter the new data.

You can alter as many fields as required on the changes screen. When all changes have been entered, the instructions at the bottom of the screen direct you to press ENTER to record the change(s). The change control screen then displays the notification CHANGE COMPLETED SUCCESSFULLY in the message section at the bottom of the screen if no errors were detected. The message PLEASE CORRECT HIGHLIGHTED FIELDS continues to appear at the bottom of the change detail screen until the changes are made correctly or the function is ended by pressing one of the other AID keys.

Deletions

Records are sometimes added in error or become obsolete after a period of

```
01/23/99                  ABC MANUFACTURING COMPANY              POVMCH2
04:03:11                      VENDOR FILE CHANGES


VENDOR CODE: A-0100-1
        NAME: AA INDUSTRIAL SUPPLIES      PHONE:   ( 301 ) 555 - 1000
                                          CONTACT: JEAN CATHERINE


ADDRESS - STREET: 555 HUDSON STREET
           CITY: NEWARK
          STATE: NJ NEW JERSEY
            ZIP: 07102


  TO ATTENTION OF: JOSEPH RAYMOND




        1. CHANGES, KEY-IN NEW DATA           - PRESS ENTER
        2. RETURN TO CHANGES CONTROL SCREEN   - PRESS PF3
        3. RETURN TO MENU                     - PRESS PF5
        4. END OF SESSION                     - PRESS CLEAR
```

Fig. 1.9 Vendor file changes detail screen.

```
01/23/99                    ABC MANUFACTURING COMPANY                        POVMDL2
05:23:54                       VENDOR FILE DELETION

VENDOR CODE: A-0100-1
        NAME: AA INDUSTRIAL SUPPLIES          PHONE:   ( 301 ) 555 - 1000
                                              CONTACT: JEAN CATHERINE

ADDRESS - STREET: 555 HUDSON STREET
            CITY: NEWARK
           STATE: NJ NEW JERSEY
             ZIP: 07102

TO ATTENTION OF: JOSEPH RAYMOND




        1. DELETIONS VERIFY DATA BEFORE DELETING    - PRESS ENTER
        2. RETURN TO DELETION CONTROL SCREEN        - PRESS PF3
        3. RETURN TO MENU                           - PRESS PF5
        4. END OF SESSION                           - PRESS CLEAR
```

Fig. 1.10 Vendor file deletions detail screen.

time. These records can be purged or deleted by a batch program or online. Our system allows the online deletion of records from the vendor master file.

The code of the vendor to be deleted is entered on a control screen and ENTER is pressed to display the delete detail screen. The vendor deletion detail screen (Fig. 1.10) is displayed. The first instruction at the lower part of the screen directs you to verify data before deleting. When the data has been checked to verify that you have the right record, press ENTER to finalize the delete. The next display would be that of the delete control screen with the message RECORD DELETED SUCCESSFULLY displayed at the bottom of the screen.

Browse Function

The browse function, like the inquiry function, is not a maintenance function, but it is often helpful to include it on a control screen as shown in Fig. 1.5. A browse is a sequential search of a file, starting at the key passed to the browse program. For example, if you wanted to search the vendor file for a code beginning with S, you would enter one character, an S, in the vendor code entry field on the control screen (see Fig. 1.5) and press PF4 to start the browse function.

The browse function will display the vendor file browse map shown in Fig. 1.11. Because you entered only one character, the browse starts its sequential search with the first vendor record beginning with an S. If you were searching for a vendor named Smith Brothers Parts, which is near the middle of the S records, it wouldn't be advisable to start your browse at the beginning of the S records. You would have to read half of the S records before reaching the desired record. This would not only be a waste of time, because sequential file searches are slow, but it would also tie up computer resources by requiring numerous unnecessary file reads.

Try to limit the scope of browse searches. Limit your search by trial and error. For instance, when searching for Smith, enter S-5 as the first two characters on the control screen (see Fig. 1.5) before initiating the browse (S-5000-0 should be near the middle of the S records). If S-5 is much greater than or less than the code of the desired vendor, reset the browse. Key in a new start browse code, a full or partial code on the bottom of the vendor file browse map (Fig. 1.11), next to the field identifier RESET VENDOR CODE;, and press PF9. For instance, try S-4, S-6, S-45, or S-55. Partial key searches of a file are referred to as *generic* searches.

After displaying a full map of vendor browse data, the user has several options corresponding to the instructions at the bottom of Fig. 1.11.

■ Press PF8, which is commonly used for forward paging, to display the next page of sequential vendor browse data. The display of succeeding pages of data can be continued by pressing PF8. The browse process of paging forward and backward is often referred to as *scrolling*. Try to be as consistent as possible in the use of function keys in all systems at your installation.

■ Press PF7, which is commonly used for backward paging, to display the

```
     01/23/99                    ABC MANUFACTURING COMPANY                    POVMBR1
     05:35:32                       VENDOR FILE BROWSE
        VENDOR CD  VENDOR NAME                  STREET             CITY / STATE
     01 S-0010-1  SABER SAWS & TOOLS         106 MULBERRY STREET  NEWARK           NJ
     02 S-0020-1  SACRET CEMENT PRODUCTS      23 RIVER DRIVE      JERSEY CITY      NJ
     03 S-0030-1  SADLER SCRAP STEEL         1103 ESSEX STREET    PASSAIC          NJ
     04 S-0035-1  SADOR DISCOUNT EQUIPMENT    310 E MAIN AVENUE   SYRACUSE         NY
     05 S-0040-1  SAFETY GLASS INSTALLERS     11 HARRIS STREET    WORCESTER        MA
     06 S-0050-1  SAFEWAY INDUSTRIAL TOOLS    48 BROADWAY         WILKES-BARRE     PA
     07 S-0060-1  SAKXON BROTHERS CHEMICALS  454 JUNCTION BLVD    RIDGEWOOD        NJ
     08 S-0065-1  SALE ITEM PAINTS           1610 BLEEKER STREET  LYNDHURST        NJ
     09 S-0070-1  SALVAGE METALS              34 UNION AVENUE     NO ARLINGTON     NJ
     10 S-0070-2  SALVAGE METALS              88 BROAD STREET     BOSTON           MA
     11 S-0080-1  SAMPSON STEEL INC.         754 AVON STREET      ORLANDO          FL
     12 S-0090-1  SANDOR INDUSTRIAL ACIDS    101 MONROE STREET    SAN FRANCISCO    CA
     13 S-0095-1  SANITARY CLEANSERS          33 EASTON DRIVE     RUTHERFORD       NJ
     14 S-0100-1  SANORA RESINS              2300 BELT PARKWAY    NO WILDWOOD      NJ
     15 S-0165-1  SANTOR CHEMICALS           1000 ERIE BLVD       NEW YORK         NY
          : SELECTION
          RESET VENDOR CODE:
     1. FWD  - PF8      4. KEY IN SELECTION      - PF6
     2. BWD  - PF7      5. KEY IN RESET VENDOR   - PF9
     3. MENU - PF5      6. END OF SESSION        - CLEAR
```

Fig. 1.11 Vendor file browse screen.

previous page of data. Normally, you are required to scroll forward and save succeeding pages before you can page backward.

- Return to the vendor file maintenance submenu (see Fig. 1.4).
- Key in a selection between 01 and 15 to select a vendor. The selected code may be passed to a different program. Some systems may be designed to have a program pass control to a browse program in order to select a code and return it to the invoking program.
- Enter a full or partial vendor code to reset the browse, then press PF9 to continue the browse from the point of the reset code.
- Press CLEAR to end the session.

The browse program example in this book is presented for ease of conveying browse concepts. Your installation might employ alphanumeric search logic and use alternate keys for its browse programs.

2

Designing User-Friendly Maps

The design of user-friendly maps requires user involvement. Users have to live with the screens and the systems, while data processing personnel only maintain the system. Almost any concept the user can define and convey to a programmer/analyst can be implemented. The best in-house systems (not packages) and their associated screens are developed through close cooperation and coordination between users and data processing personnel.

Data processing, in its simplest form, has always consisted of receiving input, processing the data, and creating some form of output. CICS is no different, although the sequence is slightly different. Generally, after initiating a transaction by entering a TRANSID, the first thing you get is output, in the form of a map, displayed on a terminal. Next, you key information on the screen and enter the input into the system, which then processes it. The design of maps, which are the major source of input and output in a CICS system, is the subject of this chapter. Later chapters explain the coding required to generate the maps.

Designing Maps

Maps define formatted screens that are user's input and output in an online environment. The map is the user's primary aid when conveying to data processing the input and output of a system. The map is used to send information to and receive data from a screen. Users will view some maps repeatedly throughout the day. Therefore, they should make sure they understand the map and feel comfortable with its format. Many installations use a screen generator, such as IBM's Screen Definition Facility (SDF), or similar tool to design their maps. The techniques used to design screens are similar no matter which tools you use to produce your maps. This chapter paints pictures of its maps on a terminal screen that contains 80 columns and 24 lines. Figure 2.1 shows the basic map format I recommend. Many terminals have nearby printers that can reproduce a screen image by pressing a designated key on the terminal keyboard. Often important for future reference is knowing the date and time when map images were printed. I recommend putting date and time on detail and browse maps. They are optional on menu maps and control screens. These different types of maps were discussed under "Screen Classifications" in chapter 1.

Put the mapname on all maps; I find the upper-right-hand corner a convenient location for this. Users often have questions or recommendations pertaining to the system; Identifying the map in question is easier if it can be referred to by a common name. Occasionally, a program comes to an ABEND; identifying where the problem occurred is easier if you can identify the map that triggered the ABEND. The center of the first line of the map is a good location for company name or system name, and the center map title on the second line. The last line of the map (line 24) is generally reserved for program-generated user-notification messages.

The area between the two heading lines and the message line contains the body of the map and user instructions. There are no rules for this part of the map, but the body of the map should generally precede the instructions. This is the area of the map where a user and an analyst can express their creativity and their good design skills.

A series of maps helps develop the picture a user receives of a system. This picture can be pleasing, neutral, or irritating. How can a map be irritating? Anything that is difficult to understand, cumbersome to work with, and causes frustration to a user is a source of irritation. Poorly planned and designed maps, as well as the sequence of map appearance in a system, can be a major irritant. Since users have to live and work with a system's screens, they should help design maps that are pleasing and logical.

I usually design and redesign a map several times before showing it to a user. The user usually offers suggestions that necessitate a few additional map alterations. This communication between screen designer and user, before programming begins, minimizes the number of changes required after a program has been written.

Map Design Guidelines

When designing maps, as in most areas of data processing, an important consideration should be, "Keep it simple and straightforward (KISS)". Some guidelines I like to apply when designing a map are:

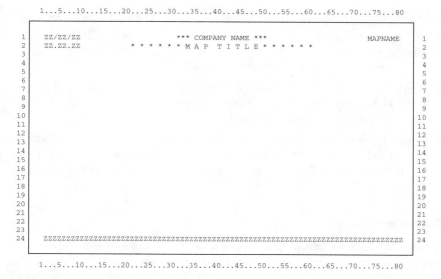

Fig. 2.1 Basic map screen format.

- Balance the data to be displayed. Don't cramp it all to the left and top of the map. You have 80 columns and 21 lines, plus 2 header lines and a message line. Don't be reluctant to use them.

- Put date and time on detail maps.

- Depending on company standards, display company, department, or system name, centered on line 1 of the map.

- Always include mapname in the upper-right corner of each map.

- Give the map a title centered on line 2 of the map.

- Start the body of the map on line 3 or lower. Leave a few blank lines, if space is available, to improve balance.

- Indicate display-only variable data (such as date and time) by Zs and data-entry fields by Xs. This may not be necessary if you are using a screen generator.

- Follow the body with instructions that will guide the user to perform the required functions.

- Number instructions when there are three or more options from which to choose.

- Generally locate program-generated operator-notification and action-required message on line 24 of the map. A notification message between the body and instructions is sometimes an asset, usually on control maps.

- Brighten all messages so that they will stand out from the rest of the map.
- Highlight the field identifiers of items that are entered incorrectly. Alternatively, you may highlight the erroneous data. This may be dictated by the standards in effect at your installation.
- Strive for consistency of format for similar functions on different maps. Users become accustomed to using the same PF key for identical functions on screens within the system.
- Reserve column 1 of all lines for map attributes (see "Map Attributes" later in this chapter). Attributes can be set in column 80 of the preceding line if you wish to display or enter data starting at column 1, but this is awkward and can lead to errors.

Consistency in Map Design

A map that is similar from one program to another is easier to reproduce and modify for new programs. Maps can be generated much more quickly for new programs if a skeleton map exists that is similar to the new map. Consistency enables you to design a prototype of a new system within a reasonable period of time using existing systems as models. Maps discussed in chapter 1 that possess similarities from one system to another are:

- Menus
- Control maps
- Detail maps
- Browse maps

Some installations like to show the field identifiers for date and time. Your installation may just want to display the date and time without descriptions. When possible, always place them in the same location on all maps. *Always* place the mapname in the same location for all maps.

Map Attributes

Each field on a map has an attribute associated with it. A field, as a user perceives it, is any displayed data or any location on a map at which data can be entered. In reality, all literals, field identifiers, displayed data, and data-entry locations are map fields. Figure 2.2 shows a menu map for the purchasing system; this is the map used to format the screen shown in Fig. 1-2. There are several fields on this map, but only one in which the terminal operator is permitted to enter data—the SELECTION field.

The common attributes with which you should be familiar are:

```
      1...5...10...15...20...25...30...35...40...45...50...55...60...65...70...75...80

  1 │                      ABC MANUFACTURING COMPANY                   POMENU1  │  1
  2 │                        PURCHASING SYSTEM MENU                              │  2
  3 │                                                                           │  3
  4 │          SELECTION: X                                                     │  4
  5 │                                                                           │  5
  6 │                    1. PURCHASE ORDER ENTRY                                 │  6
  7 │                                                                           │  7
  8 │                    2. PURCHASE ORDER MAINTENANCE                           │  8
  9 │                                                                           │  9
 10 │                    3. VENDOR FILE MAINTENANCE                              │ 10
 11 │                                                                           │ 11
 12 │                                                                           │ 12
 13 │                                                                           │ 13
 14 │                                                                           │ 14
 15 │                                                                           │ 15
 16 │                    KEY IN SELECTION - PRESS ENTER                         │ 16
 17 │                                                                           │ 17
 18 │                    END OF SESSION   - PRESS CLEAR                         │ 18
 19 │                                                                           │ 19
 20 │                                                                           │ 20
 21 │                                                                           │ 21
 22 │                                                                           │ 22
 23 │                                                                           │ 23
 24 │ ZZZZZZZZZZZZZZZZZZZZZZZZZZZZZZZZZZZZZZZZZZZZZZZZZZZZZZZZZZZZZZZZZZZZZZZZZZZZZ │ 24

      1...5...10...15...20...25...30...35...40...45...50...55...60...65...70...75...80
```

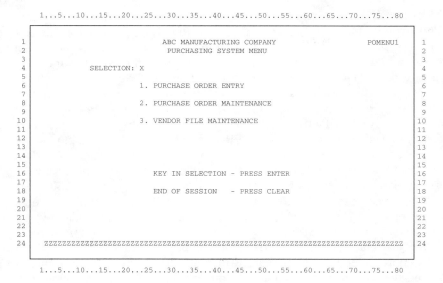

Fig. 2.2 Purchasing system menu map.

- ASKIP (Automatic SKIP)—The cursor skips over fields with this attribute.

- UNPROT (UNPROTected)—A field the cursor will stop at so that the terminal operator can enter data.

- PROT (PROTected)—This attribute sometimes immediately follows an unprotected field; data entry will be inhibited when this attribute is encountered.

- BRT (BRighTer intensity)—A field displayed at a brighter intensity than normal. A BRT field may be referred to as a *highlighted* or *high-intensity* field. Messages and field identifiers of erroneous entries are highlighted in this book.

- NORM (NORMal intensity)—The usual display for fields. When errors are corrected, their field identifiers are changed from BRT to NORM.

- DRK (DaRK intensity)—This field cannot be seen and is generally used for a password field. It is sometimes used to darken a message field on a subsequent display of the screen, when the message no longer applies.

Chapter 6, Basic Mapping Support, explains attributes in more detail.

Each attribute occupies one position on the map and controls the field that immediately follows it. All field attributes in Fig. 2.2 are defined as

ASKIP, NORM initially, except the attribute for the entry of the selection. The attribute for the selection entry is UNPROT in order to allow the user to enter the selection number. The UNPROT attribute occupies the screen position between SELECTION and the field to be entered (shown on the map by an X). The ASKIP attribute occupies screen location line 4, column 24. Without this ASKIP attribute, nothing would exist to stop the terminal operator from entering data. This attribute limits the user to one digit of data entry. An ASKIP attribute following an UNPROT field is sometimes referred to as a stopper attribute. A PROT attribute can be used in place of ASKIP if you want to stop data entry and lock the keyboard when more than one digit is entered. If another UNPROT field was on the map, the cursor would skip to the start of that field when it encountered the ASKIP attribute. The cursor never stops at an ASKIP field. When designing a screen, just keep in mind that each UNPROT field is immediately preceded by and followed by an attribute, each of which occupies one position on the screen. ASKIP attributes result the cursor skipping past a field and moving to the next unprotected field. Note that the message line starts at line 24, column 2, because column 1 is occupied by an ASKIP attribute. A program can change this attribute from ASKIP, NORM to ASKIP, BRT to ASKIP, DRK and back again in order to highlight and "erase" messages by brightening and darkening them.

The most commonly used screen or map size is 80 columns by 24 lines and contains 1920 available positions for characters and attributes. The two heading lines plus the message line take up 3 lines, or 240 of the available positions, leaving 21 lines, or 1680 positions, for the body and instructions of your map. Twenty-one lines are usually sufficient space for display and entry information and for instructions to the terminal operator. You can use two or more maps in cases where one map is insufficient for a required function.

Map Body and Instructions

The body of the map is the most important part of the display screen and, therefore, requires the most planning; in this area, you can best express creativity. Users of the most complicated and advanced system, even if it performs every function imaginable, will think the system is poorly designed if it is difficult to understand and cumbersome to use.

The body of the purchasing system menu (see Fig. 2.2) is typical of that used for a menu program. Most menus have more than three selections, which may be indicated by numbers and/or letters. On a menu with numerous entries, you may display two or more entries per line, if necessary. The user will normally key in the number or letter and press ENTER.

The instruction section of a menu map is usually rather simple, generally consisting of two entries:

```
KEY IN SELECTION - PRESS ENTER
END OF SESSION   - PRESS CLEAR
```

I do not usually number fewer than three instructions on a map, although you may choose to do so. There is no reason a map must have instructions numbered, but doing so sometimes helps a user to remember the options by association.

Designing the Control Map

The heading and message lines of the control map are similar to those of the menu and all of the maps in this book. Date and time are the basic differences on the heading lines for the vendor file inquiry control map shown in Fig. 2.3.

Body of the control map

The body of a control map is generally brief, usually consisting of one or more entries that are concatenated (joined together) to develop a key for the record which is to be acted upon. Figure 2.3 has just one item in the body, the vendor code. I like to have codes entered in a format to which the user is accustomed—for example, one alphabetic character followed by a four-digit sequence number and a one-digit location number. The vendor code and its associated attributes could be laid out in several different

```
     1...5...10...15...20...25...30...35...40...45...50...55...60...65...70...75...80

 1   ZZ/ZZ/ZZ               ABC MANUFACTURING COMPANY                    POVMIQ1    1
 2   ZZ.ZZ.ZZ               VENDOR FILE INQUIRY CONTROL                             2
 3                                                                                  3
 4                                                                                  4
 5                                                                                  5
 6                                                                                  6
 7                          VENDOR CODE: X - XXXX - X                               7
 8                                                                                  8
 9                                                                                  9
10                                                                                 10
11                                                                                 11
12              1. FOR VENDOR FILE INQUIRY - PRESS ENTER                           12
13                                                                                 13
14              2. TO BROWSE VENDOR FILE   - PRESS PF4                             14
15                                                                                 15
16              3. TO RETURN TO MENU       - PRESS PF5                             16
17                                                                                 17
18              4. TO END SESSION          - PRESS CLEAR                           18
19                                                                                 19
20                                                                                 20
21                                                                                 21
22                                                                                 22
23                                                                                 23
24   ZZZZZZZZZZZZZZZZZZZZZZZZZZZZZZZZZZZZZZZZZZZZZZZZZZZZZZZZZZZZZZZZZZZZZZZZZZZZZ   24

     1...5...10...15...20...25...30...35...40...45...50...55...60...65...70...75...80
```

Fig. 2.3 Vendor file inquiry control map.

ways, as shown in Fig. 2.4. Use the structure with which the system's users are most comfortable.

Entering data into a key field

Figure 2.4 shows four different ways a user can enter data into a field. The Xs, indicating where data would be entered, do not actually appear on the control screen. The "A" or "U" under each line indicates, respectively, the ASKIP or UNPROT attribute that would occupy the same column on the above line.

Lines 2 and 3

> Show the field to be entered with the edit characters displayed on the screen. Initially position the cursor after the first UNPROT attribute to allow entry of the first character in the vendor code. After entering the first character, the ASKIP attribute causes the cursor to move to the right of the next UNPROT attribute. After the fourth digit is entered, the cursor skips to the right of the last UNPROT attribute to enable entry of the last vendor code digit. For all fields, the trailing ASKIP attribute is called a stopper attribute.

Lines 6 and 7

> Leave a space between significant groupings of characters to be entered. The space actually contains an UNPROT attribute, which causes the cursor to skip over the space to the start of the next significant entry field.

Lines 10 and 11

> Enter the code without any editing characters displayed or implied by a space. This method becomes less effective when the size of the field to be entered increases.

Lines 14 and 15

> Enter the edit characters (dashes, -) along with the key characters. This method involves additional keying (the dashes), and in general seems to cause the most problems; avoid it if possible.

Techniques for entering and editing numeric data are discussed in chapter 20. Since there are many methods of entering data into a field on a terminal, understanding the various options enables you to be more effective in your map design.

Instructions on the control map

Control maps are often dominated by instructions, and the vendor file inquiry control map in Fig. 2.3 is no exception. The instructions occupy the area between vendor code and the message line at the bottom of the map.

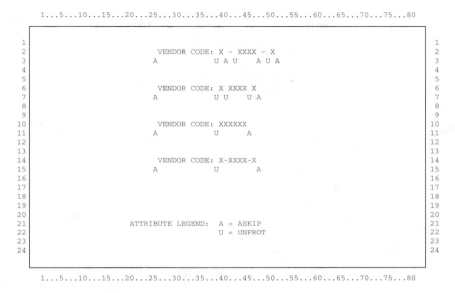

Fig. 2.4 Key field entry techniques.

Why display instructions on a map when they can be placed in a user's manual? They do occupy screen space and result in more data being transmitted to the screen, but I believe it is easier for the user to read instructions from a screen.

This book is concerned with reducing maintenance and making the user and you more productive. It is not *overly* concerned with computer efficiencies and does not attempt to minimize terminal response time. Advances in technology will bring improvements in that area. Later chapters explain techniques to minimize the transmittal of *data* when a map must be resent due to errors.

Instructions on a control map generally list a number of functions that prompt the user to press the appropriate key in order to invoke the desired function.

Messages displayed on the control map

Normally, when a programmer writes a program, checks are made for all anticipated conditions that could create a problem, and a message is displayed notifying the terminal operator of the condition. The experienced CICS programmer/analyst who has dealt with users has an instinct for the type of messages that should be displayed. Users or user-interface personnel, when testing a system, will often offer suggestions for making the messages more meaningful. A professional programmer/analyst expects this kind of feed-

```
1...5...10...15...20...25...30...35...40...45...50...55...60...65...70...75...80
```

```
 1  ZZ/ZZ/ZZ                    ABC MANUFACTURING COMPANY                POVMIQ2    1
 2  ZZ.ZZ.ZZ                        VENDOR FILE INQUIRY                              2
 3                                                                                  3
 4  VENDOR CODE: Z-ZZZZ-Z                                                           4
 5        NAME: ZZZZZZZZZZZZZZZZZZZZZZZZZZ    PHONE:   ( ZZZ ) ZZZ - ZZZZ           5
 6                                           CONTACT: ZZZZZZZZZZZZZZZZZZZZZZZZZZ     6
 7                                                                                  7
 8  ADDRESS - STREET: ZZZZZZZZZZZZZZZZZZZZ                                          8
 9            CITY: ZZZZZZZZZZZZZZZZZZ      DOLLARS COMMITTED: $Z,ZZZ,ZZZ.ZZCR      9
10           STATE: ZZ ZZZZZZZZZZZZZZ                                              10
11             ZIP: ZZZZZ                                                          11
12                                                                                 12
13  TO ATTENTION OF: ZZZZZZZZZZZZZZZZZZZZ                                          13
14                                                                                 14
15                                                                                 15
16                                                                                 16
17                                                                                 17
18         1. RETURN TO INQUIRY CONTROL SCREEN      - PRESS ENTER                  18
19         2. RETURN TO MENU                        - PRESS PF5                    19
20         3. END OF SESSION                        - PRESS CLEAR                  20
21                                                                                 21
22                                                                                 22
23                                                                                 23
24  ZZZZZZZZZZZZZZZZZZZZZZZZZZZZZZZZZZZZZZZZZZZZZZZZZZZZZZZZZZZZZZZZZZZZZZZZZZZZZZZ   24
```

```
1...5...10...15...20...25...30...35...40...45...50...55...60...65...70...75...80
```

Fig. 2.5   Vendor file inquiry detail map.

back from a user. Alterations of this type are not difficult to make. User representatives and data processing personnel realize that many of the messages displayed notify the terminal operator that an incorrect entry has been made. Nobody likes to be corrected in an abusive fashion or in a way that will make him or her feel foolish, so the professional will use care to soften messages. A word like "please" as part of a message of this type is usually an effective softener.

Detail Maps

A detail map is one displayed as a result of an entry made on a control map. Many installations do not use control maps and enter keys directly on a detail map. This has the advantage of transmitting less data to the screen and probably outweighs the drawback that the key on a detail map might be changed after a screen has been displayed. The screen could then be printed showing incorrect data for the key. The browse program in chapter 17 is an example of using a detail map without a control map. For ease of understanding, this book uses control maps for the following detail maps:

- Inquires
- Additions
- Changes
- Deletions

Inquiry map

The inquiry detail map shown in Fig. 2.5 contains data found on the vendor master record. All attributes on the inquiry map are ASKIP, NORM. The only attribute that changes on this map is the message attribute, which can change from ASKIP, NORM to ASKIP, BRT when an error message is displayed. The vendor code attribute would be UNPROT if you were not using a control map.

The body of the report displays information from the vendor master record for the code entered on the control map. The instructions prompt you for action after viewing the map.

Addition map

Figure 2.6 shows the format of the vendor file addition detail map. Unlike the inquiry map, all variable field attributes in the body of this map with the exception of vendor code and state name are UNPROT. Vendor code and state name (indicated by Zs) cannot be changed, since their attributes are ASKIP, NORM. Vendor code can only be entered on the control screen. The vendor code attribute would be UNPROT if you were not using a control map.

The body of the map contains fields into which new data can be entered. The ENTER key is then pressed to effect the addition. The design of this part of the addition map must be closely coordinated with the user, since

```
     1...5...10...15...20...25...30...35...40...45...50...55...60...65...70...75...80

 1  | ZZ/ZZ/ZZ                    ABC MANUFACTURING COMPANY                POVMAD2   | 1
 2  | ZZ.ZZ.ZZ                       VENDOR FILE ADDITION                            | 2
 3  |                                                                                | 3
 4  | VENDOR CODE: Z-ZZZZ-Z                                                          | 4
 5  |        NAME: XXXXXXXXXXXXXXXXXXXXXXXXX       PHONE:   ( XXX ) XXX - XXXX        | 5
 6  |                                             CONTACT: XXXXXXXXXXXXXXXXXXXXXXXXX  | 6
 7  |                                                                                | 7
 8  | ADDRESS - STREET: XXXXXXXXXXXXXXXXXXXX                                          | 8
 9  |            CITY: XXXXXXXXXXXXXXXXXX                                             | 9
10  |           STATE: XX ZZZZZZZZZZZZZZ                                             |10
11  |             ZIP: XXXXX                                                         |11
12  |                                                                                |12
13  |  TO ATTENTION OF: XXXXXXXXXXXXXXXXXXXX                                          |13
14  |                                                                                |14
15  |                                                                                |15
16  |                                                                                |16
17  |                                                                                |17
18  |        1. ADDITIONS, KEY IN REQUIRED DATA       - PRESS ENTER                  |18
19  |        2. RETURN TO ADDITION CONTROL SCREEN     - PRESS PF3                    |19
20  |        3. RETURN TO MENU                        - PRESS PF5                    |20
21  |        4. END OF SESSION                        - PRESS CLEAR                  |21
22  |                                                                                |22
23  |                                                                                |23
24  | ZZZZZZZZZZZZZZZZZZZZZZZZZZZZZZZZZZZZZZZZZZZZZZZZZZZZZZZZZZZZZZZZZZZZZZZZZZZZZZZZZ |24

     1...5...10...15...20...25...30...35...40...45...50...55...60...65...70...75...80
```

Fig. 2.6 Vendor file addition detail map.

the entry of data must flow smoothly. The layout of data should correspond closely with the format of the source document used for adding a new vendor. Plan the layout of the data fields carefully; for instance, it would be awkward to put PHONE on the same line as VENDOR CODE. Remember, the cursor moves from left to right, top to bottom, stopping at UNPROT fields and skipping over ASKIP fields. Placing PHONE, which is an UNPROT field, on the same line as VENDOR CODE, an ASKIP field, would position the cursor at the first UNPROT field, which is PHONE. This seems illogical for two reasons: first, it is backward to enter the phone number before keying in the vendor's name; second, it seems more logical to have the cursor positioned initially on the left side of the screen.

Another illogical and awkward situation would arise if the fields PHONE and CONTACT were moved down opposite STREET and CITY. The user, in this case, enters STREET, then PHONE, followed by CITY, CONTACT, and STATE. On a full screen, a better alternative than breaking up an address entry in this fashion is to design the screen with the entire address on the same line. For example:

```
STREET                  CITY                    STATE  ZIP
XXXXXXXXXXXXXXXXXXXXX XXXXXXXXXXXXXXXXXXXXX   XX   XXXXX
```

When a field is entered erroneously or is inadvertently missed, the field identifier describing that field should have its attribute changed to ASKIP,BRT, which highlights the description. Field identifiers should be restored to ASKIP,NORM after their corresponding fields have been corrected and should no longer display brightly. As shown in Fig. 1.8, the brightening of field identifiers is accompanied by the highlighting and display of the message field containing the message:

```
PLEASE CORRECT HIGHLIGHTED FIELDS
```

As noted previously, some systems highlight incorrectly entered data instead of its field identifier. The procedure of highlighting and restoring to normal intensity is the same regardless of which method you use.

Change map

The vendor file change map layout is shown in Fig. 2.7. Upon the initial send of a change map, the existing record's data is displayed. Each variable attribute in the body of this map is UNPROT, NORM, except for vendor code, which is ASKIP, NORM; it would be UNPROT if you were *not* using a control map.

Changes can be keyed in over the existing data that is displayed or the user can press the EOF key to clear the field before entering the new data. The TAB key can be used to skip over fields that do not require changes.

```
         1...5...10...15...20...25...30...35...40...45...50...55...60...65...70...75...80

  1 │ ZZ/ZZ/ZZ                    ABC MANUFACTURING COMPANY                    POVMCH2 │ 1
  2 │ ZZ.ZZ.ZZ                       VENDOR FILE CHANGES                               │ 2
  3 │                                                                                  │ 3
  4 │ VENDOR CODE: Z-ZZZZ-Z                                                            │ 4
  5 │       NAME: XXXXXXXXXXXXXXXXXXXXXXXXXX       PHONE:    ( XXX ) XXX - XXXX         │ 5
  6 │                                            CONTACT: XXXXXXXXXXXXXXXXXXXXXXXXX     │ 6
  7 │                                                                                  │ 7
  8 │ ADDRESS - STREET: XXXXXXXXXXXXXXXXXXXX                                            │ 8
  9 │            CITY: XXXXXXXXXXXXXXXXXX                                               │ 9
 10 │           STATE: XX ZZZZZZZZZZZZZZ                                               │ 10
 11 │             ZIP: XXXXX                                                            │ 11
 12 │                                                                                  │ 12
 13 │   TO ATTENTION OF: XXXXXXXXXXXXXXXXXXXX                                           │ 13
 14 │                                                                                  │ 14
 15 │                                                                                  │ 15
 16 │                                                                                  │ 16
 17 │                                                                                  │ 17
 18 │          1. CHANGES, KEY IN NEW DATA              - PRESS ENTER                   │ 18
 19 │          2. RETURN TO CHANGES CONTROL SCREEN      - PRESS PF3                     │ 19
 20 │          3. RETURN TO MENU                        - PRESS PF5                     │ 20
 21 │          4. END OF SESSION                        - PRESS CLEAR                   │ 21
 22 │                                                                                  │ 22
 23 │                                                                                  │ 23
 24 │ ZZZZZZZZZZZZZZZZZZZZZZZZZZZZZZZZZZZZZZZZZZZZZZZZZZZZZZZZZZZZZZZZZZZZZZZZZZZZZZZZZZ │ 24

         1...5...10...15...20...25...30...35...40...45...50...55...60...65...70...75...80
```

Fig. 2.7 Vendor file change detail map.

The ENTER key is pressed to update the record with the altered data. Do *not* put data in different locations on the various maintenance maps. Users become more easily accustomed to a system if similar fields are located in the same relative positions on all inquiry and maintenance screens.

Deletion map

The deletion detail map is shown in Fig. 2.8. The fields displayed all have attributes of ASKIP, NORM. The purpose of displaying a record before deleting it is to give the user a chance to verify that the record is the proper one to be deleted before pressing ENTER. The user could exercise one of the other options listed in the instructions if he or she did not want to delete the record. I recommend *always* displaying a record for user verification before deleting; it takes a little longer, but the additional check is worth performing.

Browse Map

The browse map, shown in Fig. 2.9, contains many of the characteristics found in the other maps discussed. The headings and message lines have the same format and occupy the same line numbers as the other maps. The body follows the headings and precedes the map instructions. The browse map functions as a detail map that does not have an associated control map. As mentioned previously, this has the advantage of transmitting less to the screen.

```
1...5...10...15...20...25...30...35...40...45...50...55...60...65...70...75...80
```

```
 1 | ZZ/ZZ/ZZ                ABC MANUFACTURING COMPANY               POVMDL2 | 1
 2 | ZZ.ZZ.ZZ                   VENDOR FILE DELETION                         | 2
 3 |                                                                         | 3
 4 | VENDOR CODE: Z-ZZZZ-Z                                                   | 4
 5 |      NAME: ZZZZZZZZZZZZZZZZZZZZZZZZ       PHONE:   ( ZZZ ) ZZZ - ZZZZ   | 5
 6 |                                         CONTACT: ZZZZZZZZZZZZZZZZZZZZZZZ | 6
 7 |                                                                         | 7
 8 | ADDRESS - STREET: ZZZZZZZZZZZZZZZZZZZZZ                                  | 8
 9 |           CITY: ZZZZZZZZZZZZZZZZZZZ                                     | 9
10 |          STATE: ZZ ZZZZZZZZZZZZZZZ                                      | 10
11 |            ZIP: ZZZZZ                                                   | 11
12 |                                                                         | 12
13 |   TO ATTENTION OF: ZZZZZZZZZZZZZZZZZZZZ                                  | 13
14 |                                                                         | 14
15 |                                                                         | 15
16 |                                                                         | 16
17 |                                                                         | 17
18 |      1. DELETIONS, VERIFY DATA BEFORE DELETING  - PRESS ENTER           | 18
19 |      2. RETURN TO DELETION CONTROL SCREEN       - PRESS PF3             | 19
20 |      3. RETURN TO MENU                          - PRESS PF5             | 20
21 |      4. END OF SESSION                          - PRESS CLEAR           | 21
22 |                                                                         | 22
23 |                                                                         | 23
24 | ZZZZZZZZZZZZZZZZZZZZZZZZZZZZZZZZZZZZZZZZZZZZZZZZZZZZZZZZZZZZZZZZZZZZZZZZZZ | 24
```

```
1...5...10...15...20...25...30...35...40...45...50...55...60...65...70...75...80
```

Fig. 2.8 Vendor file deletion detail map.

```
1...5...10...15...20...25...30...35...40...45...50...55...60...65...70...75...80
```

```
 1 | ZZ/ZZ/ZZ              ABC MANUFACTURING COMPANY              POVMBR1 | 1
 2 | ZZ.ZZ.ZZ                 VENDOR FILE BROWSE                          | 2
 3 |   VENDOR CD VENDOR NAME              STREET           CITY / STATE   | 3
 4 | 01 Z-ZZZZ-Z ZZZZZZZZZZZZZZZZZZZZZZZZZ ZZZZZZZZZZZZZZZZZZZZ ZZZZZZZZZZZZZZZZZZZZ | 4
 5 | 02 Z       Z Z                    Z Z                Z Z           Z | 5
 6 | 03 Z       Z Z                    Z Z                Z Z           Z | 6
 7 | 04 Z       Z Z                    Z Z                Z Z           Z | 7
 8 | 05 Z       Z Z                    Z Z                Z Z           Z | 8
 9 | 06 Z       Z Z                    Z Z                Z Z           Z | 9
10 | 07 Z       Z Z                    Z Z                Z Z           Z | 10
11 | 08 Z       Z Z                    Z Z                Z Z           Z | 11
12 | 09 Z       Z Z                    Z Z                Z Z           Z | 12
13 | 10 Z       Z Z                    Z Z                Z Z           Z | 13
14 | 11 Z       Z Z                    Z Z                Z Z           Z | 14
15 | 12 Z       Z Z                    Z Z                Z Z           Z | 15
16 | 13 Z       Z Z                    Z Z                Z Z           Z | 16
17 | 14 Z       Z Z                    Z Z                Z Z           Z | 17
18 | 15 Z-ZZZZ-Z ZZZZZZZZZZZZZZZZZZZZZZZZZ ZZZZZZZZZZZZZZZZZZZZ ZZZZZZZZZZZZZZZZZZZZ | 18
19 | XX : SELECTION                                                      | 19
20 |      RESET VENDOR CODE: XXXXXX                                      | 20
21 | 1. FWD  - PF8      4. KEY IN SELECTION    - PF6                     | 21
22 | 2. BWD  - PF7      5. KEY IN RESET VENDOR - PF9                     | 22
23 | 3. MENU - PF5      6. END OF SESSION      - CLEAR                   | 23
24 | ZZZZZZZZZZZZZZZZZZZZZZZZZZZZZZZZZZZZZZZZZZZZZZZZZZZZZZZZZZZZZZZZZZZZZZ | 24
```

```
1...5...10...15...20...25...30...35...40...45...50...55...60...65...70...75...80
```

Fig. 2.9 Vendor file browse map.

The attributes for this map are all ASKIP, NORM, except for those on lines 19 and 20, the SELECTION and RESET VENDOR CODE data-entry fields, which are UNPROT. The message line attribute can be changed to brighten or darken the message.

3

Basic Concepts and Terminology

This chapter introduces required CICS terminology, the CICS command format, pseudoconversational and conversational programming, CICS tables, and other background considerations.

CICS programmers usually refer to the display of a map as a *send* of the map. A CICS program issues a SEND MAP command in order to display various types of maps, such as menu, control, or detail maps. The design of the system determines the types of maps to be used and the sequence in which they are to appear. The map sent usually requires data to be entered and/or an AID key to be pressed in order to initiate the receive of the map.

A CICS program obtains the information entered by a terminal operator when an AID key is pressed. The AID keys consist of ENTER, PF, CLEAR, and PA. A CICS program issues a RECEIVE MAP command in order to initiate the action the user requests. The action indicated by the AID key pressed determines the type of processing to be performed.

Pseudoconversational Programming

CICS allows many users to log on and use CICS concurrently. Computer main-storage size is finite. If numerous users are running transactions demanding considerable main storage, a short-on-storage condition could occur, causing delays.

Pseudoconversational programming is a coding technique that results in a program being loaded into main storage when required and released when it is no longer active. For instance, when a map is displayed and the program is waiting for a user's response, the program can be released from main storage and reloaded when needed (when the user responds).

CICS loads and releases application programs from main storage automatically. High-use programs are often defined as main-storage-resident, and the system keeps them in main storage. Tables and maps, which are considered programs by CICS, are usually controlled by a program.

Generally, when using the pseudoconversational technique of processing, pressing an AID key causes a program to be loaded if it is not already in main storage. When a program is finished with a logical segment of processing, it normally sends a map, saves required data, and returns control to CICS. This allows the release of the program from main storage if storage is needed by other programs. When an AID key is pressed, the program will again be loaded into main storage if necessary, saved data will be restored, and processing will continue.

Pseudoconversational programming techniques should be used whenever possible, and all program examples in this book use this technique. Pseudoconversational programming techniques are your responsibility.

Conversational Programming

Conversational programming is a coding technique that results in a program being loaded into and remaining in main storage until a user is finished working with the program. The program is not released from main storage when not active, as in pseudoconversational programming. For instance, a conversational program displays a map and remains in main storage while waiting for a user's response.

Conversational programming techniques usually involve the send of a map, with the program remaining in main storage while the user is entering data. Unless an AID key is pressed to end the session, the program will send another map and await the user's reply, while remaining in main storage.

The conversational technique appears the same from a user's perspective as pseudoconversational programming, but the conversational technique will not release main storage until the task has completed. Getting a telephone call, taking a break, or engaging in conversation after starting a session holds main storage for excessive periods of time. The user is generally not aware of this situation, and you should design and write programs that minimize the impact of this condition.

Practical applications of conversational programming are very limited and so are not covered in this book. Since pseudoconversational programming is widely used, it is addressed because it eliminates many of the problems that occur when using conversational programming.

Master Terminal Commands

Master terminal commands can be issued by a programmer or a designated master terminal operator (MTO) in order to perform many functions including:

- Place the latest load library address of a program, table, or map into the PPT (discussed later in this chapter)
- Monitor tasks that are running (discussed later in this chapter)
- Terminate a task
- Enable, disable, or inquire as to the status of programs, transactions, or files (data sets). Files can also be opened or closed
- Put a terminal out of service

Master terminal commands may be entered on a cleared screen by keying in CEMT followed by the required entries. CEMT is a prompting transaction allowing abbreviated keywords to be entered. Just key in CEMT and press ENTER. You can enter PRO for program, TRAN for transaction, DAT for data set, etc.

CICS Tables

CICS uses many tables. Only the few that are of direct interest to the application programmer are discussed. A user initiates a compiled CICS program by clearing the screen and keying in a four-character TRANSID, which directs CICS to start a program at that terminal. Identifying the TRANSID and program to CICS and tying them together is necessary, and this is accomplished by means of two tables that are very important to the CICS programmer.

Program-control table (PCT)

The basic function of the PCT is to tie together the TRANSID the user enters with the program name. TRANSID and PROGRAM are the PCT entries of most interest to you. The user enters a TRANSID to start a transaction, then the TRANSID is matched against the PCT to determine if it is a valid entry. A TRANSID not in the PCT causes an invalid TRANSID message to display on the terminal. A match on TRANSID uses the associated program name to search the PPT for a match on PROGRAM. The program is loaded into main storage if it is not a main-storage-resident program or already in main storage.

Processing program table (PPT)

The PPT contains entries such as:

- Program name, language, and size
- The main-storage address of the program (if it has been loaded)
- A task use counter (discussed later in this chapter)
- The load library address of the program to be loaded into main storage
- An indicator whether the program is main-storage-resident (usually high-use)

A PPT entry is used to locate programs to be loaded into main storage and is required for each program, map and table the CICS system uses. When CICS is started up, the PPT is initialized with the address of the load module for all programs, maps, and tables. When a program is changed and compiled or assembled after CICS has been started up, the address of the load module in the PPT must be refreshed—a normal occurrence on the test system. The new load module address can be placed into the PPT by the following master terminal transaction entered on a cleared screen:

```
CEMT INQ PRO (progname) NEW
```

Both tables contain additional entries usually maintained by the systems programming staff. For simplicity, assume the tables contain information of only direct importance to the applications programmer.

PCT Entries	PPT Entries
TRANSID = RECV	PROGRAM = RECEIVEP
PROGRAM = RECEIVEPPGMLANG = COBOL	

Clear the screen, key in the TRANSID RECV, and press ENTER. CICS finds the TRANSID RECV and the program name RECEIVEP in the PCT. The PCT ties the transaction to the PPT entry RECEIVEP. The PPT entry is used to locate the associated program's load module and to load it into main storage.

CICS application programmers generally obtain PCT and PPT entries through their manager and the systems programming department. All examples in this book use the following tables and entries shown in Fig. 3.1 (CICS program tables and file control table (FCT) entries are discussed later in the book).

Maps, generated by an assembler program, are discussed in more detail in chapters 6 and 7. Maps and tables do not have TRANSIDs; they are controlled by CICS programs. The program language for all PPT entries for examples in this book are PGMLANG=COBOL.

* * * PCT * * * TRANSID	Program	PPT Program	PPT Map	PPT Tables	FCT Dataset
DSPL	DISPLAYP	DISPLAYP			
RECV	RECEIVEP	RECEIVEP			
POMU	POMENUPM	POMENUPM	POMENU1		
POVM	POVMAINT	POVMAINT	POVMNT1		
		JRNLPOST		T053JRSQ	JOURNAL1
POVI	POVMINQY	POVMINQY	POVMIQ1 POVMIQ2	T037LOAD	VENDMAST
POVC	POVMCHGE	POVMCHGE	POVMCH1 POVMCH2	T037LOAD	VENDMAST
POVA	POVMADDN	POVMADDN	POVMAD1 POVMAD2	T037LOAD	VENDMAST
POVD	POVMDLET	POVMDLET	POVMDL1 POVMDL2	T037LOAD	VENDMAST
POVB	POVMBROW	POVMBROW	POVMBR1		VENDMAST

Program	Description
DISPLAYP	Displays message CICS IS EASY
RECEIVEP	Receives and sends social security number
POMENUPM	Purchasing system menu
POVMAINT	Vendor file maintenance submenu
JRNLPOST	Journal file updating
POVMINQY	Vendor file inquiry
POVMCHGE	Vendor file changes
POVMADDN	Vendor file additions
POVMDLET	Vendor file deletions
POVMBROW	Vendor file browse

Fig. 3.1 CICS table entries used in this book.

Multiple PCT entries

Multiple PCT entries are permitted to refer to the same program, but multiple programs cannot be associated with the same PCT entry.

	Valid		Invalid
PCT	**PPT**	**PCT**	**PPT**
POVA	POVMADDN	POVA	POVMADDN
POVB	POVMADDN	POVA	POVMDLET

CICS Command Format

CICS commands have the general format:

```
EXEC CICS function
        option 1 (argument 1)
        option 2 (argument 2)
            .
            .
            .
END-EXEC.
```

Function may be commands such as:

```
SEND
RECEIVE
RETURN
READ
```

Options and arguments may be:

```
FROM    (WS-OUTPUT)
INTO    (WS-INPUT)
LENGTH (WS-LENGTH)
ERASE
```

Options have no required sequence, but must be used under the corresponding function. Many options are available for some CICS commands, but only a few may actually be required. This chapter presents only options required to illustrate selected functions.

Task

A task is created for each executed transaction identifier, TRANSID, recognized by CICS (found in the PCT). A task can include one or several programs. A task continues until a program returns control to CICS or issues a

RETURN command in a pseudoconversational program. Only one task can be executing at a given time, but the user may perceive that many tasks are running. CICS's ability to handle multiple tasks simultaneously is called *multitasking*. Different tasks can concurrently access the same program's load module, which is resident in main storage. Since a single load module in main storage may be accessed by several tasks, a program cannot have its procedure division instructions modified during a specific task. Each task obtains main storage for its unique copy of a program's working storage. Programs should be written so that their working storage is kept as small as possible. Keep constants, literals, and messages in the program's procedure division when practical.

CICS Multitasking and Multithreading

Figure 3.2 illustrates how multitasking and multithreading might utilize main storage. Four users at different terminals have entered the TRANSID DSPL and three other users have entered the TRANSID RECV, starting seven different tasks. The initial task for each TRANSID resulted in the corresponding program in the PCT obtaining the associated program's load library address for each program from the PPT. The load module was then loaded into main storage and its main-storage address moved into the PPT.

Each task for both programs obtained a copy of its own unique working storage in main storage as shown. As each task completes, its working storage can be released from main storage. When all tasks accessing a program are complete, a program can be released from main storage (if it is not defined as a resident program in the PPT) if main storage is required for another task.

The following master terminal transaction gives the status of all tasks active in the CICS partition or region.

```
CEMT INQ TAS
```

Entering CEMT INQ TAS at the time the tasks shown in Fig. 3.2 are active produces a display similar to that shown in Fig. 3.3. CEMT list all tasks active in the CICS region showing:

1. TAS (XXXXXX)   – TASK number

2. TRA (XXXX)   – TRANSID entered

3. FAC (XXXX)   – FACility, terminal at which the task was entered

4. ACT or SUS   – ACTive or SUSpended task

5. TER   – TERminal

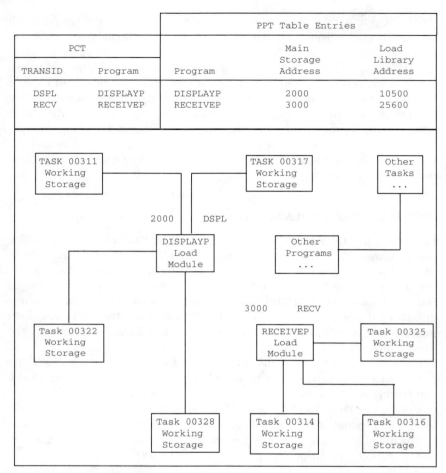

Fig. 3.2 CICS multitasking and multithreading.

Program Considerations and Restrictions

You must be aware of certain considerations and restrictions when writing programs.

Considerations

A program

- Must return control to CICS or to another program
- Cannot modify procedure division instructions because CICS programs may be shared by other tasks

- Can modify working storage since a unique copy of working storage is created for each task

Restrictions

- Do not use FILE SECTION, OPEN, CLOSE, and non-CICS READ and WRITE statements, because data management is handled by CICS
- Avoid COBOL features such as internal sorts, use of special registers, ACCEPT, DISPLAY, EXAMINE, EXHIBIT, INSPECT, STRING/UNSTRING, TRANSFORM, STOP RUN, and GOBACK. GOBACK is included in a CICS program in order to satisfy a compiler requirement but it must *never* be executed
- Use the FORMATTIME command, discussed later in this book, to obtain time and date in various formats. Avoid using CURRENT-DATE, DATE, DAY, and TIME

System and Program Security

Security is a major concern in the design of some online systems, such as payroll, and a consideration in others. The design of security techniques can be implemented at the system and/or program level. An installation can

```
INQ TAS
STATUS:  RESULTS - OVERTYPE TO MODIFY
  TAS(00311) TRA(DSPL) FAC(T022) ACT TER
  TAS(00314) TRA(RECV) FAC(T014) ACT TER
  TAS(00316) TRA(RECV) FAC(T031) ACT TER
  TAS(00317) TRA(DSPL) FAC(T005) ACT TER
  TAS(00322) TRA(DSPL) FAC(T017) ACT TER
  TAS(00325) TRA(RECV) FAC(T003) ACT TER
  TAS(00328) TRA(DSPL) FAC(T027) ACT TER




  RESPONSE: NORMAL                    TIME: 10.16.27  DATE:   99.023

PF:  1 HELP      3 END                7 SBH 8 SFH 9 MSG 10 SB 11 SF
```

Fig. 3.3 CEMT master terminal display for a task.

utilize many security techniques. Some may require extensive user interaction; others may be less obvious to a user.

System security

System security is important when some applications are restricted to certain users. For instance, if payroll is online, allowing all users of the system access to these programs would not be wise . Likewise, you may have to limit the access or update of certain files to specific users. Limiting access to certain users and limiting the time of day that certain functions may be performed may also be advisable.

Many software packages are available that can restrict access to specified files, programs, and transactions. Other security restrictions are possible, such as having the system restrict use to certain users and limit the time of day that specific functions can be used. Currently available versions of CICS will require users to use external security packages because most security functions have been removed from CICS.

Program security

Once the system's security has been passed and the user is into a transaction, you may wish to restrict access to specific record types. The safest way to restrict access is by having each program check against a table of authorized codes. The table can contain authorized items valid for users to access. A user trying to access a record on the system might get into your program, but an unauthorized message can be displayed if the record is not in the table.

A situation that often occurs is an authorized user signing on to CICS and leaving the terminal before signing off. Unauthorized personnel can use the vacated terminal. Current CICS facilities are available that can force a program to terminate if an AID key is not pressed within a predetermined time interval. This time interval should be chosen carefully, because a user who displays information on a terminal while on the phone with a customer would not want to be logged off CICS in the middle of a conversation.

Many of the techniques used by system security software can be coded into individual programs. Selected programs can contain routines to check a password against tables or files in order to determine file, record, transaction, and program authorization. Logic can be coded to permit or prohibit access between certain dates and times and on specified days of the week. Security violations can be written out to a file and printed by category by a batch program. An audible alarm can sound at the violating terminal. All of these checks require additional program code and make programs less efficient and more complicated. Let your system security software handle as many of these checks as possible, if your installation has such software.

Program security, if planned properly and implemented correctly, can run very smoothly; if not, all types of security problems will occur. Some day, access to a system by persons outside of a company may be common. This could be a major growth area for CICS usage in the years to come.

4

System and Programming Documentation Standards

Standards are uniform methods of performing required functions. A standard should serve a definite purpose. The problem with standards is that few people agree about what is beneficial and many consider documentation a wasted effort. The creation and maintenance of standards often require more time than the task they support; if not kept up to date, they become useless and can actually create problems. Most data processing personnel agree that certain standards are necessary, but the fewer the better. This chapter covers what I consider to be the most worthwhile standards for use in an online environment; many can be applied also to batch systems.

System Design Standards

The best design tool and standard is perhaps one of the easiest to create and maintain—the system structure chart. A system structure chart should show at a glance the scope of a system; it should be simple, yet comprehensive. I like to work with a structure chart that shows the major functions of a system, including related PCT and PPT entries.

Structure charts

Figure 4.1 illustrates a system structure chart that diagrams the entire purchasing system. The PCT entry, which is also referred to as the TRANSID,

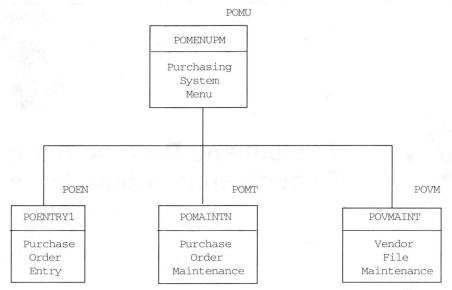

Fig. 4.1 Purchasing system structure chart.

is shown above each block. The top section of each block contains the PPT entry; it is the program's name. Each block contains a description of the associated program. This type of structure chart requires a minimal amount of effort to create and maintain, yet it is an excellent planning tool and shows the scope of a project at a glance.

Once the system structure chart has been established, drawing a subsystem structure chart as shown in Fig. 4.2 is often advantageous. The format of a subsystem structure chart is identical to that of a regular system structure chart. The value of both charts is twofold: they show what functions are contained in a system, and they also provide a picture of the scope of a system, making it easy to explain to others.

The subsystem structure chart shown in Fig. 4.2 is the structure used for programs in the text. POVMAINT, referred to as the menu program, is discussed in chapter 9. The inquiry program POVMINQY, additions program POVMADDN, change program POVMCHGE, delete program POVMDLET, and browse program POVMBROW are discussed in chapters 12, 13, 14, 15, and 17, respectively.

Programming Standards

Program standards generally are time-consuming to create and often require considerable effort to maintain. Even in the best-documented installations, the programmer/analyst who maintains a program seldom uses standards as more than a general guideline regarding what function a program should perform. Programs contain a tremendous amount of detail, and that detail is seldom completely and correctly reflected in program documentation. The best place for program documentation is in the program itself, by using meaningful comments.

Program structure charts, program comments, and style of programming all help to determine how easy or difficult a program is to maintain. The use of standard file layouts and of standard program routines can greatly aid you in the initial writing and in future maintenance of a program. Program documentation is more of an art than a science. This chapter covers many of the techniques I employ to make a program self-documenting and easy to maintain.

Program structure charts

A well-designed program structure chart informs the user viewing the chart what the major functions of a program include. The structure chart helps to simplify complex logic and is most useful to the programmer who initially designs a program; it is seldom maintained after the program has been coded and tested.

The structure chart for a menu program (Fig. 4.3) is rather straightforward and varies little from menu program to menu program. Fig. 4.3 lists

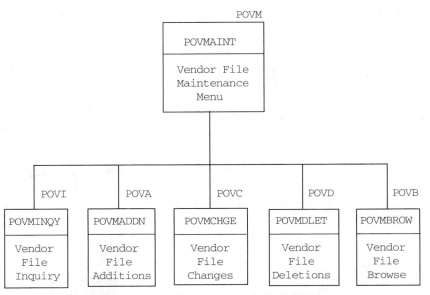

Fig. 4.2 Vendor file maintenance menu—subsystem structure chart.

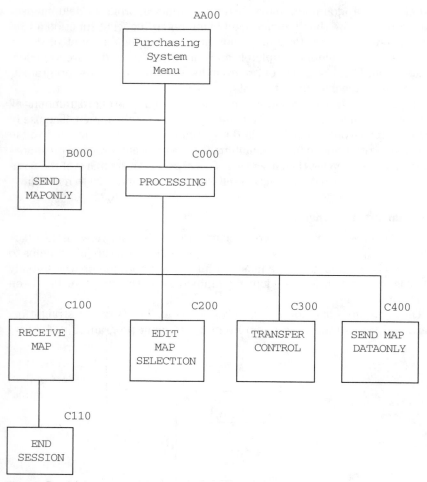

Fig. 4.3 Purchasing system menu—program structure chart.

the program section prefix at the top of each block; this prefix is usually attached to the description inside the block to form program section or paragraph names. I prefer to use sections in programs that I design and code. Sections eliminate the need to perform THRU and simplify coding. If your preference is to use paragraph names, simply eliminate the section header and code all PERFORMs with a THRU paragraph xxx-EXIT.

I generally prefix my mainline section with AA00 and the levels under it as B000, C000, etc. The next sublevel, if one exists, might be C100, C200, C300, etc.; sub-sublevels would be numbered C110, C120, C130, followed by C111, C112, etc. for even lower levels. If a program cannot be covered by this structure, it is probably too complicated and should be analyzed for a simpler design.

I find it easier to maintain several simple programs, each of which performs one function, than one large program that performs many functions. The program structure chart, if well thought out, can be an excellent tool for the initial design and future maintenance of a program. The more functions a program contains, the more beneficial a program structure chart is to you.

I include the program's structure as comments at the start of the procedure division of each program for ease of understanding. This is a good form of documentation, but is difficult to maintain in practice where many programmers, each with a different programming style, maintain a program. See the menu program example in chapter 9 for an illustration of how this is done. If your installation's standards require numeric paragraph names, you can convert B000 to 2000, C100 to 3100, D210 to 4210, etc.

Program comments

The first place a programmer generally looks when maintaining an existing program is at the latest COBOL source program listing; often this is the only place. Time spent making this listing as readable as possible is well worth the effort. Write every program as if you will have to go through it from the beginning to end six months after it has been written, explaining to another programmer/analyst what it is doing. Use meaningful program labels that describe the function of each routine. Include comments in the program, detailing the function of more complicated routines and clarifying others. Write all programs with ample comments; they can be used as models for other programs.

Keep programs short and simple

I prefer to keep programs short and simple, isolating functions into several simple programs instead of writing one large program. Maintenance functions, against the same file, usually have many common routines and use similar maps. Many designers have a tendency to put all maintenance functions into a single program. I prefer a separate program for each major function. This approach creates more PCT and PPT entry requirements for TRANSIDs, programs, and maps, but each program will be easier to code and to maintain.

Security required in the sharing of files and programs is made easier when functions, such as additions, changes, deletions, and inquiries, are put into separate programs. For example, a user may have access to inquiry and change functions, but not to add or delete functions. When each function in a system has a separate program, security is more easily maintained. Because of the constant changes in program requirements, design your programs to be as simple and flexible as possible. Since change is inevitable, you'll be glad you did.

Different Levels of Menus

A system can be designed with many levels of menus. The purchasing system defined in Figs. 4.1 and 4.2 has two levels of menus. One menu can be displayed by entering the TRANSID POMU and the other by entering the TRANSID POVM. A system can be designed to start all installation transactions through a master menu, possibly with a TRANSID of MENU. The user can enter MENU to display the master menu, make a selection to display the purchasing system menu, make another selection to display the vendor file maintenance menu, and finally, make a selection to display an inquiry map.

I am sure you would find it cumbersome to have to display three menus prior to the display of an inquiry map. Many systems do not require a user to go through three menus to reach an inquiry screen. The advantage of multimenus is that a user has fewer TRANSIDs to remember, and this approach also has some security advantages. A system can be designed requiring that all programs be started by entering a TRANSID, but this is rare in practice.

The purchasing system is designed so that a program can be initiated indirectly by a menu or directly by keying the proper TRANSID. For instance, a user can key in MENU, POMU, POVM, POVI, etc., to initiate the desired function. Your installation's security requirements and design philosophy will determine which approach you will take regarding system menus. Figure 4.4 illustrates the level of menus; any of the shown TRANSIDs will lead to the vendor file inquiry.

Passwords

Passwords provide a system with a certain degree of security because they can be used to limit system access to specific users. Personnel at a location where terminals are located must assume some responsibility for monitoring access to the system. System or program security can limit access based on specific passwords, but cannot actually monitor who enters an authorized password. Each location should be responsible for who uses a terminal. Some users at a given location may know the passwords of other employees. Unauthorized personnel can gain access to the system by using these passwords. Passwords aid system security, but they are not foolproof. At best, passwords can restrict users at specific terminals to certain transactions, programs, or files.

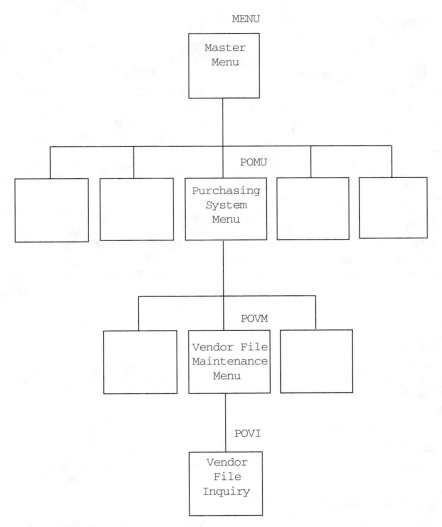

Fig. 4.4 Levels of menus.

Password requirements should be limited; continuous entering of passwords can make a system's operation cumbersome. Keying in of passwords, which are normally entered into nondisplay (DRK attribute) fields, should be limited to sign-on and to initial transaction entry screens. Carried to the ultimate, every display of a map could require the entry of a password, but the nuisance factor involved would far outweigh any security advantage gained. Passwords are a necessary part of many systems, but you must plan carefully where to use them.

Message File

The use of a message file may be considered if a system is going to be adapted for use in several countries. The key to this type of a file would probably be a four-character number, the file data being the message to be displayed on the message line (line 24) of the map. A programmer would move the key of the message to be displayed to the appropriate program area, read the message file, and then move the file's message to line 24 of the map. The advantage of a message file is that the messages can be translated into the language of the country using the system.

The disadvantages are that each program contains unique messages and that a message file can grow very large. Since a read of the message file is required to fetch the proper message, program usage and maintenance of such a file can be cumbersome. Finding an appropriate predefined message for many program conditions is often difficult. When no message exists, a new message must be added to the file. Other programmer/analysts should be notified of new messages and their codes so that they will not use the same codes or create duplicate or similar messages. For a program to contain dozens of messages is not uncommon. I recommend avoiding the use of a message file.

Program Tables

The use of tables, like the certainty of change, is inevitable in most systems. Four types of tables are commonly used, those which are:

- defined in the program itself
- loaded into main storage as needed
- set up on a VSAM file, including relational database tables
- CICS data tables held in virtual storage above the 16-megabyte line

Tables defined in a program

Tables can be coded directly in a program or may be set up in a source code library, then copied into a program when it is compiled. A change to this type of table always requires programs that use the table to be recompiled. Limit the use of such tables to those that are short and unlikely to change often; otherwise, you will design ongoing maintenance into your system.

Tables loaded into main storage

Tables can be created and stored in a load library so that they can be loaded into main storage by a program as required, then released when the program is finished with the table. This type of table requires a PPT entry and is the type used for large tables and for those requiring frequent maintenance. This kind of table requires an amount of main storage equal to the size of the table; it should be released to free main storage as soon as it is no longer needed by a program.

Maintenance of such a table requires the creation of a new table load module and may require program maintenance. The table itself does require maintenance; changes can be time-consuming and the possibility of error is great on large-volume changes.

VSAM table files

Virtual storage access method (VSAM) is a technique for accessing and updating files randomly. An individual or general purpose VSAM file can be set up to handle each table required by the system. An advantage of individual VSAM table files is that the table can be set up to be the exact size required by the table's key plus its data.

The disadvantages of individual table files are that each table has to be maintained separately and each table requires an FCT entry. A general purpose table requires only one FCT entry and can be maintained by a single program, although several programs can be used. This type of table is easy to create and maintain, but has the disadvantage of wasting disk space. A general purpose table requires the key field size to be set to the largest key in the file. For instance, a table's key might consist of a four-character prefix, followed by the key itself, and then the data in the table. A two-digit state code requires the same key size as a 15-position key.

The file can be set up with variable-length records so that less space is wasted in the data portion of the file. If you use this type of a table, I recommend that you use a general purpose table file, because it is easy to work with, flexible, and facilitates table maintenance. A general purpose file, once created, can be maintained online by a single program or by several customized programs.

Relational databases, such as DB2 and CA-DATACOM/DB, discussed in chapters 21 and 24, have facilities for creating and maintaining tables. These tables may be employed in place of the VSAM files discussed above.

CICS data tables

More recent versions of CICS enable tables to be stored and maintained in virtual storage above the 16-megabyte line. General purpose/inquiry-only tables are excellent candidates for this feature.

Source data sets are used to relate CICS data tables to a VSAM KSDS file. These files require an FCT entry and are automatically loaded into virtual storage, above the 16-megabyte line, when the table is opened to CICS. CICS data tables are accessed and maintained by using file control commands in a fashion similar to that used to read and update VSAM files. CICS file control commands, such as READ, WRITE, REWRITE, and DELETE, can be used with CICS data tables. (For detailed information on the use of CICS commands used with data tables, refer to the CICS/ESA Application Programmer's Reference manual.) Two types of data tables are supported:

CICS-maintained tables (CMTs). These tables are maintained by CICS. Changes to tables in virtual storage are automatically updated on the source data set, while changes to the source data set are loaded into virtual storage.

User-maintained tables (UMTs). Updates to these tables are not automatically made to the VSAM associated source data set.

5

Basic Program Examples

CICS, as perceived by the applications programmer, is a collection of commands interspersed in a COBOL program. CICS commands provide the ability to send and receive terminal messages, read and write files, and perform other functions. The easiest way to learn CICS is through examples used to establish concepts the creative programmer can apply to real-life situations. Simple programs are covered here, and new commands are explained as encountered.

Send a Message to a Terminal

The program DISPLAYP, shown in Fig. 5.1, is initiated by the TRANSID DSPL, which is entered on a cleared screen. That's all there is to writing a CICS program that displays the message CICS IS EASY on the screen. Two commands were introduced in this program—the SEND command and the RETURN command.

SEND command

The SEND command, as used in Fig. 5.1, is very similar in concept to the DISPLAY statement used in COBOL batch processing programs.

```
IDENTIFICATION DIVISION.

PROGRAM-ID. DISPLAYP.

*********************************************************************
*     THIS PROGRAM ILLUSTRATES CICS SEND AND RETURN COMMANDS       *
*     A MESSAGE 'CICS IS EASY' IS DISPLAYED ON THE CRT             *
*********************************************************************

ENVIRONMENT DIVISION.

DATA DIVISION.

WORKING-STORAGE  SECTION.

01  WS-MESSAGE            PIC X(12)    VALUE 'CICS IS EASY'.

LINKAGE SECTION.


PROCEDURE DIVISION.

* SEND CRT MESSAGE
     EXEC CICS SEND
               FROM   (WS-MESSAGE)
               LENGTH (12)
     END-EXEC.

* RETURN TO CICS
     EXEC CICS RETURN
     END-EXEC.
```

Fig. 5.1 Program illustrating the SEND and RETURN commands.

The SEND command is used to display small amounts of data on the
screen. WS-MESSAGE is the same as a working-storage message would be
in a batch COBOL program. CICS requires a program to specify the length
of the message being sent.

```
EXEC CICS SEND
          FROM   (WS-MESSAGE)
          LENGTH (12)
END-EXEC.
```

RETURN command

The RETURN command, conceptually much like the GOBACK command in
COBOL, returns control to CICS.

```
EXEC CICS RETURN
END-EXEC
```

Compiling a CICS Program

Most data processing installations have standard procedures set up for translating and compiling CICS programs and placing the compiled output in the appropriate CICS load library.

All CICS commands begin with EXEC CICS. The translator recognizes this and breaks down CICS commands into call statements and may print a list of the original source program. This listing is seldom used by the application programmer and is often suppressed. The translated source data is then passed through a COBOL compiler, which prints a second listing showing CICS commands translated into move-and-call statements. Additional code is also placed into the program by the compiler. The object module created is "link-edited" to produce a load module.

The translated version of the program would be similar to that shown in Fig. 5.2. Comments in this version indicate that a field called DFHEIVAR is automatically inserted at the end of working storage by the CICS translator. DFHEIVAR's subfields are inserted into a program by the translator and used to hold call parameters employed by the translated version of CICS commands. CICS commands for send and return are commented out (*), and calls are generated by the translator for CICS commands, using DFHEIVAR subfields.

Translator call fields are inserted into a program by the translator in order to set up Calls that affect CICS commands. These fields are of no direct interest to you and are only mentioned so that you will recognize them when they appear in your program.

The translator generates, in the linkage section, fields named DFHEIBLK, the execute interface block (EIB) (see App. A-1), and DFHCOMMAREA, the communication area. CICS creates a new version of the EIB, with its updated values, for program use each time a new task is initiated.

You need not be overly concerned with how the translator works; no further illustrations will be presented for the translated version of programs.

Running a Compiled Program

Once a program compiles without error, it is ready for execution (if it has the appropriate PCT and PPT entries). Refresh the PPT program address by keying in CEMT I PRO(DISPLAYP) followed by NEW at the right of the displayed line. Clear the screen to set the cursor at POS=(01,01) on the screen. Key in the TRANSID DSPL and press ENTER. The following appears, starting at POS=(01,01) of the screen:

```
DSPLCICS IS EASY
```

```
IDENTIFICATION DIVISION.
PROGRAM-ID. DISPLAYP.

***********************************************************************
*              SIMULATED TRANSLATED VERSION OF A PROGRAM              *
***********************************************************************

ENVIRONMENT DIVISION.
DATA DIVISION.

WORKING-STORAGE  SECTION.

01  WS-MESSAGE           PIC X(12)   VALUE 'CICS IS EASY'.

*  DFHEIVAR FIELDS ARE INSERTED AT THE END OF WORKING STORAGE
*           BY THE CICS TRANSLATOR

LINKAGE SECTION.

01  DFHEIBLK  COPY  DFHEIBLK.
*       (See Appendix A-1)

01  DFHCOMMAREA        PIC X.


PROCEDURE DIVISION  USING  DFHEIBLK  DFHCOMMAREA.

* SEND CRT MESSAGE
*    EXEC CICS SEND
*              FROM   (WS-MESSAGE)
*              LENGTH (12)
*    END-EXEC.

     MOVE '          ' TO DFHEIV0
     MOVE 12 TO DFHEIV11
     CALL 'DFHEI1' USING DFHEIV0 DFHDUMMY DFHDUMMY
     WS-MESSAGE DFHEIV11.


* RETURN TO CICS
*    EXEC CICS RETURN
*    END-EXEC.

     MOVE '          ' TO DFHEIV0
     CALL 'DFHEI1' USING DFHEIV0.
```

Fig. 5.2 Translated CICS program.

To display the message without DSPL, that is,

```
CICS IS EASY
```

an ERASE option must be added to the SEND command:

```
EXEC CICS SEND
          FROM   (WS-MESSAGE)
          LENGTH (12)
          ERASE
END-EXEC.
```

ERASE will clear the screen and position the cursor at line 1, column 1 of the screen prior to the send. The sequence of the options following a command is not fixed. For instance, ERASE is specified last, but results in the screen's being cleared before information is sent to it.

SEND TEXT Command

The SEND TEXT command is commonly used interchangeably with the SEND command. SEND TEXT is preferable for large amounts of text and has formatting capabilities superior to the SEND command. Lines of text are split logically from line to line, and new line characters (X'15') can be embedded within the text. Many additional options are available with this command, such as FREEKB, which unlocks the keyboard after the text has been sent. The format of this command is:

```
EXEC CICS SEND TEXT
          FROM   (WS-MESSAGE)
          LENGTH (12)
          ERASE
          FREEKB
END-EXEC.
```

Receive a Message

Now that you know how to send a message to the terminal, let's see how you might receive data entered by a user. The program in Fig. 5.3 will receive a social security number and send a message using that number.

The user keys in the TRANSID RECV, a space, and then a nine-digit social security number. The program receives the data entered and displays the message:

```
SOCIAL SECURITY NUMBER = 999999999

RECV 999999999                       (Keyed in on first screen)
SOCIAL SECURITY NUMBER = 999999999   (Displayed on next screen)
```

The program in Fig. 5.3 illustrates several new CICS concepts plus the RECEIVE command. This program receives from the input terminal a message, which consists of the TRANSID, a blank, and social security number. It then displays a message containing the social security number. The new command introduced is RECEIVE. The program receives the input

Fig. 5.3 Program illustrating the CICS RECEIVE command.

```
IDENTIFICATION DIVISION.

PROGRAM-ID. RECEIVEP.

*********************************************************************
*       THIS PROGRAM ILLUSTRATES THE CICS RECEIVE COMMAND          *
*       SOCIAL SECURITY NUMBER IS ENTERED AND THEN DISPLAYED       *
*       IN A DIFFERENT FORMAT                                      *
*********************************************************************

ENVIRONMENT DIVISION.

DATA DIVISION.

WORKING-STORAGE   SECTION.

01  WS-INPUT.
    05  WS-TRANSID            PIC X(4)          VALUE SPACES.
    05  FILLER                PIC X             VALUE SPACES.
    05  WS-INPUT-SOC-SEC-NO   PIC X(9)          VALUE ALL 'X'.

01  WSOUTPUT.
    05  FILLER                PIC X(25)         VALUE
        'SOCIAL SECURITY NUMBER = '.
    05  WS-OUTPUT-SOC-SEC-NO  PIC X(9)          VALUE SPACES.

01  WS-LENGTH                 PIC S9(4)   COMP  VALUE ZEROES.


LINKAGE SECTION.


PROCEDURE DIVISION.

AA00-MAINLINE   SECTION.

    PERFORM B000-RECEIVE-INPUT.
    PERFORM C000-SEND-OUTPUT.

* RETURN TO CICS
    EXEC CICS RETURN
    END-EXEC.


B000-RECEIVE-INPUT   SECTION.

    MOVE 14   TO   WS-LENGTH.

    EXEC CICS RECEIVE
              INTO    (WS-INPUT)
              LENGTH  (WS-LENGTH)
    END-EXEC.
```

Fig. 5.3 *Continued.*

```
    MOVE WS-INPUT-SOC-SEC-NO   TO   WS-OUTPUT-SOC-SEC-NO.

B000-EXIT.
    EXIT.


C000-SEND-OUTPUT   SECTION.

    EXEC CICS SEND
              FROM    (WS-OUTPUT)
              LENGTH (34)
              ERASE
    END-EXEC.

C000-EXIT.
    EXIT.
```

message, including the TRANSID. Note that the RECEIVE's length option is specified with an argument WS-LENGTH, which you must define in working storage as a binary halfword. LENGTH can be hard-coded in the SEND command (i.e., LENGTH (34)). You always receive *into* and send *from*.

Basically, that's all there is to the SEND and RECEIVE commands, but there are a few additional considerations when using the RECEIVE command.

The input field entered may be shorter than the specified working-storage length parameter WS-LENGTH. For instance, if only the first eight positions of a social security number were keyed in, what would happen? WS-LENGTH would be set to 13 instead of the expected 14 (TRANSID + space + social security number), and the displayed message would show an X as the last digit of the social security number. Characters keyed in are received from left to right in the input area WS-INPUT.

The input field keyed in may be greater than WS-LENGTH. What occurs if the social security number is keyed in as 10 digits in error? WS-LENGTH is set to 15 instead of the anticipated 14 characters. Unfortunately, the output message does not display the 10-digit social security number. The program comes to an ABEND. You can probably get around this condition by making WS-INPUT-SOC-SEC-NO several digits longer than required and by adjusting WS-LENGTH accordingly, but there are better ways to handle this and similar anticipated or unexpected occurrences.

The RESP Option

The RESP option enables you to test the result of the execution of any CICS command, immediately following the command. The use of the RESP option lends itself to structured code and is the recommended method of testing for conditions that may occur. Its use is similar to that of the VSAM status code as used in batch applications.

Figure 5.4 illustrates the use of the RESP option. The RECEIVE command with the RESP option, returns the value of the EIB field EIBRESP into the programmer-defined fullword binary data area named WS-RESP. A number, representing the condition resulting from the execution of a CICS command, is returned in EIBRESP after the execution of each CICS command. You must provide for an error routine if an unanticipated code is returned. Section Z999-RESPONSE-ERROR, a simplified error processing routine defined in Fig. 5.5, is used in many of the program examples in this text. Many installations have standard error processing routines that abend the task and backout updates to databases.

```
WORKING-STORAGE   SECTION.

01   WS-LENGTH                 PIC S9(4)     COMP     VALUE ZEROES.
01   WS-RESP                   PIC S9(8)     COMP     VALUE +0.
     .   .   .


PROCEDURE DIVISION.
     .   .   .


B000-RECEIVE-INPUT   SECTION.

     MOVE 14   TO   WS-LENGTH.

     EXEC CICS RECEIVE
               INTO    (WS-INPUT)
               LENGTH (WS-LENGTH)
               RESP    (WS-RESP)
     END-EXEC.

     IF WS-RESP  =   DFHRESP(NORMAL)
        MOVE WS-INPUT-SOC-SEC-NO   TO   WS-OUTPUT-SOC-SEC-NO
     ELSE
        IF WS-RESP  =   DFHRESP(LENGERR)
             MOVE 'TOO MANY DIGITS ENTERED, PLEASE CLEAR SCREE]
                  'AND TRY AGAIN'   TO   WS-OUTPUT
        ELSE
             MOVE 'B000-'   TO   WS-RESP-SECTION
             PERFORM Z999-RESPONSE-ERROR.

B000-EXIT.
     EXIT.
```

Fig. 5.4 RESP option illustration.

```
WORKING-STORAGE  SECTION.

01  WS-RESP-ERROR.
      05  FILLER            PIC X(39)     VALUE
          'PROGRAM DISPLAYP: ERROR EIBRESP CODE = '.
      05  WS-RESP-ERR-CD    PIC 99        VALUE ZEROES.
      05  FILLER            PIC X(15)     VALUE
          '  IN SECTION '.
      05  WS-RESP-SECTION   PIC X(5)   VALUE SPACES.


PROCEDURE DIVISION.
      .   .   .

Z999-RESPONSE-ERROR  SECTION.
* * * * * * * * * * * * * * * * * * * * * * * * * * * * * * * * * * * * * * * * * * * * * * * * * * * * * * * *
*  INVALID EIBRESP CODE RETURNED DURING EXECUTION OF CICS COMMAND  *
* * * * * * * * * * * * * * * * * * * * * * * * * * * * * * * * * * * * * * * * * * * * * * * * * * * * * * * *

      MOVE WS-RESP  TO  WS-RESP-ERR-CD.

      EXEC CICS SEND
              FROM    (WS-RESP-ERROR)
              LENGTH (61)
              ERASE
      END-EXEC.

      EXEC CICS RETURN
      END-EXEC.

Z999-EXIT.
      EXIT.
```

Fig. 5.5 RESP option error routine.

The RESP option is coded the same in all examples in this book—RESP (WS-RESP). CICS has a built-in function called DFHRESP that enables you to test the RESP value symbolically. This makes coding easier because you do not have to remember the numerical value of numerous response codes. Figure 5.4 shows the use of the DFHRESP built-in function as follows:

```
IF WS-RESP = DFHRESP(NORMAL)
IF WS-RESP = DFHRESP(LENGERR)
```

Alternatively, you can look up the numerical value of EIBRESP associated with these conditions and code the above statements as:

```
IF WS-RESP = 00
IF WS-RESP = 22
```

For a list of EIBRESP codes with their symbolic equivalents, refer to Appendix C of this book. Common codes used with program examples in this text will be presented as required.

HANDLE CONDITION Commands

Although the use of the RESP option is recommended in handling program conditions, many older CICS programs that you may have to maintain were coded using the CICS HANDLE CONDITION command. This is another method of handling various anticipated or unexpected CICS conditions. An example of this command is:

```
EXEC CICS HANDLE CONDITION
          ERROR (ERROR-MESSAGE)
END-EXEC.
```

The ERROR option directs a program to transfer control to ERROR-MES-SAGE if any unanticipated events occur that cause an ABEND. The program transfers control to the paragraph named ERROR-MESSAGE, which can display a message, do error processing, and cause a normal program termination. The HANDLE CONDITION command must be executed *prior* to the condition being encountered, whereas the results of the RESP option are tested *after* execution of a CICS command. CICS debugging aids, which assist CICS programmers in determining the cause of errors, are discussed in chapter 18.

CICS programmers can usually anticipate and handle most conditions that occur in a program. An option of the HANDLE CONDITION command, called LENGERR, can be used to check for a length-error condition. LENGERR and other conditions that can be provided for will take precedence over the ERROR option.

```
EXEC CICS HANDLE CONDITION
          LENGERR (LENGTH-ERROR)
          ERROR   (ERROR-MESSAGE)
END-EXEC.
```

This handle condition causes the program to pass control to the paragraph named LENGTH-ERROR if the input data is longer than the anticipated working-storage length of 14. You can make this handle condition into two separate statements as follows:

```
EXEC CICS HANDLE CONDITION
          ERROR (ERROR-MESSAGE)
END-EXEC.

EXEC CICS HANDLE CONDITION
          LENGERR (LENGTH-ERROR)
END-EXEC.
```

A program abends if an error condition not provided for occurs, and if the ERROR option of the HANDLE CONDITION command is not coded. The use of the ERROR option of a HANDLE CONDITION command is similar to providing for error processing when using the RESP option. A program might be updating several databases when an ABEND occurs. CICS has the ability to dynamically back out file updates when an abend occurs. The ER-ROR condition prevents this automatic back-out. Unless the program makes provision for a back-out in the error message routine, files can get out of sync. When you maintain programs written by others, you will most likely encounter the ERROR condition. Just remember that a specific check for a condition such as LENGERR will supersede the ERROR condition if both conditions are coded.

Figure 5.6 illustrates how the procedure division of the sample program in Fig. 5.3 appears if the HANDLE CONDITION command is added.

Note that in paragraph C000-SEND-OUTPUT of Fig. 5.3, the LENGTH option must be specified with a length of 58. This allows for the length of the larger error message in Fig. 5.6. The working-storage area WS-OUTPUT

```
 B000-RECEIVE INPUT   SECTION.

* HANDLE LENGTH ERRORS

        EXEC CICS HANDLE CONDITION
                LENGERR (B000-LENGTH-ERROR)
        END-EXEC.

        MOVE 14   TO   WS-LENGTH.

        EXEC CICS RECEIVE
                INTO   (WS-INPUT)
                LENGTH (WS-LENGTH)
        END-EXEC.

        MOVE WS-INPUT-SOC-SEC-NO   TO   WS-OUTPUT-SOC-SEC-NO.

        GO TO   B000-EXIT.

 B000-LENGTH-ERROR.

        MOVE 'TOO MANY DIGITS ENTERED, PLEASE CLEAR SCREEN AND TRY
   -      'AGAIN'   TO   WS-OUTPUT.

 B000-EXIT.
        EXIT.
```

Fig. 5.6 HANDLE CONDITION command illustration.

in Fig. 5.3 has a FILLER PIC X(24) added after WS-OUTPUT-SOC-SEC-NO to make the field 58 positions long.

If the user forgets and enters dashes as part of social security number as follows:

```
RECV 150-22-3333
```

a length error is detected because the input length is now 16 instead of the expected length of 14. The following message:

```
TOO MANY DIGITS ENTERED, PLEASE CLEAR SCREEN AND TRY AGAIN
```

is displayed instead of the anticipated message:

```
SOCIAL SECURITY NUMBER = 150223333
```

The program can have two separate SEND commands; one for displaying social security number and one for the length-error message. The advantage of this technique is the ability to eliminate ERASE from the length-error send. Without ERASE, the send would keep the original entry on the screen for user verification. The message is displayed from the last recognized position of the cursor as follows:

```
RECV 150-22-3333 TOO MANY DIGITS ENTERED, PLEASE CLEAR
    SCREEN AND TRY AGAIN
```

Cursor positioning is discussed in greater detail later in this chapter.

General information about handle conditions

- One command can have up to 16 conditions
- The last command encountered takes precedence when prior commands list the same option
- To turn off an option, list the option without an argument

In Fig. 5.7, any length errors in HANDLE-PARAGRAPH-1 cause a transfer of control to LENGERR-PARAGRAPH-1. Length errors in HANDLE-PARA-GRAPH-2 cause a branch to LENGERR-PARAGRAPH-2. HANDLE-PARA-GRAPH-3 turns off the LENGERR condition, causing the program to default to the ERROR condition and to be directed to the paragraph ERROR-MESSAGE if a LENGERR condition occurs. If a length error occurs after

```
PROCEDURE DIVISION.

      EXEC CICS HANDLE CONDITION
              ERROR (ERROR-MESSAGE)
      END-EXEC.
        .
        .
        .
HANDLE-PARAGRAPH-1.

      EXEC CICS HANDLE CONDITION
              LENGERR (LENGERR-PARAGRAPH-1)
      END-EXEC.
        .
        .
        .
HANDLE-PARAGRAPH-2.

      EXEC CICS HANDLE CONDITION
              LENGERR (LENGERR-PARAGRAPH-2)
      END-EXEC.
        .
        .
        .
HANDLE-PARAGRAPH-3.

      EXEC CICS HANDLE CONDITION
              LENGERR
      END-EXEC.
        .
        .
        .
```

Fig. 5.7 HANDLE CONDITION command priorities.

HANDLE-PARAGRAPH-3 turned off the LENGERR condition, and if the HANDLE ERROR condition was absent, the program ABENDs.

IGNORE CONDITION Command

The IGNORE CONDITION command is sometimes helpful in situations when no action is desired upon encountering a program condition. This command permits our program to ignore the LENGERR condition and continue execution at the following statement. Up to sixteen conditions can be coded on the IGNORE CONDITION command. Only conditions specified in the IGNORE CONDITION command are disabled; any other handle conditions in effect remain active. A succeeding HANDLE CONDITION command in the program's logic can reactivate a condition that was ignored. The format of this command for the LENGERR condition is:

```
LEXEC CICS IGNORE CONDITION
            LENGERR
END-EXEC.
```

The NOHANDLE Option

There is another technique for ignoring program conditions that occur when a CICS command is executed. The NOHANDLE option may be coded on any CICS command to ignore *any* condition that occurs upon execution of that command. This option applies only to the CICS command on which it is included. The use of the RESP option implies NOHANDLE. You must be careful not to include the NOHANDLE or RESP option on a RECEIVE MAP command if you are using the CICS HANDLE AID command discussed in chapter 7. NOHANDLE overrides the HANDLE AID command, and tests for PF keys are ignored. The NOHANDLE option can be coded as follows:

```
EXEC CICS RECEIVE
            INTO    (WS-INPUT)
            LENGTH (WS-LENGTH)
            NOHANDLE
END-EXEC.
```

Cursor Position (EIBCPOSN)

CICS programs have the ability to check the position of the cursor when an AID key was pressed to initiate a receive. EIBCPOSN, a field in the EIB updated each time a receive command is executed, can be tested to determine the line and column at which the cursor was positioned. The programs in Figs. 5.4 and 5.6 could have eliminated LENGERR testing by coding the following prior to the RECEIVE command:

```
IF EIBCPOSN IS GREATER THAN 14
    MOVE 'TOO MANY DIGITS ENTERED, PLEASE CLEAR SCREEN
        ' AND TRY AGAIN'  TO  WS-OUTPUT
    GO TO  B000-EXIT.
```

If the EIBCPOSN check did not precede the receive, then LENGERR can occur on the receive, causing an ABEND.

When developing applications and writing programs, it is sometimes beneficial to know the line and column at which the cursor is positioned. The cursor position for line 1, column 1 is 0; for line 2, column 1, 80; for line 3, column 1, 160; etc. The last allowable cursor position is 1918. A programmer can determine the value of EIBCPOSN for any line and column by subtracting 1 from line number, multiplying that result by 80, and adding column number minus 1. For example,

```
Line 3,   column 1
       (3 - 1) × 80 + (1 - 1) = 160 = EIBCPOSN

Line 11, column 10
       (11 - 1) ×  80 + (10 - 1) = 809 = EIBCPOSN
```

The technique of cursor positioning is sometimes used to select an item displayed on a formatted screen, if the cursor is placed next to that item, prior to pressing a designated AID key. Positioning the cursor anywhere on a line can be used as a signal to delete the record displayed on that line when a designated AID key is pressed.

6

Basic Mapping Support

Proper design of maps is essential to the success of a CICS system. This discussion of basic mapping support (BMS) will be limited to what you need to know in order to create usable maps; it will not cover every option and possibility. BMS maps, which are collections of assembler language macros, can create problems if not properly understood; chapter 7 presents examples that should help to eliminate most difficulties you may encounter. The theory presented in this chapter makes more sense when used with the commands presented in chapter 7.

The SEND command examples in chapter 5 were introduced to aid in the presentation of important concepts; in reality, most terminal communication is performed through the use of maps. A map is basically an assembler program that formats terminal screens and controls the transfer of data between a terminal and CICS programs.

Map Types

The BMS map is run through an assembler program twice in order to produce two maps; the physical map and the symbolic map. A macro is an instruction that generates additional code when passed through an assembler program. Macros generate many statements when the BMS map is assembled; these statements result in instructions that aid in controlling physical and symbolic maps.

Physical maps

Physical maps are assembly language programs created and placed in a load library. Physical maps control screen alignment plus the sending and receiving of constants and data to and from a terminal.

Symbolic maps

Symbolic maps define map fields used to store variable data referenced in a COBOL program at compile time.

Format and Structure

Figure 6.1 defines a skeleton BMS map that should aid you in understanding the format and structure of a BMS map. When BMS maps are assembled, the macros are expanded. The application programmer is generally not interested in the listing of expanded macros. Including the statement PRINT NOGEN at the beginning of the BMS map suppresses the listing of expanded macros.

BMS format rules

The basic format of a BMS entry is:

[Label] [Macro] operand=(parameter 1,[parameter 2,...]),   X

Some of the rules BMS maps follow are:

- PRINT NOGEN starts in the same column as the mapset definition (DFHMSD) macro, usually column 10.
- Mapset, mapname(s), and field name(s) start in column 1, begin with an alphabetic character, and are seven or fewer characters in length
- Macros, such as DFHMSD, map definition for individual maps   (DFHMDI) and map definition for fields (DFHMDF), usually begin in column 10 and are followed by operands and parameters
- Macros are followed by one space and then an operand, plus parameters, such as TYPE=MAP
- Additional continuation operands must start in column 16, as does CTRL=(FREEKB,FRSET).
- If an operand is to be continued from one line to the next, it must be followed by a comma and have a continuation character (usually an X) in column 72. Parameters plus a comma must end at column 71 or sooner. An operand to be continued must be followed by a comma; otherwise, the

```
1...5...10...15...20...25...30...35...40...45...50...55...60...65...70..

          PRINT NOGEN
mapset    DFHMSD TYPE=MAP,                                              X
                 CTRL=(FREEKB,FRSET),                                   X
                 LANG=COBOL,                                            X
                 MODE=INOUT,                                            X
                 TERM=3270,                                             X
                 TIOAPFX=YES
*
mapnam1   DFHMDI LINE=01,                                              X
                 COLUMN=01,                                             X
                 SIZE=(24,80)
*
field1    DFHMDF POS=(   ,  ),                                         X
                 ATTRB=(attr1,attr2,...),                              X
                 LENGTH=99,                                            X
                 INITIAL='Map Constants'
*
          DFHMDF POS=(   ,  ),                                         X
                 ATTRB=(attr1,attr2,...),                              X
                 LENGTH=99,                                            X
                 INITIAL='Map Constants'
*
field2    DFHMDF POS=(   ,  ),                                         X
                 ATTRB=(attr1,attr2,...),                              X
                 LENGTH=99
                 . . .
*
fieldN    DFHMDF POS=(   ,  ),                                         X
                 ATTRB=(attr1,attr2,...),                              X
                 LENGTH=99
*
*
mapnam2   DFHMDI
                 . . .
*
field1    DFHMDF
                 . . .
*
fieldN    DFHMDF
                 . . .
*
          DFHMSD TYPE=FINAL
          END
```

Fig. 6.1 BMS map structure.

assembler assumes it is the last operand and ignores additional operands
and parameters until it encounters the next macro

- END usually starts in the same column as the preceding DFHMSD
  TYPE=FINAL macro; it signals the end of a map

- Multiple parameters for the same operand are enclosed in parentheses,
  such as CTRL=(FREEKB,FRSET)

- The operands for all macros can be set up as shown in Fig. 6.1 or can be
  strung across a couple of lines, such as:

```
mapset   DFHMSD TYPE=MAP,CTRL=(FREEKB,FRSET),   X
               LANG=COBOL,MODE=INOUT,              X
               TERM=3270,TIOAPFX=YES
```

- The sequence of operands is free-form

- An asterisk in column 1 defines the line as a comment line; its use, as shown in Fig. 6.1, improves readability

Map structure

The BMS map structure shown in Fig. 6.1 consists of the DFHMSD, DFH-MDI, and DFHMDF macros.

Mapset definition macro (DFHMSD). DFHMSD macros vary little from map to map within an installation; usually mapset name is the only difference. All maps in this book use identical DFHMSD operands and parameters; only mapset changes from map to map. This macro applies to all individual maps within a mapset; it occurs only as the first and last macro in a BMS map. Mapset is the name assigned to the BMS map.

Most installations have standards for assigning mapset names. The name assigned to mapset *must* be supported by a PPT entry; it is the label used in a SEND MAP (mapset) command, discussed in the next chapter. Mapset name is included in the physical map's load module. The DFHMSD macro follows mapset name and is preceded and followed by a space:

$$
TYPE = \left[\begin{array}{l} MAP \\ DSECT \\ FINAL \end{array} \right.
$$

The TYPE operand may use one of the first two parameters listed above for the first DFHMSD macro. A BMS map is assembled twice in order to create two maps: a physical map and a symbolic map. When defined as TYPE=MAP, the physical map is created, and when TYPE=DSECT, the symbolic map is generated. Application programmers refer to the symbolic map as a DSECT. A proc or standard JCL generally handles the creation of both maps. Usually only one job is submitted and BMS ignores the operands not required for each individual map. Always assemble both maps at the same time, otherwise the physical and symbolic maps may become out of sync. Every BMS map ends with a DFHMSD TYPE=FINAL macro, followed on the last line by END:

```
CTRL=(FREEKB,FRSET)
```

The CTRL operand can contain several parameters. The most common are FREEKB, FRSET, and ALARM.

- FREEKB—This parameter FREEs the KeyBoard and permits the entry of data when a map is sent to the screen; this parameter is usually included.

- FRSET—Resets FSET attributes to *off* before the send of a map; modi fied data tags (MDTs), part of the attribute that was on, will be turned off. This concept is explained later in the chapter, under FSET. (When on, FSET attributes results in the transfer of data from the screen into the program.)

- ALARM—Sounds an audible alarm or beep at a terminal when a map is sent. This parameter is not used often because users generally find the alarm annoying.

LANG=COBOL. The LANG operand defines the language of the source program in which the map will be used. It is only modified if the map is used in a non-COBOL program.

MODE=INOUT. MODE=INOUT specifies that the map will be used for both input and output operations and generates input and output symbolic map labels.

.=IN — generates an input symbolic map only

.=OUT —generates an output symbolic map only

I recommend using MODE=INOUT for all maps because it is required if you use symbolic cursor positioning, which is discussed in chapter 7.

TERM=3270. This command defines the type of terminal this map will be used with.

TIOAPFX=YES. Always include this parameter; it generates a 12-byte filler at the beginning of the symbolic map in order to skip over control characters. Failure to include this operand causes the map to be misaligned when it is sent.

Mapset definition of individual maps (DFHMDI). DFHMDI macros, like DFHMSD macros, differ little from map to map within an installation; usu- ally mapname is the only difference. All maps in this book use the same DFHMDI operands and parameters; only mapname varies from map to map. A mapset can have several maps associated with it as shown in Fig. 6.1; each map would have its own mapname, DFHMDI, and DFHMDF macros.

Mapname. This is the name assigned to individual maps within a mapset. This label is used in the SEND (mapname) command, which will be discussed in chapter 7. Mapname is stored along with mapset in the physical map load module. The DFHMDI macro follows mapname and is preceded and followed by a space.

LINE=01, COLUMN=01, SIZE=(24,80). These operands and parameters specify that the map starts at line 01, column 01 and is to be displayed on a screen 24 lines deep by 80 columns wide.

Map definition for fields (DFHMDF). DFHMDF macros, unlike DFHMSD and DFHMDI macros, vary considerably from map to map. Each field to be displayed or retrieved through a map must be defined by a DFHMDF macro. The basic structure of the field macro is shown in Fig. 6.2; only the most commonly used operands and parameters are discussed.

Field name. Every map field name to be referenced in a program must have a one- to seven-character name; this name supplies the symbolic map with a field name label. The DFHMDF macro follows field name and is preceded and followed by a space.

POS=. This refers to the position of the attribute immediately preceding a field; it is usually defined as a two-digit line and column number.

ATTRB=. This defines the attribute characteristics of a field. All attributes take up 1 byte immediately preceding the field defined. ASKIP, UNPROT, and PROT attributes define how the cursor will react to a field; they are mutually exclusive.

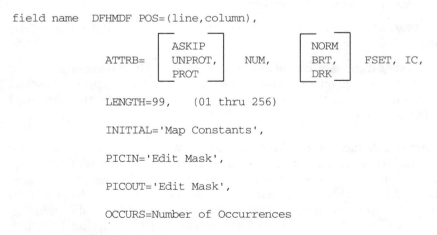

```
field name   DFHMDF POS=(line,column),

                     ┌ ASKIP  ┐              ┌ NORM ┐
             ATTRB=  │ UNPROT,│    NUM,      │ BRT, │   FSET, IC,
                     └ PROT   ┘              └ DRK  ┘

             LENGTH=99,    (01 thru 256)

             INITIAL='Map Constants',

             PICIN='Edit Mask',

             PICOUT='Edit Mask',

             OCCURS=Number of Occurrences
```

Fig. 6.2 DFHMDF—macro format.

- ASKIP—The cursor automatically skips over this field and stops at the next UNPROT field encountered. Remember that the cursor moves left to right, top to bottom; when it reaches the end of the map, it starts at the beginning of the map again. The ASKIP attribute is used as a stopper field following UNPROT fields, to skip to the next UNPROT field.

- UNPROT—The cursor stops at the first position of each UNPROT field (just to the right of the attribute) to allow for data entry. An UNPROT field should be followed by a stopper field (ASKIP or PROT), otherwise, data entry is permitted to continue until the next ASKIP or PROT field is encountered.

- PROT—Data cannot be entered into a PROT field. PROT is commonly used as a stopper field following an UNPROT field, when it is important to know if too many digits were entered into a field. PROT stops movement of the cursor in this case, whereas ASKIP skips to the next UNPROT field and allows the entry of the excess characters into that field. PROT can also be defined for map constant fields, since the cursor bypasses PROT fields and stops at the next UNPROT field. NOTE: ASKIP and PROT attributes are often used interchangeably. The major difference occurs when they are used at the end of an UNPROT field as a stopper field. PROT stops data entry, while ASKIP skips to the next UNPROT field and allows the continued entry of data.

- NUM—Data entered into a numeric field is right-justified, and unfilled positions to the left are filled with zeros. Fields not defined as NUM are left-justified and filled with spaces to the right of the last significant character entered. Unless a keyboard numeric lock feature is installed, it is possible to enter nonnumeric data into a NUM field. For instance, if "A" is entered into a NUM field, it is received as 000A. I recommend editing all input data.

- NORM—A field with this attribute is displayed at normal intensity.

- BRT—A field with bright intensity is highlighted to stand out on a screen. Data or field identifiers of items entered incorrectly are generally brightened. The cursor is positioned at the start of the first field in error, and error and operator-notification messages are highlighted.

- DRK—Fields with dark intensity are usually used for passwords or information that an onlooker is not permitted to view, since data entered into a dark field cannot be seen. Dark fields may be used to store data in unused positions of the screen in order to pass information to the same program or among different programs. I have found this use to be rare.

- FSET—When the user keys data into a field, an MDT is turned on, which causes entered data to be received into a program. Fields without the MDT on are not transmitted to a program. Specifying FSET in the BMS or symbolic map turns on the MDT. This returns data in a map field to the program on a RECEIVE MAP command, even if the user did not key data into the field. Sometimes, data sent to a screen, perhaps from a file which was read, is needed upon a succeeding receive of the map. FSET fields are turned off before the map is sent when FRSET is specified on the CTRL operand of the DFHMSD macro; the map being displayed then controls FSET attributes. This concept is very important and is discussed in detail in chapter 7.

- IC—The Insert Cursor (IC), part of an attribute, places the cursor at the first position of the map field that contains IC. Normally, only the first UN-PROT field on a map contains IC; if specified for more than one field, the *last* field specified with IC is the field at which the cursor stops. Using symbolic cursor positioning, discussed in the next chapter, the cursor is positioned at the *first* field if multiple fields are set. The cursor is positioned at screen position line 1, column 1, if IC is not specified and symbolic cursor positioning is not used. IC can be defined for an ASKIP or PROT field, but no data can be entered into the field; this is normally not done.

ASKIP,NORM is the default if ATTRB= is not defined and UNPROT,NORM is the default if only NUMeric and/or IC is specified.

LENGTH=field length. The valid values are 1 to 256 (characters).

INITIAL='map constants'. This gives an initial value to a constant or variable field. The DFHMDF macro should be assigned a field name if the field contents or its display intensity attribute is to be modified. INITIAL generally defines map constants displayed only at a predetermined intensity, and the macro does not require a field name in this case. If the map constant exceeds one line, continue the constant to column 71 of the first line, put an X in column 72, then on the next line, continue the constant, starting at column 16. Quotation marks should only occur at the beginning and at the end of the map constant. The characters ' and &, if used within an initial value, must be repeated twice. For example, O'Rourke && Sons' displays O'Rourke & Sons. The length of the constant is 15, not 17, because the extra characters do not take up any additional space on the map.

If the number of characters defined by INITIAL exceeds the value set by the length parameter, the excess characters are truncated when the map is sent.

PICIN='edit mask'. Input symbolic map fields are assigned a picture of X unless the PICIN (PICture IN) operand defines the picture differently. For example:

```
PICIN='999999'
```

PICOUT='edit mask'. Output symbolic map fields will be assigned a picture of X unless the PICOUT (PICture OUT) operand defines the picture differently. For example:

```
PICOUT='$ZZ,ZZZ.99'
```

OCCURS=number of occurrences. This generates a symbolic map OCCURS clause for the defined number of occurrences. This clause is most commonly used with map fields to be indexed, such as in a browse display. For example:

```
MAPDESC DFHMDF POS=(09,01),    X
               ATTRB=ASKIP,    X
               LENGTH=79,      X
               OCCURS=14
```

The above generates 14 lines of 79 characters, each with an ASKIP attribute in column 1 of each line. A programmer can then move a 79-character working-storage field to each MAPDESCO (map-index) symbolic map line.

BMS Map for a Menu

Figure 6.3 shows the vendor file maintenance submenu map and Fig. 6.4, the BMS map used to format the screen.

The first macro (DFHMSD) in Fig. 6.4 [1] has a label POVMNT1, the mapset name, which must be defined in the PPT. The rest of the operands and parameters are identical to those shown in Fig. 6.1.

The second macro (DFHMDI) [2] is shown with a mapname of MAPPOVM; the rest of the macro is the same as shown in Fig. 6.1. Several DFHMDI macros can be defined in one mapset. Try to limit each mapset to one map.

The last macro, DFHMSD TYPE=FINAL, followed by END [7] is standard for all maps. Other maps in this book do not refer to the last two entries or to the mapset and mapname macros; only mapset and mapname labels vary from map to map.

DFHMDF Macro Usage

Figure 6.4 demonstrates the use of many of the DFHMDF parameters discussed, and a comparison with Fig. 6.3 should make the defining of BMS macros easy to understand.

[3] *a.* Defines a map-constant field ABC MANUFACTURING COMPANY with a preceding ASKIP attribute in line 1, column 27; it is 25 characters long.

   b. The option ATTRIB=ASKIP can be omitted since it is the default; I like to include the ATTRB operand for all map fields. This helps document a map for those unfamiliar with the default settings.

   c. No label is shown in columns 1 to 7; therefore, no symbolic map entry is generated. Constant fields that may be displayed with varying

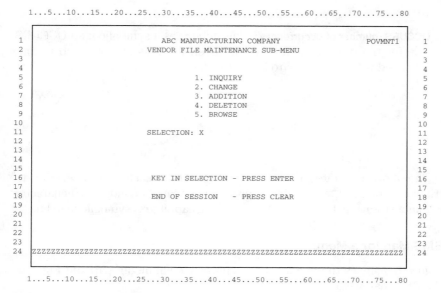

```
      1...5...10...15...20...25...30...35...40...45...50...55...60...65...70...75...80

   1                          ABC MANUFACTURING COMPANY                   POVMNT1    1
   2                        VENDOR FILE MAINTENANCE SUB-MENU                          2
   3                                                                                  3
   4                                                                                  4
   5                               1. INQUIRY                                         5
   6                               2. CHANGE                                          6
   7                               3. ADDITION                                        7
   8                               4. DELETION                                        8
   9                               5. BROWSE                                          9
  10                                                                                 10
  11                        SELECTION: X                                             11
  12                                                                                 12
  13                                                                                 13
  14                                                                                 14
  15                                                                                 15
  16                        KEY IN SELECTION - PRESS ENTER                           16
  17                                                                                 17
  18                        END OF SESSION   - PRESS CLEAR                           18
  19                                                                                 19
  20                                                                                 20
  21                                                                                 21
  22                                                                                 22
  23                                                                                 23
  24  ZZZZZZZZZZZZZZZZZZZZZZZZZZZZZZZZZZZZZZZZZZZZZZZZZZZZZZZZZZZZZZZZZZZZZZZZZZZZZZZZ  24

      1...5...10...15...20...25...30...35...40...45...50...55...60...65...70...75...80
```

Fig. 6.3 Vendor file maintenance submenu map.

    intensity (BRT, NORM, or DRK) require a label in order to generate a symbolic map field name.

    d. LENGTH must correspond to INITIAL=map constant size.

[4] *a.* Defines the field into which the user makes a selection. A symbolic map field name is generated, since this macro has a field name MS-ELECT.

    b. The attribute preceding the field starts at line 11, column 34; it is one character long.

    c. The attribute UNPROT causes the cursor to stop at a field for data entry, and IC causes the cursor to be positioned initially at the start of the field (not at the attribute) when the physical map is sent (chapter 7 explains this technique). This is the only UNPROT field on this map. IC alone can be entered in the ATTRB field, since, in this case, UNPROT is the default. Chapter 7 explains symbolic cursor positioning, which allows the program to override IC on a send that includes the symbolic map.

    d. INITIAL is often omitted for UNPROT fields unless it is desired to assign an initial default value to the field. For instance, if INQUIRY is selected much more frequently than any other item on the vendor file maintenance submenu, the DFHMDF macro is defined as follows:

```
MSELECT DFHMDF POS=(11,34),              X
               ATTRB=(UNPROT,FSET,IC),   X
               LENGTH=01,                X
               INITIAL='1'
```

Note: ATTRB= now contains FSET to turn on the MDT so that when the user presses ENTER, the selection of 1 will initially be received by the program as if the user had entered a 1, turning on the MDT. This may only be true of a receive of a map that immediately follows a send of the physical map, which is explained in chapter 7.

[5] *a.* Defines a 1-byte stopper field with an attribute of PROT; without this stopper field, the user can continue entering data into the SE-LECTION field. An attempt to enter more than one digit into the SELECTION field causes the cursor to stop, the keyboard to lock, and requires the user to press RESET in order to continue.

   b. Generally, if more than one UNPROT field exists on a map, the stopper field contains an ATTRB=ASKIP so that when one field is entered, the cursor skips to the next UNPROT field. Setting all stopper attributes to PROT requires the user to press the TAB key each time a data field is completely filled.

[6] *a.* A symbolic map field name is generated, since a field name MAPMESG is included in this field.

   b. ASKIP attribute preceding this field is in line 24, column 1.

   c. This field often has its intensity changed by the program to ASKIP, BRT when user-notification or error messages are displayed.

   d. This field is sometimes defined with an initial value and AT-TRB=(ASKIP,DRK), defined so that the message does not display until a program changes the attribute to ASKIP,BRT. I prefer not to assign an initial value to message fields and to let the program select the message to be displayed.

Refresh the PPT when a Map Changes

The PPT should be refreshed with the latest load library address of the physical map when it is reassembled; failure to do so can lead to unpredictable results. A map is considered a program by CICS and the PPT is updated by:

```
CEMT SET PRO(mapset) NEW
```

A program almost always changes when a symbolic map is altered. Make sure the BMS map is assembled correctly before compiling the changed program to ensure that the program will have the latest version of the BMS-generated symbolic map (unless you employ user-friendly symbolic maps, discussed later in this chapter). After the program has been compiled, refresh its address in the PPT:

```
CEMT SET PRO(program) NEW
```

Fig. 6.4 BMS map for vendor file maintenance submenu.

```
         PRINT NOGEN

POVMNT1  DFHMSD TYPE=MAP,                                          X
                CTRL=(FREEKB,FRSET),                               X
                LANG=COBOL,                     [1]               X
                MODE=INOUT,                                       X
                TERM=3270,                                        X
                TIOAPFX=YES
*

MAPPOVM  DFHMDI LINE=01,                                           X
                COLUMN=01,                      [2]               X
                SIZE=(24,80)
*

         DFHMDF POS=(01,27),                                       X
                ATTRB=ASKIP,                            [3] X
                LENGTH=25,                                        X
                INITIAL='ABC MANUFACTURING COMPANY'
*
         DFHMDF POS=(01,72),                                       X
                ATTRB=ASKIP,                                      X
                LENGTH=07,                                        X
                INITIAL='POVMNT1'
*
         DFHMDF POS=(02,24),                                       X
                ATTRB=ASKIP,                                      X
                LENGTH=32,                                        X
                INITIAL='VENDOR FILE MAINTENANCE SUB-MENU'
*
         DFHMDF POS=(05,34),                                       X
                ATTRB=ASKIP,                                      X
                LENGTH=10,                                        X
                INITIAL='1. INQUIRY'
*
         DFHMDF POS=(06,34),                                       X
                ATTRB=ASKIP,                                      X
                LENGTH=09,                                        X
                INITIAL='2. CHANGE'
*
         DFHMDF POS=(07,34),                                       X
                ATTRB=ASKIP,                                      X
                LENGTH=11,                                        X
                INITIAL='3. ADDITION'
```

Fig. 6.4 *Continued.*

```
*
           DFHMDF POS=(08,34),
                  ATTRB=ASKIP,
                  LENGTH=11,
                  INITIAL='4. DELETE'
*
           DFHMDF POS=(09,34),
                  ATTRB=ASKIP,
                  LENGTH=09,
                  INITIAL='5. BROWSE'
*
           DFHMDF POS=(11,23),
                  ATTRB=ASKIP,
                  LENGTH=10,
                  INITIAL='SELECTION:'
*
MSELECT DFHMDF POS=(11,34),
                  ATTRB=(UNPROT,IC),          [4]
                  LENGTH=01
*
           DFHMDF POS=(11,36),
                  ATTRB=PROT,                  [5]
                  LENGTH=01
*
           DFHMDF POS=(16,25),
                  ATTRB=ASKIP,
                  LENGTH=30,
                  INITIAL='KEY IN SELECTION - PRESS ENTER'
*
           DFHMDF POS=(18,25),
                  ATTRB=ASKIP,
                  LENGTH=30,
                  INITIAL='END OF SESSION  - PRESS CLEAR'
*
MAPMESG DFHMDF POS=(24,01),
                  ATTRB=ASKIP,                 [6]
                  LENGTH=79
*
           DFHMSD TYPE=FINAL                    [7]
                  END
```

Command-Level Interpreter

The format of a physical map can be checked by using the command-level interpreter (CECI). CECI, a transaction identifier, initiates the command level interpreter, which is a CICS application program. CECI is a translator supplied with CICS, which is useful for checking the syntax and execution of many CICS commands. The user can clear the screen, key in CECI, and press the enter key to display a list of CICS commands. Commands can be syntax-checked and executed from the list. The complete command can be keyed in when CECI is entered, if you know the syntax and want to see the results of the execution of the command. If you do not know the syntax, just key in CECI and press ENTER and the system prompts you for other entries.

The command-level interpreter is useful for testing new or changed BMS physical maps for format and entry of UNPROT fields. You just have to key in the following and press ENTER:

```
CECI SEND MAP (mapset)
```

The above command displays the same physical map as the SEND command in a program. This allows you to test your physical map before it is used in a program.

The Generated Symbolic Map

The symbolic map generated by the BMS map in Fig. 6.4 looks similar to the map in Fig. 6.5. Blank (*) lines, comments, and alignment are included to improve readability; they are not found in the actual symbolic map generated. The symbolic map can be copied into a program by using the following COPY statement.

```
*01 MAPPOVMI
            COPY POVMNT1
```

Most symbolic maps will usually contain more fields than shown in Fig. 6.5, but the format of the generated symbolic map is always the same. The first 12 bytes of the COBOL symbolic map consist of a FILLER PIC X(12). Variable fields in a map are generated with an input (I) suffix and an output (O) suffix (such as MSELECTI and MSELECTO).

The input map MAPPOVMI contains various types of fields:

- L suffix (length field)—This field contains the length of the input field keyed in on the map by a user when the program receives the map. By moving a -1 to a length field, such as MSELECTL, before issuing a SEND MAP command, the cursor is positioned at the start of that field on the screen. This is referred to as *symbolic cursor positioning* and is discussed in chapter 7. The L suffix is generally not used with fields defined as ASKIP, such as MAPMESGL.

- F suffix (flag byte)—You can use this field during input procedures to test if the terminal operator has cleared a field, such as MSELECTF, using the EOF key on the terminal. The flag byte contains hexadecimal 80 (X'80') if EOF had been pressed; otherwise, it would equal X'00' (low

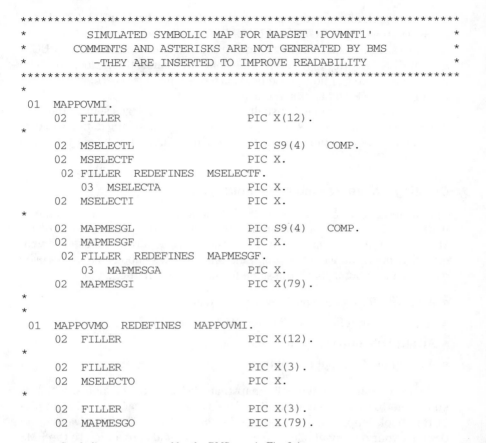

```
*********************************************************************
*              SIMULATED SYMBOLIC MAP FOR MAPSET 'POVMNT1'         *
*         COMMENTS AND ASTERISKS ARE NOT GENERATED BY BMS          *
*              -THEY ARE INSERTED TO IMPROVE READABILITY           *
*********************************************************************
*
 01   MAPPOVMI.
      02   FILLER                    PIC X(12).
*
      02   MSELECTL                  PIC S9(4)    COMP.
      02   MSELECTF                  PIC X.
       02 FILLER  REDEFINES  MSELECTF.
          03   MSELECTA              PIC X.
      02   MSELECTI                  PIC X.
*
      02   MAPMESGL                  PIC S9(4)    COMP.
      02   MAPMESGF                  PIC X.
       02 FILLER  REDEFINES  MAPMESGF.
          03   MAPMESGA              PIC X.
      02   MAPMESGI                  PIC X(79).
*
*
 01   MAPPOVMO  REDEFINES  MAPPOVMI.
      02   FILLER                    PIC X(12).
*
      02   FILLER                    PIC X(3).
      02   MSELECTO                  PIC X.
*
      02   FILLER                    PIC X(3).
      02   MAPMESGO                  PIC X(79).
```

Fig. 6.5 Symbolic map generated by the BMS map in Fig. 6.4.

values). The F suffix is not used with fields defined as ASKIP, such as MAPMESGF.

- Map redefinition of this field

- A suffix (attribute field)—This field may be used during output procedures (see SEND MAP discussed in chapter 7) to override the attribute field defined in the BMS map.

- I suffix (input field)—This field contains the data entered by the user and received into the program (see RECEIVE MAP, discussed in chapter 7).

- Map redefinition of this field.

- O suffix (output field)—This field is used to hold the output field for operations requiring the send of a map.

A close look at the symbolic map shows that F (flag) and A (attribute) fields, such as MSELECTF and MSELECTA, share the same storage location. In a similar fashion, I (input) and O (output) fields, such as MSELECTI and MSELECTO, through redefinition share the same storage location. The main determinant of how these fields are referenced is whether we are receiving a map (F and I) or sending a map (A and O).

The last line of the map is usually reserved for messages sent to the user regarding conditions that may require action, such as keying data into a certain field or notification of error conditions. Figure 6.5 labels this field MAPMESGO.

Creating a More Readable Symbolic Map

The symbolic map created by BMS is difficult to read and cumbersome to work with. Depending on your installation's standards, you may wish to create a more readable map. Many data processing departments use the generated symbolic map in their programs. All COBOL symbolic maps, not used with color attributes, have the same format as shown in Fig. 6.5:

- A 12-byte filler at the beginning of the map
- A 2-byte length field PIC S9(4) COMP for each field
- An attribute or flag byte for each field
- A data field for input and output

Figure 6.6 shows a symbolic map that contains longer labels, which is equivalent to that shown in Fig. 6.5. For ease of understanding, all examples in this book employ more readable symbolic maps. The disadvantage of defining your own symbolic map is that as new fields are added to the BMS map, it is necessary to keep the redefined map in *sync* with the BMS map. This requires additional maintenance to affected programs. See chapter 19 for color attribute considerations.

Screen Definition Facility (SDF)

IBM provides a map generator, named Screen Definition Facility (SDF), that enables the design and creation of maps to be performed in an interactive fashion. All facilities of BMS are included with SDF. The screen designer can paint a screen online, define screen attributes, name symbolic map fields, and assemble the map. The map can be viewed at various stages of development and modified as appropriate. SDF provides the capability to assign more meaningful names, up to 15 characters in length, to symbolic map fields. Symbolic maps generated by SDF with longer more meaningful labels are more readable than the BMS generated symbolic map.

Another advantage of using SDF or other screen generators is that there is no need to define your own user-friendly symbolic maps. This reduces the

```
**********************************************************************
*                    USER FRIENDLY MENU SYMBOLIC MAP                 *
**********************************************************************
*
 01  MPM-MENU-MAP.
      05  FILLER                    PIC X(12).
*
      05  MPM-L-SELECTION           PIC S9(4)      COMP.
      05  MPM-A-SELECTION           PIC X.
      05  MPM-D-SELECTION           PIC X.
*
      05  MPM-L-MESSAGE             PIC S9(4)      COMP.
      05  MPM-A-MESSAGE             PIC X.
      05  MPM-D-MESSAGE             PIC X(79).
```

Fig. 6.6 More readable menu symbolic map.

maintenance required to keep user-friendly symbolic maps in *sync* with the BMS generated symbolic map.

7

Using Assembled
BMS Maps

COBOL CICS command-level programs are generally compiled after the BMS map has been assembled. The BMS-generated symbolic map or its redefined counterpart is included in the program. The symbolic map can be copied from a copy library or coded directly into the program's working storage or linkage section. Maps are either sent from or received into working storage or the linkage section of a program. This book defines its maps in working storage, where they are commonly found. Conceptually, there is little difference in mapping, regardless of where the map is located.

This chapter covers the SEND MAP and RECEIVE MAP commands, the use of map attributes, and cursor positioning on the map. I consider this chapter the key to mastering CICS; reread it until you thoroughly understand all concepts presented. My experience has been that a large percentage of programming difficulty is caused by a lack of understanding of the function that map attributes perform in pseudoconversational programming.

Send Map Command

The SEND MAP command can be issued to send the physical and/or symbolic map in order to format a terminal screen. The format of the SEND

MAP command is as follows; only the options you are most likely to encounter are listed:

```
EXEC CICS SEND
          MAP        (mapname)
          MAPSET     (mapset)
          FROM       (data-area)
          [MAPONLY   / DATAONLY]
          [ERASE     / ERASEAUP]
          [CURSOR]
          [FREEKB]
          [FRSET]
          [ALARM]
END-EXEC.
```

FREEKB, FRSET, and ALARM can be specified on the send of a map, but because I define only one map per mapset, these options, when desired, are included in the BMS map. All three options perform the same function as described under the DFHMSD CTRL= option in chapter 6. This book includes FREEKB and FRSET in the BMS map for all examples and not on the SEND command. I do not use the ALARM parameter in this book.

The SEND MAP command uses the following options and arguments:

- MAP (mapname)—The mapname from the BMS map DFHMDI label.

- MAPSET (mapset)—The mapset from the BMS map DFHMSD label; this is the PPT entry.

- FROM (data-area)—A programmer-defined working-storage area from which the symbolic map is sent.

- MAPONLY—Only the physical map is to be sent.

- DATAONLY—Only the symbolic map is to be sent.

- ERASE—Clears the screen before sending the map. This option is not used with DATAONLY because the symbolic map's data would be sent to a screen that has no constant data displayed.

- ERASEAUP—Erases all UNPROT fields; it is used only with a send of DATAONLY. ASKIP or PROT fields, such as constants and message fields, would not be erased by this option.

- CURSOR—This option is used with symbolic cursor positioning (discussed later in this chapter) in order to place the cursor at the required field.

Types of SEND Commands

The SEND MAP command is similar to the send of a message as presented in chapter 5. Three command types are frequently selected when using the

SEND MAP command: SEND MAP AND DATA, SEND MAP DATAONLY, and SEND MAP MAPONLY. You must thoroughly understand these command types to design and use maps properly in CICS programs.

SEND MAP AND DATA

The format of this send is:

```
EXEC CICS SEND
          MAP     (mapname)
          MAPSET  (mapset)
          [FROM   (data-area)]
          ERASE
          [CURSOR]
END-EXEC.
```

This option sends both physical and symbolic maps, which are merged together on the screen. Always specify ERASE with SEND MAP AND DATA in order to clear the screen prior to the send. Use CURSOR with symbolic cursor positioning to set the cursor to the proper location on the screen. If CURSOR is not included on this send, the BMS map controls cursor positioning. Use this send if variable data is on the initial send; for instance, date and time.

When FROM is omitted, the program sends its map from the working storage map, which is generated by BMS and must be copied into the program at compile time. With FROM specified, the program will send its symbolic map's data from the programmer-created easier-to-read symbolic map, which is placed in working storage.

SEND MAP MAPONLY

The format of this send is:

```
EXEC CICS SEND
          MAP     (mapname)
          MAPSET  (mapset)
          ERASE
          MAPONLY
END-EXEC.
```

It sends only the physical map and is generally used for the initial send of a map when there is no variable data to be sent to the screen. MAPONLY is also used to send information or help screens that do not require a user to enter data. Help screens are, in a sense, online instructions that supplement user guides. MAPONLY is usually sent only once in a program, to a cleared screen. The cursor position for this option is determined by the BMS map IC attribute. The cursor is set at screen POS=(01,01) if the BMS map did not specify an IC attribute.

SEND MAP DATAONLY

The format of this send is:

```
EXEC CICS SEND
          MAP      (mapname)
          MAPSET (mapset)
          [FROM    (data-area)]
          DATAONLY
          [CURSOR]
END-EXEC.
```

It sends the symbolic map. This send is generally used after the physical map has been sent by one of the previously described SEND MAP commands. Only variable data has to be sent when the physical map is showing on the screen. This format of the SEND MAP command is generally used to send error and operator messages, as well as to highlight fields that contain errors. Do not specify ERASE with this option of the send; otherwise, you will display a screen that contains only the variable data from the symbolic map.

Symbolic Cursor Positioning

Cursor positioning can be controlled by specifying IC in an attribute field on the BMS map and then issuing a send that includes the physical map (not DATAONLY). This method works fine if the cursor is always located at the same position, which is often not the case. On an addition or change map, a variety of fields may be entered incorrectly, and you might position the cursor at the first field in error. Symbolic cursor positioning provides this facility. The cursor is positioned at the start of the designated field and overrides IC if specified in the BMS map. For example:

```
MOVE - 1 TO mapfldL
```

This places the cursor at the start of the map field. Sometimes multiple errors are encountered when a map's fields are edited. A –1 is moved to the length field of each item incorrectly entered. If more than one length field contains a –1, the first such field encountered controls the cursor position. The cursor is set at the start of the field when a SEND MAP command is issued.

To use symbolic cursor positioning:

1. The BMS map must specify MODE=INOUT on the DFHMSD macro.
2. CURSOR must be specified on a SEND MAP command that includes the symbolic map (not MAPONLY).
3. The program must move –1 to the symbolic map length field of the item at which the CURSOR is to be positioned, prior to issuing a SEND MAP command. If CURSOR is not specified on a DATAONLY send, the cursor is set at POS=(01,01).

SEND MAP Transaction ABEND

During the execution of a SEND MAP command, an unanticipated condition sometimes occurs, causing a program to come to an ABEND. A message is displayed on the screen indicating that an APCT abend has occurred.

The ABEND code APCT is displayed if the map has not been defined in the PPT or if the map has been disabled. Use the CEMT I PRO(mapname) to determine if the map is in the PPT and if so, if it is ENAbled or DISabled.

Disabling a Program

Programs, maps, and tables are occasionally disabled by the use of the master terminal command CEMT in order to prevent the access of problem modules. A program is also disabled if no load module is found when the CICS system references the module. This condition will lead to an APCT ABEND for maps sent and a PGMIDERR handle condition for programs and tables that a program attempts to bring into main storage.

Low-Values Are Not Transmitted

Low-values are the characters of least value known to the computer system; they are represented by hexadecimal zeros (X'00'). Low-values are not transmitted between a program and a terminal when a map is sent or received; therefore, it is good practice to initialize symbolic maps. A program should initialize the symbolic map to low-values prior to a receive of a map and prior to formatting the map with data to be sent. A map formatted with spaces results in the transmission of those spaces during a send operation, resulting in unnecessary traffic over transmission lines. Sometimes, a field such as a message that is displayed on the screen, must be blanked out on a subsequent send of the map. Moving low-values to the field to be blanked out does not eliminate the display of a field, because low-values are not transmitted. Move spaces to any symbolic map fields to be blanked out by the SEND MAP command, since spaces *are* transmitted.

RECEIVE MAP Command

The following RECEIVE MAP command facilitates the receive of the symbolic map into working storage or the linkage section:

```
EXEC CICS RECEIVE
          MAP     (mapname)
          MAPSET  (mapset)
          [INTO   (data-area)  |
          SET     (ptr-ref)    |
          SET     (ADDRESS OF struc) ]
END-EXEC.
```

The program can receive the map into the working-storage area or linkage section area defined by the symbolic map generated by BMS. This area is copied into the program at compile time from a copy library. The program can also receive the map into a redefined symbolic map in working storage (data-area) that you can define.

Remember to initialize the symbolic map's working storage to low-values before issuing the RECEIVE MAP command. All fields containing significant data (not low-values) are received into the symbolic map when the RECEIVE MAP command is issued, provided that their MDTs are turned on (see "FSET" in chapter 6). Remember, data may appear on the screen and not be returned to the program on a RECEIVE MAP command if the MDT for the field is turned off.

Locate Mode Processing

All program examples in this text use the *move* mode of processing in which program I/O areas are placed in working storage. In practice, you may find that programs you have to maintain use the linkage area for program I/O. This is referred to as the *locate* mode of processing. The locate mode of processing uses BLL Cells in OS/VS COBOL, which are explained in chapter 10. VS COBOL II can use the linkage section for its I/O, but has eliminated the need for BLL Cells as explained in chapter 25. For your convenience of reference, where appropriate, all CICS commands have their I/O area presented as shown in the preceding RECEIVE MAP command:

```
[INTO (data-area)   |
 SET  (ptr-ref)     |
 SET  (ADDRESS OF struc) ]
```

where:

- INTO (data-area)—refers to a programmer-defined working storage I/O area. This is used in the move mode of processing by programs in this text.

- SET (ptr-ref)—refers to the setting of a BLL Cell pointer by OS/VS COBOL programs that use the locate mode of processing.

- SET (ADDRESS OF struc)—sets the ADDRESS special register to the address of a *struc*ture, which is essentially an I/O area, in VS COBOL II programs (explained in chapter 25).

Map Attributes

It has been my experience that misuse of map attributes and of MDTs causes more confusion and program errors than does any other area of

CICS application programming. Attributes control individual map fields on the screen. The user is given the ability to automatically skip over a field (ASKIP) or to enter data into a unprotected field (UNPROT), or is prevented from entering data into a protected field (PROT). The BMS map or program can determine the intensity at which a map field displays: BRT, NORM or DRK. A field can be received as alphanumeric data (left-justified, padded with spaces) or numeric (NUM) data (right-justified, padded with zeros). The cursor can be set by specifying IC in the BMS map or through program symbolic cursor positioning. Specifying FSET for a field in the BMS or symbolic map turns on its MDT when the map is sent. Symbolic map attributes override BMS map attributes. The user turns on the MDT when a map field is keyed into. Including FRSET in the CTRL operand of the BMS map's DFHMSD macro causes all MDTs to be turned off before a map is sent. The combination of all the above considerations causes the best of programmers some grief.

Standard Attribute Characters

CICS has available a list of standard attribute characters in the form of a copy book called DFHBMSCA. The standard attribute control list is a set of standard control characters used by CICS, which can be copied into a program. Many data processing departments create their own list of the more commonly used attribute characters, assigning more meaningful labels.

As shown in Fig. 7.1, all DFHBMSCA fields begin with DFHBM..., and the last three characters are not very descriptive. These fields do not cover many of the attribute configurations required by the application programmer. The programmer may move certain attribute characters directly to the

```
01      DFHBMSCA  COPY  DFHBMSCA.
        02  DFHBMPEM    PIC X    VALUE ' '.
        02  DFHBMPNL    PIC X    VALUE ' '.
        02  DFHBMASK    PIC X    VALUE '0'.
        02  DFHBMUNP    PIC X    VALUE ' '.
        02  DFHBMUNN    PIC X    VALUE '&'.
        02  DFHBMPRO    PIC X    VALUE '-'.
        02  DFHBMBRY    PIC X    VALUE 'H'.
        02  DFHBMDAR    PIC X    VALUE '<'.
        02  DFHBMFSE    PIC X    VALUE 'A'.
        02  DFHBMPRF    PIC X    VALUE '/'.
        02  DFHBMASF    PIC X    VALUE '1'.
        02  DFHBMASB    PIC X    VALUE '8'.
        02  DFHBMEOF    PIC X    VALUE ' '.
```

Fig. 7.1 DFHBMSCA fields.

symbolic map prior to issuing a SEND MAP command. The following illustrates the alignment of the more commonly used attribute names found in the list above (DFHBMSCA) and in Appendix B (STWSATTR):

DFHBMSCA	Descriptive	Value
DFHBMASK	ASKIP-NORM	'0'.
DFHBMUNP	UNPROT-NORM	SPACE.
DFHBMUNN	UNPROT-NUM	'&'.
DFHBMBRY	UNPROT-BRT	'H'.
DFHBMFSE	UNPROT-FSET	'A'.
DFHBMASF	ASKIP-FSET	'1'.
DFHBMASB	ASKIP-BRT	'8'.

The application programmer may move any of the equivalent characters, during execution of an application program, to the symbolic map's attribute field. For example:

```
MOVE DFHBMASB   TO  mapfldA.
MOVE ASKIP-BRT  TO    "
MOVE '8'        TO    "
```

This book will use the attribute characters shown in App. B for all program examples. You should be aware of DFHBMSCA characters, since you may encounter them in programs which you have to maintain. I recommend using a list of characters similar to STWSATTR and making it a standard copy library member at your installation. Chapter 19 will discuss DFHBMSCA sub fields that are used if color monitors are in use at your installation.

Testing for EOF Key

The DFHBMEOF attribute character, in the DFHBMSCA copy member, is commonly used to test if a CRT user has pressed the EOF key. DFHBMEOF is defined with a value of hexadecimal 80 (X'80'). A field's flag (attribute) byte on the symbolic map can be tested after a RECEIVE MAP command for a value of hexadecimal 80, to determine if EOF has been pressed as follows:

```
IF MPM-A-SELECTION  =  DFHBMEOF
   MOVE SPACES  TO  CA-SELECTION.
```

　　　　or

```
IF MSELECTF  =  DFHBMEOF
   MOVE SPACES  TO  CA-SELECTION.
```

Programs that you have to maintain sometimes define their own version of DFHBMEOF. Some of the more commonly encountered redefinitions are similar to the following:

```
05  EOF-COMP-3      PIC S999  COMP-3    VALUE +800.
05  FILLER   REDEFINES   EOF-COMP-3.
    10  EOF        PIC X.
    10  FILLER     PIC X.
```

or

```
05  EOF-COMP        PIC S9999   COMP     VALUE +128.
05  FILLER   REDEFINES   EOF-COMP.
    10  FILLER     PIC X.
    10  EOF        PIC X.
```

It is common practice to save map fields in a communications area (DFH-COMMAREA) during editing. This can minimize the transmission of screen data. When a field has been entered correctly it is saved in the communications area and does not need to be transmitted on subsequent sends or receives of a screen. The communications area is discussed in more detail in chapter 8 and succeeding chapters.

Changing Map Attributes

Changing the map attributes frequently causes confusion because it is often not understood how physical and symbolic maps interact. The BMS physical map sends a string of data to the terminal, while the symbolic map can overlay that data. There are many factors to consider in the interaction of physical and symbolic maps. It is also important to understand how modified data tags affect the transfer of data from the screen.

Physical Map Strings

Physical maps can be visualized as a string of data consisting of control characters, a data length field, an attribute byte, and a data field. The map also contains an offset number indicating the position on the screen where a field should display. Length fields determine the length of the data to be sent, as specified on the BMS map. The attribute field contains the attribute specified in the BMS map, while data fields contain initial values given to fields in the BMS map. If no initial value was specified, then the data field contains low-values and no data is transmitted on a send of only the physical map. Actual data strings are more complicated. Fortunately, BMS handles the formatting of data strings for you.

Physical and symbolic map considerations

A symbolic map name is generated for BMS map fields defined with a DFH-MDF macro field name. No symbolic map entry is generated for screen constants defined without a field name in the BMS map. Constants are normally defined on the BMS map with an attribute of ASKIP or ASKIP,BRT, and no field name. The program cannot change their attribute, because no symbolic map field is generated.

Field identifiers can be set to ASKIP in the BMS map and can be turned on to ASKIP,BRT through the symbolic map if the field was not entered correctly. Alternately, the data entry field itself may be highlighted if entered incorrectly. The attribute of a field, which contains a symbolic map entry, can be changed each time a map is sent. Data-entry fields generally have UNPROT attributes and can have some combination of UNPROT, such as UNPROT,BRT, or UNPROT,FSET.

Message fields are usually defined in the BMS map with an attribute of ASKIP. Sometimes a program detects an error condition or wants to display an operator-notification message. To highlight the message, the program sends the map with the attribute of the appropriate field in the symbolic map changed to ASKIP,BRT. The BMS map can set an initial value for the message field by defining its attribute as ATTRB=(ASKIP,DRK). When the appropriate program condition is encountered, the program highlights the message field (making it visible) by sending the symbolic map with the message field's attribute changed to ASKIP,BRT. The message can be erased on a subsequent send by changing the attribute back to ASKIP,DRK.

Physical map stopper fields, like constants, are usually defined without a BMS map field name. The primary purpose of stopper fields is to limit the size of the preceding UNPROT data-entry field. Stopper fields are defined in the physical map with attributes of ASKIP or PROT.

Physical map interaction with symbolic map

Understanding how the three types of SEND MAP commands handle attributes and data fields is important.

SEND ONLY physical map. The SEND MAP MAPONLY command with the ERASE option specified erases the screen before the send and transmits the constants and attributes defined in the BMS map to the screen. The symbolic map is never used with a MAPONLY send; therefore, no variable data is transmitted. This book refers to input data and attributes as being received from the screen and to symbolic map output data and attributes as being sent to the screen.

SEND both physical and symbolic maps. The SEND MAP AND DATA command with the ERASE option specified erases the screen before sending the combined physical and symbolic maps. Visualize the physical map as initially being sent to the screen, then as being overlaid by corresponding attribute and data fields from the symbolic map. Remember, if the symbolic map contains low-values in any attribute or data field, then no transmission takes place for those items. On a SEND MAP AND DATA command, the physical map BMS-defined attribute takes effect if the symbolic map attribute contains low-values. When the symbolic map contains a significant attribute, it will override the physical map attribute.

SEND ONLY symbolic map. The SEND MAP DATAONLY command does not normally erase the screen before sending only the symbolic map. Prior to this send, one of the other two SEND MAP commands would have been executed. The prior send would have formatted the screen with constants from the BMS map and with attributes from the BMS map and/or symbolic map. The SEND MAP AND DATA command could have sent data from the symbolic map. Once again, visualize the existing data and attributes on the screen as being overlaid by the symbolic map's data and attributes.

Manipulating MDTs

An *on* MDT, which is part of the attribute byte, causes data on the screen to be returned to the program when a map is received. MDTs can be turned on by:

1. Specifying FSET as part of the attribute on the BMS map, then issuing a send that includes the physical map. Do not overlay the BMS map's attribute with the symbolic map's attribute on a send of map and data. Symbolic map attributes equal to low-values do *not* overlay the BMS attributes. The MDT can be set *on* by coding FSET as part of the attribute of fields defined on the BMS map as follows:

   ```
   ATTRB=(attr1,FSET),
   ```

2. Moving a standard attribute containing FSET to the symbolic map's attribute before issuing a send that includes the symbolic map, such as:

   ```
   MOVE UNPROT-FSET  TO   mapfldA
   ```

3. Keying data into an UNPROT field on the screen because entering data into a field always turns its MDT on.

FRSET

Specifying FRSET in the BMS map (or on the SEND MAP command) causes all MDTs on the screen to be turned off prior to sending a map. This requires the physical map field attribute or the symbolic override to control the MDT status of an attribute. A user can key data into a field, turning on its MDT. A receive of the map and a subsequent send of the map turns the MDT off if CTRL=FRSET was specified in the DFHMSD macro of the BMS map. If CTRL=FRSET was not specified, the MDTs would remain on.

Confusion often results when data appearing on the screen is not received into the program because its MDT is not turned on. I recommend specifying the appropriate attributes in the BMS map and in the symbolic map so that they are properly set prior to a send. For instance, if the user enters data into a field, the MDT turns on. Let's suppose that the program, when it receives the map, detects an error on a different field and resends the map with an error message. The MDTs of all fields turn off prior to the send because FRSET was specified. Correctly entered fields are not received into the program on a subsequent receive map, even though they appear on the screen, because their MDTs were turned off. You can ensure that required fields are returned by moving the UNPROT,FSET attribute to the appropriate symbolic map field before issuing the send. Once a field has been keyed in and verified, you may not want the user to be allowed to change it, but it must be returned to the program on a subsequent receive. Including the attributes ASKIP,FSET in the symbolic map prior to issuing a send ensures that the field is returned to the program on a subsequent receive. The communications area (COMMAREA) discussed in chapter 8 is usually employed to store the most recent data entered. This technique minimizes the transfer of data between the screen and the program. With practice, the use of attributes and the manner in which FRSET works should become clear.

Attribute Usage Summary

Figure 7.2 and the following outlines summarize the more common attribute considerations. Control of attribute fields depends upon the type of SEND MAP command:

1. MAP AND DATA (specify ERASE)
   a. Symbolic map attributes override the physical map attributes defined by the BMS map.

SEND MAP Options	Type of Map Sent Symbolic	Type of Map Sent Physical	Physical Map Only	*** Attribute Sent to Screen *** Symbolic Map Attribute Field Contains Attribute	*** Attribute Sent to Screen *** Symbolic Map Attribute Field Contains Low Values
MAP and Data	X	X		SYM	BMS
MAPONLY		X	BMS		
DATAONLY	X			SYM	Screen

Fig. 7.2 Attribute usage summary.

  b. Low-values in an attribute field causes the BMS map attribute to be sent to the screen.

2. MAPONLY (specify ERASE)
   The BMS-map-defined attributes will be sent to the screen.

3. DATAONLY (omit ERASE)
    a. Attributes in the symbolic map override existing screen attributes.
    b. Low-values in an attribute field do not change the existing attributes on the screen.

MDTs can be turned on in an attribute field by:

1. The BMS map FSET parameter
2. The user's keying data into a field
3. Moving a program-defined FSET-containing attribute to a field before a send that includes the symbolic map.

 Specifying FRSET in CTRL=(FREEKB,FRSET) of the BMS map DFHMSD macro turns off the attribute MDTs of all fields on the screen immediately prior to the send of the map to the screen when a SEND MAP command is issued.

RECEIVE MAP Considerations

The RECEIVE MAP command, as presented earlier in the chapter, is easy to understand and use. However, there are additional considerations when a map is received:

1. The length of the data keyed into a map field is received as the result of executing a RECEIVE MAP command.
2. A MAPFAIL condition occurs if no data is received from the map; if this condition is not properly handled, a program ABEND occurs.
3. The AID key pressed by the user can be tested and acted upon in several different ways.

Length Field on Map Receive

When a map is received, the symbolic map length field can be tested for two conditions:

1. If data were entered into a field
2. If the required number of characters were entered

Length field indicative of data entry. Many programs test if the symbolic map length field is greater than zero. A positive value is an indication that the user entered data into the field. For example,

```
IF  mapfldL  IS GREATER THAN  ZERO
     MOVE mapfldI  TO  WS-INPUT-DATA.
```

Here, mapfldL represents a map length field and mapfldI an input field.

Monitoring number of characters entered. Sometimes a program must know the exact number of characters keyed in; for example, when a field requires a specific number of characters or digits. Valid entry of a social security number, for instance, requires nine digits, and a program can test if MSOCSECL is equal to nine.

MAPFAIL conditions

A MAPFAIL, indicating that no characters were passed from the screen on a RECEIVE MAP command, occurs when

1. The CLEAR key is pressed.
2. PA1, PA2, or PA3 is pressed.
3. Any other AID key is pressed without data being entered on the screen, and no map field being FSET.

MAPFAIL, which causes a program ABEND if not provided for, can be controlled by:

1. Issuing an IGNORE CONDITION MAPFAIL command before the receive. This command states that if a MAPFAIL occurs on a receive of a map, ignore the condition and continue processing. This is the preferred method when using the HANDLE AID command discussed later in this chapter. For example:

```
EXEC CICS IGNORE CONDITION
          MAPFAIL
END-EXEC.
```

2. Including the RESP option on the RECEIVE MAP command. Programs in this text employ this method for examples that do not employ the HANDLE AID command. You test the code returned as follows:

```
EXEC CICS RECEIVE
          MAP     (mapname)
          MAPSET  (mapset)
```

```
                INTO   (WS-MAP-AREA)
                RESP   (WS-RESP)
        END-EXEC.

        IF WS-RESP    =   DFHRESP (NORMAL)     OR
           WS-RESP    =   DFHRESP (MAPFAIL)
           NEXT SENTENCE
        ELSE
             MOVE 'C100-'  TO  WS-RESP-SECTION
             PERFORM Z999-RESPONSE-ERROR.
```

3. Including the NOHANDLE option instead of the RESP option on the RE-CEIVE MAP command. A disadvantage in using this option is that all re-sulting conditions are ignored. *Never* use this option if using the HANDLE AID command.

4. Issuing a HANDLE CONDITION MAPFAIL before the receive. For example:

```
EXEC CICS HANDLE CONDITION
          MAPFAIL (C100-MAPFAIL)
END-EXEC.
```

This HANDLE CONDITION command directs that if a MAPFAIL occurs, then control is to be transferred to paragraph C100-MAPFAIL.

5. Coding a 1-byte BMS map field with an attribute of ASKIP,DRK,FSET so that at least 1 byte of data is always returned on a receive. If this method is employed, it is best to standardize the byte location on the screen at a position not likely to be used.

6. Executing the HANDLE AID command, discussed later in this chapter, in order to direct control to the proper routines if the CLEAR or PA key is pressed. PA keys can be handled by the ANYKEY option.

7. Testing data-entry AID keys (see below) in order to direct control to the proper routines if the CLEAR or a PA key is pressed.

Sending a message to the user indicating that no data was keyed in (when data is required) seems more logical than sending a message indicating that an invalid entry was made. There are situations when a receive without data being entered is valid: for example, pressing a PF key to end an inquiry and return to a control screen. MAPFAIL sounds complicated, but controlling it in your program is easy. The following examples should help to clarify the required techniques.

Testing data-entry AID keys

When the user presses an AID key, an indicator is stored in the EIB field EIBAID. The AID fields in DFHAID (see Appendix A-3) are generally copied into working storage. They are compared against EIBAID to determine which AID key was pressed in order to determine the flow of program logic.

Valid AID keys are ENTER; CLEAR; PF1 through PF24; PA1, PA2, and PA3; and ANYKEY. DFHAID fields are DFHENTER; DFHCLEAR; DFHPF1 through DFHPF24; and DFHPA1, DFHPA2, and DFHPA3.

Options for testing EIBAID. EIBAID can be tested in three ways:

1. Compare EIBAID against one of the DFHAID fields. For instance, to test if the AID key PF1 was pressed, code:

```
IF EIBAID = DFHPF1
```

2. Execute a HANDLE AID command; for example

```
EXEC CICS HANDLE AID
          PF1 (C100-EXIT)
```

3. Test EIBAID against its actual value (see Appendix A-3); for example:

```
IF EIBAID = 1
```

Testing EIBAID fields against DFHAID fields. Unlike the CICS-supplied list of standard attributes, the DFHAID fields are often used in application programs. Copy DFHAID (supplied with CICS) into the working-storage section of your program.

Any AID key the user presses can be tested and acted upon as soon as the program is entered. These checks can be made at the beginning of the main line of a program, before or after a receive, or almost any place in the program. For ease of maintenance, I recommend being consistent regarding where you check EIBAID against DFHAID fields. I prefer to keep these checks in the RECEIVE MAP section of my program whenever possible.

EIBAID remains unchanged throughout a program and a task until another AID key is pressed. It can be tested and used as a switch throughout the program or task. An AID key pressed prior to a receive in one program can be tested by another program in the same task [i.e., a program XCTLed or linked to (see chapter 8, "Program Control")].

Figure 7.3 illustrates typical usage of DFHAID fields. AID keys for ENTER, PF1, PF2, PF3, and PF4 are valid data-entry keys in this example. The program receives the map and continues processing if any of the keys are pressed. EIBAID can be tested later in the program to determine the flow of logic. The RESP option is included on the receive and the programmer-defined field WS-RESP is tested immediately after the receive. A G is moved to STATUS-OF-RECEIVE if a normal receive is completed. An F is moved to STATUS-OF-RECEIVE, if a MAPFAIL condition occurs.

```
C100-RECEIVE-CONTROL-MAP   SECTION.

    MOVE LOW-VALUES   TO  VM-CONTROL-MAP.

    IF EIBAID  =  DFHENTER   OR
                  DFHPF1     OR
                  DFHPF2     OR
                  DFHPF3     OR
                  DFHPF4

        EXEC CICS RECEIVE
                MAP    ('MAPPOVC')
                MAPSET ('POVMNT1')
                INTO   (VM-CONTROL-MAP)
                RESP   (WS-RESP)
        ENDEXEC

        IF WS-RESP  =  DFHRESP(NORMAL)
            MOVE 'G'  TO  STATUS-OF-RECEIVE
        ELSE
            IF WS-RESP  =  DFHRESP(MAPFAIL)
                MOVE 'F'  TO  STATUS-OF-RECEIVE
            ELSE
                MOVE 'C100-'  TO  WS-RESP-SECTION
                PERFORM Z999-RESPONSE-ERROR
    ELSE
        IF EIBAID  =  DFHCLEAR
            PERFORM C110-END-SESSION
        ELSE
        IF EIBAID  =  DFHPF5
            PERFORM C120-TRANSFER-XCTL-TO-MENU
        ELSE
            MOVE 'I'         TO  STATUS-OF-RECEIVE
            MOVE 'INVALID KEY PRESSED   PLEASE TRY AGAIN'
                             TO  MVC-D-MESSAGE
            MOVE ASKIP-BRT   TO  MVC-A-MESSAGE.

C100-EXIT.
    EXIT.
```

Fig. 7.3 Illustration of EIBAID with RESP option.

STATUS-OF-RECEIVE can be tested by the routine that performed C100-RECEIVE-CONTROL-MAP.

Other valid AID keys that be pressed are CLEAR and PF5. All other keys would cause an I to be moved to STATUS-OF-RECEIVE and an INVALID KEY PRESSED message to be moved to the map message field.

HANDLE AID command. The HANDLE AID command is similar to the HANDLE CONDITION command discussed in chapter 5 in format and in transfer of control. HANDLE AID is invoked upon the completion of a receive map command. If you use this technique, I recommend placing the command in your RECEIVE MAP program section. Its basic format is:

```
EXEC CICS HANDLE AID
          AID KEY (section/paragraph)
              .
              .
              .
END-EXEC.
```

HANDLE AID illustration. Figure 7.4 illustrates the use of the HANDLE AID command; it performs the same functions as the example in Fig. 7.3. AID keys ENTER, PF1, PF2, PF3, and PF4 are valid data-entry keys. Unless

Fig. 7.4 Illustration of the HANDLE AID command.

```
C100-RECEIVE-CONTROL-MAP   SECTION.

    MOVE LOW-VALUES  TO  VM-CONTROL-MAP.

    EXEC CICS HANDLE AID
              PF1
              PF2
              PF3
              PF4
              PF5    (C100-RETURN-TO-MENU)
              CLEAR  (C100-END-OF-SESSION)
              ANYKEY (C100-INVALID-KEY)
    END-EXEC.

    EXEC CICS HANDLE CONDITION
              MAPFAIL (C100-MAPFAIL)
    END-EXEC.

    EXEC CICS RECEIVE
              MAP    ('MAPPOVC')
              MAPSET ('POVMNT1')
              INTO   (VM-CONTROL-MAP)
    END-EXEC.

    MOVE 'G'  TO  STATUS-OF-RECEIVE.
*
* WILL REACH THIS POINT IF PF1, PF2, PF3, PF4 OR ENTER KEY PRESSED
*      AND DATA WAS ENTERED - OTHERWISE A MAPFAIL OCCURS
*  PF5, CLEAR AND OTHER KEYS PASS CONTROL TO INDICATED PARAGRAPHS
*
    GO TO  C100-EXIT.
C100-RETURN-TO-MENU.
```

Fig. 7.4 *Continued.*

```
      PERFORM C120-TRANSFER-XCTL-TO-MENU.

 * PRECEDING PERFORM DOES NOT RETURN - IT TRANSFERS CONTROL TO MENU


 C100-END-SESSION.

      PERFORM C110-END-SESSION.

 * PRECEDING PERFORM DOES NOT RETURN - CONTROL IS RETURNED TO CICS
 C100-INVALID-KEY.

         MOVE 'I'         TO   STATUS-OF-RECEIVE.
         MOVE 'INVALID KEY PRESSED   PLEASE TRY AGAIN'
                          TO   MVC-D-MESSAGE.
         MOVE ASKIP-BRT  TO   MVC-A-MESSAGE.
         GO TO   C100-EXIT.


 C100-MAPFAIL.

         MOVE 'F'   TO   STATUS-OF-RECEIVE.

 C100-EXIT.
      EXIT
```

there is a MAPFAIL on the receive, the program falls through to the statement following the receive. Pressing the CLEAR key always causes a MAP-FAIL to occur, but since HANDLE AID takes precedence over HANDLE CONDITION, MAPFAIL is overridden by the transfer of control to C100-END-OF-SESSION. A MAPFAIL would direct control to C100-MAPFAIL if it resulted from the entry of other PF keys.

PF5 is the only other valid AID key; it overrides a MAPFAIL and transfers control to C100-RETURN-TO-MENU. For any unspecified AID key, except ENTER, ANYKEY directs control to C100-INVALID-KEY. ENTER always passes control to the statement immediately following the receive, if not specified on the AID command.

HANDLE AID considerations. You must be aware of the following when writing a program:

1. Up to 16 AID keys can be specified on one command. Use two or more commands if required.

2. The last AID command encountered takes precedence and overrides AID keys specified in prior commands.

3. ANYKEY should be included to cover any key not specifically mentioned.

4. A specified AID key overrides ANYKEY.

5. If ENTER is not specified in the HANDLE AID command, control passes to the statement that follows the RECEIVE MAP command. ENTER is not included in ANYKEY.

6. AID keys listed in a HANDLE AID command without a paragraph name fall through to the statement following a RECEIVE MAP command.

7. HANDLE AID commands take precedence over HANDLE CONDITION commands, such as MAPFAIL.

8. Do not include the RESP or NOHANDLE option on the receive map command because they override the HANDLE AID command, and the PF key directives are ignored.

Testing EIBAID against its value.   Testing EIBAID against its actual value is handled in an identical fashion to comparing EIBAID against DFHAID fields. The only difference is that instead of using DFHAID fields, the actual value is used (see Fig. 7.3 for similarities). This option is seldom encountered, and its use is *not* recommended.

```
IF EIBAID  =  QUOTE    OR
                 1      OR
                 2      OR
                 3      OR
                 4
     MOVE 'F'   TO   STATUS-OF-RECEIVE
```

8

Program
Control

Program-control commands facilitate returning control to the CICS system; passing control from one program to another; and loading and releasing programs, tables, and maps to or from main storage. An understanding of program logical levels is required to follow the flow of program control. A communications area is used to pass data from one program to another when using program-control commands. These commands include:

- RETURN—Return control to CICS or to an invoking program (see "LINK" below).

- XCTL—Transfer control to another program without returning. This is conceptually similar to a GO TO statement in a COBOL program.

- LINK—Pass control to another program that returns control to the in voking program, after performing its logic. This command is similar in concept to a PERFORM command in a COBOL program.

- LOAD—Access and load a table, program, or map into main storage.

- RELEASE—When a table, program, or map is no longer required, this command releases it from main storage.

Program Logical Levels

Programs of the type presented in chapter 5 are basically started by keying in a TRANSID and pressing an AID key. CICS, shown at level 0 in Fig. 8.1,

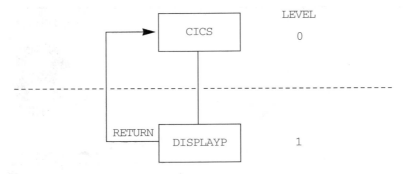

Fig. 8.1 Single program logical levels.

then passes control to the program associated with the TRANSID. A program initiated by CICS is at the highest logical level, level 1. (A program's logical level refers to its executing sequence relative to the CICS system, which is by definition at level zero.) When a RETURN command is issued in the level 1 program, control is returned to CICS.

Transactions, such as those represented in Fig. 8.1, are not as common as systems of programs that communicate with one another. Menu programs are commonly started by a TRANSID. The menu program then transfers control (XCTL) to another program at the same logical level as itself. The program transferred to can either end the session by returning to CICS or can transfer control back to the menu program. The menu program can then either return to CICS or transfer control to another program.

Programs at level 1 can always return to CICS. A program can transfer control to any program at the same level, including a program that has directly or indirectly transferred control to itself. Figure 8.2 shows this interaction.

Often a menu program transfers control to a submenu at the same logical level. POVMAINT, a submenu program, transfers control to individual inquiry, maintenance, and browse functions. A program to which control is transferred is always at the same logical level as the transferring program. Figure 8.3 illustrates how POMENUPM at level 1 can transfer control to three programs: POVMAINT, POMAINTN, and POENTRY1. POVMAINT can then transfer control to one of five programs, all at the same logical level. Any program shown in Fig. 8.3 at logical level 1 can return control to CICS. Each program at level 1 can be written so that it can transfer control to any other program shown at the same level. By definition, an XCTLed-to program is at the same logical level as the invoking program.

Normally, an XCTLed-to program is not intended to immediately transfer control back to the invoking program. XCTL can be considered an absolute transfer of control to another program, with an option to return. Often system development requires an unconditional return from a program to which control has been passed. A change program, prior to changing a record, might write a before-journal record, and, following the change, write an after-journal record. A common program is often employed to handle such postings; our system calls this program JRNLPOST. Figure 8.4 shows how a linked program appears at a lower logical level than the linking program.

POMENUPM is initiated by keying in the TRANSID POMU. Vendor file maintenance is selected and POMENUPM XCTLs-to POVMAINT. POVMAINT displays its submenu and the change function is selected, resulting in an XCTL-to POVMCHGE. POMENUPM, POVMAINT, and POVMCHGE are all at the same logical level, level 1. The change program, POVMCHGE, needs to record the before-and-after image of all changes. This type of logic is commonly handled by a linked program. A linked program, JRNLPOST level 2, is always at a lower logical level than the invoking program, POVMCHGE level 1. When a RETURN command is issued in the linked program,

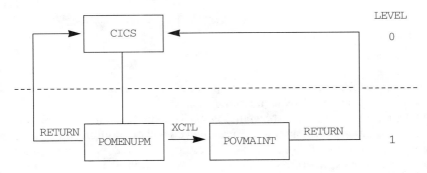

Fig. 8.2 Menu program logical levels.

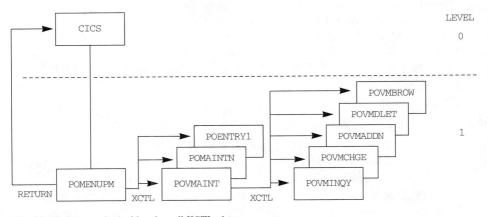

Fig. 8.3 Multimenu logical levels—all XCTLed-to.

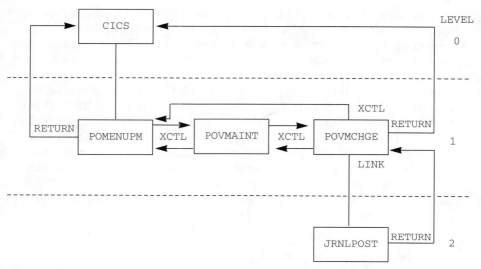

Fig. 8.4 Logical levels with LINKed-to program.

control is passed back to the invoking program at the next sequential instruction following the LINK command.

The logical level structure shown in Fig. 8.4 is generally sufficient to handle most design and programming situations you will encounter. Keep your
logical level structure design simple and modular; it makes maintenance
easier. Occasionally, a situation might arise that requires a more complicated logical level structure. Keep in mind that if a program links to another
program, the linked program is always at a lower logical level. A RETURN
command issued in any program at the next lower level always returns to
the linking program at the next higher logical level.

Figure 8.5 illustrates how an extended logical level structure functions.
POVMCHGE can be initiated by entering the TRANSID POVC. POVMCHGE
then links to JRNLPOST. After the link to JRNLPOST, several paths can be
followed:

1. JRNLPOST can issue a RETURN command, which passes control up to
   the next higher logical level, back to POVMCHGE.

2. JRNLPOST might XCTL-to PROGRAMX. If PROGRAMX issues a RE-
   TURN command, control passes up to the next higher logical level, program POVMCHGE.

3. PROGRAMX can link to PROGRAMY, which can return to PROGRAMX
   or XCTL-to PROGRAMZ. A RETURN command issued in PROGRAMZ
   passes control up to PROGRAMX. When PROGRAMX issues a RE-

TURN command, control passes up to the next higher logical level, POVMCHGE.

Task Number Considerations

Each time a new transaction is initiated, a task number is assigned to the task. The task number assigned is stored in the EIB field EIBTASKN. The task number remains unchanged until a RETURN command is issued at the highest logical level, level 1.

Communications Area

A communications area (COMMAREA) is a data area in working storage or the linkage section used for passing data from one program to another. The practical maximum length of COMMAREA is 32K, but most data passed in

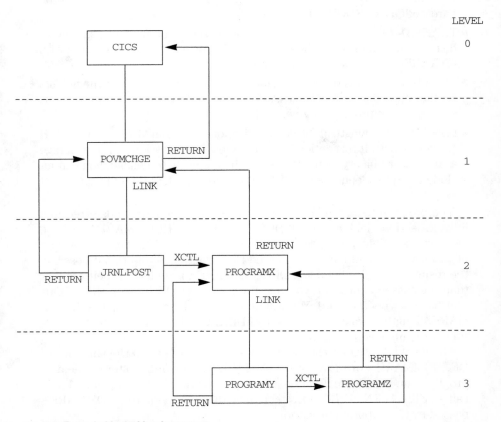

Fig. 8.5 Extended logical level structure.

a COMMAREA is generally small in size, often less than 100 bytes. When COMMAREA is passed to another program, the receiving program retrieves the passed data in a linkage-section field called DFHCOMMAREA.

COMMAREA can be passed between programs by using the RETURN. XCTL, and LINK commands. The COMMAREA is specified for the above commands as follows:

```
EXEC CICS ...
          [PROGRAM  (WS-PROGRAM-NAME) / ('progname')]
          [TRANSID  (TRID)]
           COMMAREA (WS-COMMAREA)
           LENGTH   (WS-CA-LENGTH)   or   LENGTH (15)
END-EXEC.
```

- PROGRAM—Defines the name of a linked or XCTLed-to-program. PRO-GRAM would not be included on a RETURN. WS-PROGRAM-NAME, or your label, can be defined in working storage as PIC X(8), or it could be hard-coded as PROGRAM ("POVMCHGE").

- TRANSID—The transaction identifier (TRID) or the next transaction to be initiated at a terminal. It is only specified on a RETURN command with a TRANSID, discussed later in this chapter.

- COMMAREA—This refers to a data area in working storage or the linkage section named WS-COMMAREA. (You can refer to this communications area by any appropriate name.)

- LENGTH—The length of the communications area named WS-CA-LENGTH (or your label). If this option is used, it must be defined in working storage as a halfword binary value. If the length is unlikely to change, you can include the actual length in the LENGTH option, i.e., LENGTH (15).

The program to which control passes receives the data transferred in a linkage-section field called DFHCOMMAREA. DFHCOMMAREA should, whenever possible, be the same length as the passed data. Sometimes data of various types and lengths is passed to a program. Avoid this if possible: the results are unpredictable if DFHCOMMAREA is defined as being longer than the passed data and if your program accesses DFHCOMMAREA fields that have not been passed. You will minimize problems if the passed COM-MAREA length is equal to the length of DFHCOMMAREA in the linkage section of the invoked program.

The invoked program can access passed data directly in the subfields of DFHCOMMAREA or move DFHCOMMAREA to a working-storage field. A program can determine if data has been passed to it by testing an EIB field called EIBCALEN. EIBCALEN contains the length of the COMMAREA passed by the initiating program.

EIBCALEN, the COMMAREA length, is often referred to as a *first-time switch.* A program initiated by entering a TRANSID, or one which is invoked by another program without a COMMAREA being passed to it, has an EIBCALEN equal to 0. Subsequent entries into the program can return with a COMMAREA of length 1; COMMAREA is not required to contain any significant data. This is done so that EIBCALEN equals the length of the COMMAREA or 1, and not 0, as it does upon initial entry. Statements similar to the following are commonly found in the main line of CICS programs:

```
IF EIBCALEN = ZERO
    PERFORM (first time processing)
ELSE
    MOVE DFHCOMMAREA TO WS-COMMAREA
    PERFORM (second time processing).
```

COMMAREA is sometimes used as a first-time switch or to direct the flow of program logic in pseudoconversational programs. Often, a value is moved to a WS-COMMAREA subfield; I call this field CA-SWITCH, before issuing a return to a program. The subfield is tested upon a subsequent reentry into the program in order to determine program flow. For example:

```
IF EIBCALEN = 0
    PERFORM (first time processing)
ELSE
    MOVE DFHCOMMAREA TO WS-COMMAREA
    IF CA-SWITCH = 2
        PERFORM (second time processing)
    ELSE
    IF CA-SWITCH = 3
        PERFORM (third time processing)
    ELSE
    IF CA-SWITCH = 4
        .
        .
        .
```

Some of these techniques are employed in program examples in future chapters. As you work with the COMMAREA concept, you will find it easy to understand and master.

RETURN Command

The RETURN command, as used in the programs in chapter 5, returned control to CICS and terminated a transaction. Most CICS systems and programs are not that simple. A program is usually initiated by a TRANSID, XCTL, or LINK command. The initiated program often sends a map upon which the user enters data. The program then executes a return to itself in order to receive and process the map's data. If invalid data had been entered, the program sends an error message, allows the user to correct the data, and issues a return to itself.

The format of the RETURN command used in previous examples to return to CICS was:

```
EXEC CICS RETURN
END-EXEC.
```

This format, when issued at the highest logical level, always terminates a task and returns control to CICS. This format is also executed at a lower logical level to return control to an invoking program that issued a LINK command.

Return with a TRANSID

The format of the RETURN command that is used in pseudoconversational programming is:

```
EXEC CICS RETURN
          TRANSID   ('TRAN')
          COMMAREA  (WS-COMMAREA)
          LENGTH    (WS-CA-LENGTH)
END-EXEC.
```

This format can only be issued in a program returning to CICS from the highest logical level, level 1. Using this format in a lower-logical-level program results in the INVREQ (INValid REQuest) handle condition being invoked. Never use this option in a linked program or in programs at or below the logical level of the linked program.

This format of the RETURN command returns control back to CICS and ends the task. The program associated with the TRANSID in the RETURN command is initiated when an AID key is pressed. This RETURN command is used to set a first-time switch. A return is issued with a one-character WS-COMMAREA and a length of 1. EIBCALEN equals 1 when an AID key is pressed to initiate the program again. The first time the program is initiated, EIBCALEN should be equal to 0 in order to use EIBCALEN as a first-time switch.

COMMAREA can be used to return a variety of switches and/or data to a program. A program may send a map, receive the map, and store data from the map or program in COMMAREA. When this format of the RETURN command is executed and the program is reentered, DFHCOMMAREA will contain the data returned in COMMAREA.

Transactions accessed frequently may use COMMAREA to store "valid" map data. If errors occur that necessitate the resend and receive of the map, the valid data saved in COMMAREA need not be retransmitted to or from the map.

A RETURN command with a TRANSID can be used to initiate a new program associated with a TRANSID that differs from the one that issued the return. You can design a system so that one program sends a map, then issues a return with a TRANSID in order to initiate a different program. The new program can receive and process the map and, when finished, either return with a TRANSID, which initiates the send program again, or ends the session. This technique has the advantage of using less main storage because it is more modular. I do not, however, recommend this technique, because I find systems using this method more difficult to maintain. Sending and receiving a map in the same program is more logical.

XCTL Command

The XCTL command is used to pass control to a program at the same logical level. Transfer is made by releasing the current program and loading the new program into main storage. Programs can be written to transfer control to another program and have the new program in turn transfer control back to the original program. This type of processing is common when a menu program transfers control to a selected program. The new program processes in the pseudoconversational mode and, when finished, transfers control back to the menu.

The format of the XCTL command is:

```
EXEC CICS XCTL
          PROGRAM   (WS-PROGRAM-NAME)
          [COMMAREA (WS-COMMAREA)]
          [LENGTH   (WS-CA-LENGTH)]
          [RESP     (WS-RESP)]
END-EXEC.
```

An XCTL command can be executed with or without COMMAREA and length being specified:

1. A program invoked without COMMAREA and LENGTH being specified on an XCTL command is similar in its initial entry to that of a program started by entering a TRANSID, in that EIBCALEN equals zero.

2. If COMMAREA and LENGTH are specified on the XCTL command, EIB-CALEN of the new program is equal to the length of the COMMAREA passed to it. DFHCOMMAREA in the new program will contain the data passed from the COMMAREA of the initiating program.

The program initiated by the XCTL command can have data of varying length passed to it from the COMMAREA of different programs. Try to avoid this in your system design; when possible, keep the passing program's COMMAREA the same length as the invoked program's DFHCOMMAREA. If your program attempts to access data in the linkage-section field DFH-

COMMAREA, which is longer than the length of the COMMAREA passed, the results are unpredictable.

The handle condition PGMIDERR (ProGraM IDentification ERRor) occurs if the XCTLed-to program is not in the PPT or if it has been disabled. This condition most likely occurs in testing. It might also occur if a program selected from a menu is disabled when changes are made. Rather than have your program abend if this condition occurs, you can include the RESP option on the XCTL command and test as follows:

```
IF WS-RESP  =  DFHRESP(PGMIDERR)
    MOVE 'PROGRAM progname NOT AVAILABLE'
        TO  MAP-D-MESSAGE
    PERFORM B110-SEND-MAP-DATAONLY
    PERFORM B120-RETURN-TO-CICS.
```

LINK Command

The LINK command is similar in format to the XCTL command; however, its function is much different. A LINK command passes control to a program at a lower logical level, with the intent of returning. A RETURN command issued in a program at the next lower level returns to the next sequential instruction in the invoking program, immediately following the LINK command. Linking to a program is costly in term of computer system resources which are tied up. A LINK command holds the linking program in main storage as well as the linked-to program. Figure 8.5 shows how a link can require several programs to be in main storage simultaneously. Avoid using the LINK command unless absolutely necessary because it requires more main storage and results in slower response time.

The format of the LINK command is:

```
EXEC CICS LINK
          PROGRAM   (WS-PROGRAM-NAME)
         [COMMAREA (WS-COMMAREA)]
         [LENGTH    (WS-CA-LENGTH)]
         [RESP      (WS-RESP)]
END-EXEC.
```

A program which links to another program generally passes a COMMAREA to the linked program. There are other methods of passing data. Actually, the address of WS-COMMAREA in the issuing program is passed to the linked program. The data passed in COMMAREA is accessed under DFHCOMMAREA in the invoked program. Any data changes made under DFHCOMMAREA in the linked program are available under WS-COMMAREA when control is returned to the invoking program (see Fig. 8.5). If POVMCHGE passed a COMMAREA to JRNLPOST via a LINK command, DFHCOMMAREA in JRNLPOST points to the same address and data as WS-COMMAREA in the invoking program POVMCHGE. If JRNLPOST with

COMMAREA (DFHCOMMAREA) XCTLed to PROGRAMX, DFHCOMM-
AREA in PROGRAMX points to the same WS-COMMAREA in POVMCHGE.
Any changes made under DFHCOMMAREA in PROGRAMX are reflected
under WS-COMMAREA in POVMCHGE, when PROGRAMX issued a RE-
TURN command to POVMCHGE. If JRNLPOST XCTLed to PROGRAMX
with COMMAREA (WS-NEW-COMMAREA), only changes made by JRNL-
POST are reflected in WS-COMMAREA of POVMCHGE when PROGRAMX
issued a RETURN command. An additional new copy of COMMAREA, containing the data passed from WS-NEW-COMMAREA, would be created, and
this new copy of COMMAREA would be received in DFHCOMMAREA of
PROGRAMX. This type of logic can get confusing and is difficult to maintain. Design your systems so that when a program links to another, the required functions are performed in that program. When processing is
complete, return immediately to the invoking program.

When a program that has issued a LINK command is returned to, then working storage, all handle aids, handle conditions, etc., except possibly, COMM-
AREA, are restored to their status prior to the issue of the LINK command.

The handle condition PGMIDERR occurs if the linked-to program is not
in the PPT or if it has been disabled. The RESP option can be included on
the LINK command and can be tested in the same fashion as shown for the
XCTL command already discussed.

Load Command

The LOAD command is used to access and load a table, map, or program
into main storage. It can be used to load program tables, such as a state
code table, a sales force table, or a cost table into main storage. The table
accessed is addressed through a linkage-section pointer called base loca-
tor for linkage or BLL cells if using OS/VS COBOL (chapter 25 shows you
how this is handled by VS COBOL II). The format of the LOAD command
is:

```
EXEC CICS LOAD
          PROGRAM    (progname)
          SET        (ptr-ref)
          HOLD
          [RESP      (WS-RESP)]
END-EXEC.
```

- PROGRAM—Program name of the table, map, or program that is to be
  loaded into main storage.

- SET—Sets the BLL-pointer to address of the loaded program.

- HOLD—Indicates that the program is to be held in main storage, even after the task is terminated. The program is deleted from main storage only
  when a RELEASE command is executed in the current or in a future task.

Chapter 10 illustrates the load of a highly used table defined in the PPT as a main-storage resident table. This chapter also demonstrates the use of BLL-pointers for setting addressability to a table.

The handle condition PGMIDERR will occur if the program to be loaded is not in the PPT or if it has been disabled. The RESP option can be included on the LOAD command and can be tested in the same fashion as shown for the XCTL command discussed above.

RELEASE Command

This command is issued in order to release a table, program, or map from main storage. A RELEASE command should be issued in order to free main storage as soon as the program loaded is no longer required. The format of the RELEASE command is:

```
EXEC CICS RELEASE
          PROGRAM (progname)
       [RESP     (WS-RESP)]
          END-EXEC.
```

[(progname) is the name of the table, map, or program which is to be released from main storage.]

You must execute this command to release programs loaded with the HOLD option. The program loaded is automatically released when the task is completed if hold was not specified on the LOAD command. Load tables as close as possible to their point of use; then release them as soon as they are no longer required.

The handle condition PGMIDERR can occur if the program to be released is not in the PPT or if it has been disabled. The RESP option can be included on the RELEASE command and can be tested in the same fashion as shown for the XCTL command.

9

The Menu Program

You have learned many important CICS concepts and commands. Practical application programs help you pull together the theory you have been reading. The purchase order menu program and the vendor file maintenance menu programs are similar; this chapter discusses the latter and concepts such as pseudoconversational programming and the communications area. SEND MAP, RECEIVE MAP, and MAPFAIL commands and conditions are used as well as the program-control commands RETURN, RETURN with a TRANSID, XCTL, and LINK.

The standard attention identifier list (DFHAID) is used as a comparison with the EIB field EIBAID in order to determine the AID key the user presses. EIB fields as well as translator call fields are copied into the linkage and working-storage sections, respectively, for all programs at compile time. COPY statements generated by the translator accomplish this. EIB fields, such as EIBCALEN, are used and discussed.

This chapter lays the foundation for sample programs in succeeding chapters. The explanation of the example presented is more thorough than those in following chapters, which only detail new commands and concepts as they are encountered.

Most installations have one or more menu programs. Their basic function is to initiate other programs. A user keys in a TRANSID and presses ENTER to display a menu screen, then keys a selection and presses ENTER to effect the transfer of control to the chosen program.

Often a main menu cannot accommodate all the required functions. This is not the case in the purchase order system; I just want to show how it would be done. A selection of 3 entered on the purchase system menu (Fig. 2.2) would display the submenu shown by the screen layout in Fig. 6.3.

The vendor file maintenance menu program structure chart, which is similar for most menu programs, was illustrated in Fig. 4.3. The BMS map was shown in Fig. 6.4 and its BMS-generated symbolic map in Fig. 6.5. The more-readable symbolic map used by this program was shown in Fig. 6.6.

Vendor File Maintenance Submenu

Figure 9.1 presents the vendor file maintenance menu program. The remarks in your CICS programs should contain sufficient information to enable someone unfamiliar with the program to understand its basic function. Be brief yet thorough; a program's comments are among the first references for a maintenance programmer. Include just enough comments to make the intent of the program clear to someone unfamiliar with it. Write all of your programs as if you have to explain them to your co-workers. All programs should be written with ease of understanding and future change in mind. Write them as if you or your fellow workers have to make changes in them six months from today. You will! I like to include in the remarks the program title, the method of program initiation, and the basic program functions.

Fig. 9.1 Vendor file maintenance submenu program.

```
IDENTIFICATION DIVISION.
PROGRAM-ID. POVMAINT.
*
***********************************************************************
*   VENDOR FILE MAINTENANCE SUB MENU - STARTED BY TRANSID 'POVM'   *
*          OR BY ANOTHER MENU       PROGRAM FUNCTIONS:       *
*       A) SEND MENU SCREEN                                        *
*       B) RECEIVE MENU MAP AND DEPENDING ON SELECTION - XCTL TO: *
*          1) INQUIRY          2) CHANGE          3) ADD          *
*          4) DELETE           5) BROWSE                          *
***********************************************************************
ENVIRONMENT DIVISION.
DATA DIVISION.
*
WORKING-STORAGE SECTION.
*
01  WS-PROGRAM-FIELDS.
    05  FILLER       PIC X(22)     VALUE 'POVMAINT - START OF WS'.
*
    05  WS-CRT-MESSAGE       PIC X(17)      VALUE 'SESSION COMPLETED'.
    05  WS-XCTL-PROGRAM      PIC X(8)       VALUE SPACES.
    05  WS-COMMAREA          PIC X          VALUE SPACE.
    05  WS-RESP              PIC S9(8)      VALUE +0      COMP.

01  WS-RESP-ERROR.
```

Fig. 9.1 *Continued.*

```
      05  FILLER                  PIC X(39)       VALUE
          'PROGRAM POVMAINT: ERROR EIBRESP  CODE = '.
      05  WS-RESP-ERR-CD          PIC 99          VALUE ZEROES.
      05  FILLER                  PIC X(15)       VALUE
          '  IN SECTION '.
      05  WS-RESP-SECTION         PIC X(5)        VALUE SPACES.
 *
  01  MPM-MENU-MAP.
      05  FILLER                      PIC X(12).
      05  MPM-L-SELECTION             PIC S9(4)       COMP.
      05  MPM-A-SELECTION             PIC X.
      05  MPM-D-SELECTION             PIC X.
      05  MPM-L-MESSAGE               PIC S9(4)       COMP.
      05  MPM-A-MESSAGE               PIC X.
      05  MPM-D-MESSAGE               PIC X(79).
 *
 *01  WS-STATUS-FIELDS.
      COPY   STWSSTAT.
 *01  ATTRIBUTE-LIST.
      COPY   STWSATTR.
 *
      COPY   DFHAID.
 *
      COPY   DFHBMSCA.
 *
  01  END-OF-WORKING-STORAGE   PIC X(15)  VALUE 'END WS POVMAINT'.
 *
  LINKAGE SECTION.
 *
  01  DFHCOMMAREA        PIC X.
 *
  PROCEDURE DIVISION.
 **********************************************************************
 *              PROGRAM STRUCTURE IS:                                *
 *                  AA00-MAINLINE                                    *
 *                      B000-SEND-MAPONLY                            *
 *                      C000-PROCESSING                             *
 *                          C100-RECEIVE-MAP                        *
 *                              C110-END-SESSION                    *
 *                                  C200-EDIT-MAP-SELECTION         *
 *                                  C300-TRANSFER-CONTROL           *
 *                                  C400-SEND-MAP-DATAONLY          *
 **********************************************************************
  AA00-MAINLINE  SECTION.
 *
      IF EIBCALEN  =  ZERO
          PERFORM B000-SEND-MAPONLY

      ELSE
          PERFORM C000-PROCESSING.
 *
      EXEC CICS RETURN
```

Fig. 9.1 *Continued.*

```
                        TRANSID  ('POVM')
                        COMMAREA (WS-COMMAREA)
                        LENGTH   (1)
            END-EXEC.
*
*
B000-SEND-MAPONLY  SECTION.
***********************************************************************
*                  SEND MAPONLY - PHYSICAL MAP                        *
*                  PERFORMED FROM:  AA00-MAINLINE                     *
*   ONLY PERFORMED ONCE, UPON INITIAL ENTRY WHEN EIBCALEN = 0         *
***********************************************************************
*
            EXEC CICS SEND
                        MAP     ('MAPPOVM')
                        MAPSET  ('POVMNT1')
                        MAPONLY
                        ERASE
            END-EXEC.
*
B000-EXIT.
     EXIT.
*
*
C000-PROCESSING  SECTION.
***********************************************************************
*                      MAIN PROCESSING MODULE                         *
*                      PERFORMED FROM:  AA00-MAINLINE                  *
*   RECEIVE AND PROCESS SELECTION SCREEN - IF VALID RECEIVE, AND       *
*        SELECTION - TRANSFER CONTROL TO SELECTED PROGRAM ELSE         *
*             SEND MAP MESSAGE DEPENDING ON STATUS:                   *
*        1) STATUS-OF-RECEIVE    = 'I'  INVALID KEY PRESSED            *
*        2) STATUS-OF-RECIEVE    = 'M'  MAPFAIL - NO SELECTION MADE    *
*        3) STATUS-OF-SELECTION  = 'E'  INVALID SELECTION KEYED-IN     *
***********************************************************************
*
            PERFORM C100-RECEIVE-MAP.
            IF GOOD-RECEIVE
            PERFORM C200-EDIT-MAP-SELECTION
            IF VALID-SELECTION
                        PERFORM C300-TRANSFER-CONTROL
            ELSE
                        PERFORM C400-SEND-MAP-DATAONLY
            ELSE
            IF STATUS-OF-RECEIVE  =  'M'
                        MOVE 'NO SELECTION WAS MADE - PLEASE ENTER SELECTION'
                                     TO  MPM-D-MESSAGE
                        MOVE ASKIP-BRT  TO  MPM-A-MESSAGE
                        PERFORM C400-SEND-MAP-DATAONLY
             ELSE
                        PERFORM C400-SEND-MAP-DATAONLY.
*
```

Fig. 9.1 *Continued.*

```
 C000-EXIT.
     EXIT.
 *
 *
 C100-RECEIVE-MAP  SECTION.
 ***********************************************************************
 *               PERFORMED FROM:  C000-PROCESSING               *
 *               ONLY ENTER AND CLEAR KEYS ARE VALID            *
 *          OTHER CONDITIONS CHANGE STATUS-OF-RECEIVE           *
 *     GOOD-RECEIVE = 'G'     INVALID-KEY  = 'I'     MAPFAIL = 'M'  *
 ***********************************************************************
 *
     IF EIBAID  =  DFHENTER
 *
         EXEC CICS RECEIVE
                   MAP     ('MAPPOVM')

                      MAPSET ('POVMNT1')
                      INTO   (MPM-MENU-MAP)
                      RESP   (WS-RESP)
             END-EXEC
 *
             IF WS-RESP  =  DFHRESP(NORMAL)
                 MOVE 'G'  TO  STATUS-OF-RECEIVE
             ELSE
                 IF WS-RESP  =  DFHRESP(MAPFAIL)
                     MOVE 'M'  TO  STATUS-OF-RECEIVE
             ELSE
                     MOVE 'C100-'  TO  WS-RESP-SECTION
                     PERFORM Z999-RESPONSE-ERROR
 *
             ELSE
                     IF EIBAID  =  DFHCLEAR
                     PERFORM C110-END-SESSION
             ELSE
                     MOVE 'I'           TO  STATUS-OF-RECEIVE
                     MOVE 'ENTER AND CLEAR KEYS ARE ONLY VALID KEYS - PLEA -
                      'SE TRY AGAIN'  TO  MPM-D-MESSAGE
                     MOVE ASKIP-BRT     TO  MPM-A-MESSAGE
                     MOVE UNPROT-FSET TO  MPM-A-SELECTION.
 *
 C100-EXIT.
     EXIT.
 *
 *
 C110-END-SESSION  SECTION.
 ***********************************************************************
 *            OPERATOR PRESSED CLEAR - END SESSION            *
 *               PERFORMED FROM:  C100-RECEIVE-MAP           *
 ***********************************************************************
 *
     EXEC CICS SEND
```

Fig. 9.1 *Continued.*

```
                FROM    (WS-CRT-MESSAGE)
                LENGTH (17)
                ERASE
      END-EXEC.
*
      EXEC CICS RETURN
      END-EXEC.
*
 C110-EXIT.
      EXIT.
*
*
 C200-EDIT-MAP-SELECTION   SECTION.
********************************************************************
*            EDIT SELECTION MADE BY THE CRT OPERATOR          ***
*                PERFORMED FROM:  C000-PROCESSING             ***
********************************************************************
*
      MOVE 'G'  TO  STATUS-OF-SELECTION.
*
      IF MPM-D-SELECTION =  '1'  MOVE 'POVMINQY' TO WS-XCTL-PROGRAM
        ELSE
      IF MPM-D-SELECTION =  '2'  MOVE 'POVMCHGE' TO WS-XCTL-PROGRAM
        ELSE
      IF MPM-D-SELECTION =  '3'  MOVE 'POVMADDN' TO WS-XCTL-PROGRAM
        ELSE
      IF MPM-D-SELECTION =  '4'  MOVE 'POVMDLET' TO WS-XCTL-PROGRAM
        ELSE
      IF MPM-D-SELECTION =  '5'  MOVE 'POVMBROW' TO WS-XCTL-PROGRAM
        ELSE
          MOVE 'E'       TO  STATUS-OF-SELECTION
          MOVE 'INVALID SELECTION - PLEASE RE-ENTER YOUR SELECTION'
                         TO  MPM-D-MESSAGE
          MOVE ASKIP-BRT  TO  MPM-A-MESSAGE.
*
 C200-EXIT.
      EXIT.
*
*
 C300-TRANSFER-CONTROL   SECTION.
********************************************************************
*          TRANSFER CONTROL 'XCTL' TO SELECTED PROGRAM          *
*                PERFORMED FROM:  C000-PROCESSING               *
********************************************************************
*
      EXEC CICS XCTL
                PROGRAM (WS-XCTL-PROGRAM)
                RESP    (WS-RESP)
      END-EXEC.
*
      IF WS-RESP =  DFHRESP (PGMIDERR)
          MOVE 'PROGRAM SELECTION NOT AVAILABLE'
```

Fig. 9.1 *Continued.*

```
                                TO  MPM-D-MESSAGE
        MOVE ASKIP-BRT     TO  MPM-A-MESSAGE
        PERFORM C400-SEND-MAP-DATAONLY
    ELSE
        MOVE 'C300-'  TO  WS-RESP-SECTION
        PERFORM Z999-RESPONSE-ERROR.
*
 C300-EXIT.
    EXIT.
*
*
 C400-SEND-MAP-DATAONLY  SECTION.
 *********************************************************************
 *           SEND MAP DATAONLY - SYMBOLIC MAP               *
 *           PERFORMED FROM:  C000-PROCESSING               *
 *        WHEN INVALID CONDITIONS ARE DETECTED              *
 *********************************************************************
 *
    EXEC CICS SEND
            MAP       ('MAPPOVM')
            MAPSET    ('POVMNT1')
            FROM      (MPM-MENU-MAP)
            DATAONLY
    END-EXEC.
*
 C400-EXIT.
    EXIT.
*
*
 Z999-RESPONSE-ERROR  SECTION.
 *********************************************************************
 * INVALID EIBRESP CODE RETURNED DURING EXECUTION OF CICS COMMAND *
 *********************************************************************
 *
    MOVE WS-RESP  TO  WS-RESP-ERR-CD.
*
    EXEC CICS SEND
            FROM    (WS-RESP-ERROR)
            LENGTH  (61)
            ERASE
    END-EXEC.
*
    EXEC CICS RETURN
    END-EXEC.
*
 Z999-EXIT.
    EXIT.
```

I generally start the working-storage section with the program name and a literal indicating that this is the beginning of working storage, i.e., POV-MAINT - START OF WS. For examples in this text, a literal SESSION COM-PLETED is included in programs that may be terminated by pressing the CLEAR key. This message is displayed on an erased screen.

I like to end a program's working storage with a literal followed by the program's name (i.e., END WS POVMAINT). These literals often help in program debugging.

Try to be consistent from program to program in your label names. Give them meaningful names. Use your source code Copy library to store linkage section, working-storage, and procedure division code that is used in more than one program. BMS-generated symbolic maps are usually copied into working storage. More-readable symbolic maps can either be copied or hard-coded in the program's working storage.

Working-storage section

It is good practice to keep working storage as small as possible, since each task obtains its own unique copy of this section. Avoid unnecessarily storing literals and messages in this section; instead hard-code them in the procedure division. Some installations have standards that may require you to code messages in working storage. Fields used in this program and their meaning are as follows:

- WS-CRT-MESSAGE—Contains the literal SESSION COMPLETED, which is displayed when a program at the highest logical level returns to CICS. In practice, your program may return to a higher level menu, or display a standard termination map or message.

- WS-XCTL-PROGRAM—Based on the selection made by the user, the program to be transferred to is moved to this field before a common XCTL command is executed.

- WS-COMMAREA—Communications area used to return with a COMM-AREA and LENGTH. This is used as a first-time switch in this program. In later programs, you will see how it is used to pass data from one transaction to another.

- WS-RESP—This user-defined binary fullword is used to hold the value of EIBRESP following the execution of CICS commands containing the RESP option.

- WS-RESP-ERROR—A message displayed for unanticipated response codes returned when using the RESP option. Most installations have standard procedures for handling unanticipated errors, which are more comprehensive than the simplified error handling in this text.

- MPM-MENU-MAP—Chapter 6 showed how to create more-readable symbolic maps.

- WS-STATUS-FIELDS—Program status fields found in the copy library (see STWSSTAT in Appendix B). These fields contain the status of program functions such as RECEIVE MAP, SELECTION, EDIT, READ, WRITE, CHANGE, and DELETE RECORDS, etc.
- ATTRIBUTE-LIST—Easier-to-read standard attribute character list (see STWSATTR in appendix B).
- DFHAID—AID fields (see appendix A.3).

Linkage section

The only field defined in this program's linkage section is DFHCOMMAREA (see Fig. 9.1). The translator automatically generates a 1-byte DFHCOM-MAREA, even if it is not coded. The size of this communication area is determined by the size of the data area passed using the COMMAREA option.

Procedure division

The procedure division contains the program's logic and comments that assist the programmer who has to test and maintain the program.

Program comments and section-naming conventions. I start the procedure division with comments describing the program's structure and use descriptive paragraph names, which are the actual names of program sections. This practice is often difficult to maintain in the real world of data processing. It is included for your ease of understanding. I label my mainline section AA00-MAINLINE. All other section names begin with an alphabetic character followed by three digits and then a description of the function performed. I indent the program structure section name four spaces to reflect sections performed from a higher level section.

Sections performed from another section are listed following the literal PERFORMED FROM:, which is contained within the comments following each program section name. The rest of the comment area for each section contains information that should aid somebody unfamiliar with the program to understand the intent of the section. Do not put unnecessary information in this area, just enough to clarify.

I strongly recommend using modular, structured programming techniques. They aid in development, debugging, and maintenance. Keep your structured code straightforward and simple. KISS will make your job much easier.

AA00-MAINLINE. Many programs contain initial or first-entry processing logic that is performed only once. Succeeding entries into the program follow a different logic path.

Initial program entry. On initial entry into the vendor file maintenance menu program, EIBCALEN is equal to zero because the program is initiated either by entering the TRANSID POVM or by a transfer of control from the purchasing system menu (POMENUPM, see Fig. 2.2). EIBCALEN always equals zero when a program is initiated by entering a TRANSID. Any program that transfers control to this program does so without COMMAREA and LENGTH specified. This results in EIBCALEN equaling zero on initial entry. Transferring control to this program with COMMAREA and LENGTH specified would require that the program be written differently. EIBCALEN would be greater than 0. This program can test a switch, or program name, sent in the COMMAREA in order to determine program flow. It can test an EIB field EIBTRNID, the TRANSID, to determine how the program was initiated. The browse program in chapter 17 employs EIBTRNID.

When EIBCALEN equals 0, the program sends the vendor file maintenance submenu screen shown in Fig. 6.3 and returns to CICS with a TRANSID, COMMAREA, and LENGTH. Return with a TRANSID is the main technique used in pseudoconversational programming. This enables the user to initiate the next execution of the program by pressing an AID key instead of entering a TRANSID. Specifying an invalid TRANSID or a RETURN command causes the task to ABEND with an INVALID TRANSACTION IDENTIFICATION message displayed on the screen. When a program returns with a TRANSID, the current task is terminated. The program can be released from main storage, unless the program is defined in the PPT as being main-storage resident, and storage can be used for other tasks. Each program obtains its unique copy of working storage, and when a task ends, this copy is released from main storage. Each time CICS initiates a program, working storage reverts to its initial values. For this reason a program cannot pass data from one task to another through working storage. When you issue a return with COMMAREA and TRANSID, the contents of the communication area are saved. The stored data is available under DFHCOMMAREA of the same program when an AID key is pressed. You have so far learned two methods which can be used to transfer data between tasks: through a map and the COMMAREA. This program is not concerned with passing data through the COMMAREA. It only returns with a COMMAREA containing a space and a length of 1, in order to set the communication area length, EIBCALEN, for succeeding entries into the program. This technique is referred to as using EIBCALEN as a first-time switch.

Second and succeeding program entries.   The first entry into the program sent the initial map, MAPONLY, and returned to CICS with a TRANSID and a length of 1. On succeeding entries into the program, EIBCALEN is equal to 1, and the program performs C000-PROCESSING. If a RETURN command was issued with TRANSID, but without COMMAREA and LENGTH specified, EIBCALEN equals 0 and the program loops, performing B000-SEND-MAPONLY each time an AID key was pressed.

When a valid selection is made, control is transferred to the selected program. Invalid conditions, such as pressing an invalid AID key, not entering a selection (MAPFAIL), and making an invalid selection, result in a DATAONLY map send and the execution of the return with TRANSID. The return with TRANSID, COMMAREA, and length after the send of the DATAONLY map allows the user to correct the map's data. The user reads the error message, keys in a valid selection, and presses the proper AID key (ENTER); then this program is initiated again. Upon reentry into the program, EIBCALEN equals 1 and the program will perform C000-PROCESS-ING again. This process is repeated as often as required until a correct selection is entered. Transfer of control takes place, or the user presses CLEAR to end the session.

An understanding of the technique presented in the menu program should aid you in learning pseudoconversational programming. Pseudo-conversational programming basically involves the send of a map and the release of the program from main storage if storage is required for another task. The map can be received without having to enter a TRANSID again since the RETURN command is issued with a TRANSID. Then, if the map's data is valid, the required logic is performed. When invalid data is entered, the map is resent with an indicative message. This process continues until valid data is entered or the session is ended.

B000-SEND-MAPONLY. This section is performed only once, upon initial entry into the program, when EIBCALEN equals 0. The program specifies MAPONLY in the send because the initial map contains no variable data. Only the physical map, which contains constants, needs to be sent. Maps containing variable data, such as date and time, eliminate MAPONLY from the send and send both map and data (physical and symbolic maps).

C000-PROCESSING. This section is executed for all entries into the program after the first time. EIBCALEN is *not* be equal to 0. Section functions are:

1. Perform C100-RECEIVE-MAP—Receives the selection entered on the map

2. Perform C200-EDIT-MAP-SELECTION—Validate the selection

3. Perform C300-TRANSFER-CONTROL—Transfer control to the selected program if a valid selection was entered

4. Perform C400-SEND-MAP-DATAONLY—Send only the symbolic map if any invalid conditions are encountered, such as:
   a. Invalid AID key pressed
   b. MAPFAIL (encountered when no selection is entered)
   c. An invalid selection was entered

C100-RECEIVE-MAP. The RECEIVE MAP section checks which AID key was pressed in order to determine a logic path to follow. The only valid AID keys are ENTER and CLEAR. Any other AID key pressed results in an invalid key message displayed on the screen. I check which AID key was pressed by comparing the EIB field EIBAID against one of the attention identifier fields listed in appendix A.3. Figure 7.3 showed an alternate method of testing which AID key was pressed; that method is used in the browse program in chapter 17. EIBAID can be tested and used as a switch at any point in the program.

EIBAID equals DFHENTER. The RESP option is included on the RECEIVE MAP command. The value of EIBRESP, the response code, is returned in WS-RESP when the map is received. A code of G is moved to STATUS-OF-RECEIVE if this field indicates a normal response. A response that indicates a MAPFAIL results in an M being moved to STATUS-OF-RECEIVE. Any other response code indicates a serious error and control passes to Z999-RESPONSE-ERROR. MAPFAIL is invoked on the receive of a map if no field is FSET. If the EOF key is pressed prior to a receive, MAPFAIL does not occur.

The RECEIVE MAP command receives the map into the working-storage area MPM-MENU-MAP. Although not required by this program, the flag (attribute) byte MPM-A-SELECTION could have been tested for hexadecimal 80 (DFHBMEOF) to determine if the EOF key had been pressed. In all other cases, the flag byte equals X'00' (low-values). The L suffix (length field) can be tested after a RECEIVE MAP command to determine if data has been keyed into a field. Its length is greater than 0 if data has been entered.

EIBAID equals DFHCLEAR. If the CLEAR key is pressed, the program performs C110-END-SESSION. The end-of-session section sends a message and returns control to CICS. Any AID key(s) can be programmed to perform this function.

EIBAID not equal to DFHENTER or DFHCLEAR. This program considers any AID key other than ENTER or CLEAR an invalid entry. An I is moved to STATUS-OF-RECEIVE and a message moved to the map output field MPM-D-MESSAGE. The attribute character ASKIP,BRT is moved to the map message attribute field MPM-A-MESSAGE. UNPROT,FSET is moved to the SELECTION field attribute MPM-A-SELECTION; otherwise, the selection code is not returned on a subsequent read of the map. The DFHMSD macro of the BMS map defines CTRL=(FREEKB,FRSET). FRSET turns off all MDTs before a map is sent. The selection is displayed on the screen, but is not returned to the program when a RECEIVE MAP command is executed because its MDT is not on. Moving UNPROT,FSET to the attribute field prior to the SEND MAP DATAONLY command turns the MDT on. This results in the selection being returned in its prior state if it is not changed.

C110-END-SESSION. The RECEIVE MAP section performs the C110-END-SESSION when the user presses the CLEAR key. It displays the message SESSION COMPLETED. The length of the message (17) must be specified. ERASE clears the screen before the send. Since this program is at the highest logical level, the execution of the CICS RETURN command returns control to CICS. No TRANSID is specified on the RETURN command; therefore, if the user presses an AID key after the message is displayed, an invalid transaction message appears on the screen.

C200-EDIT-MAP-SELECTION. The selection entered by the user is edited in this section. The appropriate program is moved to WS-XCTL-PROGRAM if the selection is valid. On an invalid selection, an E is placed in STATUS-OF-SELECTION. A message is then moved to the map's message field and ASKIP,BRT is moved to the map's field attribute. Unlike section C100-RE-CEIVE-MAP, it is *not* necessary to move UNPROT,FSET to the map's selection attribute. When an invalid selection is keyed in, it is not required to be returned on a subsequent receive of the map; the correct selection should be entered. What do you think would happen if, after displaying the invalid selection message, the user presses ENTER without keying in any selection? The invalid selection displayed on the screen is returned to the program since the send with FRSET turns off its MDT. Low-values are returned. Section C000-PROCESSING moves NO SELECTION WAS MADE . . . to the message field and resends the map. All the while, the invalid selection shows on the screen. The user might press the EOF key to erase the invalid entry and then press ENTER. This does not cause a MAPFAIL. Low-values are transmitted on a RECEIVE MAP command, but the flag byte MPM-A-SELECTION contains X'80'. In this case, the selection is treated as invalid by section C200-EDIT-MAP-SELECTION. The flag byte received is equal to low-values (X'00') if EOF is not pressed or if a selection has been entered. The flag byte is generally tested to determine if the EOF key had been pressed. Data returned in an EOFed field is treated as spaces or zeroes as appropriate. Remember that the flag and attribute bytes occupy the same field. Also keep in mind that BMS map A and F suffix fields are shown only as A fields on the more-readable maps employed by examples in this text. BMS map suffix fields I and O are shown as data (D) fields on these symbolic maps.

C300-TRANSFER-CONTROL. After section C200-EDIT-MAP-SELECTION moves the selection program name to WS-XCTL-PROGRAM, this section immediately transfers control to the selected program. The new program is loaded into main storage if necessary, and control is transferred to the program. The menu program can be released from main storage, if it's not required by another task or if it's not defined in the PPT as a main-storage resident program. The EIB fields, task number (EIBTASKN), and TRANSID (EIBTRNID) remains unchanged in the new program until it issues a RETURN command at the highest logical level.

The handle condition PGMIDERR is invoked if the program has not been defined in the PPT or if the program has been disabled. The RESP option is included on the XCTL command and WS-RESP is tested for DFHRESP(PGMIDERR) if control is not transferred. If RESP is NORMAL, control is transferred to the desired program and the WS-RESP test is not reached. For simplicity, I will not include the test for PGMIDERR on the XCTL command in future programs.

Programs initiated by this section are entered with a communications area length (EIBCALEN) equal to 0. This program can transfer control with data, in which case, the XCTL command requires the COMMAREA and LENGTH options.

C400-SEND-MAP-DATAONLY. This section is performed from C000-PROCESSING when an invalid condition has been detected, such as invalid key pressed, MAPFAIL, or an invalid selection. This send does not include the physical map. Only the symbolic map (DATAONLY) is sent. The physical map previously should have been sent by either a SEND MAP MAPONLY command or a SEND MAP AND DATA command. Do not specify ERASE on the DATAONLY option of the SEND MAP command because you will display variable data on a screen that has no physical constants. When the FROM option is not specified on a SEND MAP command, the output symbolic map generated by BMS, MAPPOVMO in Fig. 6.5, is the default.

If CURSOR was specified in this SEND MAP DATAONLY command, −1 would have to be moved to one of the symbolic map length field's (L suffix). The cursor is set at map POS=(01,01) if −1 was not moved to a length field when CURSOR is specified.

Z999-RESPONSE-ERROR. This is a simplified error processing routine that is performed when an unanticipated RESP is returned in WS-RESP. It is used by all programs in this text.

10

The Linked Program

When one program links to another, the original program remains and the linked program is loaded into main storage. Since linked programs tie-up more main storage, you should limit their use. The journal-posting program discussed in this chapter is a linked program. It utilizes the COMMAREA for passing data to the linked program and for returning data to the linking program.

Some new commands are introduced - ASKTIME, FORMATTIME and the file control command WRITE, which is covered in more detail in chapter 11. BLL pointers are presented and explained.

Many systems require the posting of audit records when transactions change the contents of a record. Rather than having each transaction write its own audit record, one program may be designated as a journal-posting program that writes audit records for several files. This program posts audit transactions for the following files: vendor master, purchase order master, and item master. Programs in this book write a before-and/or after-record for the following file maintenance transactions: changes, additions, and deletions.

Many systems contain separate programs that perform all update maintenance against a system's files. These are often linked-to or *called* programs.

Linking Routine

An audit record can be written only for designated significant field changes or whenever any field in a record changes. *All* changes, additions, and deletions in the vendor master file maintenance programs write an audit record. Change programs write a before-and after-record, additions an after-record, and deletions a before-record.

```
E121-POST-JOURNAL-RECORD   SECTION.
*********************************************************************
*     POST JOURNAL ENTRY - LINK TO JOURNAL PROGRAM 'JRNLPOST'      *
*********************************************************************
*
      MOVE 'VM'                    TO   JR-PREFIX.
      MOVE VENDOR-MASTER-RECORD    TO   JRRECORD-DATA.
      MOVE SPACES                  TO   JR-PASSWORD.
*
      EXEC CICS LINK
              PROGRAM   ('JRNLPOST')
              COMMAREA  (JOURNAL-RECORD)
              LENGTH    (524)
      END-EXEC.
*
 E121-EXIT.
     EXIT.
```

Fig. 10.1 LINKing program section.

Figure 10.1 contains the section of program code used to invoke the journal-posting program JRNLPOST. The record layout for JOURNAL-RECORD can be found in the copy library [see App. B, JRNLRECD].

A B (before) is moved to JR-TYPE in JOURNAL-RECORD by maintenance programs immediately after reading a record for update and prior to a change or delete being executed. An A (after) is moved to JR-TYPE in JOURNAL-RECORD immediately after rewriting a changed record or after writing an added record to the vendor master file. Chapter 11 discusses all file control commands. After moving an A or B to JR-TYPE, all maintenance programs perform E121-POST-JOURNAL-RECORD.

E121-POST-JOURNAL-RECORD

This section formats the simplified journal record prior to executing a LINK command. Depending upon your installation's security requirements, a password might have to be entered on the maintenance screen or in a prior program. The password is then passed to the journal-posting program. The user's sign-on ID is commonly included in an audit record. The ASSIGN command is used to retrieve the user's ID from the system as follows

```
EXEC CICS ASSIGN
        USERID (WS-USERID)
END-EXEC.
```

where WS-USERID is an eight-character programmer-defined working storage data area. Another use of the ASSIGN command is discussed in chapter 12.

The LINK command invokes the program JRNLPOST, which is by definition at a lower logical level. The linking program remains in main storage while the linked program, if necessary, is loaded into main storage. Task number remains the same. JOURNAL-RECORD in COMMAREA and its length (524) are passed to JRNLPOST.

Journal-Posting Program

Figure 10.2 is the linked program JRNLPOST. The working-storage section contains the journal record layout (JRNLRECD) found in appendix B.

```
IDENTIFICATION DIVISION.
PROGRAM-ID. JRNLPOST.
*
**********************************************************************
*                     JOURNAL POSTING PROGRAM                       *
*      POST A JOURNAL RECORD FOR ITEMS PASSED TO THIS PROGRAM       *
*           IN THE COMMAREA BY A LINK FROM ANOTHER PROGRAM.         *
**********************************************************************
ENVIRONMENT DIVISION.
DATA DIVISION.
*
WORKING-STORAGE SECTION.
*
01   WS-PROGRAM-FIELDS.
     05   FILLER          PIC X(22)   VALUE 'JRNLPOST - START OF WS'.
     05   JR-REC-LENGTH  PIC S9(4)   VALUE +524    COMP.
*
01   JOURNAL-RECORD   COPY    JRNLRECD.
*
01  END-OF-WORKING-STORAGE   PIC X(15)   VALUE 'END WS JRNLPOST'.
*
LINKAGE SECTION.
*
01   DFHCOMMAREA                 PIC X(524).
*
01   BLL-CELLS.
     02   FILLER                 PIC S9(8)    COMP.
     02   BLL-SEQ-TABLE-ADDRESS  PIC S9(8)    COMP.
*
01   T053-SEQUENCE-TABLE.
     05   T053-SEQUENCE-NUMBER   PIC S9(5)    COMP-3.
*
PROCEDURE DIVISION.
```

Fig. 10.2 LINKed program JRNLPOST.

Fig. 10.2 *Continued.*

```
***********************************************************************
*                 PROGRAM STRUCTURE IS:                               *
*                 AA00-MAINLINE                                       *
*                      B000-LOAD-SEQUENCE-TABLE                       *
*                      C000-FORMAT-JOURNAL-RECORD                     *
*                      D000-WRITE-JOURNAL-RECORD                      *
***********************************************************************
*
 AA00-MAINLINE  SECTION.
*
*    SERVICE RELOAD BLL-CELLS.
*
     MOVE DFHCOMMAREA  TO  JOURNAL-RECORD.
*
     PERFORM B000-LOAD-SEQUENCE-TABLE.
*
     PERFORM C000-FORMAT-JOURNAL-RECORD.
*
     PERFORM D000-WRITE-JOURNAL-RECORD.
*
     MOVE JOURNAL-RECORD  TO  DFHCOMMAREA.
*
* RETURN TO LINKED FROM PROGRAM
     EXEC CICS RETURN
     END-EXEC.
*

 B000-LOAD-SEQUENCE-TABLE  SECTION.
***********************************************************************
*          SET ADDRESS OF MAIN STORAGE RESIDENT TABLE                 *
*                 PERFORMED FROM:  AA00-MAINLINE                       *
***********************************************************************
*
     EXEC CICS LOAD
             PROGRAM ('T053JRSQ')
             SET     (BLL-SEQ-TABLE-ADDRESS)
     ENDEXEC.
*
*    SERVICE RELOAD T053-SEQUENCE-TABLE.
*
 B000EXIT.
     EXIT.
*
 C000-FORMAT-JOURNAL-RECORD  SECTION.
***********************************************************************
*          FORMAT JOURNAL RECORD - PRIOR TO WRITING                   *
*                 PERFORMED FROM:  AA00-MAINLINE                       *
***********************************************************************
```

Fig. 10.2 *Continued.*

```
*
       MOVE T053-SEQUENCE-NUMBER  TO  JR-SEQUENCE-NUMBER.
       ADD 1                      TO  T053-SEQUENCE-NUMBER.
*
       EXEC CICS ASKTIME
       END-EXEC.
*
       MOVE EIBDATE   TO  JR-EIBDATE.
       MOVE EIBTIME   TO  JR-EIBTIME.
       MOVE EIBTRMID  TO  JR-EIBTRMID.
*
   C000EXIT.
       EXIT.
*


   D000WRITEJOURNALRECORD  SECTION.
 *********************************************************************
 *            ADD A 'BEFORE' OR 'AFTER' JOURNAL RECORD              *
 *                 PERFORMED FROM:  AA00MAINLINE                    *
 *      INCLUDING SEQUENCE NUMBER AS PART OF KEY ELIMINATES         *
 *      POSSIBILITY OF DUPREC HANDLE CONDITION ON FOLLOWING WRITE   *
 *********************************************************************
*
       EXEC CICS WRITE
                 DATASET ('JOURNAL1')
                 FROM    (JOURNALRECORD)
                 RIDFLD  (JRKEY)
                 LENGTH  (JR-REC-LENGTH)
       END-EXEC.
*
   D000-EXIT.
       -EXIT.
```

Linkage section

DFHCOMMAREA is defined in the linkage section as a 524-byte field. This is the length passed by the invoking maintenance program. DFHCOM-MAREA, moved to JOURNAL-RECORD upon entering the program, can contain subfields corresponding to JOURNAL-RECORD fields, if data were required to be returned to the linking program. JRNLPOST issues a WRITE command from the journal record.

BLL cells definition. BLL cells are pointers that must immediately follow DFHCOMMAREA in the linkage section. The filler following BLL-CELLS points to the BLL cell list itself. Each labeled 02 field under FILLER can be set to point to the corresponding 01 field that follows the BLL cell list. This program sets BLL-SEQ-TABLE-ADDRESS to point to T053-SEQUENCE-

TABLE. BLL-cell usage is explained further as we examine the procedure division of JRNLPOST. Chapter 25 demonstrates how BLL cells are eliminated when you use VS COBOL II.

Procedure division

The program structure is defined as comments at the start of the procedure division.

AA00-MAINLINE. The SERVICE RELOAD statement must be issued at the start of the program to ensure proper linkage-section addressability if your installation uses an OS/VS COBOL or OS COBOL Version 4 compiler. The SERVICE RELOAD statement should be issued whenever the address of a BLL cell is changed. The SERVICE RELOAD statement is shown commented out in all program examples. SERVICE RELOAD is not needed or permitted if you are using VS COBOL II as explained in chapter 25.

DFHCOMMAREA, which contains the journal record data passed from the linking program, is moved to JOURNAL-RECORD. A sequence table is loaded. The journal record is then formatted and written to the journal file. JOURNAL-RECORD is then moved to DFHCOMMAREA and a RETURN command, without TRANSID, is executed in order to return to the higher-logical-level linking program. Control returns to the statement following the LINK command (E121-EXIT) in Fig. 10.1. Any JOURNAL-RECORD fields changed by JRNLPOST are available in the working-storage communications area, JOURNAL-RECORD, of the linking program (e.g. from section E121-POST-JOURNAL-RECORD in Fig. 10.1), not in DFHCOMMAREA.

B000-LOAD-SEQUENCE-TABLE. The LOAD command sets a BLL address pointer to the journal sequence table (T053-SEQUENCE-TABLE), in the linkage section. BLL-SEQ-TABLE-ADDRESS has addressability to T053-SEQUENCE-TABLE. T053-SEQUENCE-NUMBER can be referenced and changed. Define the sequence table in the PPT as a main-storage resident table. For nonresident tables, it is good practice to release the table as soon as it is no longer required.

The PGMIDERR handle condition is invoked if T053JRSQ is not in the PPT. You can include the RESP option on the LOAD command and test it after execution for the PGMIDERR condition [IF WS-RESP = DFHRESP (PGMIDERR) PERFORM program 'not found' condition] or you can just let the program abend if the table is not found.

BLL cells usage. Define BLL cells as shown in the linkage section, as binary full words. Each BLL cell can address only 4096 bytes of main storage. If a table exceeds 4096 bytes, the additional positions must be addressed in multiples of 4096, even if fewer than 4096 additional bytes are needed. Figure 10.3 illustrates how this works. Table 2 requires 9606 bytes or two full blocks

of 4096 plus one partial block. Three BLL cells are required to address this
table as shown. The LOAD command addresses the first 4096 bytes; then
4096 is added to the first address in order to set the address pointer to the

```
LINKAGE SECTION.
*
01  DFHCOMMAREA                        PIC X.
*
01  BLL-CELLS.  ←
    02  BLL-CELLS-ADDRESS              PIC S9(8)    COMP. ⟩
*
    02  BLL-TABLE-1-ADDRESS            PIC S9(8)    COMP. ⟩
*
    02  BLL-TABLE-2-ADDRESS-1          PIC S9(8)    COMP.
    02  BLL-TABLE-2-ADDRESS-2          PIC S9(8)    COMP.
    02  BLL-TABLE-2-ADDRESS-3          PIC S9(8)    COMP.
*
    02  BLL-TABLE-3-ADDRESS            PIC S9(8)    COMP. ⟩
*
01  TABLE-1                            PIC X(10). ←
*
01  TABLE-2                            PIC X(9606). ←
*
01  TABLE-3                            PIC X(4000). ←
*
*
PROCEDURE DIVISION.
        .
        .
        .

    EXEC CICS LOAD
            PROGRAM ('T002BIGT')
            SET     (BLL-TABLE-2-ADDRESS-1)
    END-EXEC.
*
    ADD 4096  BLL-TABLE-2-ADDRESS-1
       GIVING BLL-TABLE-2-ADDRESS-2.
*
    ADD 4096  BLL-TABLE-2-ADDRESS-2
       GIVING BLL-TABLE-2-ADDRESS-3.
*
*   SERVICE RELOAD TABLE-2.
        .
        .
        .
```

Fig. 10.3 Establishing BLL addressability for large table.

```
05  FO-ABSTIME          PIC S9(16)   COMP VALUE ZEROES.
05  FO-TIME             PIC X(8)     VALUE SPACES.
05  FO-TIMESEP          PIC X        VALUE '.'.
05  FO-DATESEP          PIC X        VALUE '.'.
05  FO-YYDDD            PIC X(6)     VALUE SPACES.
05  FO-YYMMDD           PIC X(8)     VALUE SPACES.
05  FO-YYDDMM           PIC X(8)     VALUE SPACES.
05  FO-MMDDYY           PIC X(8)     VALUE SPACES.
05  FO-DDMMYY           PIC X(8)     VALUE SPACES.
05  FO-DAYCOUNT         PIC S9(8)    COMP VALUE ZEROES.
05  FO-DAYOFWEEK        PIC S9(8)    COMP VALUE ZEROES.
05  FO-DAYOFMONTH       PIC S9(8)    COMP VALUE ZEROES.
05  FO-MONTHOFYEAR      PIC S9(8)    COMP VALUE ZEROES.
05  FO-YEAR             PIC S9(8)    COMP VALUE ZEROES.


EXEC CICS FORMATTIME
            ABSTIME       (FO-ABSTIME)
            TIME          (FO-TIME)
            TIMESEP       (FO-TIMESEP)
            DATESEP       (FO-DATESEP)
            YYDDD         (FO-YYDDD)
            YYMMDD        (FO-YYMMDD)
            YYDDMM        (FO-YYDDMM)
            MMDDYY        (FO-MMDDYY)
            DDMMYY        (FO-DDMMYY)
            DAYCOUNT      (FO-DAYCOUNT)
            DAYOFWEEK     (FO-DAYOFWEEK)
            DAYOFMONTH    (FO-DAYOFMONTH)
            MONTHOFYEAR   (FO-MONTHOFYEAR)
            YEAR          (FO-YEAR)
END-EXEC.
```

Fig. 10.4 FORMATTIME options.

next 4096 bytes. Finally, 4096 is added to the second address to set the address pointer to the third block of 4096. If required, you have to issue a SERVICE RELOAD command to establish addressability as shown in Fig. 10.3.

C000-FORMAT-JOURNAL-RECORD. This section formats the journal record prior to writing it. The journal record's data is passed in DFHCOMMAREA from the linking program. When a task is initiated, the EIB is established with initial values. In a long-running task, it may be desirable to refresh the value of certain EIB fields such as EIBDATE and EIBTIME. Most likely, EIBDATE won't change, but EIBTIME might. The ASKTIME command updates the fields EIBTIME and EIBDATE when it is issued. Its format is:

```
EXEC CICS ASKTIME
END-EXEC.
```

See FORMATTIME later in this chapter for the ABSTIME option of ASKTIME.

The journal record's key consists of EIBDATE, EIBTIME, and a sequence number. The sequence number is obtained from the sequence table and is incremented by 1 each time it is used. The sequence number is needed as part of the key to ensure that no multiple record keys occur. The EIB TeRMinal IDentification (EIBTRMID) field is moved to the journal record as a data element for audit reporting. This is a simplified example and many additional fields are most likely moved to your audit record.

The journal file can be closed off line and its data written to another file by a batch program. Journal-file records can be deleted, and the next day's processing can begin with an empty file. The batch file extracted from the journal file can be used for audit reporting and saved if required.

D000-WRITE-JOURNAL-RECORD.   The journal record formatted in section C000-FORMAT-JOURNAL-RECORD is written out to a file called JOURNAL1. The WRITE command is covered in chapter 11, "File Control."

FORMATTIME

The FORMATTIME command is used to set time and date in various formats in programmer-defined fields. This command requires an input field that is passed by using the ABSTIME option. ABSTIME is defined as the elapsed time in milliseconds since zero hours on January 1, 1900. It can be calculated or derived for the current date and time by including the ABSTIME option on the ASKTIME command as follows:

```
EXEC CICS ASKTIME
        ABSTIME (FO-ABSTIME)
END-EXEC.
```

FO-ABSTIME must be defined as a doubleword (8 bytes). Its contents can be stored in a record as part of a key field or as a data element. EIBTIME, sometimes used as part of a record's key for time-stamping audit records, may not always change between file writes because of the computer's speed of processing. This can result in a duplicate key condition and may require additional logic to reexecute ASKTIME and to again process the write. The use of ABSTIME should break time down to a fine enough interval to eliminate this problem. The options of FORMATTIME most likely to be used along with representative working-storage fields are as shown in Fig. 10.4.

Only the desired options need be specified on the FORMATTIME command, and the results of the execution are found in the appropriate working-storage fields. The options of FORMATTIME are

- ABSTIME—The argument of this required entry may be derived from the execution of the ASKTIME command, may have been saved in a data record, or may be calculated. It must be defined as a doubleword (8 bytes). ABSTIME can be calculated (zero time) by multiplying days since 1/1/00 X 86,400 s/day X 1000 ms/s.

- TIME—An eight-character field in hh:mm:ss format depending on the separator defined by TIMESEP.

- TIMESEP—A separator character used to split time into hh.mm.ss format. If this option is specified without an argument, then the default separator is a colon (:). A six-character field without separators is returned if this option is omitted.

- DATESEP—A separator character used to split date into an appropriate format. If this option is specified without an argument, then the default separator is a slash (/). A field without separators is returned if this option is omitted.

- YYDDD—The date is returned to a six-character working-storage field for this option in Julian date format, with or without separator characters, depending on whether DATESEP is specified.

- YYMMDD, YYDDMM, MMDDYY, and DDMMYY—The date is returned to an eight-character working-storage field for these options in the indicated format, with or without separator characters, depending on whether you specify DATESEP.

- DAYCOUNT—The argument to this option receives the number of days since January 1, 1900. This option should be helpful in determining the number of days between two dates. Specify the receiving field as a binary fullword.

- DAYOFWEEK—The argument to this option receives a relative number that represents the day of the week: Sunday = 0, Saturday = 6. Specify the receiving field as a binary fullword.

- DAYOFMONTH—The argument to this option receives the day of the month. Specify the receiving field as a binary fullword.

- MONTHOFYEAR—The argument to this option receives the month of the year. Specify the receiving fieldas a binary fullword.

- YEAR—The year is returned to working storage as a four-digit year. Define the receiving field as a binary fullword.

11

File Control

File control seems to be one of the easier concepts for CICS programmers to understand, especially those who have worked on batch systems using virtual storage access methods (VSAM). Knowledge of VSAM is helpful, but not required, to understand this chapter. You should be familiar with the concept of random access file processing in order to gain maximum benefit from the material presented.

This chapter addresses file control using VSAM key-sequenced data sets (VSAM KSDS), the file structure used for all examples in this book. Files are opened dynamically by CICS when the file is first accessed, and closed when CICS is brought down. CICS applications programs must never open or close a file.

All CICS files must be defined in a table called the file control table (FCT). Some FCT entries are: data set name; access method (KSDS for examples in this text); and permissible file service requests such as update, browse, add, and delete. You generally need only to specify data set name, key field, and the data-area name of a record's I/O area. For program examples, all required entries are assumed to have been made in the FCT for files containing fixed-length records. VENDMAST and JOURNAL1 are the two files used, and they permit the use of all file control commands required for examples in this book. The FCT is generally maintained by the system programming staff.

Opening and Closing Files

Files used by CICS are opened dynamically when they are first required by a program. CICS files must be closed if they need to be changed by a batch

```
IF WS-RESP   =   DFHRESP (NORMAL)
    NEXT SENTENCE
ELSE
    IF WS-RESP   =   DFHRESP (NOTOPEN)
            OR       DFHRESP (DISABLED)
        MOVE 'FILE IS NOT OPEN - PLEASE TRY LATER'
                        TO MAP-D-MESSAGE
        MOVE ASKIP-BRT    TO MAP-A-MESSAGE
        PERFORM B110-SEND-MAP-AND-DATA
        PERFORM B120-RETURN-TO-CICS
    ELSE
        IF . . .
            . . .
        ELSE
            MOVE 'B100-' TO WS-RESP-SECTION
            PERFORM Z999-RESPONSE-ERROR.
```

Fig. 11.1 RESP options to test for NOTOPEN or DISABLED condition.

program, since they cannot be updated by both CICS and batch systems at the same time. Occasionally, users get an indicative message that files have been closed; they are most likely needed by a batch program. Whenever practical, data processing gives notice to users before closing and reopening files. The condition NOTOPEN or DISABLED is raised by file control commands if a file is closed or disabled. A task ABENDs if a file cannot be accessed and if a test is not made for this condition. Including the RESP option on file control commands and testing for these conditions as follows is good practice (see Fig. 11.1).

Depending on the file control command being used, you will most likely test for additional conditions, such as record not found, end of file, etc. For simplicity of illustration, file available tests are not coded on program examples in this book, but their inclusion is recommended on programs you code.

File Control Commands

The most common file control commands are:

- READ command—Read a file for inquiry or access without update intended.

- READ FOR UPDATE—Read a file with the intent of changing and updating a record.

- WRITE—Write a new record to a file.

- REWRITE—Rewrite a record read for update.

- UNLOCK—Release a record read for update if processing indicates that updating is not required.

- DELETE—Remove a record from the file.

- STARTBR—Establish a starting point for a browse (sequential reads against a file).

- READNEXT—Read the next record after a STARTBR or after a prior READNEXT command.

- READPREV—Read the preceding record after a STARTBR or after a prior READPREV command.

- ENDBR—Terminate a browse function initiated by the STARTBR command.

- RESETBR—End the previous browse and start a new browse.

Options Common to Many File Control Commands

- DATASET (FCT entry)—The FCT entry uses up to eight alphanumeric characters for the file's name. The FCT entry may be enclosed in single quotes, or may refer to an eight-character alphanumeric data area in working storage, for instance:

```
DATASET ('VENDMAST')
```
    or
```
DATASET (WS-FILE-NAME)
```

- INTO (data-area) / FROM (data-area)—Program-defined working-storage area used to hold your program's input and/or output area. These options are used by most text program examples.

- SET (ptr-ref) | (ADDRESS OF struc)—Used for locate mode processing for OS/VS COBOL and VS COBOL II respectively, as explained in chapter 7 (see "Locate Mode Processing").

- RIDFLD (data-area)—RIDFLD (Record IDentification FieLD) contains the key of the record to be operated upon. This field may be defined as part of the record's key or it may be defined in working storage.

- RESP (data-area)—The recommended RESP option can be included on all CICS commands and tested following execution of the command. This text uses the programmer-defined data-area named WS-RESP to hold the response returned from EIBRESP. Data-area is defined as a fullword binary value.

- LENGTH (data-value)—Program defined length of the data area into which a record is to be retrieved, or from which it is to be written. The *actual* length of a record is available in this area at the completion of a read command. Length is defined in working storage as a halfword binary value. This option is required for variable-length records and is optional for fixed-length records.

READ Command

The READ command reads a record into a data area defined in working storage or the linkage section. After a successful read, the record's data is available to the program.

The READ command format is:

```
EXEC CICS READ
          DATASET (FCT entry)
          [INTO   (data-area)  |
          SET     (ptr-ref)  |
          SET     (ADDRESS OF struc) ]
          RIDFLD  (data-area)
          LENGTH  (data-value)
          RESP    (data-area)
END-EXEC.
```

- Conditions Raised—Record NOT FouND (NOTFND), file NOTOPEN, and file DISABLED are the conditions most often encountered when using the READ command. I recommend you use the RESP option to check for all anticipated conditions.

WRITE Command

The WRITE command writes a record *from* an area defined in working storage or the linkage section. The required data must be moved to the working-storage or linkage section area of the record to be added, prior to issuing a WRITE command. When a write is successful, the record is added to the file.

The WRITE command format is:

```
EXEC CICS WRITE
          DATASET (FCT entry)
          FROM    (data-area)
          RIDFLD  (data-area)
          LENGTH  (data-value)
          RESP    (data-area)
END-EXEC
```

- Conditions Raised—Record already exists on the file [DUPlicate RECord (DUPREC)] is the condition generally checked for when using the WRITE command. NOSPACE occurs if a file to which a record is being added is full. DISABLED or NOTOPEN conditions may also occur. I recommend that you use the RESP option to check for all anticipated conditions.

READ for UPDATE Command

The READ for UPDATE version of the READ command reads a record into an area defined in working storage or the linkage section, with the intent of updating the record. Normally, fields to be updated have new data moved into the I/O area of the record to be changed, before the record is rewritten (see REWRITE command below). After a successful read, the record's data is available in its defined data area.

A record read for update should be read as close to the update command as possible in order to prevent file lockout of other tasks. If you determine that a record read for update will not be rewritten, issue the UNLOCK command as soon as you determine that the record will not be rewritten (see "Exclusive Control" below).

The format of the READ for UPDATE option of the READ command is identical to the regular READ command, except that you must specify the option UPDATE.

```
EXEC CICS READ     UPDATE
           DATASET (FCT entry)
          [INTO    (data-area)   |
           SET     (ptr-ref)  |
           SET     (ADDRESS OF struc) ]
           RIDFLD  (data-area)
           LENGTH  (data-value)
           RESP    (data-area)
END-EXEC.
```

- Conditions Raised—Record NOT FouND (NOTFND), file NOTOPEN, and file DISABLED are the conditions most often encountered when using the READ command. I recommend that you use the RESP option to check for all anticipated conditions.

REWRITE Command

The REWRITE command updates a record from a data area defined in working storage or the linkage section. Prior to issuing a REWRITE command, the required data must be moved to the data area of the record to be changed. The key field within the record must not be changed. When a rewrite is successful, the record's new data replaces the old data in the designated record. A rewrite is only successful against a record found when read for update.

The REWRITE command format is:

```
EXEC CICS REWRITE
          DATASET (FCT entry)
          FROM    (data-area)
          LENGTH  (data-value)
          RESP    (data-area)
END-EXEC.
```

- Conditions Raised—The condition INVREQ occurs if a rewrite is attempted against a record not read for update. Generally, you do not need to check for any conditions other than a normal response after issuing a REWRITE command.

Ensuring Data Integrity

Most systems can have more than one person update records in a file. A user may read a record from a file and display data fields to be updated. A different user may, at the same time, display the same record with the intent of updating the same fields with different data. When both users make their changes on the screen and press an AID key to update the record, changes made by the first user are overriden by those made by the second user. A common practice is to save the full record to be updated in a scratchpad area, such as the COMMAREA or in temporary storage (see chapter 16). The program then sends a map upon which the user keys in changes and then presses an AID key. Upon reentry into the program, the record to be modified is read for update. This current record can be compared against the old record saved in a scratchpad area. If the records are equal, no changes have been made to the record since it was originally read by the program. If the record has been changed since it was originally read, an indicative user notification message can be displayed. The user must reenter changes against the altered record. This is inconvenient, but should not occur often, and the increased file integrity is worth the occasional inconvenience.

Exclusive Control

File control gives exclusive control to the control interval containing a record read for update. Exclusive control prevents reading of the same record, or any record in the control interval for update, until the record read for update has been rewritten or released. A lockout occurs when a task tries to read another record for update or attempts to add a record before a record read for update in the same control interval is rewritten, deleted, or unlocked. Sometimes it is determined that a record read for update will not be changed. When you can determine the point at which a record does not need to be written, exclusive control should be released by issuing the UNLOCK command. Rewriting or deleting a record read for update as well as terminating a task releases exclusive control of the control interval. Exclusive control is not released for a recoverable file until the task ends or a syncpoint is issued.

You must release exclusive control of a record read for update before reading another record in the same file for update. Failure to do this results in an INValid REQuest (INVREQ) condition being raised. It is good practice to read files that may be updated, in the same sequence in all programs to prevent a lockout from occurring between two different tasks. Limit the number of programs that can directly update a file. Many systems link to or call a program that performs all updating against one or more files.

UNLOCK Command

The UNLOCK command should be used in programs containing much processing, after it is known that a record will not be rewritten. Exclusive control is released by issuing the UNLOCK command.

The UNLOCK command format is:

```
EXEC CICS UNLOCK
          DATASET (FCT entry)
END-EXEC.
```

DELETE Command

Although it is not required, I recommend reading a record prior to deletion. You might display the record in an inquiry format with a message DO YOU WISH TO DELETE THIS RECORD? To delete the record, you might have the user key in YES and press a designated AID key or some similar action. The common practice is to write the record to an audit file that can be used later offline to print a batch-processing listing of transactions that updated the file. A record read prior to deletion must be read with the UPDATE option.

The format for the DELETE command when read first is:

```
EXEC CICS DELETE
          DATASET (FCT entry)
END-EXEC.
```

Only the DATASET option is required when the file is read for update prior to issuing the DELETE command. You must not specify the RIDFLD option. If the record is *not* read prior to deletion, the RIDFLD option must be included as follows:

```
EXEC CICS DELETE
```

```
          DATASET (FCT entry)
          RIDFLD  (data-area)
END-EXEC.
```

You must move the key of the record to be deleted to the data-area prior to issuing the delete.

- Conditions Raised—I generally read a record first before deleting it and do not test for any expected conditions. INVREQ can occur on this delete if no previous read for update was executed. NOTFND can occur for the delete without a preceding READ for UPDATE, if the key specified in the RIDFLD data-area is not on the file.

FILE BROWSE Commands and Considerations

Some applications require a program to start at a specified item in the file and then to display records sequentially beginning from that point. A record cannot be updated using browse commands; it must first be read for update. A vendor file could be in alphabetical sequence by vendor code prefix; assume the code is of the format A-9999-9, with the first character being A through Z. The next four digits can position the vendor alphabetically within the alphabetic prefix and the last digit might be used for vendor location. The user may want to search the file for vendors that have a name starting with the letter M. The browse can be initiated by entering vendor code M00000 or just M. The program moves the entered vendor code to the data-area specified in the RIDFLD option and issue the browse command to establish a position at the record, or at the first record with a greater key value.

STARTBR command

The STARTBR (START BRowse) command sets the beginning position for a browse. The READNEXT and READPREV commands read records sequentially, starting at the position established by the STARTBR command. No record is read by the STARTBR command; a starting point in the file is established for the first READNEXT or READPREV command.

The STARTBR command format is:

```
EXEC CICS STARTBR
          DATASET (FCT entry)
          RIDFLD  (data-area)
      [GTEQ | EQUAL]
END-EXEC.
```

Low-values in RIDFLD's data-area position the browse at the beginning of the file. High-values position it at the end of the file.

- GTEQ—The Greater Than or EQual to (GTEQ) operand of the STARTBR command specifies that if the RIDFLD record key is not found, the browse is to set the file starting point at the next sequential record. EQUAL may be specified in place of GTEQ.

- Conditions Raised—NOTFND occurs if GTEQ is not specified and an exact hit is not made for the record in RIDFLD. NOTFND also occurs if GTEQ is included and the record specified in RIDFLD has a key greater than the last key in the file. INVREQ occurs if a STARTBR command is issued against a file not defined in the FCT with the browse option.

Browse inefficiencies

Browse operations are inefficient because many records must be read from a file. Limit a browse by providing the ability to reset its starting key.

READNEXT command

The format of the READNEXT command is similar to that of the READ command. The first time READNEXT is executed following a STARTBR command, the record retrieved is the record positioned at by the STARTBR command. Succeeding READNEXT executions retrieve records sequentially from that position in the file. The data-area specified in the RIDFLD option is updated with the entire record key each time a READNEXT command is executed. Records in the file could be skipped by changing the key in data-area to a key greater than that of the last record read. This is called "skip sequential processing."

The READNEXT command format is:

```
EXEC CICS READNEXT
          DATASET (FCT entry)
          [INTO   (data-area)  |
          SET     (ptr-ref)    |
          SET     (ADDRESS OF struc) ]
          RIDFLD  (data-area)
          LENGTH  (data-value)
          RESP    (data-area)
END-EXEC.
```

- Conditions Raised—ENDFILE occurs when the end of a file is reached. NOTFND may occur if, in the same program, data-area specified in the RIDFLD option is set to a key lower than the last key read. If this occurs, the program should execute a RESETBR or an ENDBR command (discussed later in this chapter). INVREQ occurs if no preceding STARTBR command was executed.

Generic search

A generic (partial key) search can be used with the STARTBR command.

The generic search requires the move of the generic key to the first portion of RIDFLD's data-area and the specification of the KEYLENGTH and GENERIC options on the STARTBR command.

The format of the STARTBR command with the GENERIC option is:

```
EXEC CICS STARTBR
          DATASET (FCT entry)
          RIDFLD  (data-area)
          GTEQ
          KEYLENGTH (data-value)
          GENERIC
END-EXEC.
```

- GTEQ—This operand specifies that if the RIDFLD record key is not found, the browse is to set the file starting point at the next sequential record.

- KEYLENGTH (data-value)—This is a working-storage entry defined as a halfword binary field. The length of the portion of the key to be searched for must be moved to this field prior to execution of the GENERIC option of the STARTBR command. A generic STARTBR command establishes position at the start of the file if KEYLENGTH (0) is specified.

- GENERIC—This statement must be included along with KEYLENGTH for a generic search.

- Conditions Raised—NOTFND occurs if GTEQ is omitted and an exact hit is not made for the value in RIDFLD. NOTFND also occurs if GTEQ is included and the record specified in RIDFLD contains a key greater than the last key in the file. INVREQ occurs if a STARTBR command is issued against a file not defined in the FCT with the browse option.

READPREV command

The READPREV command functions similarly to the READNEXT command, following the execution of a STARTBR command. The first time READPREV is executed following a STARTBR command and the record retrieved is the record at which position was established by the STARTBR command. Succeeding READPREV executions retrieve records containing keys sequentially lower than the previous record. The data-area specified in the RIDFLD option is updated with the entire record key each time a READPREV command is executed. READPREV cannot be issued following a browse initiated with the GENERIC option of the STARTBR command. If a READNEXT command is followed by a READPREV command, the READPREV reads the same record read by the READNEXT. Issue another READPREV to read the desired record. Skip sequential processing cannot be used with a backward browse.

The READPREV command format is:

```
EXEC CICS READPREV
          DATASET (FCT entry)
          [INTO    (data-area)  |
          SET     (ptr-ref)  |
          SET     (ADDRESS OF struc) ]
          RIDFLD  (data-area)
          LENGTH  (data-value)
          RESP    (data-area)
END-EXEC.
```

■ Conditions Raised—ENDFILE occurs when the "beginning" of the file is reached. INVREQ occurs if no preceding STARTBR command was executed or if the STARTBR command had a GENERIC option specified. NOTFND occurs if an immediately preceding STARTBR did not get an EQUAL hit. For this reason, it is preferable to issue a READ*NEXT* following a STARTBR and then follow with a READPREV command.

End browse (ENDBR) command

The ENDBR command is issued in order to terminate a browse. Executing a new STARTBR command against the same file in a task without having ended a previous browse results in an INVREQ condition. Terminate all browses with the ENDBR command as soon as possible.

The ENDBR command format is:

```
EXEC CICS ENDBR
          DATASET (FCT entry)
END-EXEC.
```

■ Conditions Raised—INVREQ occurs if no preceding STARTBR command was executed.

Reset browse (RESETBR) command

The RESETBR command resets a browse to the original or to a new browse starting point. It has the same effect as an ENDBR command followed by a STARTBR command. You can use RESETBR commands to skip sequentially through a file.

The RESETBR command format is similar to STARTBR:

```
EXEC CICS RESETBR
          DATASET (FCT entry)
          RIDFLD  (data-area)
```

```
      [GTEQ | EQUAL]
       KEYLENGTH (data-value)
       GENERIC
  END-EXEC.
```

Low-values in RIDFLD position the browse at the beginning of the file. High-values position it at the end of the file.

- GTEQ—This operand of the RESETBR command specifies that if the RIDFLD record key is not found, the browse is to set the file starting point at the next sequential record. EQUAL may also be specified.

- Conditions Raised—NOTFND occurs if GTEQ is not specified and an exact hit is not made for the value in RIDFLD. NOTFND also occurs if GTEQ is included and if the record specified in RIDFLD has a key greater than the last key in the file. INVREQ occurs if a RESETBR command is issued against a file not defined in the FCT with the browse option.

12

The Inquiry Program

An inquiry program is one of the first programs you should write after an online file is created. This is not a maintenance program, but I include it on many maintenance menus. Inquiries generally list most fields contained on the record being displayed. Inquiry and maintenance programs are helpful during the testing stage of a system and are necessary once the system is running in a production environment.

Control and detail maps are used for the inquiry program. The control map, shown in Fig. 2.3, requires the user to key in a vendor code and press ENTER to display the inquiry detail map. The user also has the option of transferring control to the vendor file browse program, of returning to the vendor file maintenance submenu (see Fig. 6.3), or of ending the session. The vendor file inquiry detail map shown in Fig. 2.5 is displayed when the user enters a vendor code on the control screen and then presses ENTER. The detail screen displays all fields contained on the vendor's record. The user can view the vendor's data and then press ENTER in order to return to the control screen. The detail screen also permits the user to return to the submenu or to end the session.

BMS Maps

Figures 12.1 and 12.2 show the BMS maps for the control and detail maps shown in Figs. 2.3 and 2.5, respectively. The DFHMSD and DFHMDI macros are the same as those on previous maps except for the mapset and map-name labels.

Fig. 12.1 Vendor file inquiry BMS control map.

```
          PRINT NOGEN
POVMIQ1                          DFHMSD              TYPE=MAP,
X
                                              TIOAPFX=YES,
X
                                    CTRL=(FRSET,FREEKB),
X
          TERM=3270,                                        X
          LANG=COBOL,                                       X
          MODE=INOUT
*
MAPPOVC                  DFHMDI              SIZE=(24,80),
X
          COLUMN=01,                                        X
          LINE=01
*
MCDATE                 DFHMDF              POS=(01,01),
X
          LENGTH=08,                                        X
          ATTRB=ASKIP
*
                              DFHMDF      POS=(01,27),
X
          LENGTH=25,                                        X
                                    ATTRB=ASKIP,
X
          INITIAL='ABC MANUFACTURING COMPANY'
*
                              DFHMDF      POS=(01,72),
X
          LENGTH=07,                                        X
                                    ATTRB=ASKIP,
X
          INITIAL='POVMIQ1'
*
MCTIME                 DFHMDF              POS=(02,01),
X
          LENGTH=08,                                        X
          ATTRB=ASKIP
*
                              DFHMDF      POS=(02,26),
X
          LENGTH=27,                                        X
```

Fig. 12.1 *Continued.*

```
*
                                         DFHMDF    POS=(07,40),
X
              LENGTH=01,                                        X
                                                   ATTRB=ASKIP,
X
                INITIAL='-'
*
MCVCOD2                     DFHMDF                  POS=(07,42),
X
              LENGTH=04,                                        X
                ATTRB=UNPROT
*
                                         DFHMDF    POS=(07,47),
X
              LENGTH=01,                                        X
                                                   ATTRB=ASKIP,
X
                INITIAL='-'
*
MCVCOD3                     DFHMDF                  POS=(07,49),
X
              LENGTH=01,                                        X
                ATTRB=UNPROT
*
                                         DFHMDF    POS=(07,51),
X
              LENGTH=01,                                        X
                ATTRB=ASKIP
*
                                         DFHMDF    POS=(12,19),
X
              LENGTH=40,                                        X
                                                   ATTRB=ASKIP,
X
                INITIAL='1. FOR VENDOR FILE INQUIRY - PRESS EN-
TER'
*
                                         DFHMDF    POS=(14,19),
X
              LENGTH=38,                                        X
                                                   ATTRB=ASKIP,
X
```

Fig. 12.1 *Continued.*

```
MCMESSG                  DFHMDF                  POS=(24,01),
X
                                                 LENGTH=79,
X
              ATTRB=ASKIP
*
```

Fig. 12.2 Vendor file inquiry BMS detail map.

```
         PRINT NOGEN
POVMIQ2                          DFHMSD                  TYPE=MAP,
X
                                             TIOAPFX=YES,
X
                                 CTRL=(FRSET,FREEKB),
X
                                              TERM=3270,
X
                                              LANG=COBOL,
X
              MODE=INOUT
*
MAPPOVD                          DFHMDI            SIZE=(24,80),
X
                                                  COLUMN=01,
X
              LINE=01
*
MDDATE                  DFHMDF                  POS=(01,01),
X
                                                 LENGTH=08,
X
              ATTRB=ASKIP
*
                                   DFHMDF    POS=(01,27),
X
                                              LENGTH=25,
X
                                              ATTRB=ASKIP,
X
              INITIAL='ABC MANUFACTURING COMPANY'
*
                                   DFHMDF    POS=(01,72),
```

Fig. 12.2 *Continued.*

```
                  INITIAL='VENDOR FILE INQUIRY'
*
                                      DFHMDF     POS=(04,01),
X
                                                 LENGTH=12,
X
                                                 ATTRB=ASKIP,
X
                  INITIAL='VENDOR CODE:'
*
MDVNDCD                      DFHMDF                 POS=(04,14),
X
                                                   LENGTH=08,
X
                  ATTRB=ASKIP
*
                                      DFHMDF     POS=(05,08),
X
                                                 LENGTH=05,
X
                                                 ATTRB=ASKIP,
X
                  INITIAL='NAME:'
*
MDVNDNM                      DFHMDF                 POS=(05,14),
X
                                                   LENGTH=25,
X
                  ATTRB=ASKIP
*
                                      DFHMDF     POS=(05,45),
X
                                                 LENGTH=06,
X
                                                 ATTRB=ASKIP,
X
                  INITIAL='PHONE:'
*
                                      DFHMDF     POS=(05,54),
X
                                                 LENGTH=01,
X
                                                 ATTRB=ASKIP,
```

Fig. 12.2 *Continued.*

```
                                        DFHMDF     POS=(05,66),
X
                                                   LENGTH=01,
X
                                                   ATTRB=ASKIP,
X
              INITIAL='-'
*
MDPHON2                    DFHMDF                   POS=(05,68),
X
                                                   LENGTH=04,
X
              ATTRB=ASKIP
*
                                        DFHMDF     POS=(06,45),
X
                                                   LENGTH=08,
X
                                                   ATTRB=ASKIP,
X
              INITIAL='CONTACT:'
*
MDCONTA                    DFHMDF                   POS=(06,54),
X
                                                   LENGTH=25,
X
              ATTRB=ASKIP
*
                                        DFHMDF     POS=(08,01),
X
                                                   LENGTH=17,
X
                                                   ATTRB=ASKIP,
X
              INITIAL='ADDRESS - STREET:'
*
MDSTRET                    DFHMDF                   POS=(08,19),
X
                                                   LENGTH=20,
X
              ATTRB=ASKIP
*
                                        DFHMDF     POS=(08,45),
```

Fig. 12.2 *Continued.*

```
                    INITIAL='CITY:'
*
MDCITY                    DFHMDF                    POS=(09,19),
X
              LENGTH=18,                                         X
              ATTRB=ASKIP
*
                                    DFHMDF          POS=(10,12),
X
              LENGTH=06,                                         X
                                    ATTRB=ASKIP,
X
                    INITIAL='STATE:'
*
MDSTATE                   DFHMDF                    POS=(10,19),
X
              LENGTH=02,                                         X
              ATTRB=ASKIP
*
MDSTANM                   DFHMDF                    POS=(10,22),
X
              LENGTH=14,                                         X
              ATTRB=ASKIP
*
                                    DFHMDF          POS=(11,14),
X
              LENGTH=04,                                         X
                                    ATTRB=ASKIP,
X
                    INITIAL='ZIP:'
*
MDZIP                     DFHMDF                    POS=(11,19),
X
              LENGTH=05,                                         X
              ATTRB=ASKIP
*
                                    DFHMDF          POS=(13,02),
X
              LENGTH=16,                                         X
                                    ATTRB=ASKIP,
X
                    INITIAL='TO ATTENTION OF:'
*
```

Fig. 12.2 *Continued.*

```
                                    DFHMDF      POS=(19,10),
X
              LENGTH=54,                                    X
              ATTRB=ASKIP,                                  X
               INITIAL='2. RETURN TO MENU                   -
PRX
              ESS PF5'
*
                                    DFHMDF      POS=(20,10),
X
              LENGTH=56,                                    X
              ATTRB=ASKIP,                                  X
               INITIAL='3. END OF SESSION                   -
PRX
              ESS CLEAR'
*
MDMESSG                             DFHMDF          POS=(24,01),
X
              LENGTH=79,                                    X
```

BMS control map

All control map fields have ASKIP attributes, except for vendor code, which is UNPROT. The first vendor code entry field, MCVCOD1, has IC specified as part of its attribute. This results in the cursor being positioned under this field if the program issued a SEND MAP MAPONLY command, or if the command-level interpreter (CECI, discussed in chapter 6) is used to test the physical map. This program specifies CURSOR as part of its SEND MAP commands and uses symbolic cursor positioning. Stopper fields are not required following BMS map labels MCVCOD1 and MCVCOD2 because the following hyphens have ASKIP attributes. MCVCOD3 is followed by a stopper field, an unlabeled 1-byte ASKIP attribute in POS=(07,51).

BMS detail map

All inquiry detail map attributes are defined as ASKIP. All BMS maps can be generated with ASKIP attributes defined for every field. Programs can control attributes by modifying them prior to a send that includes the symbolic map. No IC attribute is defined on the BMS map because when the map is sent, the cursor should be set at POS=(01,01). The cursor defaults to this position when the map is sent, unless CURSOR is specified on a send which includes the symbolic map, and –1 is moved to a map length field.

More-Readable Symbolic Maps

More readable symbolic maps that correspond to the BMS-generated maps are shown in the copy library (appendix B, members MAPVMCTL and

MAPVDTL1). Each field defined on the BMS map has a corresponding more-readable map field (see chapter 6).

Inquiry Program Source Code

The inquiry program source code shown in Fig. 12.3 follows the format used in previous examples. I will discuss only sections that contain new commands and concepts or those that need reinforcement.

Working-storage section

Copy library members, for all program examples, are found in the copy library (appendix B). You can find DFHAID in appendix A.3.

Linkage section

The BLL cells in this program are used to establish addressability to two fields, the common work area (CWA) and state code table. The CWA is a system area common to all command-level CICS programs. It can be initialized by a system initiator program run on a daily basis. Member STLNKCWA in appendix B contains a typical group of fields you might find in the CWA. The only CWA field to which program examples in this book refer is CWA-CURRENT-DATE. The CWA and state table are discussed in more detail in the procedure division. The CWA, used by many older CICS systems to pass dates, is included to familiarize you with its use. The data obtained from the CWA for examples in this book can be easily obtained by executing the FORMATTIME command.

Fig. 12.3 Vendor file inquiry program source code.

```
 IDENTIFICATION DIVISION.
 PROGRAM-ID. POVMINQY.
*
********************************************************************
*           PURCHASING SYSTEM - VENDOR FILE INQUIRY           *
*   - STARTED BY PURCHASING SYSTEM SUB-MENU PROGRAM 'POVMAINT'   *
*           COULD ALSO BE STARTED BY TRANSID 'POVI'           *
********************************************************************
 ENVIRONMENT DIVISION.
 DATA DIVISION.
*
 WORKING-STORAGE  SECTION.
*
 01  WS-PROGRAM-FIELDS.
     05  FILLER       PIC X(22)     VALUE 'POVMINQY - START OF WS'.
     05  WS-CRT-MESSAGE   PIC X(17)    VALUE 'SESSION COMPLETED'.
     05  WS-RESP          PIC S9(8)    VALUE +0      COMP.

 01  WS-RESP-ERROR.
     05  FILLER   PIC X(39)     VALUE
         'PROGRAM POVMINQY: ERROR EIBRESP CODE = '.
     05  WS-RESP-ERR-CD     PIC 99          VALUE ZEROES.
```

Fig. 12.3 *Continued.*

```
      05  FILLER    PIC X(39)    VALUE
          'PROGRAM POVMINQY: ERROR EIBRESP CODE = '.
      05  WS-RESP-ERR-CD    PIC 99       VALUE ZEROES.
      05  FILLER   PIC X(15)    VALUE
          '  IN SECTION '.
      05  WS-RESP-SECTION   PIC X(5)   VALUE SPACES.
*
*01  VENDOR-MASTER-RECORD
                              COPY    VENDMAST.
*01  WS-COMMAREA
                              COPY    POWSVMCA.
*01  WS-STATUS-FIELDS
                              COPY    STWSSTAT.
*01  VM-CONTROL-MAP
                              COPY    MAPVMCTL.
*01  VM-DETAIL-MAP
                              COPY    MAPVDTL1.
*01  WS-DATE-AND-TIME
                              COPY    STWSDTTM.
*01  WS-STATE-CODE-SEARCH-ENTRIES
                              COPY    STWST037.
*01  ATTRIBUTE-LIST
                              COPY    STWSATTR.
*01  DFHAID
                              COPY    DFHAID.
*
 01  END-OF-WORKING-STORAGE   PIC X(15)   VALUE 'END WS POVMINQY'.
*
 LINKAGE SECTION.
*
 01  DFHCOMMAREA              PIC X(8).
*
 01  BLL-CELLS.
      05  FILLER         PIC S9(8)  COMP.
      05  BLL-CWA-ADDRESS        PIC S9(8)  COMP.
      05  BLL-T037-STATE-TABLE-ADDRESS  PIC S9(8)   COMP.
*
*01  CWA-DATA
                              COPY    STLNKCWA.
*01  T037-STATE-TABLE
                              COPY    T037STAT.
*
 PROCEDURE DIVISION.
*****************************************************************
*       PROGRAM STRUCTURE IS:                                  *
*              AA00-MAINLINE                                    *
*                B000-INITIAL-ENTRY                             *
*                  B100-SEND-CONTROL-MAP-AND-DATA              *
*                    B110-GET-DATE-AND-TIME                     *
*                                                              *
*                C000-PROCESS-CONTROL-MAP                       *
*                  C100-RECEIVE-CONTROL-MAP                     *
*                    C110-END-SESSION                          *
```

Fig. 12.3 *Continued.*

```
*                              C120-TRANSFER-XCTL-TO-MENU              *
*                              C130-TRANSFER-XCTL-TO-BROWSE            *
*                        C200-VERIFY-VENDOR-FORMAT                     *
*                        C400-VERIFY-VENDOR-FILE-STATUS                *
*                              C410-READ-VENDOR-FILE                   *
*                        C500-SEND-DETAIL-MAP-AND-DATA                 *
*                              B110-GET-DATE-AND-TIME                  *
*                              C530-FORMAT-DETAIL-MAP                  *
*                                 C531-GET-STATE-NAME                  *
*                        C600-SEND-CONTROL-MAP-DATAONLY                *
*                                                                      *
*                   D000-INQUIRY-PROCESSING                            *
*                        D100-RECEIVE-DETAIL-MAP                       *
*                              C110-END-SESSION                        *
*                              C120-TRANSFER-XCTL-TO-MENU              *
*                  B100-SEND-CONTROL-MAP-AND-DATA                      *
*                  D200-SEND-DETAIL-MAP-DATAONLY                       *
************************************************************************
*
 AA00-MAINLINE  SECTION.
*
*     SERVICE RELOAD BLL-CELLS.
*
      IF EIBCALEN  =  0
          PERFORM B000-INITIAL-ENTRY
      ELSE
          MOVE DFHCOMMAREA  TO  WS-COMMAREA
          IF CA-BROWSE
              MOVE SPACE         TO  CA-FUNCTION-CODE
              MOVE LOW-VALUES  TO  VM-CONTROL-MAP
              PERFORM C400-VERIFY-VENDOR-FILE-STATUS
              IF GOOD-VERIFY
                  PERFORM C500-SEND-DETAIL-MAP-AND-DATA
              ELSE
                  PERFORM B100-SEND-CONTROL-MAP-AND-DATA
           ELSE
               IF CA-RECEIVE-CTL-MAP
                   PERFORM C000-PROCESS-CONTROL-MAP
               ELSE
                   PERFORM D000-INQUIRY-PROCESSING.
*
      EXEC CICS RETURN
               TRANSID  ('POVI')
               COMMAREA (WS-COMMAREA)
               LENGTH   (8)
      END-EXEC.
*
 B000-INITIAL-ENTRY  SECTION.
************************************************************************
*          INITIAL ENTRY INTO PROGRAM - ONLY EXECUTED ONCE            *
*                  PERFORMED FROM:  AA00-MAINLINE                      *
************************************************************************
```

Fig. 12.3 *Continued.*

```
*
     MOVE LOW-VALUES  TO  VM-CONTROL-MAP.
     PERFORM B100-SEND-CONTROL-MAP-AND-DATA.
*
 B000-EXIT.
     EXIT.
*
 B100-SEND-CONTROL-MAP-AND-DATA  SECTION.
**********************************************************************
*          SEND CONTROL MAP - SYMBOLIC AND PHYSICAL MAPS         *
*                PERFORMED FROM:  B000-INITIAL-ENTRY             *
*                    D000-INQUIRY-PROCESSING                     *
**********************************************************************
*
     PERFORM B110-GET-DATE-AND-TIME.
     MOVE WS-CURRENT-DATE  TO  MVC-D-DATE.
     MOVE WS-MAP-TIME      TO  MVC-D-TIME.
*
     MOVE -1  TO  MVC-L-VEND-CD-1.
     MOVE '1'  TO  CA-MAP-CONTROL.
*
     EXEC CICS SEND
             MAP    ('MAPPOVC')
             MAPSET ('POVMIQ1')
             FROM   (VM-CONTROL-MAP)
             ERASE
             CURSOR
     END-EXEC.
*
 B100-EXIT.
     EXIT.
*
 B110-GET-DATE-AND-TIME  SECTION.
**********************************************************************
*          STPDDTTM - OBTAIN DATE FROM CWA AND FORMAT TIME      *
*          PERFORMED FROM:  B100-SEND-CONTROL-MAP-AND-DATA      *
*                C500-SEND-DETAIL-MAP-AND-DATA                  *
**********************************************************************
*
     COPY   STPDDTTM.
*
 B110-EXIT.
     EXIT.
*
 C000-PROCESS-CONTROL-MAP  SECTION.
**********************************************************************
*                     PERFORMED FROM:  AA00-MAINLINE           *
*             PROCESS CONTROL MAP - IF VALID SEND DETAIL MAP    *
*                ELSE SEND CONTROL MAP WITH INVALID MESSAGE:    *
*   1) STATUS-OF-RECEIVE  =  'I'   INVALID KEY PRESSED          *
*   2) STATUS-OF-RECEIVE  =  'M'   MAPFAIL - NO DATA ENTERED    *
```

Fig. 12.3 *Continued.*

```
*    3) STATUS-OF-FORMAT    = 'E'   INVALID VENDOR KEYED FORMAT  *
*    4) STATUS-OF-VERIFY    = 'E'   VENDOR FILE STATUS ERROR     *
*****************************************************************
*
     PERFORM C100-RECEIVE-CONTROL-MAP.
     IF GOOD-RECEIVE
         PERFORM C200-VERIFY-VENDOR-FORMAT
         IF VALID-FORMAT
             PERFORM C400-VERIFY-VENDOR-FILE-STATUS
             IF GOOD-VERIFY
                 PERFORM C500-SEND-DETAIL-MAP-AND-DATA
             ELSE
                 PERFORM C600-SEND-CONTROL-MAP-DATAONLY
         ELSE
             PERFORM C600-SEND-CONTROL-MAP-DATAONLY
     ELSE
         IF MAPFAIL-ON-RECEIVE
             MOVE 'VENDOR CODE MUST BE ENTERED - PLEASE KEY-IN'
                             TO MVC-D-MESSAGE
             MOVE ASKIP-BRT  TO MVC-A-MESSAGE
             PERFORM C600-SEND-CONTROL-MAP-DATAONLY
         ELSE
             PERFORM C600-SEND-CONTROL-MAP-DATAONLY.
*
 C000-EXIT.
     EXIT.
*
 C100-RECEIVE-CONTROL-MAP  SECTION.
*****************************************************************
*          PERFORMED FROM:  C000-PROCESS-CONTROL-MAP    *
*             ENTER IS ONLY VALID DATA ENTRY KEY             *
*  CLEAR KEY - ENDS TERMINAL SESSION    PF5 - RETURNS TO MENU *
*                                       PF4 - XCTL TO BROWSE  *
*             ALL OTHER AID KEYS ARE INVALID                 *
*          STATUS-OF-RECEIVE  =  'G'  =  GOOD RECEIVE        *
*                                'M'  =  MAPFAIL             *
*                                'I'  =  INVALID KEY PRESSED *
*****************************************************************
*
     MOVE LOW-VALUES  TO  VM-CONTROL-MAP.
*
     IF EIBAID  =  DFHENTER
*
         EXEC CICS RECEIVE
                 MAP     ('MAPPOVC')
                 MAPSET  ('POVMIQ1')
                 INTO    (VM-CONTROL-MAP)
                 RESP    (WS-RESP)
         END-EXEC
*
         IF WS-RESP  =  DFHRESP(NORMAL)
```

Fig. 12.3 *Continued.*

```
                       MOVE 'G'  TO   STATUS-OF-RECEIVE
                 ELSE
                    IF WS-RESP  =  DFHRESP(MAPFAIL)
                        MOVE 'M'  TO   STATUS-OF-RECEIVE
                    ELSE
                            MOVE 'C100-'  TO   WS-RESP-SECTION
                            PERFORM Z999-RESPONSE-ERROR
               ELSE
                    IF EIBAID  =  DFHCLEAR
                        PERFORM C110-END-SESSION
                    ELSE
                    IF EIBAID  =  DFHPF5
                        PERFORM C120-TRANSFER-XCTL-TO-MENU
                    ELSE
                    IF EIBAID  =  DFHPF4
                        PERFORM C130-TRANSFER-XCTL-TO-BROWSE
                    ELSE
                        MOVE 'I'             TO  STATUS-OF-RECEIVE
                        MOVE 'INVALID KEY PRESSED - PLEASE TRY AGAIN'
                                             TO   MVC-D-MESSAGE
                        MOVE ASKIP-BRT  TO   MVC-A-MESSAGE.
 *
 C100-EXIT.
     EXIT.
 *
 C110-END-SESSION   SECTION.
 ***********************************************************************
 *     CRT OPERATOR PRESSED CLEAR KEY TO END TERMINAL SESSION        *
 *           PERFORMED FROM:  C100-RECEIVE-CONTROL-MAP                *
 *                            D100-RECEIVE-DETAIL-MAP                 *
 ***********************************************************************
 *
     EXEC CICS SEND
               FROM   (WS-CRT-MESSAGE)
               LENGTH (17)
               ERASE
     END-EXEC.
 *
     EXEC CICS RETURN
     END-EXEC.
 *
 C110-EXIT.
     EXIT.
 *
 C120-TRANSFER-XCTL-TO-MENU   SECTION.
 ***********************************************************************
 *           OPERATOR PRESSED PF5 TO RETURN TO MENU PROGRAM          *
 *           PERFORMED FROM:  C100-RECEIVE-CONTROL-MAP                *
 *                            D100-RECEIVE-DETAIL-MAP                 *
 ***********************************************************************
```

Fig. 12.3 *Continued.*

```
*
     EXEC CICS XCTL
               PROGRAM ('POVMAINT')
     END-EXEC.
*
 C120-EXIT.
     EXIT.
*
 C130-TRANSFER-XCTL-TO-BROWSE  SECTION.
************************************************************************
*        OPERATOR PRESSED PF4 TO TRANSFER CONTROL TO BROWSE          *
*             PERFORMED FROM:  C100-RECEIVE-CONTROL-MAP              *
************************************************************************
*
     MOVE LOW-VALUES  TO  WS-COMMAREA.
     MOVE 'I'         TO  CA-FUNCTION-CODE.
*
     EXEC CICS XCTL
               PROGRAM  ('POVMBROW')
               COMMAREA (WS-COMMAREA)
               LENGTH   (8)
     END-EXEC.
*
 C130-EXIT.
     EXIT.
*
 C200-VERIFY-VENDOR-FORMAT  SECTION.
************************************************************************
*        VERIFY FORMAT OF VENDOR CODE KEYED-IN = A-9999-9            *
*             PERFORMED FROM:  C000-PROCESS-CONTROL-MAP              *
*    IF VALID FORMAT - MOVE CODE TO WS-COMMAREA FIELDS (CA- )        *
************************************************************************
*
     IF (MVC-D-VEND-CD-1  IS  ALPHABETIC
                    AND
        MVC-D-VEND-CD-1  IS NOT =  SPACE)
        AND
         MVC-D-VEND-CD-2  IS  NUMERIC
        AND
         MVC-D-VEND-CD-3  IS  NUMERIC
           MOVE MVC-D-VEND-CD-1  TO  CA-VEND-1
           MOVE MVC-D-VEND-CD-2  TO  CA-VEND-2
           MOVE MVC-D-VEND-CD-3  TO  CA-VEND-3
           MOVE 'G'              TO  STATUS-OF-FORMAT
        ELSE
             MOVE 'E'         TO  STATUS-OF-FORMAT
             MOVE 'VENDOR CODE FORMAT MUST BE: A-9999-9 - PLEASE RE-EN
                  'TER'       TO  MVC-D-MESSAGE
             MOVE ASKIP-BRT  TO  MVC-A-MESSAGE. *
```

Fig. 12.3 *Continued.*

```
 C200-EXIT.
     EXIT.
*
 C400-VERIFY-VENDOR-FILE-STATUS  SECTION.
 **************************************************************
 *          PERFORMED FROM:  C000-PROCESS-CONTROL-MAP         *
 *          MUST BE A VENDOR RECORD FOR INQUIRIES             *
 **************************************************************
 *
     MOVE 'G'  TO  STATUS-OF-VERIFY.
*
     PERFORM C410-READ-VENDOR-FILE.
*
     IF RECORD-NOT-FOUND
         MOVE 'E'     TO   STATUS-OF-VERIFY
         MOVE 'VENDOR RECORD NOT ON FILE'
                      TO   MVC-D-MESSAGE
         MOVE ASKIP-BRT  TO  MVC-A-MESSAGE.
*
 C400-EXIT.
     EXIT.
*
 C410-READ-VENDOR-FILE  SECTION.
 **************************************************************
 *      PERFORMED FROM:  C400-VERIFY-VENDOR-FILE-STATUS       *
 **************************************************************
 *
     EXEC CICS READ
             DATASET ('VENDMAST')
             INTO    (VENDOR-MASTER-RECORD)
             RIDFLD  (CA-VENDOR-CODE)
             RESP    (WS-RESP)
     END-EXEC.
*
     IF WS-RESP  =  DFHRESP(NORMAL)
         MOVE 'G' TO  STATUS-OF-READ
     ELSE
         IF WS-RESP  =  DFHRESP(NOTFND)
             MOVE 'E' TO  STATUS-OF-READ
         ELSE
             MOVE 'C410-' TO  WS-RESP-SECTION
             PERFORM Z999-RESPONSE-ERROR.
*
 C410-EXIT.
     EXIT.
*
 C500-SEND-DETAIL-MAP-AND-DATA  SECTION.
 **************************************************************
 *       SEND DETAIL MAP - PHYSICAL AND SYMBOLIC MAPS        *
 *           PERFORMED FROM:  C000-PROCESS-CONTROL-MAP       *
 *   SENT WHEN ALL VALIDATION AND EDIT CONDITIONS HAVE BEEN MET   *
 **************************************************************
```

Fig. 12.3 *Continued.*

```
*
      MOVE LOW-VALUES   TO   VM-DETAIL-MAP.
*
      PERFORM B110-GET-DATE-AND-TIME.
      MOVE WS-CURRENT-DATE   TO   MVD-D-DATE.
      MOVE WS-MAP-TIME       TO   MVD-D-TIME.
*
      PERFORM C530-FORMAT-DETAIL-MAP.
*
      MOVE '2'  TO   CA-MAP-CONTROL.
*
      EXEC CICS SEND
               MAP     ('MAPPOVD')
               MAPSET  ('POVMIQ2')
               FROM    (VM-DETAIL-MAP)
               ERASE
      END-EXEC.
*
  C500-EXIT.
     EXIT.
*


  C530-FORMAT-DETAIL-MAP   SECTION.
  *********************************************************************
  *         PERFORMED FROM:  C500-SEND-DETAIL-MAP-AND-DATA           *
  *********************************************************************
  *
  * FORMAT VENDOR CODE: A-9999-9   WS- FIELDS ARE AT END OF VENDMAST
        MOVE CA-VEND-1             TO   WS-VENDOR-CD-1.
        MOVE CA-VEND-2             TO   WS-VENDOR-CD-2.
        MOVE CA-VEND-3             TO   WS-VENDOR-CD-3.
        MOVE WS-VENDOR-CODE        TO   MVD-D-VENDOR-CODE.
  *
        MOVE VM-AREA-CD            TO   MVD-D-PHONE-AREA-CD.
        MOVE VM-PHONE-1-3          TO   MVD-D-PHONE-1.
        MOVE VM-PHONE-4-7          TO   MVD-D-PHONE-2.
        MOVE VM-VENDOR-NAME        TO   MVD-D-VENDOR-NAME.
        MOVE VM-CONTACT            TO   MVD-D-CONTACT.
        MOVE VM-STREET-ADDRESS     TO   MVD-D-STREET.
        MOVE VM-CITY               TO   MVD-D-CITY.
        MOVE VM-STATE              TO   MVD-D-STATE-CODE.
  *
        MOVE VM-STATE              TO   WS-STATE-CODE.
        PERFORM C531-GET-STATE-NAME.
        MOVE WS-STATE-NAME         TO   MVD-D-STATE-NAME.
  *
        MOVE VM-ZIP-CODE           TO   MVD-D-ZIP-CODE.
        MOVE VM-TO-ATTN-OF         TO   MVD-D-ATTENTION-OF.
        MOVE VM-DOLLARS-COMMITTED  TO   MVD-D-DLRS-COMMITTED.
  *
  C530-EXIT.
     EXIT.
```

Fig. 12.3 *Continued.*

```
*
 C531-GET-STATE-NAME  SECTION.
 *******************************************************************
 *                 LOAD AND SEARCH STATE CODE TABLE                *
 *          PERFORMED FROM:  C530-SEND-DETAIL-MAP-AND-DATA          *
 *******************************************************************
 *
     COPY    STPDT037.
 *
 C531-EXIT.
     EXIT.
 *
 C600-SEND-CONTROL-MAP-DATAONLY  SECTION.
 *******************************************************************
 *            SEND CONTROL MAP DATAONLY - SYMBOLIC MAP             *
 *            PERFORMED FROM:  C000-PROCESS-CONTROL-MAP            *
 *                  SENT FOR INVALID CONDITIONS                    *
 *******************************************************************
 *
     MOVE '1'  TO  CA-MAP-CONTROL.
     MOVE -1   TO  MVC-L-VEND-CD-1.
 *
     MOVE UNPROT-FSET  TO  MVC-A-VEND-CD-1
                          MVC-A-VEND-CD-2
                          MVC-A-VEND-CD-3.
 *
     EXEC CICS SEND
             MAP       ('MAPPOVC')
             MAPSET    ('POVMIQ1')
             FROM      (VM-CONTROL-MAP)
             DATAONLY
             CURSOR
     END-EXEC.
 *
 C600-EXIT.
     EXIT.
 *
 D000-INQUIRY-PROCESSING  SECTION.
 *******************************************************************
 *                PERFORMED FROM:  AA00-MAINLINE                   *
 *        DETAIL MAP IS SENT IF AN INVALID KEY WAS PRESSED         *
 *******************************************************************
 *
     PERFORM D100-RECEIVE-DETAIL-MAP.
 *
     IF GOOD-RECEIVE
         PERFORM B100-SEND-CONTROL-MAP-AND-DATA
     ELSE
         PERFORM D200-SEND-DETAIL-MAP-DATAONLY.
 *
 D000-EXIT.
```

Fig. 12.3 *Continued.*

```
      EXIT.
*
 D100-RECEIVE-DETAIL-MAP  SECTION.
***********************************************************************
*             PERFORMED FROM:  D000-INQUIRY-PROCESSING               *
*  ENTER - RETURN TO CONTROL SCREEN       CLEAR - ENDS SESSION       *
*                   PF5   - RETURN TO MENU                           *
*             ALL OTHER KEYS ARE INVALID                             *
*          STATUS-OF-RECEIVE  =  'G'  =  GOOD RECEIVE                 *
*                              'I'  =  INVALID KEY PRESSED           *
***********************************************************************
*
      MOVE LOW-VALUES  TO  VM-DETAIL-MAP.
*
      IF EIBAID  =  DFHENTER
*
          EXEC CICS RECEIVE
                  MAP        ('MAPPOVD')
                  MAPSET     ('POVMIQ2')
                  INTO       (VM-DETAIL-MAP)
                  RESP       (WS-RESP)
          END-EXEC
*
          IF WS-RESP  =  DFHRESP(NORMAL)   OR
             WS-RESP  =  DFHRESP(MAPFAIL)
             MOVE 'G'  TO  STATUS-OF-RECEIVE
          ELSE
             MOVE 'D100-'  TO  WS-RESP-SECTION
             PERFORM Z999-RESPONSE-ERROR
*
      ELSE
          IF EIBAID  =  DFHCLEAR
             PERFORM C110-END-SESSION
      ELSE
          IF EIBAID  =  DFHPF5
             PERFORM C120-TRANSFER-XCTL-TO-MENU
          ELSE
              MOVE 'I'       TO  STATUS-OF-RECEIVE
              MOVE 'INVALID KEY PRESSED - PLEASE TRY AGAIN'
                            TO  MVD-D-MESSAGE
              MOVE ASKIP-BRT  TO  MVD-A-MESSAGE.
*
 D100-EXIT.
      EXIT.
*
 D200-SEND-DETAIL-MAP-DATAONLY  SECTION.
***********************************************************************
*          SEND DETAIL MAP DATA ONLY - SYMBOLIC MAP                  *
*          PERFORMED FROM:  D000-INQUIRY-PROCESSING                  *
*  SENT IF INVALID KEY IS PRESSED ON A RECEIVE OF THE DETAIL MAP *
***********************************************************************
*
```

Fig. 12.3 *Continued.*

```
      MOVE '2'  TO  CA-MAP-CONTROL.
*
      EXEC CICS SEND
                MAP     ('MAPPOVD')
                MAPSET  ('POVMIQ2')
                FROM    (VM-DETAIL-MAP)
                DATAONLY
      END-EXEC.
*
 D200-EXIT.
      EXIT.
*
 Z999-RESPONSE-ERROR   SECTION.
 ******************************************************************
 * INVALID EIBRESP CODE RETURNED DURING EXECUTION OF CICS COMMAND *
 ******************************************************************
 *
      MOVE WS-RESP  TO  WS-RESP-ERR-CD.
*
      EXEC CICS SEND
                FROM    (WS-RESP-ERROR)
                LENGTH  (61)
                ERASE
      END-EXEC.
*
      EXEC CICS RETURN
      END-EXEC.
*
 Z999-EXIT.
      EXIT.
```

Procedure division

The program structure for all sample programs is shown at the start of the procedure division. This documentation is included for your ease of understanding. I find this format an acceptable and easier-to-maintain substitute for a drawn block program structure chart. Even this form of the program structure chart requires maintenance. Many installations have several programmers maintaining the same program at different times. This type of documentation is seldom kept up-to-date. As you develop or enhance your standards, you must decide on the level of documentation you want to maintain.

AA00-MAINLINE.   This section is similar to that of previously discussed programs. On the first entry into the program, EIBCALEN is equal to 0 and the program performs B000-INITIAL-ENTRY. On succeeding entries, EIB-CALEN equals 8 (see the RETURN command) and DFHCOMMAREA is moved to WS-COMMAREA. The contents of the COMMAREA field CA-MAP-CONTROL (see appendix B, POWSVMCA) are used as a switch to determine whether the program receives the control or detail map. The program issues a RETURN command, with a TRANSID of POVO and a COMMAREA 8 bytes long. When the user presses an AID key, this program is initiated again. This program may be returned to by an XCTL from the browse program discussed in chapter 17. This is tested for by checking CA-FUNCTION-CODE for a B (CA-BROWSE).

B100-SEND-CONTROL-MAP-AND-DATA. This command issues a PERFORM command to obtain date and time and then moves them to the control map. A 1 is moved to CA-MAP-CONTROL. This is a signal on a subsequent entry into the program that the control map is to be received. A –1 is moved to the map's vendor code length field to set the cursor at the first position of that field on the SEND MAP command that contains the symbolic map and the CURSOR option.

B110-GET-DATE-AND-TIME. The get-date-and-time routine is found in the copy library (appendix B, member STPDDTTM). Two new CICS commands are introduced: the ASSIGN and ADDRESS commands. The ASSIGN command allows a program to access values outside the program. The most commonly accessed value is the length of the CWA. The CWA, as mentioned earlier in the chapter, is an area used by the system to pass common data to a program. Before attempting to establish addressability and access CWA data, it is good practice to make sure the CWA is available to CICS. The copy library member used for the CWA should be the proper length.

```
EXEC CICS ASSIGN
     CWALENG (WS-CWA-LENGTH)
END-EXEC.
```

Execution of this command makes the length of the CWA available in a working-storage data-area WS-CWA-LENGTH, which must be defined as a halfword binary value.

The ADDRESS command is used to establish addressability to the CWA and other system areas. It is similar in effect to the LOAD command in that it sets the address so that the BLL cell points to the CWA. Once addressability has been established, the program can access all data defined in the CWA.

```
EXEC CICS ADDRESS
         CWA (BLL-CWA-ADDRESS)
END-EXEC.
```

The execution of this command sets the linkage-section pointer BLL-CWA-ADDRESS to the address of CWA-DATA and makes the CWA data available to the program.

Time is obtained from the EIB field EIBTIME and formatted to HH.MM.SS. I am using this simplified example to illustrate the use of the CWA. If the only required fields were date and time, they could be obtained by executing the FORMATTIME command (explained in chapter 10) with the following options:

```
EXEC CICS FORMATTIME
          MMDDYY  (WS-CURRENT-DATE)
          DATESEP ('/')
          TIME    (WS-EIBTIME)
          TIMESEP (':')
END-EXEC.
```

C000-PROCESS-CONTROL-MAP. This section, similar for all maintenance functions, receives the control map, then verifies the format of vendor code. The status of the vendor file is checked to make sure a record is available to display; if so, a formatted detail map is sent. Invalid conditions, which prevent the display of the detail map, result in the control map's being sent with an appropriate highlighted ASKIP,BRT message displayed.

C100-RECEIVE-CONTROL-MAP. This section receives the symbolic map into the working-storage area VM-CONTROL-MAP and invokes the end-of-session or the transfer of control to the submenu or to the browse program. The RESP option is used to check for MAPFAIL.

C120-TRANSFER-XCTL-TO-MENU. This section transfers control to the vendor file maintenance submenu, program POVMAINT (see Fig. 6.3). No COMMAREA is returned to the menu program.

C130-TRANSFER-XCTL-TO-BROWSE. This section transfers control to the vendor file browse program POVMBROW, discussed in chapter 17. This program can pass an entered vendor code to POVMBROW. For simplicity, enter the code in the browse program. An I moved to CA-FUNCTION-CODE signals the browse program that control was transferred to POVMBROW by the inquiry program POVMINQY. The browse program uses this code to signal a return of control to POVMINQY if desired. The addition, change, and delete programs, respectively, move an A, C, or D to CA-FUNCTION-CODE.

C200-VERIFY-VENDOR-FORMAT. This section verifies that the keyed-in vendor code is of the proper format A-9999-9. If the format is correct, the vendor code is moved to the working-storage area WS-COMMAREA; otherwise, an error message and indicator are returned.

C400-VERIFY-VENDOR-FILE-STATUS. This section performs a read of the vendor file to make sure the vendor entered is on the file. If the vendor is not on the file, an error indicator is set and an error message returned. This section can also be coded as follows:

```
PERFORM C410-READ-VENDOR-FILE.

IF WS-RESP = DFHRESP (NORMAL)
    MOVE 'G' TO STATUS-OF-VERIFY
ELSE
    MOVE 'E' TO STATUS-OF-VERIFY
    . . .
```

C410-READ-VENDOR-FILE. The RESP option is included on the READ command. If the record is on the file, it is read into the working-storage area VENDOR-MASTER-RECORD, and a G is moved to STATUS-OF-READ. If no record is found, an E is moved to STATUS-OF-READ. RIDFLD was set in section C200-VERIFY-VENDOR-FORMAT.

C500-SEND-DETAIL-MAP-AND-DATA. This section performs a format of the detail map and moves a 2 to CA-MAP-CONTROL, so that on a succeeding entry into this program, the detail map is received. Physical and symbolic maps are sent; the symbolic map is located in the working-storage area VM-DETAIL-MAP.

C530-FORMAT-DETAIL-MAP. This section moves vendor master file data to the appropriate map fields.

C531-GET-STATE-NAME. Logic for obtaining state name is found in the copy library (appendix B, member STPDT037). This logic is included in the system to demonstrate the use of a nonresident table, which is released from main storage as soon as it is no longer required.

```
EXEC CICS LOAD
        PROGRAM ('T037LOAD')
        SET     (BLL-T037-STATE-TABLE-ADDRESS)
END-EXEC.
```

This LOAD command establishes addressability to the state code table. The state name obtained is moved to the working-storage field WS-STATE-NAME. If a state is not found, all * are moved to WS-STATE-NAME.

After the search of the state table is complete, the following command releases the state table from main storage:

```
EXEC CICS RELEASE
        PROGRAM ('T037LOAD')
END-EXEC.
```

C600-SEND-CONTROL-MAP-DATAONLY. This is performed when an invalid condition occurs. UNPROT,FSET attributes are moved to the map's vendor code fields so that if vendor code was entered correctly, it is returned on a subsequent receive of the map. FRSET on the BMS map's

DFHMSD parameter turns off all MDT's prior to a send; −1 is moved to the symbolic map's length field. Specify CURSOR on the send to set the cursor at the first position of vendor code.

D100-RECEIVE-DETAIL-MAP. This section receives the detail map and, if the ENTER key was pressed, returns to the invoking section. The RESP option is included on the RECEIVE command, and the MAPFAIL condition is treated as a valid receive. A MAPFAIL condition always occurs on the receive of this map because no data is received and no map fields are FSET. Programs that do *not* include the RESP option on a RECEIVE MAP command (see Browse program in chapter 17) ignore a MAPFAIL condition as follows:

```
EXEC CICS IGNORE CONDITION
          MAPFAIL
END-EXEC.
```

This command directs that if the specified condition (in this case MAP-FAIL) occurs, the condition should be ignored. MAPFAIL is a common occurrence on many types of maps that do not require the entry of data. This command permits program logic to fall through to the command following the receive. You can achieve the same result on a MAPFAIL if a HANDLE CONDITION command directed control as follows:

```
    EXEC CICS HANDLE CONDITION
              MAPFAIL (D100-MOVE-G-TO-STATUS)
    END-EXEC.
        .
        .
        .
D100-MOVE-G-TO-STATUS.
    MOVE 'G'  TO  STATUS-OF-RECEIVE.
```

If the CLEAR key or PF5 key is pressed, this section directs control to C110-END-SESSION or C120-TRANSFER-XCTL-TO-MENU, respectively. Any other key results in an invalid key message being displayed on the detail map.

D200-SEND-DETAIL-MAP-DATAONLY. If an invalid key was pressed prior to the receive of the detail map, this section sends the detail symbolic map only. A 2 is moved to CA-MAP-CONTROL so that the mainline section AA00-MAINLINE directs control to the receive of the detail map on a subsequent entry into this program.

13

The Addition Program

After a file has been created and an inquiry program written to check the status of various fields, you might have to make new additions to the file. This chapter discusses the addition program.

The addition program uses control and detail maps. The control map requires the user to key in a vendor code and to press ENTER to display the addition detail map. The user also has the option of transferring control to the vendor file browse, returning to the vendor file maintenance submenu (see Fig. 6.3), or ending the session. The map shown in Fig. 2.6 defines the vendor file addition detail screen. This screen displays when the user keys in a vendor code on the control screen, which is not currently on the vendor file.

The detail map shows as Xs all fields that can be added to the vendor's record. The map permits the user to key in the vendor's data and then press ENTER to add the record. The detail map gives a user the option of returning to the addition control screen without adding the record, returning to the submenu, or ending the session.

BMS Maps

Figures 13.2 and 13.3 show the BMS maps for the control and detail maps shown in Figs. 13.1 and 2.6, respectively.

```
      1...5...10...15...20...25...30...35...40...45...50...55...60...65...70...75...80

  1  | ZZ/ZZ/ZZ                    ABC MANUFACTURING COMPANY                    POVMAD1  |  1
  2  | ZZ.ZZ.ZZ                    VENDOR FILE ADDITIONS CONTROL                         |  2
  3  |                                                                                  |  3
  4  |                                                                                  |  4
  5  |                                                                                  |  5
  6  |                                                                                  |  6
  7  |                            VENDOR CODE: X - XXXX - X                              |  7
  8  |                                                                                  |  8
  9  |                                                                                  |  9
 10  |                                                                                  | 10
 11  |                                                                                  | 11
 12  |              1. TO ADD VENDOR RECORD      - PRESS ENTER                           | 12
 13  |                                                                                  | 13
 14  |              2. TO BROWSE VENDOR FILE     - PRESS PF4                             | 14
 15  |                                                                                  | 15
 16  |              3. TO RETURN TO MENU         - PRESS PF5                             | 16
 17  |                                                                                  | 17
 18  |              4. TO END SESSION            - PRESS CLEAR                           | 18
 19  |                                                                                  | 19
 20  |                                                                                  | 20
 21  |                                                                                  | 21
 22  |                                                                                  | 22
 23  |                                                                                  | 23
 24  | ZZZZZZZZZZZZZZZZZZZZZZZZZZZZZZZZZZZZZZZZZZZZZZZZZZZZZZZZZZZZZZZZZZZZZZZZZZZZZZZZ   | 24

      1...5...10...15...20...25...30...35...40...45...50...55...60...65...70...75...80
```

Fig. 13.1 Vendor file additions control map.

BMS control map

Figure 13.2 shows only the differences between this map and the BMS control map for the inquiry program (see Fig. 12.1). Keeping fields in the same position for similar maps makes the creation of new maps easy. An existing map serves as a model for others.

BMS detail map

All addition detail map attributes can be defined as ASKIP. The program then controls the attributes by modifying them prior to a send that includes the symbolic map. I have defined data-entry fields as UNPROT because this makes the initial testing of the map's format easier. The data-entry fields can be checked by using the command-level interpreter (CECI) discussed in chapter 6 to display the map and check its format. All UNPROT fields have either a trailing ASKIP field or a following stopper field to limit the size of the data-entry field. Fields requiring data to be entered on an addition screen have field names assigned. For instance, NAME;, a required field, is assigned a field name MDCVMNM. This results in a symbolic map label being generated when the BMS map is assembled. Include more-readable symbolic map entries for all field identifiers of items that will be referenced. For instance, see the easier-to-read map label MVD-C-A-VENDOR-NAME for member MAPVDTL2 in Appendix B. The program has the ability to brighten and darken field identifiers as required when testing for the entry of valid data. No IC attribute is defined on this map because the program sets the cursor by moving −1 to the appropriate length field in the symbolic map. The map is then sent with CURSOR specified.

More-Readable Symbolic Maps

More-readable symbolic maps created to correspond to generated BMS maps are shown in the copy library (Appendix B, members MAPVMCTL and MAPVDTL2). Note the inclusion of additional names for the field identifiers on the detail symbolic map. They are used by the addition program to highlight field identifiers of incorrectly entered items. As mentioned previously, many systems do not highlight field identifiers of fields that contain invalid data; instead they highlight the data itself. Determine your approach based on standards in effect at your installation.

Addition Program Source Code

The addition program source code shown in Fig. 13.4 follows the format used in previous examples. I will discuss only sections that differ from previous examples.

Procedure Division

AA00-MAINLINE. This section is similar to that of the inquiry program in Chapter 12 except that the perform E000-ADDITION-PROCESSING replaces D000-INQUIRY-PROCESSING and TRANSID POVA replaces POVI.

C400-VERIFY-VENDOR-FILE-STATUS. This section performs a read of the vendor file to make sure that the vendor to be added is not already on the file. If the vendor is on the file, an error indicator is set and an error message is returned.

C410-READ-VENDOR-FILE. The RESP option is included on the READ command and WS-RESP is checked following execution. If the record is on the file, it is read into the working-storage area VENDOR-MASTER-RECORD and a G is moved to STATUS-OF-READ. A "not found" condition results in an E being moved to STATUS-OF-READ. A vendor record should not be found for a record being added, and a "record-found" condition is treated as an error in the invoking section (C400-VERIFY-VENDOR-FILE-STATUS).

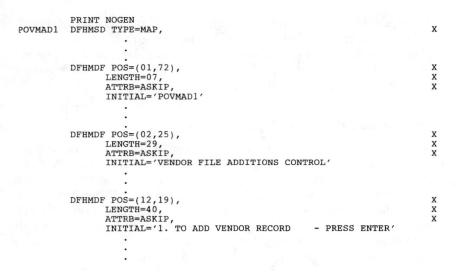

```
       PRINT NOGEN
POVMAD1 DFHMSD TYPE=MAP,                                              X
              .
              .
       DFHMDF POS=(01,72),                                           X
              LENGTH=07,                                            X
              ATTRB=ASKIP,                                          X
              INITIAL='POVMAD1'
              .
              .
       DFHMDF POS=(02,25),                                          X
              LENGTH=29,                                            X
              ATTRB=ASKIP,                                          X
              INITIAL='VENDOR FILE ADDITIONS CONTROL'
              .
              .
       DFHMDF POS=(12,19),                                          X
              LENGTH=40,                                            X
              ATTRB=ASKIP,                                          X
              INITIAL='1. TO ADD VENDOR RECORD    - PRESS ENTER'
              .
              .
```

Fig. 13.2 Vendor file additions BMS control map.

C500-SEND-DETAIL-MAP-AND-DATA. This section is similar to that of the Inquiry program in chapter 12. The differences are:

1. Perform C520-SET-MAP-ATTRIBUTES.
2. MOVE -1 TO MVD-L-VENDOR-NAME. Moving a –1 to the symbolic map length field sets the cursor initially at this item.

C520-SET-MAP-ATTRIBUTES. This section turns on the MDT for all data entry fields by moving the UNPROT,FSET attribute to each field prior to the SEND MAP command. The MDT turns on any time data is keyed into a field. A map can be received after data has been keyed into its fields in order to edit and process the fields. The editing might detect errors in some of the fields and send the map DATAONLY with the field identifiers of the incorrectly entered fields highlighted. The map is sent with a brightened error message. When you specify FRSET on the BMS map DFHMSD macro, a SEND MAP command turns off all MDTs. This section ensures that all data-entry fields on the map are returned on subsequent receives of the map. There is a more efficient way to handle this situation, but this is one of the easier to understand methods. The more efficient method is discussed below (under E110-EDIT-MAP-VM-RECORD). Vendor code is not a data-entry field on the detail map; its BMS map attribute is ASKIP.

C530-FORMAT-DETAIL-MAP. Moves vendor code fields obtained from WS-COMMAREA subfields to the appropriate map locations prior to the send of the detail map. There are no vendor record fields to display since no record exists.

E100-ADD-VENDOR-RECORD. Performs an edit of map data and a format of the vendor record. If the edit and format are successful, a write of the vendor record is performed. The message RECORD SUCCESSFULLY ADDED is normally returned and displayed on the control screen. The message RECORD TO BE ADDED – ALREADY ON VENDOR FILE only displays if a user at another terminal adds the same record you are attempting to add, after you have entered vendor code on the control screen. This program would have previously read the vendor file for the entered vendor code (in section C410-READ-VENDOR-FILE) and determined that it was not online, in order to reach this point.

E110-EDIT-MAP-FORMAT-VM-RECORD. This section expects that all fields entered are available each time the detail map is received, because section C520-SET-MAP-ATTRIBUTES resets the MDTs each time the detail map is sent. There are many different acceptable ways to validate input data received from a screen. This section employs several different methods: checking for numeric fields, fields with low values or spaces, and field length.

A field can be checked for data expected to be numeric, such as area code, phone number, and zip code.

Fields containing low-values or spaces may be considered invalid. Using the techniques chosen for the maintenance programs, a field contains low-values only if nothing was keyed into the field or if the EOF key was pressed. Spaces are present in a field only if the user keyed in at least one space, or if the program moved spaces to a map field prior to a send.

Field length can be tested to determine if data has been keyed into a field. The field's length is greater than zero if at least one character was entered. Be careful how you use the length field because it is sometimes different on the initial receive of a map than it is on subsequent receives of the same map. When a user enters data, the initial receive of the map returns the actual length keyed in. Subsequent receives of the same map, if the program sets the attribute to FSET and if a field was not rekeyed, return the full length of the field regardless of how many characters were originally entered.

I have chosen the technique of highlighting (ASKIP,BRT) the field identifiers of items entered incorrectly or for which data has been omitted. I move an error indicator to STATUS-OF-EDIT for invalid fields. On subsequent receives of the same map, the ASKIP,NORM attribute is moved to the field identifier of correctly entered fields. At the end of this section, I check if STATUS-OF-EDIT equals E, and, if so, move the message PLEASE CORRECT HIGHLIGHTED FIELDS to the detail map message field. The detail map is sent DATAONLY in section E000-ADDITION-PROCESSING.

Fig. 13.3 Vendor file additions BMS detail map.

```
           PRINT NOGEN
POVMAD2    DFHMSD TYPE=MAP,                                              X
                  TIOAPFX=YES,                                          X
                  CTRL=(FRSET,FREEKB),                                  X
                  TERM=3270,                                            X
                  LANG=COBOL,                                           X
                  MODE=INOUT
*
MAPPOVD    DFHMDI SIZE=(24,80),                                         X
                  COLUMN=01,                                            X
                  LINE=01
*
MDDATE     DFHMDF POS=(01,01),                                          X
                  LENGTH=08,                                            X
                  ATTRB=ASKIP
*
           DFHMDF POS=(01,27),                                          X
                  LENGTH=25,                                            X
                  ATTRB=ASKIP,                                          X
                  INITIAL='ABC MANUFACTURING COMPANY'
*
           DFHMDF POS=(01,72),                                          X
                  LENGTH=07,                                            X
                  ATTRB=ASKIP,                                          X
                  INITIAL='POVMAD2'
*
MDTIME DFHMDF POS=(02,01),                                              X
                  LENGTH=08,                                            X
                  ATTRB=ASKIP
*
           DFHMDF POS=(02,30),                                          X
                  LENGTH=20,                                            X
                  ATTRB=ASKIP,                                          X
                  INITIAL='VENDOR FILE ADDITION'
*
           DFHMDF POS=(04,01),                                          X
                  LENGTH=12,                                            X
                  ATTRB=ASKIP,                                          X
                  INITIAL='VENDOR CODE:'
*
MDVNDCD    DFHMDF POS=(04,14),                                          X
                  LENGTH=08,                                            X
                  ATTRB=ASKIP
*
MDCVMNM    DFHMDF POS=(05,08),                                          X
                  LENGTH=05,                                            X
                  ATTRB=ASKIP,                                          X
                  INITIAL='NAME:'
*
MDVNDNM    DFHMDF POS=(05,14),                                          X
                  LENGTH=25,                                            X
                  ATTRB=(UNPROT,IC)
*
           DFHMDF POS=(05,40),                                          X
                  LENGTH=01,                                            X
                  ATTRB=ASKIP
*
MDCPHON    DFHMDF POS=(05,45),                                          X
                  LENGTH=06,                                            X
                  ATTRB=ASKIP,                                          X
                  INITIAL='PHONE:'
*
           DFHMDF POS=(05,54),                                          X
                  LENGTH=01,                                            X
                  ATTRB=ASKIP,                                          X
                  INITIAL='('
*
MDAREAC    DFHMDF POS=(05,56),                                          X
```

Fig. 13.3 *Continued.*

```
                    LENGTH=03,                                              X
                    ATTRB=UNPROT
        *
                    DFHMDF POS=(05,60),                                     X
                    LENGTH=01,                                              X
                    ATTRB=ASKIP,                                            X
                    INITIAL=')'
        *
MDPHON1 DFHMDF POS=(05,62),                                                 X
                    LENGTH=03,                                              X
                    ATTRB=UNPROT
        *
                    DFHMDF POS=(05,66),                                     X
                    LENGTH=01,                                              X
                    ATTRB=ASKIP,                                            X
                    INITIAL='-'
        *
MDPHON2 DFHMDF POS=(05,68),                                                 X
                    LENGTH=04,                                              X
                    ATTRB=UNPROT
        *
                    DFHMDF POS=(05,73),                                     X
                    LENGTH=01,                                              X
                    ATTRB=ASKIP
        *
                    DFHMDF POS=(06,45),                                     X
                    LENGTH=08,                                              X
                    ATTRB=ASKIP,                                            X
                    INITIAL='CONTACT:'
        *
MDCONTA DFHMDF POS=(06,54),                                                 X
                    LENGTH=25,                                              X
                    ATTRB=UNPROT
        *
                    DFHMDF POS=(06,80),                                     X
                    LENGTH=01,                                              X
                    ATTRB=(ASKIP,DRK)
        *
MDCSTRT DFHMDF POS=(08,01),                                                 X
                    LENGTH=17,                                              X
                    ATTRB=ASKIP,                                            X
                    INITIAL='ADDRESS - STREET:'
        *
MDSTRET DFHMDF POS=(08,19),                                                 X
                    LENGTH=20,                                              X
                    ATTRB=UNPROT
        *
                    DFHMDF POS=(08,40),                                     X
                    LENGTH=01,                                              X
                    ATTRB=ASKIP
        *
MDCCITY DFHMDF POS=(09,13),                                                 X
                    LENGTH=05,                                              X
                    ATTRB=ASKIP,                                            X
                    INITIAL='CITY:'
        *
MDCITY  DFHMDF POS=(09,19),                                                 X
                    LENGTH=18,                                              X
                    ATTRB=UNPROT
        *
                    DFHMDF POS=(09,38),                                     X
                    LENGTH=01,                                              X
                    ATTRB=ASKIP
        *
MDCSTAT DFHMDF POS=(10,12),                                                 X
                    LENGTH=06,                                              X
                    ATTRB=ASKIP,                                            X
                    INITIAL='STATE:'
        *
```

Fig. 13.3 *Continued.*

```
MDSTATE DFHMDF POS=(10,19),                                              X
               LENGTH=02,                                               X
               ATTRB=UNPROT
*
MDSTANM DFHMDF POS=(10,22),                                              X
               LENGTH=14,                                               X
               ATTRB=ASKIP
*
MDCZIP DFHMDF POS=(11,14),                                              X
              LENGTH=04,                                                X
              ATTRB=ASKIP,                                              X
              INITIAL='ZIP:'
*
MDZIP DFHMDF POS=(11,19),                                              X
             LENGTH=05,                                                X
             ATTRB=UNPROT
*
       DFHMDF POS=(11,25),                                             X
              LENGTH=01,                                               X
              ATTRB=ASKIP
*
       DFHMDF POS=(13,02),                                             X
              LENGTH=16,                                               X
              ATTRB=ASKIP,                                             X
              INITIAL='TO ATTENTION OF:'
*
MDATTOF DFHMDF POS=(13,19),                                             X
               LENGTH=20,                                              X
               ATTRB=UNPROT
*
       DFHMDF POS=(13,40),                                             X
              LENGTH=01,                                               X
              ATTRB=ASKIP
*
       DFHMDF POS=(18,10),                                             X
              LENGTH=56,                                               X
              ATTRB=ASKIP,                                             X
              INITIAL='1. ADDITIONS, KEY IN REQUIRED DATA        - PRX
              ESS ENTER'
*
       DFHMDF POS=(19,10),                                             X
              LENGTH=54,                                               X
              ATTRB=ASKIP,                                             X
              INITIAL='2. RETURN TO ADDITION CONTROL SCREEN      - PRX
              ESS PF3'
*
       DFHMDF POS=(20,10),                                             X
              LENGTH=54,                                               X
              ATTRB=ASKIP,                                             X
              INITIAL='3. RETURN TO MENU                         - PRX
              ESS PF5'
*
       DFHMDF POS=(21,10),                                             X
              LENGTH=56,                                               X
              ATTRB=ASKIP,                                             X
              INITIAL='4. END OF SESSION                         - PRX
              ESS CLEAR'
*
MDMESSG DFHMDF POS=(24,01),                                             X
               LENGTH=79,                                              X
               ATTRB=ASKIP
*
       DFHMSD TYPE=FINAL
              END
```

Fig. 13.4 Vendor file addition program source code.

```
IDENTIFICATION DIVISION.
PROGRAM-ID. POVMADDN.
*
*********************************************************************
*            PURCHASING SYSTEM - VENDOR FILE ADDITIONS             *
*     - STARTED BY PURCHASING SYSTEM SUB-MENU PROGRAM 'POVMAINT'    *
*            COULD ALSO BE STARTED BY TRANSID 'POVA'               *
*********************************************************************
ENVIRONMENT DIVISION.
DATA DIVISION.
*WORKING-STORAGE  SECTION.
*
 01  WS-PROGRAM-FIELDS.
     05  FILLER        PIC X(22)    VALUE 'POVMADDN - START OF WS'.
     05  WS-CRT-MESSAGE   PIC X(17)   VALUE 'SESSION COMPLETED'.
     05  WS-RESP          PIC S9(8)   VALUE +0      COMP.

 01  WS-RESP-ERROR.
     05  FILLER          PIC X(39)    VALUE
         'PROGRAM POVMADDN: ERROR EIBRESP CODE = '.
     05  WS-RESP-ERR-CD    PIC 99        VALUE ZEROES.
     05  FILLER           PIC X(15)     VALUE
         ' IN SECTION '.
     05  WS-RESP-SECTION   PIC X(5)    VALUE SPACES.
*
*01  VENDOR-MASTER-RECORD
                                  COPY    VENDMAST.
*01  JOURNAL-RECORD
                                  COPY    JRNLRECD.
*01  WS-COMMAREA
                                  COPY    POWSVMCA.
*01  WS-STATUS-FIELDS
                                  COPY    STWSSTAT.
*01  VM-CONTROL-MAP
                                  COPY    MAPVMCTL.
*01  VM-DETAIL-MAP
                                  COPY    MAPVDTL2.
*01  WS-DATE-AND-TIME
                                  COPY    STWSDTTM.
*01  WS-STATE-CODE-SEARCH-ENTRIES
                                  COPY    STWST037.
*01  ATTRIBUTE-LIST
                                  COPY    STWSATTR.
*01  DFHAID
```

Fig. 13.4 *Continued.*

```
                                    COPY    DFHAID.
*
 01   END-OF-WORKING-STORAGE    PIC X(15)    VALUE 'END WS POVMADDN'.
*
 LINKAGE SECTION.
*
 01   DFHCOMMAREA              PIC X(8).
*
 01   BLL-CELLS.
      05   FILLER                        PIC S9(8)    COMP.
      05   BLL-CWA-ADDRESS               PIC S9(8)    COMP.
      05   BLL-T037-STATE-TABLE-ADDRESS  PIC S9(8)    COMP.
*
*01   CWA-DATA
                        COPY    STLNKCWA.
*01   T037-STATE-TABLE
                        COPY    T037STAT.
 PROCEDURE DIVISION.
**********************************************************************
*     PROGRAM STRUCTURE IS:                                         *
*          AA00-MAINLINE                                            *
*             B000-INITIAL-ENTRY                                    *
*                B100-SEND-CONTROL-MAP-AND-DATA                     *
*                   B110-GET-DATE-AND-TIME                          *
*                                                                  *
*             C000-PROCESS-CONTROL-MAP                              *
*                C100-RECEIVE-CONTROL-MAP                           *
*                   C110-END-SESSION                                *
*                   C120-TRANSFER-XCTL-TO-MENU                      *
*                   C130-TRANSFER-XCTL-TO-BROWSE                    *
*                C200-VERIFY-VENDOR-FORMAT                          *
*                C400-VERIFY-VENDOR-FILE-STATUS                     *
*                   C410-READ-VENDOR-FILE                           *
*                C500-SEND-DETAIL-MAP-AND-DATA                      *
*                      B110-GET-DATE-AND-TIME                       *
*                   C520-SET-MAP-ATTRIBUTES                         *
*                   C530-FORMAT-DETAIL-MAP                          *
*                      C531-GET-STATE-NAME                          *
*                C600-SEND-CONTROL-MAP-DATAONLY                     *
*                                                                  *
*          E000-ADDITION-PROCESSING                                *
*             D100-RECEIVE-DETAIL-MAP                               *
*                C110-END-SESSION                                   *
*                C120-TRANSFER-XCTL-TO-MENU                         *
*             E100-ADD-VENDOR-RECORD                                *
*                E110-EDIT-MAP-FORMAT-VM-RECORD                     *
*                   C531-GET-STATE-NAME                             *
```

Fig. 13.4 *Continued.*

```
*                    E120-WRITE-VENDOR-RECORD                    *
*                      E121-POST-JOURNAL-RECORD                  *
*              B100-SEND-CONTROL-MAP-AND-DATA                    *
*              D200-SEND-DETAIL-MAP-DATAONLY                     *
*                 C520-SET-MAP-ATTRIBUTES                        *
*****************************************************************
*
 AA00-MAINLINE  SECTION.
*
*     SERVICE RELOAD BLL-CELLS.
*
     MOVE LOW-VALUES  TO  VM-CONTROL-MAP.
*
     IF EIBCALEN  =  0
         PERFORM B000-INITIAL-ENTRY
     ELSE
         MOVE DFHCOMMAREA  TO  WS-COMMAREA
         IF CA-BROWSE
             MOVE SPACE        TO  CA-FUNCTION-CODE
             MOVE LOW-VALUES  TO  VM-CONTROL-MAP
             PERFORM C400-VERIFY-VENDOR-FILE-STATUS
             IF GOOD-VERIFY
                 PERFORM C500-SEND-DETAIL-MAP-AND-DATA
             ELSE
                 PERFORM B100-SEND-CONTROL-MAP-AND-DATA
         ELSE
             IF CA-RECEIVE-CTL-MAP
                 PERFORM C000-PROCESS-CONTROL-MAP
             ELSE
                 PERFORM E000-ADDITION-PROCESSING.
*
     EXEC CICS RETURN
             TRANSID  ('POVA')
             COMMAREA (WS-COMMAREA)
             LENGTH   (8)
     END-EXEC.
*
 B000-INITIAL-ENTRY  SECTION.
*****************************************************************
*                 PERFORMED FROM:  AA00-MAINLINE                *
*****************************************************************
*
     MOVE LOW-VALUES  TO  VM-CONTROL-MAP.
     PERFORM B100-SEND-CONTROL-MAP-AND-DATA.
*
 B000-EXIT.
```

Fig. 13.4 *Continued.*

```
    EXIT.
*
B100-SEND-CONTROL-MAP-AND-DATA  SECTION.
************************************************************************
*                PERFORMED FROM:  B000-INITIAL-ENTRY         *
*                                 E000-ADDITION-PROCESSING    *
************************************************************************
*
    PERFORM B110-GET-DATE-AND-TIME.
    MOVE WS-CURRENT-DATE  TO  MVC-D-DATE.
    MOVE WS-MAP-TIME      TO  MVC-D-TIME.
*
    MOVE -1   TO  MVC-L-VEND-CD-1.
    MOVE '1'  TO  CA-MAP-CONTROL.
*
    EXEC CICS SEND
            MAP    ('MAPPOVC')
            MAPSET ('POVMAD1')
            FROM   (VM-CONTROL-MAP)
            ERASE
            CURSOR
    END-EXEC.
*
 B100-EXIT.
    EXIT.
*
B110-GET-DATE-AND-TIME  SECTION.
************************************************************************
*       STPDDTTM - OBTAIN DATE FROM CWA AND FORMAT TIME      *
*          PERFORMED FROM:  B100-SEND-CONTROL-MAP-AND-DATA   *
*                           C500-SEND-DETAIL-MAP-AND-DATA    *
************************************************************************
*
    COPY STPDDTTM.
*
 B110-EXIT.
    EXIT.
*
C000-PROCESS-CONTROL-MAP  SECTION.
************************************************************************
*                PERFORMED FROM:  AA00-MAINLINE             *
*          PROCESS CONTROL MAP - IF VALID SEND DETAIL MAP    *
*            ELSE SEND CONTROL MAP WITH INVALID MESSAGE:     *
*    1) STATUS-OF-RECEIVE    =  'I'   INVALID KEY PRESSED    *
*    2) STATUS-OF-RECEIVE    =  'M'   MAPFAIL - NO DATA ENTERED *
*    3) STATUS-OF-FORMAT     =  'E'   INVALID VENDOR KEYED FORMAT *
```

Fig. 13.4 *Continued.*

```
*    4) STATUS-OF-VERIFY      =  'E'   VENDOR FILE STATUS ERROR    *
*******************************************************************
*
     PERFORM C100-RECEIVE-CONTROL-MAP.
     IF GOOD-RECEIVE
         PERFORM C200-VERIFY-VENDOR-FORMAT
         IF VALID-FORMAT
             PERFORM C400-VERIFY-VENDOR-FILE-STATUS
             IF GOOD-VERIFY
                 PERFORM C500-SEND-DETAIL-MAP-AND-DATA
             ELSE
                 PERFORM C600-SEND-CONTROL-MAP-DATAONLY
         ELSE
                 PERFORM C600-SEND-CONTROL-MAP-DATAONLY
     ELSE
         IF MAPFAIL-ON-RECEIVE
             MOVE 'VENDOR CODE MUST BE ENTERED - PLEASE KEY-IN'
                         TO MVC-D-MESSAGE
             MOVE ASKIP-BRT  TO MVC-A-MESSAGE
             PERFORM C600-SEND-CONTROL-MAP-DATAONLY
         ELSE
             PERFORM C600-SEND-CONTROL-MAP-DATAONLY.
*
 C000-EXIT.
     EXIT.
*
 C100-RECEIVE-CONTROL-MAP  SECTION.
*******************************************************************
*              PERFORMED FROM:  C000-PROCESS-CONTROL-MAP          *
*              ENTER IS ONLY VALID DATA ENTRY KEY                 *
*  CLEAR KEY - ENDS TERMINAL SESSION       PF5 - RETURNS TO MENU  *
*                                          PF4 - XCTL TO BROWSE   *
*              ALL OTHER AID KEYS ARE INVALID                     *
*         STATUS-OF-RECEIVE  =  'G' =   GOOD RECEIVE              *
*                             'M' =   MAPFAIL                     *
*                             'I' =   INVALID KEY PRESSED         *
*******************************************************************
*
     MOVE LOW-VALUES   TO  VM-CONTROL-MAP.
*
     IF EIBAID  =  DFHENTER
*
             EXEC CICS RECEIVE
                     MAP     ('MAPPOVC')
                     MAPSET ('POVMAD1')
                     INTO    (VM-CONTROL-MAP)
```

Fig. 13.4 *Continued.*

```
                RESP    (WS-RESP)
       END-EXEC
*
       IF WS-RESP  =  DFHRESP(NORMAL)
            MOVE 'G'  TO  STATUS-OF-RECEIVE
       ELSE
            IF WS-RESP  =  DFHRESP(MAPFAIL)
                 MOVE 'M'  TO  STATUS-OF-RECEIVE
       ELSE
                 MOVE 'C100-'  TO  WS-RESP-SECTION
                 PERFORM Z999-RESPONSE-ERROR
*
       ELSE
           IF EIBAID  =  DFHCLEAR
                PERFORM C110-END-SESSION
           ELSE
           IF EIBAID  =  DFHPF5
                PERFORM C120-TRANSFER-XCTL-TO-MENU
           ELSE
           IF EIBAID  =  DFHPF4
                PERFORM C130-TRANSFER-XCTL-TO-BROWSE
           ELSE
                MOVE 'I'         TO  STATUS-OF-RECEIVE
                MOVE 'INVALID KEY PRESSED - PLEASE TRY AGAIN'
                                 TO  MVC-D-MESSAGE
                MOVE ASKIP-BRT  TO  MVC-A-MESSAGE.
*
  C100-EXIT.
      EXIT.
*
  C110-END-SESSION  SECTION.
  ******************************************************************
  *    CRT OPERATOR PRESSED CLEAR KEY TO END TERMINAL SESSION      *
  *          PERFORMED FROM:  C100-RECEIVE-CONTROL-MAP             *
  *                           D100-RECEIVE-DETAIL-MAP              *
  ******************************************************************
  *
       EXEC CICS SEND
                FROM   (WS-CRT-MESSAGE)
                LENGTH (17)
                ERASE
       END-EXEC.
*
       EXEC CICS RETURN
       END-EXEC.
*
```

Fig. 13.4 *Continued.*

```
 C110-EXIT.
     EXIT.
*
 C120-TRANSFER-XCTL-TO-MENU  SECTION.
**********************************************************************
*       OPERATOR PRESSED PF5 TO RETURN TO MENU PROGRAM             *
*           PERFORMED FROM:  C100-RECEIVE-CONTROL-MAP              *
*                            D100-RECEIVE-DETAIL-MAP               *
**********************************************************************
*
     EXEC CICS XCTL
             PROGRAM ('POVMAINT')
     END-EXEC.
*
 C120-EXIT.
     EXIT.
*
 C130-TRANSFER-XCTL-TO-BROWSE  SECTION.
**********************************************************************
*       OPERATOR PRESSED PF4 TO TRANSFER CONTROL TO BROWSE        *
*           PERFORMED FROM:  C100-RECEIVE-CONTROL-MAP              *
*                            D100-RECEIVE-DETAIL-MAP               *
**********************************************************************
*
     MOVE LOW-VALUES   TO  WS-COMMAREA.
     MOVE 'A'          TO  CA-FUNCTION-CODE.
*
     EXEC CICS XCTL
             PROGRAM  ('POVMBROW')
             COMMAREA (WS-COMMAREA)
             LENGTH   (8)
     END-EXEC.
*
 C130-EXIT.
     EXIT.
*
 C200-VERIFY-VENDOR-FORMAT  SECTION.
**********************************************************************
*       VERIFY FORMAT OF VENDOR CODE KEYED-IN = A-9999-9          *
*           PERFORMED FROM:  C000-PROCESS-CONTROL-MAP             *
*   IF VALID FORMAT - MOVE CODE TO WS-COMMAREA FIELDS (CA- )      *
**********************************************************************
*
     IF (MVC-D-VEND-CD-1  IS  ALPHABETIC
                   AND
         MVC-D-VEND-CD-1     IS NOT =  SPACE)
```

Fig. 13.4 *Continued.*

```
                   AND
      MVC-D-VEND-CD-2      IS   NUMERIC
                   AND
      MVC-D-VEND-CD-3      IS   NUMERIC
      MOVE MVC-D-VEND-CD-1   TO   CA-VEND-1
      MOVE MVC-D-VEND-CD-2   TO   CA-VEND-2
      MOVE MVC-D-VEND-CD-3   TO   CA-VEND-3
      MOVE 'G'             TO   STATUS-OF-FORMAT
   ELSE
      MOVE 'E'     TO   STATUS-OF-FORMAT
      MOVE 'VENDOR CODE FORMAT MUST BE: A-9999-9 - PLEASE RE-EN
-'TER' TO           MVC-D-MESSAGE
                   MOVE ASKIP-BRT   TO   MVC-A-MESSAGE.
*
 C200-EXIT.
    EXIT.
*
 C400-VERIFY-VENDOR-FILE-STATUS   SECTION.
*********************************************************************
*          PERFORMED FROM:  C000-PROCESS-CONTROL-MAP            *
*          MUST NOT BE A VENDOR RECORD FOR ADDITIONS            *
*********************************************************************
*
    MOVE 'G'   TO   STATUS-OF-VERIFY.
*
    PERFORM C410-READ-VENDOR-FILE.
*
    IF RECORD-NOT-FOUND
        NEXT SENTENCE
    ELSE
        MOVE 'E'         TO   STATUS-OF-VERIFY
        MOVE 'VENDOR     TO BE ADDED IS ALREADY ON THE FILE'
                         TO   MVC-D-MESSAGE
        MOVE ASKIP-BRT   TO   MVC-A-MESSAGE.
*
 C400-EXIT.
    EXIT.
*
 C410-READ-VENDOR-FILE   SECTION.
*********************************************************************
*          PERFORMED FROM:  C400-VERIFY-VENDOR-FILE-STATUS       *
*********************************************************************
*
    EXEC CICS   READ
              DATASET ('VENDMAST')
              INTO    (VENDOR-MASTER-RECORD)
```

Fig. 13.4 *Continued.*

```
                     RIDFLD  (CA-VENDOR-CODE)
                     RESP    (WS-RESP)
          END-EXEC.
*
          IF WS-RESP  =  DFHRESP(NORMAL)
              MOVE 'G'  TO  STATUS-OF-READ
          ELSE
              IF WS-RESP  =  DFHRESP(NOTFND)
                  MOVE 'E'  TO  STATUS-OF-READ
              ELSE
                  MOVE 'C410-'  TO  WS-RESP-SECTION
                  PERFORM Z999-RESPONSE-ERROR.
*
    C410-EXIT.
          EXIT.
*
    C500-SEND-DETAIL-MAP-AND-DATA  SECTION.
    *********************************************************************
    *        SEND DETAIL MAP - PHYSICAL AND SYMBOLIC MAPS              *
    *           PERFORMED FROM:  C000-PROCESS-CONTROL-MAP              *
    *   SENT WHEN ALL VALIDATION AND EDIT CONDITIONS HAVE BEEN MET     *
    *********************************************************************
*
          MOVE LOW-VALUES  TO  VM-DETAIL-MAP.
*
          PERFORM B110-GET-DATE-AND-TIME.
          MOVE WS-CURRENT-DATE  TO  MVD-D-DATE.
          MOVE WS-MAP-TIME      TO  MVD-D-TIME.
*
          PERFORM C520-SET-MAP-ATTRIBUTES.
          PERFORM C530-FORMAT-DETAIL-MAP.
*
          MOVE -1  TO  MVD-L-VENDOR-NAME.
          MOVE '2'  TO  CA-MAP-CONTROL.
*
          EXEC CICS SEND
                     MAP    ('MAPPOVD')
                     MAPSET ('POVMAD2')
                     FROM   (VM-DETAIL-MAP)
                     ERASE
                     CURSOR
          END-EXEC.
*
    C500-EXIT.
          EXIT.
*
```

Fig. 13.4 *Continued.*

```
C520-SET-MAP-ATTRIBUTES  SECTION.
**********************************************************************
*          PERFORMED FROM:  C500-SEND-DETAIL-MAP-AND-DATA            *
*                           D200-SEND-DETAIL-MAP-DATAONLY            *
**********************************************************************
*
     MOVE UNPROT-FSET  TO  MVD-A-PHONE-AREA-CD
                           MVD-A-PHONE-1
                           MVD-A-PHONE-2
                           MVD-A-VENDOR-NAME
                           MVD-A-CONTACT
                           MVD-A-STREET
                           MVD-A-CITY
                           MVD-A-STATE-CODE
                           MVD-A-ZIP-CODE
                           MVD-A-ATTENTION-OF.
*
 C520-EXIT.
     EXIT.
*
 C530-FORMAT-DETAIL-MAP  SECTION.
**********************************************************************
*             FORMAT DETAIL MAP FOR INITIAL SEND                     *
*        PERFORMED FROM:  C500-SEND-DETAIL-MAP-AND-DATA              *
**********************************************************************
*
* FORMAT VENDOR CODE: A-9999-9   WS- FIELDS ARE AT END OF VENDMAST
     MOVE CA-VEND-1      TO  WS-VENDOR-CD-1.
     MOVE CA-VEND-2      TO  WS-VENDOR-CD-2.
     MOVE CA-VEND-3      TO  WS-VENDOR-CD-3.
     MOVE WS-VENDOR-CODE TO  MVD-D-VENDOR-CODE.
*
 C530-EXIT.
     EXIT.
*

 C531-GET-STATE-NAME  SECTION.
**********************************************************************
*             LOAD AND SEARCH STATE CODE TABLE                      *
*        PERFORMED FROM:  E110-EDIT-MAP-FORMAT-VM-RECORD            *
**********************************************************************
*
     COPY STPDT037.
*
 C531-EXIT.
     EXIT.
*
```

Fig. 13.4 *Continued.*

```
C600-SEND-CONTROL-MAP-DATAONLY  SECTION.
***********************************************************************
*              SEND CONTROL MAP DATAONLY - SYMBOLIC MAP               *
*              PERFORMED FROM:  C000-PROCESS-CONTROL-MAP              *
*                   SENT FOR INVALID CONDITIONS                       *
***********************************************************************
*
     MOVE '1'  TO  CA-MAP-CONTROL.
     MOVE -1   TO  MVC-L-VEND-CD-1.
*
     MOVE UNPROT-FSET  TO  MVC-A-VEND-CD-1
                           MVC-A-VEND-CD-2
                           MVC-A-VEND-CD-3.
*
     EXEC CICS SEND
             MAP     ('MAPPOVC')
             MAPSET  ('POVMAD1')
             FROM    (VM-CONTROL-MAP)
             DATAONLY
             CURSOR
     END-EXEC.
*
C600-EXIT.
     EXIT.
*
D100-RECEIVE-DETAIL-MAP  SECTION.
***********************************************************************
*            PERFORMED FROM:  E000-ADDITION-PROCESSING               *
*  ENTER - PROCESSES TRANSACTION          CLEAR - ENDS SESSION        *
*  PF3 - SETS DISPLAY OF CTL MAP          PF5   - RETURNS TO MENU      *
*              ALL OTHER KEYS ARE INVALID                             *
*            STATUS-OF-RECEIVE  =  'G'  =  GOOD RECEIVE               *
*                                  'C'  =  RETURN TO CTL-MAP          *
*                                  'I'  =  INVALID KEY PRESSED        *
***********************************************************************
*
     MOVE LOW-VALUES  TO  VM-DETAIL-MAP.
*
     IF EIBAID  =  DFHENTER
*
         EXEC CICS RECEIVE
                 MAP     ('MAPPOVD')
                 MAPSET  ('POVMAD2')
                 INTO    (VM-DETAIL-MAP)
                 RESP    (WS-RESP)
         END-EXEC
*
```

Fig. 13.4 *Continued.*

```
        IF WS-RESP  =  DFHRESP(NORMAL)    OR
           WS-RESP  =  DFHRESP(MAPFAIL)
            MOVE 'G'  TO  STATUS-OF-RECEIVE
        ELSE
            MOVE 'D100-'  TO  WS-RESP-SECTION
            PERFORM Z999-RESPONSE-ERROR
*
        ELSE
          IF EIBAID  =  DFHCLEAR
              PERFORM C110-END-SESSION
          ELSE
          IF EIBAID   =  DFHPF3
              MOVE 'C'  TO  STATUS-OF-RECEIVE
          ELSE
          IF EIBAID  =  DFHPF5
              PERFORM C120-TRANSFER-XCTL-TO-MENU
          ELSE
              MOVE 'I'       TO  STATUS-OF-RECEIVE
              MOVE 'INVALID KEY PRESSED - PLEASE TRY AGAIN'
                             TO  MVD-D-MESSAGE
              MOVE ASKIP-BRT  TO  MVD-A-MESSAGE.
*
 D100-EXIT.
     EXIT.
*
 D200-SEND-DETAIL-MAP-DATAONLY  SECTION.
******************************************************************
*          SEND DETAIL MAP DATA ONLY - SYMBOLIC MAP             *
*          PERFORMED FROM:  E000-ADDITION-PROCESSING            *
* SENT IF INVALID KEY IS PRESSED ON A RECEIVE OF THE DETAIL MAP  *
******************************************************************
*
     MOVE '2'  TO  CA-MAP-CONTROL.
*
     PERFORM C520-SET-MAP-ATTRIBUTES.
*
     EXEC CICS SEND
              MAP       ('MAPPOVD')
              MAPSET    ('POVMAD2')
              FROM      (VM-DETAIL-MAP)
              DATAONLY
              CURSOR
     END-EXEC.
*
 D200-EXIT.
     EXIT.
```

Fig. 13.4 *Continued.*

```
*
 E000-ADDITION-PROCESSING   SECTION.
*********************************************************************
*                 PERFORMED FROM:  AA00-MAINLINE                   *
*        DETAIL MAP IS SENT IF AN INVALID KEY WAS PRESSED          *
*                OR IF ADD WAS UNSUCCESSFUL                         *
*********************************************************************
*
     PERFORM D100-RECEIVE-DETAIL-MAP.
*
     IF GOOD-RECEIVE
         PERFORM E100-ADD-VENDOR-RECORD
         IF GOOD-ADD
             PERFORM B100-SEND-CONTROL-MAP-AND-DATA
     ELSE
             PERFORM D200-SEND-DETAIL-MAP-DATAONLY
     ELSE
         IF RETURN-TO-CTL-MAP
         PERFORM B100-SEND-CONTROL-MAP-AND-DATA
     ELSE
         PERFORM D200-SEND-DETAIL-MAP-DATAONLY.
*
 E000-EXIT.
     EXIT.
*
 E100-ADD-VENDOR-RECORD SECTION.
*********************************************************************
*               PERFORMED FROM:  E000-ADDITION-PROCESSING          *
*          PERFORMS EDITS AND FORMATS VENDOR-MASTER-RECORD         *
*               IF GOOD EDIT - ADDS RECORD TO THE FILE            *
*  RECORD ALREADY ON FILE MESSAGE COULD ONLY OCCUR IF RECORD WAS  *
*   ADDED BY ANOTHER TERMINAL SINCE KEYED-IN ON CONTROL SCREEN    *
*********************************************************************
*
     MOVE SPACES          TO   VENDOR-MASTER-RECORD.
     MOVE CA-VENDOR-CODE  TO   VM-VENDOR-CODE.
*
     MOVE 'E'  TO   STATUS-OF-ADD.
*
     PERFORM E110-EDIT-MAP-FORMAT-VM-RECORD.
*
     IF GOOD-EDIT
         PERFORM E120-WRITE-VENDOR-RECORD
         IF GOOD-WRITE
             MOVE 'RECORD SUCCESSFULLY ADDED'
                              TO   MVC-D-MESSAGE
```

Fig. 13.4 *Continued.*

```
                MOVE ASKIP-BRT   TO   MVC-A-MESSAGE
                MOVE 'G'         TO   STATUS-OF-ADD
           ELSE
                MOVE 'RECORD TO BE ADDED -ALREADY ON VENDOR FILE'
                              TO  MVD-D-MESSAGE
                MOVE ASKIP-BRT   TO   MVD-A-MESSAGE.
 *
  E100-EXIT.
     EXIT.
 *
  E110-EDIT-MAP-FORMAT-VM-RECORD   SECTION.
  **********************************************************************
  *       EDIT DETAIL MAP DATA - FORMAT VENDOR MASTER RECORD          *
  *            PERFORMED FROM:  E100-ADD-VENDOR-RECORD                 *
  *         HIGHLIGHT FIELDS WHICH CONTAIN INCORRECT DATA             *
  *              OR WHICH ARE MISSING REQUIRED ENTRIES                *
  **********************************************************************
  *
      MOVE 'G'  TO  STATUS-OF-EDIT.
  *
  * ASSUME ALL PHONE DIGITS SHOULD BE NUMERIC
  *
      IF MVD-D-PHONE-AREA-CD   IS   NUMERIC
                      AND
         MVD-D-PHONE-1         IS   NUMERIC
                      AND
         MVD-D-PHONE-2         IS   NUMERIC
           MOVE MVD-D-PHONE-AREA-CD   TO   VM-AREA-CD
           MOVE MVD-D-PHONE-1              TO   VM-PHONE-1-3
           MOVE MVD-D-PHONE-2              TO   VM-PHONE-4-7
           MOVE ASKIP-NORM                TO   MVD-C-A-PHONE
      ELSE
           MOVE -1          TO   MVD-L-PHONE-AREA-CD
           MOVE ASKIP-BRT   TO   MVD-C-A-PHONE
           MOVE 'E'         TO   STATUS-OF-EDIT.
  *
      IF MVD-D-VENDOR-NAME   =   LOW-VALUES   OR   SPACES
           MOVE -1          TO   MVD-L-VENDOR-NAME
           MOVE ASKIP-BRT   TO   MVD-C-A-VENDOR-NAME
           MOVE 'E'         TO   STATUS-OF-EDIT
      ELSE
           MOVE MVD-D-VENDOR-NAME   TO   VM-VENDOR-NAME
           MOVE ASKIP-NORM TO   MVD-C-A-VENDOR-NAME.
  *
  * 'CONTACT' AND 'TO ATTENTION OF' ARE OPTIONAL FIELDS
  *
      IF MVD-L-CONTACT   =   ZERO
```

Fig. 13.4 *Continued.*

```
              MOVE SPACES              TO   VM-CONTACT
         ELSE
              MOVE MVD-D-CONTACT  TO   VM-CONTACT.
    *
         IF MVD-L-STREET   =   0     OR
              MVD-D-STREET   =   SPACES
              MOVE -1            TO   MVD-L-STREET
              MOVE ASKIP-BRT  TO   MVD-C-A-STREET
              MOVE 'E'           TO   STATUS-OF-EDIT
         ELSE
              MOVE MVD-D-STREET  TO   VM-STREET-ADDRESS
              MOVE ASKIP-NORM   TO   MVD-C-A-STREET.
    *
              MOVE ZEROES   TO   VM-DOLLARS-COMMITTED.
    *
         IF MVD-D-CITY   =   LOW-VALUES   OR   SPACES
              MOVE -1            TO   MVD-L-CITY
              MOVE ASKIP-BRT  TO   MVD-C-A-CITY
              MOVE 'E'           TO   STATUS-OF-EDIT
         ELSE
              MOVE MVD-D-CITY  TO   VM-CITY
              MOVE ASKIP-NORM  TO   MVD-C-A-CITY.
    *
              MOVE MVD-D-STATE-CODE   TO   WS-STATE-CODE.
              PERFORM C531-GET-STATE-NAME.
              IF STATE-FOUND
                   MOVE MVD-D-STATE-CODE  TO   VM-STATE
                   MOVE WS-STATE-NAME                 TO   MVD-D-STATE-NAME
                   MOVE ASKIP-NORM                    TO   MVD-C-A-STATE
         ELSE
                   MOVE ALL '*'    TO   MVD-D-STATE-NAME
                   MOVE -1  TO   MVD-L-STATE-CODE
                   MOVE ASKIP-BRT  TO   MVD-C-A-STATE
                   MOVE 'E' TO   STATUS-OF-EDIT.
    *
         IF MVD-D-ZIP-CODE   IS   NUMERIC
              MOVE MVD-D-ZIP-CODE  TO   VM-ZIP-CODE
              MOVE ASKIP-NORM      TO   MVD-C-A-ZIP-CODE
         ELSE
              MOVE -1                   TO   MVD-L-ZIP-CODE
              MOVE ASKIP-BRT         TO   MVD-C-A-ZIP-CODE
              MOVE 'E'                  TO   STATUS-OF-EDIT.
    *
         IF MVD-L-ATTENTION-OF   =   ZERO
              MOVE SPACES                TO   VM-TO-ATTN-OF
         ELSE
              MOVE MVD-D-ATTENTION-OF  TO   VM-TO-ATTN-OF.
```

Fig. 13.4 *Continued.*

```
*
     IF STATUS-OF-EDIT  =  'E'
        MOVE 'PLEASE CORRECT HIGHLIGHTED FIELDS'
                        TO  MVD-D-MESSAGE
        MOVE ASKIP-BRT  TO  MVD-A-MESSAGE.
*
 E110-EXIT.
     EXIT.
*
 E120-WRITE-VENDOR-RECORD   SECTION.
*****************************************************************
*        WRITE VENDOR RECORD - PERFORM JOURNAL POSTING          *
*           PERFORMED FROM:   E100-ADD-VENDOR-RECORD            *
*****************************************************************
*
     EXEC CICS WRITE
               DATASET ('VENDMAST')
               FROM    (VENDOR-MASTER-RECORD)
               RIDFLD  (CA-VENDOR-CODE)
               RESP    (WS-RESP)
     END-EXEC.
*
     IF WS-RESP  =  DFHRESP(NORMAL)
         MOVE 'G'  TO  STATUS-OF-WRITE
     ELSE
         IF WS-RESP  =  DFHRESP(DUPREC)
             MOVE 'E'  TO  STATUS-OF-WRITE
     ELSE
             MOVE 'E120-'  TO  WS-RESP-SECTION
             PERFORM Z999-RESPONSE-ERROR.
*
             MOVE 'A'  TO  JR-TYPE.
             PERFORM E121-POST-JOURNAL-RECORD.
*
 E120-EXIT.
     EXIT.
*
 E121-POST-JOURNAL-RECORD   SECTION.
*****************************************************************
*    POST JOURNAL ENTRY - LINK TO JOURNAL PROGRAM 'JRNLPOST'    *
*         PERFORMED FROM:  E120-WRITE-VENDOR-RECORD            *
*****************************************************************
*
     MOVE 'VM'                 TO  JR-PREFIX.
     MOVE VENDOR-MASTER-RECORD TO  JR-RECORD-DATA.
     MOVE SPACES               TO  JR-PASSWORD.
*
```

Fig. 13.4 *Continued.*

```
      EXEC CICS LINK
                PROGRAM    ('JRNLPOST')
                COMMAREA  (JOURNAL-RECORD)
                LENGTH    (524)
      END-EXEC.
*
 E121-EXIT.
     EXIT.
*
*
 Z999-RESPONSE-ERROR   SECTION.
 ****************************************************************
 * INVALID EIBRESP CODE RETURNED DURING EXECUTION OF CICS COMMAND *
 ****************************************************************
 *
      MOVE WS-RESP   TO   WS-RESP-ERR-CD.
*
      EXEC CICS SEND
                FROM    (WS-RESP-ERROR)
                LENGTH (61)
                ERASE
      END-EXEC.
*
      EXEC CICS RETURN
      END-EXEC.
*
 Z999-EXIT.
     EXIT.
```

A more efficient technique you can use for your editing when you master the basic approach is to use the COMMAREA to hold validated data. This approach employs the COMMAREA to hold data entered on the screen; data is edited using the communication area data fields. If any errors are detected, an appropriate message is sent to the screen. Only incorrectly entered data keyed in immediately before a succeeding RECEIVE MAP, is returned to the program. Other fields are not FSET by the prior SEND MAP, nor are they FSET by the entry of data into the fields. This is more efficient because it minimizes the amount of data required to be transmitted. The COMMAREA length must be increased to accommodate the additional data. Figure 13.5 shows typical coding.

Note that field-2 is edited before field-1. Editing is typically performed from the bottom field on a map up to the top field, so that an error message associated with an incorrectly entered field corresponds to the first erroneous field when multiple errors exist.

```
MOVE 'G'  TO  STATUS-OF-EDIT.

    IF MAP-A-FIELD-2  =  DFHBMEOF
        MOVE SPACES  TO  CA-FIELD-2
    ELSE
        IF MAP-L-FIELD-2  >  0
            MOVE MAP-D-FIELD-2  TO  CA-FIELD-2.

    IF CA-FIELD-2  =  SPACES  OR  LOW-VALUES
        MOVE 'E'           TO  STATUS-OF-EDIT
        MOVE -1            TO  MAP-L-FIELD-2
        MOVE '???'         TO  MAP-D-FIELD-2
        MOVE 'FIELD-2 MUST BE ENTERED'
                           TO  MAP-D-MESSAGE
        MOVE UNPROT-BRT  TO  MAP-A-MESSAGE.

    IF MAP-A-FIELD-1  =  DFHBMEOF
        MOVE ZEROES  TO  CA-FIELD-1
    ELSE
        IF MAP-L-FIELD-1  >  0
            MOVE MAP-D-FIELD-1  TO  CA-FIELD-1.

    IF CA-FIELD-1  >  ZEROES
        NEXT SENTENCE
    ELSE
        MOVE 'E'           TO  STATUS-OF-EDIT
        MOVE -1            TO  MAP-L-FIELD-1
        MOVE ZEROES        TO  MAP-D-FIELD-1
        MOVE 'FIELD-1 MUST BE GREATER THAN 0'
                           TO  MAP-D-MESSAGE
        MOVE UNPROT-BRT  TO  MAP-A-MESSAGE.
```

Fig. 13.5 Typical coding to store data in COMMAREA.

E120-WRITE-VENDOR-RECORD. Write the addition record to the vendor master file. If the record is already on the file, the DUPREC condition is invoked and an E is returned in STATUS-OF-WRITE. A good write returns a G in STATUS-OF-WRITE. An after (A) journal record posting is performed; there is no before-record for an add. The DUPREC indicator is invoked only if an operator at another terminal has already added the same record you are attempting to add.

14

The Change
Program

After a file has been created, records added to the file, and an inquiry program written to check the status of various fields, it is often necessary to change records in the file. This chapter discusses the change program.

Control and detail maps are used for the change program. The control map shown in Fig. 14.1 requires the user to key in a vendor code and to press ENTER to display the change detail screen. The user also has the option of transferring control to the vendor file browse, returning to the vendor file maintenance submenu (see Fig. 6.3), or ending the session.

The vendor file change program detail map shown in Fig. 2.7 displays when the user keys in an existing vendor code on the control screen and then presses ENTER. The detail map shows all vendor file fields that can be changed on the vendor's record.

The detail change screen permits the user to key in the vendor's new data and then press ENTER to update the record. The program then returns to the control screen to allow entry of another vendor's code. The detail screen also permits the user to return to the change control screen without changing the record, to return to the submenu, or to end the session.

BMS Maps

Figures 14.2 and 14.3 show the BMS maps for the control and detail screens, respectively.

```
        1...5...10...15...20...25...30...35...40...45...50...55...60...65...70...75...80

 1 | ZZ/ZZ/ZZ                    ABC MANUFACTURING COMPANY                    POVMCH1 | 1
 2 | ZZ.ZZ.ZZ                    VENDOR FILE CHANGES CONTROL                          | 2
 3 |                                                                                  | 3
 4 |                                                                                  | 4
 5 |                                                                                  | 5
 6 |                                                                                  | 6
 7 |                            VENDOR CODE: X - XXXX - X                             | 7
 8 |                                                                                  | 8
 9 |                                                                                  | 9
10 |                                                                                  | 10
11 |                                                                                  | 11
12 |             1. TO CHANGE VENDOR RECORD - PRESS ENTER                             | 12
13 |                                                                                  | 13
14 |             2. TO BROWSE VENDOR FILE    - PRESS PF4                              | 14
15 |                                                                                  | 15
16 |             3. TO RETURN TO MENU        - PRESS PF5                              | 16
17 |                                                                                  | 17
18 |             4. TO END SESSION           - PRESS CLEAR                            | 18
19 |                                                                                  | 19
20 |                                                                                  | 20
21 |                                                                                  | 21
22 |                                                                                  | 22
23 |                                                                                  | 23
24 | ZZZZZZZZZZZZZZZZZZZZZZZZZZZZZZZZZZZZZZZZZZZZZZZZZZZZZZZZZZZZZZZZZZZZZZZZZZZZZZZZZZZ | 24

        1...5...10...15...20...25...30...35...40...45...50...55...60...65...70...75...80
```

Fig. 14.1 Vendor file changes control map.

```
        PRINT NOGEN
POVMCH1 DFHMSD TYPE=MAP,                                                    X
               .
               .
               .
        DFHMDF POS=(01,72),                                                 X
               LENGTH=07,                                                   X
               ATTRB=ASKIP,                                                 X
               INITIAL='POVMCH1'
               .
               .
               .
        DFHMDF POS=(02,26),                                                 X
               LENGTH=27,                                                   X
               ATTRB=ASKIP,                                                 X
               INITIAL='VENDOR FILE CHANGES CONTROL'
               .
               .
               .
        DFHMDF POS=(12,19),                                                 X
               LENGTH=40,                                                   X
               ATTRB=ASKIP,                                                 X
               INITIAL='1. TO CHANGE VENDOR RECORD - PRESS ENTER'
```

Fig. 14.2 Vendor file changes BMS control map.

```
          PRINT NOGEN
POVMCH2   DFHMSD TYPE=MAP,                                          X
                .
                .
                .
          DFHMDF POS=(01,72),                                       X
                LENGTH=07,                                          X
                ATTRB=ASKIP,                                        X
                INITIAL='POVMCH2'
                .
                .
                .
          DFHMDF POS=(02,30),                                       X
                LENGTH=19,                                          X
                ATTRB=ASKIP,                                        X
                INITIAL='VENDOR FILE CHANGES'
                .
                .
                .
          DFHMDF POS=(18,10),                                       X
                LENGTH=56,                                          X
                ATTRB=ASKIP,                                        X
                INITIAL='1. CHANGES, KEY IN NEW DATA        - PRX
      *         ESS ENTER'

          DFHMDF POS=(19,10),                                       X
                LENGTH=54,                                          X
                ATTRB=ASKIP,                                        X
                INITIAL='2. RETURN TO CHANGES CONTROL SCREEN - PRX
      *         ESS PF3'

          DFHMDF POS=(20,10),                                       X
                LENGTH=54,                                          X
                ATTRB=ASKIP,                                        X
                INITIAL='3. RETURN TO MENU                   - PRX
      *         ESS PF5'

          DFHMDF POS=(21,10),                                       X
                LENGTH=56,                                          X
                ATTRB=ASKIP,                                        X
                INITIAL='4. END OF SESSION                   - PRX
      *         ESS CLEAR'
                .
                .
                .
```

Fig. 14.3 Vendor file changes BMS detail map.

BMS control map

Figure 14.2 shows only the differences between this map and the BMS control map for the inquiry program (see Fig. 12.1).

BMS detail map

This map is similar to the addition detail map shown in Fig. 13.3. Figure 14.3 shows only the differences. Keep map fields in similar columns; for related maps, it makes map creation easy.

More-Readable Symbolic Maps

The copy library (appendix B, members MAPVMCTL and MAPVDTL2) shows more-readable symbolic maps created to correspond to the generated BMS maps.

Change Program Source Code

The change program source code, shown in Fig. 14.4, follows the format used in previous examples. I will discuss only the sections that differ from previous examples.

Fig. 14.4 Vendor file changes program source code.

```
 IDENTIFICATION DIVISION.
 PROGRAM-ID. POVMCHGE.
*
**********************************************************************
*            PURCHASING SYSTEM - VENDOR FILE CHANGES                *
*    - STARTED BY PURCHASING SYSTEM SUB-MENU PROGRAM 'POVMAINT'      *
*            COULD ALSO BE STARTED BY TRANSID 'POVC'                 *
**********************************************************************
 ENVIRONMENT DIVISION.
 DATA DIVISION.
*
 WORKING-STORAGE  SECTION.
*
 01  WS-PROGRAM-FIELDS.
     05  FILLER       PIC X(22)      VALUE 'POVMCHGE - START OF WS'.
     05  WS-CRT-MESSAGE    PIC X(17)    VALUE 'SESSION COMPLETED'.
     05  WS-RESP          PIC S9(8)     VALUE +0     COMP.

 01  WS-RESP-ERROR.
     05  FILLER           PIC X(39)     VALUE
         'PROGRAM POVMCHGE: ERROR EIBRESP CODE = '.
     05  WS-RESP-ERR-CD    PIC 99      VALUE ZEROES.
     05  FILLER            PIC X(15)    VALUE
         '  IN SECTION '.
     05  WS-RESP-SECTION    PIC X(5)    VALUE SPACES.
*
*01  VENDOR-MASTER-RECORD
```

Fig. 14.4 *Continued.*

```
                              COPY    VENDMAST.
*01  JOURNAL-RECORD
                              COPY    JRNLRECD.
*01  WS-COMMAREA
                              COPY    POWSVMCA.
*01  WS-STATUS-FIELDS
                              COPY    STWSSTAT.
*01  VM-CONTROL-MAP
                              COPY    MAPVMCTL.
*01  VM-DETAIL-MAP
                              COPY    MAPVDTL2.
*01  WS-DATE-AND-TIME
                              COPY    STWSDTTM.
*01  WS-STATE-CODE-SEARCH-ENTRIES
                              COPY    STWST037.
*01  ATTRIBUTE-LIST
                              COPY    STWSATTR.
*01  DFHAID
                              COPY    DFHAID.
*
 01  END-OF-WORKING-STORAGE    PIC X(15)   VALUE 'END WS POVMCHGE'.
*
 LINKAGE SECTION.
*
 01  DFHCOMMAREA               PIC X(8).
*
 01  BLL-CELLS.
     05  FILLER                     PIC S9(8)   COMP.
     05  BLL-CWA-ADDRESS            PIC S9(8)   COMP.
     05  BLL-T037-STATE-TABLE-ADDRESS  PIC S9(8)   COMP.
*
*01  CWA-DATA
              COPY    STLNKCWA.
*01  T037-STATE-TABLE
              COPY    T037STAT.
 PROCEDURE DIVISION.
*********************************************************************
*      PROGRAM STRUCTURE IS:                                       *
*         AA00-MAINLINE                                            *
*           B000-INITIAL-ENTRY                                     *
*             B100-SEND-CONTROL-MAP-AND-DATA                       *
*               B110-GET-DATE-AND-TIME                             *
*                                                                 *
*           C000-PROCESS-CONTROL-MAP                               *
*             C100-RECEIVE-CONTROL-MAP                             *
*               C110-END-SESSION                                   *
*               C120-TRANSFER-XCTL-TO-MENU                         *
*               C130-TRANSFER-XCTL-TO-BROWSE                       *
```

Fig. 14.4 *Continued.*

```
*                    C200-VERIFY-VENDOR-FORMAT
*                    C400-VERIFY-VENDOR-FILE-STATUS
*                      C410-READ-VENDOR-FILE
*                    C500-SEND-DETAIL-MAP-AND-DATA
*                      B110-GET-DATE-AND-TIME
*                      C520-SET-MAP-ATTRIBUTES
*                      C530-FORMAT-DETAIL-MAP
*                        C531-GET-STATE-NAME
*                    C600-SEND-CONTROL-MAP-DATAONLY
*
*              F000-CHANGE-PROCESSING
*                    D100-RECEIVE-DETAIL-MAP
*                      C110-END-SESSION
*                      C120-TRANSFER-XCTL-TO-MENU
*                    F100-CHANGE-VENDOR-RECORD
*                      F110-READ-VENDOR-FOR-UPDATE
*                        E121-POST-JOURNAL-RECORD
*                      E110-EDIT-MAP-FORMAT-VM-RECORD
*                        C531-GET-STATE-NAME
*                      F120-REWRITE-VENDOR-RECORD
*                        E121-POST-JOURNAL-RECORD
*                    B100-SEND-CONTROL-MAP-AND-DATA
*                    D200-SEND-DETAIL-MAP-DATAONLY
*                      C520-SET-MAP-ATTRIBUTES
***************************************************************
*
 AA00-MAINLINE   SECTION.
*
*     SERVICE RELOAD BLL-CELLS.
*
      MOVE LOW-VALUES  TO  VM-CONTROL-MAP.
*
      IF EIBCALEN  =  0
          PERFORM B000-INITIAL-ENTRY
      ELSE
          MOVE DFHCOMMAREA  TO  WS-COMMAREA
          IF CA-BROWSE
              MOVE SPACE        TO  CA-FUNCTION-CODE
              MOVE LOW-VALUES  TO  VM-CONTROL-MAP
              PERFORM C400-VERIFY-VENDOR-FILE-STATUS
              IF GOOD-VERIFY
                 PERFORM C500-SEND-DETAIL-MAP-AND-DATA
              ELSE
                 PERFORM B100-SEND-CONTROL-MAP-AND-DATA ELSE
              IF CA-RECEIVE-CTL-MAP
                 PERFORM C000-PROCESS-CONTROL-MAP
              ELSE
                  PERFORM F000-CHANGE-PROCESSING.
```

Fig. 14.4 *Continued.*

```
*
     EXEC CICS RETURN
              TRANSID  ('POVC')
               COMMAREA (WS-COMMAREA)
               LENGTH   (8)
     END-EXEC.
*
 B000-INITIAL-ENTRY  SECTION.
**********************************************************************
*                    PERFORMED FROM:  AA00-MAINLINE                 *
**********************************************************************
*
     MOVE LOW-VALUES  TO  VM-CONTROL-MAP.
     PERFORM B100-SEND-CONTROL-MAP-AND-DATA.
*
 B000-EXIT.
     EXIT.
*
 B100-SEND-CONTROL-MAP-AND-DATA  SECTION.
**********************************************************************
*        SEND CONTROL MAP - SYMBOLIC AND PHYSICAL MAPS             *
*             PERFORMED FROM:  B000-INITIAL-ENTRY                  *
*                              F000-CHANGE-PROCESSING              *
**********************************************************************
*
     PERFORM B110-GET-DATE-AND-TIME.
     MOVE WS-CURRENT-DATE  TO  MVC-D-DATE.
     MOVE WS-MAP-TIME       TO  MVC-D-TIME.
*
     MOVE -1   TO  MVC-L-VEND-CD-1.
     MOVE '1'  TO  CA-MAP-CONTROL.
*
     EXEC CICS SEND
              MAP     ('MAPPOVC')
              MAPSET  ('POVMCH1')
              FROM    (VM-CONTROL-MAP)
              ERASE
              CURSOR
     END-EXEC.
*
     B100-EXIT.
         EXIT.
*
 B110-GET-DATE-AND-TIME  SECTION.
**********************************************************************
*         STPDDTTM - OBTAIN DATE FROM CWA AND FORMAT TIME          *
*         PERFORMED FROM:  B100-SEND-CONTROL-MAP-AND-DATA          *
*                          C500-SEND-DETAIL-MAP-AND-DATA           *
```

Fig. 14.4 *Continued.*

```
**************************************************************
*
      COPY    STPDDTTM.
*
 B110-EXIT.
      EXIT.
*
 C000-PROCESS-CONTROL-MAP  SECTION.
**************************************************************
*                 PERFORMED FROM:  AA00-MAINLINE             *
*           PROCESS CONTROL MAP - IF VALID SEND DETAIL MAP    *
*            ELSE SEND CONTROL MAP WITH INVALID MESSAGE:      *
*  1) STATUS-OF-RECEIVE  =  'I'   INVALID KEY PRESSED         *
*  2) STATUS-OF-RECEIVE  =  'M'   MAPFAIL - NO DATA ENTERED   *
*  3) STATUS-OF-FORMAT   =  'E'   INVALID VENDOR KEYED FORMAT *
*  4) STATUS-OF-VERIFY   =  'E'   VENDOR FILE STATUS ERROR    *
**************************************************************
*
      PERFORM C100-RECEIVE-CONTROL-MAP.
      IF GOOD-RECEIVE
         PERFORM C200-VERIFY-VENDOR-FORMAT
         IF VALID-FORMAT
             PERFORM C400-VERIFY-VENDOR-FILE-STATUS
             IF GOOD-VERIFY
                 PERFORM C500-SEND-DETAIL-MAP-AND-DATA
             ELSE
                 PERFORM C600-SEND-CONTROL-MAP-DATAONLY
         ELSE
             PERFORM C600-SEND-CONTROL-MAP-DATAONLY
      ELSE
         IF MAPFAIL-ON-RECEIVE
             MOVE 'VENDOR CODE MUST BE ENTERED - PLEASE KEY-IN'
                              TO MVC-D-MESSAGE
             MOVE ASKIP-BRT  TO MVC-A-MESSAGE
             PERFORM C600-SEND-CONTROL-MAP-DATAONLY
         ELSE
             PERFORM C600-SEND-CONTROL-MAP-DATAONLY.
*
 C000-EXIT.
      EXIT.
*
 C100-RECEIVE-CONTROL-MAP  SECTION.
**************************************************************
*          PERFORMED FROM:  C000-PROCESS-CONTROL-MAP         *
*              ENTER IS ONLY VALID DATA ENTRY KEY            *
*  CLEAR KEY - ENDS TERMINAL SESSION      PF5 - RETURNS TO MENU  *
```

Fig. 14.4 *Continued.*

```
*                                                  PF4 - XCTL TO BROWSE     *
*                        ALL OTHER AID KEYS ARE INVALID                     *
*                STATUS-OF-RECEIVE  =  'G'  =  GOOD RECEIVE                  *
*                                       'M'  =  MAPFAIL                      *
*                                       'I'  =  INVALID KEY PRESSED          *
****************************************************************************
*
      MOVE LOW-VALUES   TO   VM-CONTROL-MAP.
*
      IF EIBAID  =  DFHENTER
*
          EXEC CICS RECEIVE
                  MAP     ('MAPPOVC')
                  MAPSET  ('POVMCH1')
                  INTO    (VM-CONTROL-MAP)
                  RESP    (WS-RESP)
          END-EXEC
*
          IF WS-RESP  =  DFHRESP(NORMAL)
              MOVE 'G'  TO   STATUS-OF-RECEIVE
          ELSE
              IF WS-RESP  =  DFHRESP(MAPFAIL)
                  MOVE 'M'  TO   STATUS-OF-RECEIVE
              ELSE
                  MOVE 'C100-'  TO   WS-RESP-SECTION
                  PERFORM Z999-RESPONSE-ERROR
*
      ELSE
          IF EIBAID  =  DFHCLEAR
              PERFORM C110-END-SESSION
          ELSE
          IF EIBAID  =  DFHPF5
              PERFORM C120-TRANSFER-XCTL-TO-MENU
          ELSE
          IF EIBAID  =  DFHPF4
              PERFORM C130-TRANSFER-XCTL-TO-BROWSE
          ELSE
              MOVE 'I'          TO   STATUS-OF-RECEIVE
              MOVE 'INVALID KEY PRESSED - PLEASE TRY AGAIN'
                          TO   MVC-D-MESSAGE
              MOVE ASKIP-BRT  TO   MVC-A-MESSAGE.
*
 C100-EXIT.
      EXIT.
*
 C110-END-SESSION   SECTION.
 ****************************************************************************
```

Fig. 14.4 *Continued.*

```
*     CRT OPERATOR PRESSED CLEAR KEY TO END TERMINAL SESSION          *
*             PERFORMED FROM:  C100-RECEIVE-CONTROL-MAP               *
*                             D100-RECEIVE-DETAIL-MAP                 *
*********************************************************************
*
      EXEC CICS SEND
               FROM   (WS-CRT-MESSAGE)
               LENGTH (17)
               ERASE
      END-EXEC.
*
      EXEC CICS RETURN
      END-EXEC.
*
 C110-EXIT.
      EXIT.
*
 C120-TRANSFER-XCTL-TO-MENU   SECTION.
*********************************************************************
*            OPERATOR PRESSED PF5 TO RETURN TO MENU PROGRAM          *
*             PERFORMED FROM:  C100-RECEIVE-CONTROL-MAP              *
*                             D100-RECEIVE-DETAIL-MAP                *
*********************************************************************
*
      EXEC CICS XCTL
               PROGRAM ('POVMAINT')
      END-EXEC.
*
 C120-EXIT.
      EXIT.
*
 C130-TRANSFER-XCTL-TO-BROWSE   SECTION.
*********************************************************************
*      OPERATOR PRESSED PF4 TO TRANSFER CONTROL TO BROWSE           *
*             PERFORMED FROM:  C100-RECEIVE-CONTROL-MAP             *
*********************************************************************
*
      MOVE LOW-VALUES     TO  WS-COMMAREA.
      MOVE 'C'            TO  CA-FUNCTION-CODE.
*
      EXEC CICS XCTL
               PROGRAM  ('POVMBROW')
               COMMAREA (WS-COMMAREA)
               LENGTH   (8)
      END-EXEC.
*
 C130-EXIT.
      EXIT.
```

Fig. 14.4 *Continued.*

```
*
 C200-VERIFY-VENDOR-FORMAT   SECTION.
*******************************************************************
*       VERIFY FORMAT OF VENDOR CODE KEYED-IN = A-9999-9          *
*            PERFORMED FROM:  C000-PROCESS-CONTROL-MAP            *
*    IF VALID FORMAT - MOVE CODE TO WS-COMMAREA FIELDS (CA- )     *
*******************************************************************
*
     IF (MVC-D-VEND-CD-1   IS  ALPHABETIC
                   AND
        MVC-D-VEND-CD-1   IS NOT =  SPACE)
       AND
        MVC-D-VEND-CD-2   IS  NUMERIC
       AND
        MVC-D-VEND-CD-3   IS  NUMERIC
          MOVE MVC-D-VEND-CD-1   TO   CA-VEND-1
          MOVE MVC-D-VEND-CD-2   TO   CA-VEND-2
          MOVE MVC-D-VEND-CD-3   TO   CA-VEND-3
          MOVE 'G'              TO   STATUS-OF-FORMAT
       ELSE
          MOVE 'E'        TO   STATUS-OF-FORMAT
          MOVE 'VENDOR CODE FORMAT MUST BE: A-9999-9 - PLEASE RE-EN -
               'TER'      TO   MVC-D-MESSAGE
          MOVE ASKIP-BRT   TO   MVC-A-MESSAGE.
*
 C200-EXIT.
     EXIT.
*
 C400-VERIFY-VENDOR-FILE-STATUS   SECTION.
*******************************************************************
*           PERFORMED FROM:  C000-PROCESS-CONTROL-MAP            *
*           MUST BE A VENDOR RECORD FOR CHANGES                  *
*******************************************************************
*
     MOVE 'G'  TO  STATUS-OF-VERIFY.
*
     PERFORM C410-READ-VENDOR-FILE.
*
     IF RECORD-NOT-FOUND
          MOVE 'E'        TO   STATUS-OF-VERIFY
          MOVE 'VENDOR RECORD NOT ON FILE'
                          TO   MVC-D-MESSAGE
          MOVE ASKIP-BRT   TO   MVC-A-MESSAGE.
*
 C400-EXIT.
     EXIT.
*
 C410-READ-VENDOR-FILE   SECTION.
*******************************************************************
```

Fig. 14.4 *Continued.*

```
*        PERFORMED FROM:  C400-VERIFY-VENDOR-FILE-STATUS
****************************************************************
*
     EXEC CICS READ
              DATASET ('VENDMAST')
              INTO    (VENDOR-MASTER-RECORD)
              RIDFLD  (CA-VENDOR-CODE)
              RESP    (WS-RESP)
     END-EXEC.
*
     IF WS-RESP  =  DFHRESP(NORMAL)
         MOVE 'G'  TO  STATUS-OF-READ
     ELSE
         IF WS-RESP  =  DFHRESP(NOTFND)
             MOVE 'E'  TO  STATUS-OF-READ
         ELSE
             MOVE 'C410-'  TO  WS-RESP-SECTION
             PERFORM Z999-RESPONSE-ERROR.
*
 C410-EXIT.
     EXIT.
*
*
 C500-SEND-DETAIL-MAP-AND-DATA  SECTION.
****************************************************************
*         SEND DETAIL MAP - PHYSICAL AND SYMBOLIC MAPS        *
*            PERFORMED FROM:  C000-PROCESS-CONTROL-MAP        *
*   SENT WHEN ALL VALIDATION AND EDIT CONDITIONS HAVE BEEN MET *
****************************************************************
*
     MOVE LOW-VALUES  TO  VM-DETAIL-MAP.
*
     PERFORM B110-GET-DATE-AND-TIME.
     MOVE WS-CURRENT-DATE  TO  MVD-D-DATE.
     MOVE WS-MAP-TIME TO  MVD-D-TIME.
*
     PERFORM C520-SET-MAP-ATTRIBUTES.
*
     PERFORM C530-FORMAT-DETAIL-MAP.
*
     MOVE -1   TO  MVD-L-VENDOR-NAME.
     MOVE '2'  TO  CA-MAP-CONTROL.
*
     EXEC CICS SEND
              MAP     ('MAPPOVD')
              MAPSET ('POVMCH2')
              FROM    (VM-DETAIL-MAP)
```

Fig. 14.4 *Continued.*

```
                ERASE
                CURSOR
     END-EXEC.
*
 C500-EXIT.
     EXIT.
*
 C520-SET-MAP-ATTRIBUTES  SECTION.
****************************************************************
*          PERFORMED FROM:  C500-SEND-DETAIL-MAP-AND-DATA      *
*                           D200-SEND-DETAIL-MAP-DATAONLY       *
****************************************************************
*
     MOVE UNPROT-FSET   TO  MVD-A-PHONE-AREA-CD
                            MVD-A-PHONE-1
                            MVD-A-PHONE-2
                            MVD-A-VENDOR-NAME
                            MVD-A-CONTACT
                            MVD-A-STREET
                            MVD-A-CITY
                            MVD-A-STATE-CODE
                            MVD-A-ZIP-CODE
                            MVD-A-ATTENTION-OF.
*
 C520-EXIT.
     EXIT.
*
 C530-FORMAT-DETAIL-MAP  SECTION.
****************************************************************
*          PERFORMED FROM:  C500-SEND-DETAIL-MAP-AND-DATA      *
****************************************************************
*
* FORMAT VENDOR CODE: A-9999-9      WS- FIELDS ARE AT END OF VENDMAST
     MOVE CA-VEND-1          TO  WS-VENDOR-CD-1.
     MOVE CA-VEND-2          TO  WS-VENDOR-CD-2.
     MOVE CA-VEND-3          TO  WS-VENDOR-CD-3.
     MOVE WS-VENDOR-CODE     TO  MVD-D-VENDOR-CODE.
*
     MOVE VM-AREA-CD         TO  MVD-D-PHONE-AREA-CD.
     MOVE VM-PHONE-1-3       TO  MVD-D-PHONE-1.
     MOVE VM-PHONE-4-7       TO  MVD-D-PHONE-2.
     MOVE VM-VENDOR-NAME     TO  MVD-D-VENDOR-NAME.
     MOVE VM-CONTACT         TO  MVD-D-CONTACT.
     MOVE VM-STREET-ADDRESS  TO  MVD-D-STREET.
     MOVE VM-CITY            TO  MVD-D-CITY.
     MOVE VM-STATE           TO  MVD-D-STATE-CODE.
*
```

Fig. 14.4 *Continued.*

```
      MOVE VM-STATE              TO   WS-STATE-CODE.
      PERFORM C531-GET-STATE-NAME.
      MOVE WS-STATE-NAME         TO   MVD-D-STATE-NAME.
*
      MOVE VM-ZIP-CODE           TO   MVD-D-ZIP-CODE.
      MOVE VM-TO-ATTN-OF         TO   MVD-D-ATTENTION-OF.
*
 C530-EXIT.
     EXIT.
*
 C531-GET-STATE-NAME  SECTION.
************************************************************************
*              LOAD AND SEARCH STATE CODE TABLE                    *
*      PERFORMED FROM:  C530-SEND-DETAIL-MAP-AND-DATA              *
*                 E110-EDIT-MAP-FORMAT-VM-RECORD                    *
************************************************************************
*
      COPY    STPDT037.
*
 C531-EXIT.
     EXIT.
*
 C600-SEND-CONTROL-MAP-DATAONLY  SECTION.
************************************************************************
*           SEND CONTROL MAP DATAONLY - SYMBOLIC MAP               *
*           PERFORMED FROM:  C000-PROCESS-CONTROL-MAP              *
*                 SENT FOR INVALID CONDITIONS                       *
************************************************************************
*
      MOVE UNPROT-FSET  TO   MVC-A-VEND-CD-1
                             MVC-A-VEND-CD-2
                             MVC-A-VEND-CD-3.
*
      MOVE -1   TO   MVC-L-VEND-CD-1.
      MOVE '1'  TO   CA-MAP-CONTROL.
*
      EXEC CICS SEND
                MAP        ('MAPPOVC')
                MAPSET     ('POVMCH1')
                FROM       (VM-CONTROL-MAP)
                DATAONLY
                CURSOR
      END-EXEC.
*
 C600-EXIT.
     EXIT.
*
 D100-RECEIVE-DETAIL-MAP  SECTION.
```

Fig. 14.4 *Continued.*

```
**********************************************************************
*            PERFORMED FROM:  F000-CHANGE-PROCESSING                 *
*  ENTER - PROCESSES TRANSACTION         CLEAR - ENDS SESSION        *
*  PF3   - SET DISPLAY OF CTL MAP        PF5   - RETURNS TO MENU      *
*                ALL OTHER KEYS ARE INVALID                          *
*        STATUS-OF-RECEIVE  =  'G'  =  GOOD RECEIVE                   *
*                              'C'  =  RETURN TO CTL-MAP              *
*                              'I'  =  INVALID KEY PRESSED            *
**********************************************************************
*
         MOVE LOW-VALUES  TO  VM-DETAIL-MAP.
*
     IF EIBAID  =  DFHENTER
*
     EXEC CICS RECEIVE
               MAP     ('MAPPOVD')
               MAPSET  ('POVMCH2')
               INTO    (VM-DETAIL-MAP)
               RESP    (WS-RESP)
     END-EXEC
*
     IF WS-RESP  =  DFHRESP(NORMAL)   OR
        WS-RESP  =  DFHRESP(MAPFAIL)
        MOVE 'G'  TO   STATUS-OF-RECEIVE
     ELSE
        MOVE 'D100-'  TO  WS-RESP-SECTION
        PERFORM Z999-RESPONSE-ERROR
*
     ELSE
         IF EIBAID  =  DFHCLEAR
             PERFORM C110-END-SESSION
         ELSE
         IF EIBAID   =  DFHPF3
             MOVE 'C' TO   STATUS-OF-RECEIVE
         ELSE
         IF EIBAID  =  DFHPF5
             PERFORM C120-TRANSFER-XCTL-TO-MENU
         ELSE
             MOVE 'I'        TO  STATUS-OF-RECEIVE
             MOVE 'INVALID KEY PRESSED - PLEASE TRY AGAIN'
                             TO  MVD-D-MESSAGE
             MOVE ASKIP-BRT  TO  MVD-A-MESSAGE.
*
 D100-EXIT.
     EXIT.
*
 D200-SEND-DETAIL-MAP-DATAONLY  SECTION.
**********************************************************************
```

Fig. 14.4 *Continued.*

```
*                SEND DETAIL MAP DATA ONLY - SYMBOLIC MAP        *
*                PERFORMED FROM:  F000-CHANGE-PROCESSING         *
* SENT IF INVALID KEY IS PRESSED ON A RECEIVE OF THE DETAIL MAP *
****************************************************************
*
     MOVE '2'  TO  CA-MAP-CONTROL.
*
     PERFORM C520-SET-MAP-ATTRIBUTES.
*
     EXEC CICS SEND
               MAP        ('MAPPOVD')
               MAPSET     ('POVMCH2')
               FROM       (VM-DETAIL-MAP)
               DATAONLY
               CURSOR
     END-EXEC.
*
 D200-EXIT.
     EXIT.
*
*
 E110-EDIT-MAP-FORMAT-VM-RECORD   SECTION.
****************************************************************
*      EDIT DETAIL MAP DATA - FORMAT VENDOR MASTER RECORD       *
*          PERFORMED FROM:  F100-CHANGE-VENDOR-RECORD           *
*        HIGHLIGHT FIELDS WHICH CONTAIN INCORRECT DATA          *
*             OR WHICH ARE MISSING REQUIRED ENTRIES             *
****************************************************************
*
     MOVE 'G'  TO  STATUS-OF-EDIT.
*
* ASSUME ALL PHONE DIGITS SHOULD BE NUMERIC
*
     IF MVD-D-PHONE-AREA-CD  IS  NUMERIC
        AND
         MVD-D-PHONE-1         IS  NUMERIC
        AND
         MVD-D-PHONE-2         IS  NUMERIC
         MOVE MVD-D-PHONE-AREA-CD   TO  VM-AREA-CD
         MOVE MVD-D-PHONE-1         TO  VM-PHONE-1-3
         MOVE MVD-D-PHONE-2         TO  VM-PHONE-4-7
         MOVE ASKIP-NORM            TO  MVD-C-A-PHONE
     ELSE
         MOVE -1          TO  MVD-L-PHONE-AREA-CD
         MOVE ASKIP-BRT   TO  MVD-C-A-PHONE
         MOVE 'E'         TO  STATUS-OF-EDIT.
*
```

Fig. 14.4 *Continued.*

```
    IF MVD-D-VENDOR-NAME   =  LOW-VALUES   OR   SPACES
        MOVE -1          TO   MVD-L-VENDOR-NAME
        MOVE ASKIP-BRT   TO   MVD-C-A-VENDOR-NAME
        MOVE 'E'         TO   STATUS-OF-EDIT
    ELSE
        MOVE MVD-D-VENDOR-NAME   TO   VM-VENDOR-NAME
        MOVE ASKIP-NORM          TO   MVD-C-A-VENDOR-NAME.
*
* 'CONTACT' AND 'TO ATTENTION OF' ARE OPTIONAL FIELDS
*
    IF MVD-L-CONTACT   =   ZERO
        MOVE SPACES          TO   VM-CONTACT
    ELSE
        MOVE MVD-D-CONTACT   TO   VM-CONTACT.
*
    IF MVD-L-STREET   =   0              OR
       MVD-D-STREET   =   SPACES
        MOVE -1          TO   MVD-L-STREET
        MOVE ASKIP-BRT   TO   MVD-C-A-STREET
        MOVE 'E'         TO   STATUS-OF-EDIT
    ELSE
        MOVE MVD-D-STREET   TO   VM-STREET-ADDRESS
        MOVE ASKIP-NORM     TO   MVD-C-A-STREET.
*
    MOVE ZEROES   TO   VM-DOLLARS-COMMITTED.
*
    IF MVD-D-CITY   =   LOW-VALUES   OR   SPACES
        MOVE -1          TO   MVD-L-CITY
        MOVE ASKIP-BRT   TO   MVD-C-A-CITY
        MOVE 'E'         TO   STATUS-OF-EDIT
    ELSE
        MOVE MVD-D-CITY   TO   VM-CITY
        MOVE ASKIP-NORM   TO   MVD-C-A-CITY.
*
    MOVE MVD-D-STATE-CODE   TO   WS-STATE-CODE.
    PERFORM C531-GET-STATE-NAME.
    IF STATE-FOUND
        MOVE MVD-D-STATE-CODE   TO   VM-STATE
        MOVE WS-STATE-NAME      TO   MVD-D-STATE-NAME
        MOVE ASKIP-NORM         TO   MVD-C-A-STATE
    ELSE
        MOVE ALL '*'        TO   MVD-D-STATE-NAME
        MOVE -1             TO   MVD-L-STATE-CODE
        MOVE ASKIP-BRT      TO   MVD-C-A-STATE
        MOVE 'E'            TO   STATUS-OF-EDIT.
*
    IF MVD-D-ZIP-CODE   IS   NUMERIC
```

Fig. 14.4 *Continued.*

```
        MOVE MVD-D-ZIP-CODE    TO   VM-ZIP-CODE
        MOVE ASKIP-NORM        TO   MVD-C-A-ZIP-CODE
    ELSE
        MOVE -1                TO   MVD-L-ZIP-CODE
        MOVE ASKIP-BRT         TO   MVD-C-A-ZIP-CODE
        MOVE 'E'               TO   STATUS-OF-EDIT.
*
    IF MVD-L-ATTENTION-OF  =  ZERO
        MOVE SPACES                 TO   VM-TO-ATTN-OF
    ELSE
        MOVE MVD-D-ATTENTION-OF  TO   VM-TO-ATTN-OF.
*
    IF STATUS-OF-EDIT  =  'E'
        MOVE 'PLEASE CORRECT HIGHLIGHTED FIELDS'
                        TO   MVD-D-MESSAGE
        MOVE ASKIP-BRT   TO   MVD-A-MESSAGE.
*
 E110-EXIT.
    EXIT.
*
*
 E121-POST-JOURNAL-RECORD  SECTION.
 **********************************************************************
 *     POST JOURNAL ENTRY - LINK TO JOURNAL PROGRAM 'JRNLPOST'      *
 *         PERFORMED FROM:  F110-READ-VENDOR-FOR-UPDATE             *
 *                          F120-REWRITE-VENDOR-RECORD             *
 **********************************************************************
 *
    MOVE 'VM'                  TO   JR-PREFIX.
    MOVE VENDOR-MASTER-RECORD  TO   JR-RECORD-DATA.
    MOVE SPACES                TO   JR-PASSWORD.
*
    EXEC CICS LINK
            PROGRAM  ('JRNLPOST')
            COMMAREA (JOURNAL-RECORD)
            LENGTH   (524)
    END-EXEC.
*
 E121-EXIT.
    EXIT.
*
 F000-CHANGE-PROCESSING  SECTION.
 **********************************************************************
 *                 PERFORMED FROM:  AA00-MAINLINE                  *
 *      DETAIL MAP IS SENT IF INVALID KEY WAS PRESSED             *
 *                OR IF CHANGE WAS UNSUCCESSFUL                    *
 **********************************************************************
 *
```

Fig. 14.4 *Continued.*

```
      PERFORM D100-RECEIVE-DETAIL-MAP.
*
      IF GOOD-RECEIVE
          PERFORM F100-CHANGE-VENDOR-RECORD
          IF GOOD-CHANGE
              PERFORM B100-SEND-CONTROL-MAP-AND-DATA
          ELSE
              PERFORM D200-SEND-DETAIL-MAP-DATAONLY
      ELSE
          IF RETURN-TO-CTL-MAP
              PERFORM B100-SEND-CONTROL-MAP-AND-DATA
          ELSE
              PERFORM D200-SEND-DETAIL-MAP-DATAONLY.
*
  F000-EXIT.
      EXIT.
*
  F100-CHANGE-VENDOR-RECORD  SECTION.
**********************************************************************
*            PERFORMED FROM:  F000-CHANGE PROCESSING               *
*    READ RECORD FOR UPDATE, EDIT MAP DATA AND REWRITE RECORD      *
*    RECORD NOT FOUND COULD NOT OCCUR UNLESS RECORD WAS DELETED    *
*    BY ANOTHER TERMINAL SINCE BEING KEYED-IN ON CONTROL SCREEN    *
**********************************************************************
*
      MOVE 'E'  TO  STATUS-OF-CHANGE.
*
      PERFORM F110-READ-VENDOR-FOR-UPDATE.
*
      IF RECORD-NOT-FOUND
          MOVE 'UPDATE VENDOR RECORD - NOT FOUND'
                          TO  MVD-D-MESSAGE
          MOVE ASKIP-BRT  TO  MVD-A-MESSAGE
      ELSE
          PERFORM E110-EDIT-MAP-FORMAT-VM-RECORD
          IF GOOD-EDIT
              PERFORM F120-REWRITE-VENDOR-RECORD
              MOVE 'CHANGE COMPLETED SUCCESSFULLY'
                              TO  MVC-D-MESSAGE
              MOVE ASKIP-BRT  TO  MVC-A-MESSAGE
              MOVE 'G'        TO  STATUS-OF-CHANGE.
*
  F100-EXIT.
      EXIT.
*
  F110-READ-VENDOR-FOR-UPDATE  SECTION.
```

Fig. 14.4 *Continued.*

```
*********************************************************************
*    READ VENDOR RECORD FOR UPDATE - POST BEFORE JOURNAL RECORD    *
*             PERFORMED FROM:  F100-CHANGE-VENDOR-RECORD           *
*********************************************************************
*
     EXEC CICS READ    UPDATE
                       DATASET ('VENDMAST')
                       INTO    (VENDOR-MASTER-RECORD)
                       RIDFLD  (CA-VENDOR-CODE)
                       RESP    (WS-RESP)
     END-EXEC.
*
     IF WS-RESP  =  DFHRESP(NORMAL)
         MOVE 'G'  TO  STATUS-OF-READ
     ELSE
         IF WS-RESP  =  DFHRESP(NOTFND)
             MOVE 'E'  TO  STATUS-OF-READ
         ELSE
             MOVE 'F110-'  TO  WS-RESP-SECTION
             PERFORM Z999-RESPONSE-ERROR.
*
     MOVE 'B'  TO  JR-TYPE.
     PERFORM E121-POST-JOURNAL-RECORD.
*
 F110-EXIT.
     EXIT.
*
 F120-REWRITE-VENDOR-RECORD  SECTION.
*********************************************************************
*     REWRITE VENDOR RECORD - POST 'AFTER' JOURNAL RECORD          *
*          PERFORMED FROM:  F100-CHANGE-VENDOR-RECORD              *
*********************************************************************
*
     EXEC CICS REWRITE
               DATASET ('VENDMAST')
               FROM    (VENDOR-MASTER-RECORD)
     END-EXEC.
*
     MOVE 'A'  TO  JR-TYPE.
     PERFORM E121-POST-JOURNAL-RECORD.
*
 F120-EXIT.
     EXIT.
*
*
 Z999-RESPONSE-ERROR  SECTION.
```

Fig. 14.4 *Continued.*

```
******************************************************************
* INVALID EIBRESP CODE RETURNED DURING EXECUTION OF CICS COMMAND *
******************************************************************
*
     MOVE WS-RESP  TO  WS-RESP-ERR-CD.
*
     EXEC CICS SEND
               FROM   (WS-RESP-ERROR)
               LENGTH (61)
               ERASE
     END-EXEC.
*
     EXEC CICS RETURN
     END-EXEC.
*
 Z999-EXIT.
     EXIT.
```

Procedure division

AA00-MAINLINE. This section is similar to that of the inquiry program in chapter 12, except that F000-CHANGE-PROCESSING replaces D000-IN-QUIRY-PROCESSING and TRANSID POVC replaces POVI.

C400-VERIFY-VENDOR-FILE-STATUS. This section performs a read of the vendor file to make sure the vendor record exists. If the vendor is not on the file, an error indicator is set and an error message is returned.

C410-READ-VENDOR-FILE. The RESP option is included on the READ command and WS-RESP is tested following execution of the read. If the record is on the file, it is read into the working-storage area VENDOR-MAS-TER-RECORD, and a G is moved to STATUS-OF-READ. If a record is not found, an E is moved to STATUS-OF-READ. A vendor record should be on the file for a record being changed. A "record-not-found" condition is treated as an error in the invoking section.

F100-CHANGE-VENDOR-RECORD. This section reads the change record for update. If the record is not found, an indicative message is displayed on the detail map. If the record is found, the map's data is edited and the vendor's record is formatted. If the edit and format are successful, a rewrite of the vendor record is performed. The message CHANGE COMPLETED SUC-CESSFULLY normally displays on the control screen. The message UPDATE VENDOR RECORD - NOT FOUND is only displayed if a user at another terminal had deleted the same record you are attempting to read for update, after you had entered the vendor code on the control screen. This program has previously read the vendor file for the entered vendor code (in section C410-READ-VENDOR-FILE) and determined that it was online in order to reach this point.

F110-READ-VENDOR-FOR-UPDATE. This section reads the change vendor record for update. If the record is not on the file, the NOTFND condition will be turned on and an E will be returned in STATUS-OF-READ. A good read will return a G in STATUS-OF-READ. A before (B) journal record posting is performed. The after-record will be posted after the rewrite in section F120-REWRITE-VENDOR-RECORD. The NOTFND indicator is only invoked if a user at another terminal has deleted the same record you are attempting to change, after you had keyed in vendor code on the control screen.

A situation that occasionally occurs is that after you have read a record and displayed its data, a user at another terminal may display the same record with intent of updating the record. The changes made by the first user who updates the record may be lost when the other user updates the same record. This may be prevented by saving an image of the record when it is first read, and then comparing that image against the record when it is read again for update. The indication is that if the saved record image is different from the record read for update, the record has been changed by another user. A user notification message can be displayed notifying the user of this condition and requesting that the changes be reentered. This is an inconvenience for the second user, who must reenter the same changes once again, but is better than entering incorrect changes. The saved record image can be stored in the COMMAREA or in a temporary storage queue (discussed in chapter 16).

F120-REWRITE-VENDOR-RECORD. Rewrite the changed vendor record. An after (A) journal record posting is performed. When the program reaches this point, it has read the vendor record for update and has established exclusive control of the record to be changed.

15

The Delete Program

After a record has been on a file for a period of time, circumstances some-times require the record to be deleted from the file. This chapter discusses the delete program.

Control and detail maps are used for the delete program. The control map shown in Fig. 15.1 requires the user to key in a vendor code and to press ENTER to display the delete detail screen. The user also has the option of transferring control to the vendor file browse, returning to the vendor file maintenance submenu (see Fig. 6.3), or ending the session. The vendor file delete program detail map shown in Fig. 2.8 displays when the user enters an existing vendor code on the control screen (Fig. 15.1). The delete detail screen permits the user to verify the vendor's data to make sure the correct record is being deleted. The user then presses ENTER to delete the record. The detail screen also permits the user to return to the delete control screen without deleting the record, to return to the submenu, or to end the session.

BMS Maps

Figures 15.2 and 15.3 show the BMS maps for the control and detail screens, respectively.

```
1...5...10...15...20...25...30...35...40...45...50...55...60...65...70...75...80
```

```
 1  │ ZZ/ZZ/ZZ                    ABC MANUFACTURING COMPANY             POVMDL1 │  1
 2  │ ZZ.ZZ.ZZ                    VENDOR FILE DELETIONS CONTROL                 │  2
 3  │                                                                          │  3
 4  │                                                                          │  4
 5  │                                                                          │  5
 6  │                                                                          │  6
 7  │                      VENDOR CODE: X - XXXX - X                            │  7
 8  │                                                                          │  8
 9  │                                                                          │  9
10  │                                                                          │ 10
11  │                                                                          │ 11
12  │            1. TO DELETE VENDOR RECORD - PRESS ENTER                       │ 12
13  │                                                                          │ 13
14  │            2. TO BROWSE VENDOR FILE    - PRESS PF4                        │ 14
15  │                                                                          │ 15
16  │            3. TO RETURN TO MENU        - PRESS PF5                        │ 16
17  │                                                                          │ 17
18  │            4. TO END SESSION           - PRESS CLEAR                      │ 18
19  │                                                                          │ 19
20  │                                                                          │ 20
21  │                                                                          │ 21
22  │                                                                          │ 22
23  │                                                                          │ 23
24  │ ZZZZZZZZZZZZZZZZZZZZZZZZZZZZZZZZZZZZZZZZZZZZZZZZZZZZZZZZZZZZZZZZZZZZZZZZZZZZ │ 24
```

```
1...5...10...15...20...25...30...35...40...45...50...55...60...65...70...75...80
```

Fig. 15.1 Vendor file deletions control map.

BMS control map

Figure 15.2 shows only the differences between this map and the BMS control map for the inquiry program (see Fig. 12.1).

BMS detail map

This map is similar to the inquiry detail map shown in Fig. 12.2. Figure 15.3 shows only the differences.

More-Readable Symbolic Maps

The copy library (appendix B, members MAPVMCTL and MAPVDTL1) shows more-readable symbolic maps that correspond to BMS-generated maps.

Delete Program Source Code

The delete program source code shown in Fig. 15.4 follows the format used in previous examples. I will only discuss sections that differ from previous examples.

Procedure division

AA00-MAINLINE. This section is similar to that of the inquiry program in chapter 12 except that perform G000-DELETE-PROCESSING replaces D000-INQUIRY-PROCESSING and TRANSID POVD replaces POVI.

C400-VERIFY-VENDOR-FILE-STATUS. This section performs a read of the vendor file to make sure the vendor to be deleted is on the file. If the vendor is not on the file, an error indicator is set and an error message returned.

C410-READ-VENDOR-FILE. A record should be on the file for a vendor being deleted. A NOTFND condition is treated as an error in the invoking section.

F110-READ-VENDOR-FOR-UPDATE. A before (B) journal record posting is performed. There is no after-record on a delete function.

G100-DELETE-VENDOR-RECORD. This section reads the delete record for update. If the record is not found, an indicative message displays on the detail map. You need not read the record for update prior to deleting if no

```
          PRINT NOGEN
POVMDL1   DFHMSD TYPE=MAP,                                      X
             .
             .
             .
          DFHMDF POS=(01,72),                                   X
             LENGTH=07,                                         X
             ATTRB=(ASKIP),                                     X
             INITIAL='POVMDL1'
             .
             .
          DFHMDF POS=(02,25),                                   X
             LENGTH=29,                                         X
             ATTRB=(ASKIP),                                     X
             INITIAL='VENDOR FILE DELETIONS CONTROL'
             .
             .
          DFHMDF POS=(12,19),                                   X
             LENGTH=40,                                         X
             ATTRB=(ASKIP),                                     X
             INITIAL='1. TO DELETE VENDOR RECORD-PRESS ENTER'
             .
             .
             .
```

Fig. 15.2 Vendor file deletions BMS control map.

```
        PRINT NOGEN
POVMDL2  DFHMSD TYPE=MAP,                                              X
                .
                .
                .
        DFHMDF POS=(01,72),                                           X
               LENGTH=07,                                            X
               ATTRB=(ASKIP),                                        X
               INITIAL='POVMDL2'
                .
                .
                .
        DFHMDF POS=(02,30),                                           X
               LENGTH=20,                                            X
               ATTRB=(ASKIP),                                        X
               INITIAL='VENDOR FILE DELETION'
                .
                .
                .
        DFHMDF POS=(18,10),                                           X
               LENGTH=56,                                            X
               ATTRB=(ASKIP),                                        X
               INITIAL='1. DELETIONS, VERIFY DATA BEFORE DELETING  -PRX
*              ESS ENTER'
        DFHMDF POS=(19,10),                                           X
               LENGTH=54,                                            X
               ATTRB=(ASKIP),                                        X
               INITIAL='2. RETURN TO DELETION CONTROL SCREEN      -PRX
*              ESS PF3'
        DFHMDF POS=(20,10),                                           X
               LENGTH=54,                                            X
               ATTRB=(ASKIP),                                        X
               INITIAL='2. RETURN TO MENU                         -PRX
*              ESS PF5'
        DFHMDF POS=(21,10),                                           X
               LENGTH=56,                                            X
               ATTRB=(ASKIP),                                        X
               INITIAL='3. END OF SESSION                         -PRX
               ESS CLEAR'
                .
                .
                .
```

Fig. 15.3 Vendor file deletions BMS detail map.

journal record was posted. In that case, the DELETE command must contain the RIDFLD option. A successfully read record is deleted and the message RECORD DELETED SUCCESSFULLY displays on the control screen. The message RECORD TO BE DELETED - NOT FOUND only displays if a user at another terminal deleted the same record you are attempting to delete, after you have entered vendor code on the control screen. The program would have previously read the vendor file for the entered vendor code (in section C410-READ-VENDOR-FILE) and determined that it was online in order to reach this point.

G110-DELETE-VM-RECORD. Delete the vendor record read for update. You can post a before (B) journal record in this section instead of in section F110-READ-VENDOR-FOR-UPDATE, in which the logic was performed. When the program reaches this point, it has read the vendor record for update and has established exclusive control of the record to be deleted.

Fig. 15.4 Vendor file deletions program source code.

```
 IDENTIFICATION DIVISION.
 PROGRAM-ID. POVMDLET.
*****************************************************************
*              PURCHASING SYSTEM - VENDOR FILE DELETIONS       *
*       - STARTED BY PURCHASING SYSTEM SUB-MENU PROGRAM 'POVMAINT'  *
*              COULD ALSO BE STARTED BY TRANSID 'POVD'          *
*****************************************************************
 ENVIRONMENT DIVISION.
 DATA DIVISION.
*
 WORKING-STORAGE  SECTION.
*
 01  WS-PROGRAM-FIELDS.
     05  FILLER        PIC X(22)     VALUE 'POVMDLET - START OF WS'.
     05  WS-CRT-MESSAGE  PIC X(17)   VALUE 'SESSION COMPLETED'.
     05  WS-RESP        PIC S9(8)    VALUE +0     COMP.

 01  WS-RESP-ERROR.
     05  FILLER    PIC X(39)     VALUE
         'PROGRAM POVMDLET: ERROR EIBRESP CODE = '.
     05  WS-RESP-ERR-CD   PIC 99       VALUE ZEROES.
     05  FILLER         PIC X(15)      VALUE
         ' IN SECTION '.
     05  WS-RESP-SECTION   PIC X(5)    VALUE SPACES.
*
*01  VENDOR-MASTER-RECORD
                             COPY    VENDMAST.
*01  JOURNAL-RECORD
                             COPY    JRNLRECD.
*01  WS-COMMAREA
                             COPY    POWSVMCA.
*01  WS-STATUS-FIELDS
                             COPY    STWSSTAT.
*01  VM-CONTROL-MAP
                             COPY    MAPVMCTL.
```

Fig. 15.4 *Continued.*

```
*01  VM-DETAIL-MAP
                                 COPY    MAPVDTL1.
*01  WS-DATE-AND-TIME
                                 COPY    STWSDTTM.
*01  WS-STATE-CODE-SEARCH-ENTRIES
                                 COPY    STWST037.
*01  ATTRIBUTE-LIST
                                 COPY    STWSATTR.
*01  DFHAID
                                 COPY    DFHAID.
*
01  END-OF-WORKING-STORAGE   PIC X(15)   VALUE 'END WS POVMDLET'.
*
LINKAGE SECTION.
*
 01  DFHCOMMAREA               PIC X(8).
*
 01  BLL-CELLS.
     05  FILLER                        PIC S9(8)   COMP.
     05  BLL-CWA-ADDRESS               PIC S9(8)   COMP.
     05  BLL-T037-STATE-TABLE-ADDRESS  PIC S9(8)   COMP.
*
*01  CWA-DATA
                        COPY    STLNKCWA.
*01  T037-STATE-TABLE
                        COPY    T037STAT.
        PROCEDURE DIVISION.
********************************************************************
*      PROGRAM STRUCTURE IS:                                      *
*          AA00-MAINLINE                                          *
*                 B000-INITIAL-ENTRY                              *
*                     B100-SEND-CONTROL-MAP-AND-DATA              *
*                         B110-GET-DATE-AND-TIME                  *
*                                                                 *
*                 C000-PROCESS-CONTROL-MAP                        *
*                     C100-RECEIVE-CONTROL-MAP                    *
*                         C110-END-SESSION                        *
*                         C120-TRANSFER-XCTL-TO-MENU              *
*                         C130-TRANSFER-XCTL-TO-BROWSE            *
*                     C200-VERIFY-VENDOR-FORMAT                   *
*                     C400-VERIFY-VENDOR-FILE-STATUS              *
*                         C410-READ-VENDOR-FILE                   *
*                     C500-SEND-DETAIL-MAP-AND-DATA               *
*                         B110-GET-DATE-AND-TIME                  *
*                         C530-FORMAT-DETAIL-MAP                  *
*                             C531-GET-STATE-NAME                 *
*                     C600-SEND-CONTROL-MAP-DATAONLY              *
```

Fig. 15.4 *Continued.*

```
*                    G000-DELETE-PROCESSING                    *
*                       D100-RECEIVE-DETAIL-MAP                *
*                          C110-END-SESSION                    *
*                          C120-TRANSFER-XCTL-TO-MENU          *
*                       G100-DELETE-VENDOR-RECORD              *
*                          F110-READ-VENDOR-FOR-UPDATE         *
*                             E121-POST-JOURNAL-RECORD         *
*                          G110-DELETE-VM-RECORD               *
*                       B100-SEND-CONTROL-MAP-AND-DATA         *
*                       D200-SEND-DETAIL-MAP-DATAONLY          *
*****************************************************************
*
 AA00-MAINLINE   SECTION.
*
*     SERVICE RELOAD BLL-CELLS.
*
     IF EIBCALEN  =  0
          PERFORM B000-INITIAL-ENTRY
     ELSE
          MOVE DFHCOMMAREA  TO  WS-COMMAREA
          IF CA-BROWSE
               MOVE SPACE        TO  CA-FUNCTION-CODE
               MOVE LOW-VALUES   TO  VM-CONTROL-MAP
               PERFORM C400-VERIFY-VENDOR-FILE-STATUS
               IF GOOD-VERIFY
                    PERFORM C500-SEND-DETAIL-MAP-AND-DATA
               ELSE
                    PERFORM B100-SEND-CONTROL-MAP-AND-DATA
          ELSE
               IF CA-RECEIVE-CTL-MAP
                    PERFORM C000-PROCESS-CONTROL-MAP
               ELSE
                    PERFORM G000-DELETE-PROCESSING.
*
          EXEC CICS RETURN
                    TRANSID  ('POVD')
                    COMMAREA (WS-COMMAREA)
                    LENGTH   (8)
          END-EXEC.
*
 B000-INITIAL-ENTRY  SECTION.
*****************************************************************
*              PERFORMED FROM:  AA00-MAINLINE                  *
*****************************************************************
*
     MOVE LOW-VALUES  TO  VM-CONTROL-MAP.
     PERFORM B100-SEND-CONTROL-MAP-AND-DATA.
```

Fig. 15.4 *Continued.*

```
*
 B000-EXIT.
     EXIT.
*
 B100-SEND-CONTROL-MAP-AND-DATA  SECTION.
 ***********************************************************************
 *         SEND CONTROL MAP - SYMBOLIC AND PHYSICAL MAPS           *
 *             PERFORMED FROM:  B000-INITIAL-ENTRY                 *
 *                              G000-DELETE-PROCESSING             *
 ***********************************************************************
 *
     PERFORM B110-GET-DATE-AND-TIME.
     MOVE WS-CURRENT-DATE   TO  MVC-D-DATE.
     MOVE WS-MAP-TIME       TO  MVC-D-TIME.
 *
     MOVE -1   TO  MVC-L-VEND-CD-1.
     MOVE '1'  TO  CA-MAP-CONTROL.
 *
     EXEC CICS SEND
               MAP    ('MAPPOVC')
               MAPSET ('POVMDL1')
               FROM   (VM-CONTROL-MAP)
               ERASE
               CURSOR
     END-EXEC.
 *
 B100-EXIT.
     EXIT.
*
 B110-GET-DATE-AND-TIME  SECTION.
 ***********************************************************************
 *         STPDDTTM - OBTAIN DATE FROM CWA AND FORMAT TIME         *
 *             PERFORMED FROM:  B100-SEND-CONTROL-MAP-AND-DATA     *
 *                              C500-SEND-DETAIL-MAP-AND-DATA      *
 ***********************************************************************
 *
     COPY   STPDDTTM.
 *
 B110-EXIT.
     EXIT.
*
 C000-PROCESS-CONTROL-MAP  SECTION.
 ***********************************************************************
 *              PERFORMED FROM:  AA00-MAINLINE                     *
 *          PROCESS CONTROL MAP - IF VALID SEND DETAIL MAP         *
 *            ELSE SEND CONTROL MAP WITH INVALID MESSAGE:          *
 *  1) STATUS-OF-RECEIVE  =  'I'   INVALID KEY PRESSED            *
 *  2) STATUS-OF-RECEIVE  =  'M'   MAPFAIL - NO DATA ENTERED      *
```

Fig. 15.4 *Continued.*

```
*   3) STATUS-OF-FORMAT    =  'E'   INVALID VENDOR KEYED FORMAT   *
*   4) STATUS-OF-VERIFY    =  'E'   VENDOR FILE STATUS ERROR      *
******************************************************************
*
     PERFORM C100-RECEIVE-CONTROL-MAP.
     IF GOOD-RECEIVE
         PERFORM C200-VERIFY-VENDOR-FORMAT
         IF VALID-FORMAT
             PERFORM C400-VERIFY-VENDOR-FILE-STATUS
             IF GOOD-VERIFY
                 PERFORM C500-SEND-DETAIL-MAP-AND-DATA
             ELSE
                 PERFORM C600-SEND-CONTROL-MAP-DATAONLY
         ELSE
             PERFORM C600-SEND-CONTROL-MAP-DATAONLY
      ELSE
         IF MAPFAIL-ON-RECEIVE
             MOVE 'VENDOR CODE MUST BE ENTERED - PLEASE KEY-IN'
                          TO MVC-D-MESSAGE
             MOVE ASKIP-BRT  TO MVC-A-MESSAGE
             PERFORM C600-SEND-CONTROL-MAP-DATAONLY
         ELSE
             PERFORM C600-SEND-CONTROL-MAP-DATAONLY.
*
 C000-EXIT.
     EXIT.
*
 C100-RECEIVE-CONTROL-MAP  SECTION.
******************************************************************
*            PERFORMED FROM:  C000-PROCESS-CONTROL-MAP          *
*               ENTER IS ONLY VALID DATA ENTRY KEY             *
*  CLEAR KEY - ENDS TERMINAL SESSION     PF5 - RETURNS TO MENU  *
*                                        PF4 - XCTL TO BROWSE   *
*            ALL OTHER AID KEYS ARE INVALID                     *
*            STATUS-OF-RECEIVE = 'G' =  GOOD RECEIVE            *
*                               'M' =  MAPFAIL                  *
*                               'I' =  INVALID KEY PRESSED      *
******************************************************************
*
     MOVE LOW-VALUES  TO  VM-CONTROL-MAP.
*
     IF EIBAID  =  DFHENTER
*
     EXEC CICS RECEIVE
             MAP     ('MAPPOVC')
             MAPSET  ('POVMDL1')
             INTO    (VM-CONTROL-MAP)
             RESP    (WS-RESP)
```

Fig. 15.4 *Continued.*

```
      END-EXEC
*
      IF WS-RESP  =  DFHRESP(NORMAL)
          MOVE 'G'  TO  STATUS-OF-RECEIVE
      ELSE
          IF WS-RESP  =  DFHRESP(MAPFAIL)
              MOVE 'M'  TO  STATUS-OF-RECEIVE
          ELSE
              MOVE 'C100-'  TO  WS-RESP-SECTION
              PERFORM Z999-RESPONSE-ERROR
*
          ELSE
              IF EIBAID  =  DFHCLEAR
                  PERFORM C110-END-SESSION
              ELSE
              IF EIBAID  =  DFHPF5
                  PERFORM C120-TRANSFER-XCTL-TO-MENU
              ELSE
              IF EIBAID  =  DFHPF4
                  PERFORM C130-TRANSFER-XCTL-TO-BROWSE
              ELSE
                  MOVE 'I'         TO  STATUS-OF-RECEIVE
                  MOVE 'INVALID KEY PRESSED - PLEASE TRY AGAIN'
                                   TO  MVC-D-MESSAGE
                  MOVE ASKIP-BRT  TO  MVC-A-MESSAGE.
*
  C100-EXIT.
      EXIT.
*
  C110-END-SESSION  SECTION.
  ********************************************************************
  *    CRT OPERATOR PRESSED CLEAR KEY TO END TERMINAL SESSION       *
  *         PERFORMED FROM:  C100-RECEIVE-CONTROL-MAP               *
  *                          D100-RECEIVE-DETAIL-MAP                *
  ********************************************************************
  *
      EXEC CICS SEND
              FROM   (WS-CRT-MESSAGE)
              LENGTH (17)
              ERASE
      END-EXEC.
*
      EXEC CICS RETURN
      END-EXEC.
*
  C110-EXIT.
```

Fig. 15.4 *Continued.*

```
     EXIT.
*
 C120-TRANSFER-XCTL-TO-MENU  SECTION.
 **********************************************************************
 *        OPERATOR PRESSED PF5  TO RETURN TO MENU PROGRAM            *
 *           PERFORMED FROM:  C100-RECEIVE-CONTROL-MAP               *
 *                            D100-RECEIVE-DETAIL-MAP                *
 **********************************************************************
 *
     EXEC CICS XCTL
             PROGRAM ('POVMAINT')
     END-EXEC.
*
 C120-EXIT.
     EXIT.
*
 C130-TRANSFER-XCTL-TO-BROWSE  SECTION.
 **********************************************************************
 *        OPERATOR PRESSED PF4 TO TRANSFER CONTROL TO BROWSE         *
 *           PERFORMED FROM: C100-RECEIVE-CONTROL-MAP                *
 **********************************************************************
 *
     MOVE LOW-VALUES  TO  WS-COMMAREA.
     MOVE 'D'  TO  CA-FUNCTION-CODE.
*
     EXEC CICS XCTL
             PROGRAM  ('POVMBROW')
             COMMAREA (WS-COMMAREA)
             LENGTH   (8)
     END-EXEC.
*
 C130-EXIT.
     EXIT.
*
 C200-VERIFY-VENDOR-FORMAT  SECTION.
 **********************************************************************
 *        VERIFY FORMAT OF VENDOR CODE KEYED-IN = A-9999-9           *
 *           PERFORMED FROM:   C000-PROCESS-CONTROL-MAP              *
 *   IF VALID FORMAT - MOVE CODE TO WS-COMMAREA FIELDS (CA- )        *
 **********************************************************************
 *
     IF (MVC-D-VEND-CD-1  IS  ALPHABETIC
                  AND
         MVC-D-VEND-CD-1  IS NOT =  SPACE)
     AND
         MVC-D-VEND-CD-2  IS  NUMERIC
```

Fig. 15.4 *Continued.*

```
      AND
          MVC-D-VEND-CD-3  IS  NUMERIC
          MOVE MVC-D-VEND-CD-1  TO  CA-VEND-1
          MOVE MVC-D-VEND-CD-2  TO  CA-VEND-2
          MOVE MVC-D-VEND-CD-3  TO  CA-VEND-3
          MOVE 'G'              TO  STATUS-OF-FORMAT
      ELSE
          MOVE 'E'         TO  STATUS-OF-FORMAT
          MOVE 'VENDOR CODE FORMAT MUST BE: A-9999-9 - PLEASE RE-EN
-             'TER'       TO  MVC-D-MESSAGE
          MOVE ASKIP-BRT  TO  MVC-A-MESSAGE.
 *
  C200-EXIT.
      EXIT.
 *
  C400-VERIFY-VENDOR-FILE-STATUS  SECTION.
 ********************************************************************
 *          PERFORMED FROM:  C000-PROCESS-CONTROL-MAP              *
 *            MUST BE A VENDOR RECORD FOR DELETIONS                *
 ********************************************************************
 *
      MOVE 'G' TO  STATUS-OF-VERIFY.
 *
      PERFORM C410-READ-VENDOR-FILE.
 *
      IF RECORD-NOT-FOUND
          MOVE 'E'      TO  STATUS-OF-VERIFY
          MOVE 'VENDOR RECORD NOT ON FILE'
                        TO  MVC-D-MESSAGE
          MOVE ASKIP-BRT  TO  MVC-A-MESSAGE
      ELSE
          IF VM-DOLLARS-COMMITTED  GREATER THAN  ZERO
              MOVE 'E'       TO    STATUS-OF-VERIFY
              MOVE 'DOLLARS COMMITTED ARE SIGNIFICANT - CAN
-                 ' NOT DELETE'    TO  MVC-D-MESSAGE
              MOVE ASKIP-BRT  TO    MVC-A-MESSAGE.
 *
  C400-EXIT.
      EXIT.
 *
  C410-READ-VENDOR-FILE  SECTION.
 ********************************************************************
 *          PERFORMED FROM:  C400-VERIFY-VENDOR-FILE-STATUS        *
 ********************************************************************
 *
      EXEC CICS READ
```

Fig. 15.4 *Continued.*

```
                DATASET ('VENDMAST')
                INTO    (VENDOR-MASTER-RECORD)
                RIDFLD  (CA-VENDOR-CODE)
                RESP    (WS-RESP)
       END-EXEC.
*
       IF WS-RESP  =  DFHRESP(NORMAL)
           MOVE 'G'  TO  STATUS-OF-READ
       ELSE
           IF WS-RESP  =  DFHRESP(NOTFND)
               MOVE 'E'  TO  STATUS-OF-READ
           ELSE
               MOVE 'C410-'  TO  WS-RESP-SECTION
               PERFORM Z999-RESPONSE-ERROR.
*
   C410-EXIT.
       EXIT.
*
*
   C500-SEND-DETAIL-MAP-AND-DATA   SECTION.
   ********************************************************************
   *         SEND DETAIL MAP - PHYSICAL AND SYMBOLIC MAPS            *
   *            PERFORMED FROM:  C000-PROCESS-CONTROL-MAP            *
   *   SENT WHEN ALL VALIDATION AND EDIT CONDITIONS HAVE BEEN MET   *
   ********************************************************************
*
       MOVE LOW-VALUES  TO  VM-DETAIL-MAP.
*
       PERFORM B110-GET-DATE-AND-TIME.
       MOVE WS-CURRENT-DATE  TO  MVD-D-DATE.
       MOVE WS-MAP-TIME       TO  MVD-D-TIME.
*
       PERFORM C530-FORMAT-DETAIL-MAP.
*
       MOVE '2'  TO  CA-MAP-CONTROL.
*
       EXEC CICS SEND
               MAP     ('MAPPOVD')
               MAPSET  ('POVMDL2')
               FROM    (VM-DETAIL-MAP)
               ERASE
       END-EXEC.
*
   C500-EXIT
       EXIT.
```

Fig. 15.4 *Continued.*

```
*
 C530-FORMAT-DETAIL-MAP  SECTION.
*******************************************************************
*         PERFORMED FROM:  C500-SEND-DETAIL-MAP-AND-DATA          *
*******************************************************************
*
* FORMAT VENDOR CODE: A-9999-9    WS- FIELDS ARE AT END OF VENDMAST
      MOVE CA-VEND-1              TO  WS-VENDOR-CD-1.
      MOVE CA-VEND-2              TO  WS-VENDOR-CD-2.
      MOVE CA-VEND-3              TO  WS-VENDOR-CD-3.
      MOVE WS-VENDOR-CODE         TO  MVD-D-VENDOR-CODE.
*
      MOVE VM-AREA-CD             TO  MVD-D-PHONE-AREA-CD.
      MOVE VM-PHONE-1-3           TO  MVD-D-PHONE-1.
      MOVE VM-PHONE-4-7           TO  MVD-D-PHONE-2.
      MOVE VM-VENDOR-NAME         TO  MVD-D-VENDOR-NAME.
      MOVE VM-CONTACT             TO  MVD-D-CONTACT.
      MOVE VM-STREET-ADDRESS      TO  MVD-D-STREET.
      MOVE VM-CITY                TO  MVD-D-CITY.
      MOVE VM-STATE               TO  MVD-D-STATE-CODE.
*
      MOVE VM-STATE               TO  WS-STATE-CODE.
      PERFORM C531-GET-STATE-NAME.
      MOVE WS-STATE-NAME          TO  MVD-D-STATE-NAME.
*
      MOVE VM-ZIP-CODE            TO  MVD-D-ZIP-CODE.
      MOVE VM-TO-ATTN-OF          TO  MVD-D-ATTENTION-OF.
      MOVE VM-DOLLARS-COMMITTED   TO  MVD-D-DLRS-COMMITTED.
*
 C530-EXIT.
     EXIT.
*
 C531-GET-STATE-NAME  SECTION.
*******************************************************************
*              LOAD AND SEARCH STATE CODE TABLE                   *
*         PERFORMED FROM:  C530-SEND-DETAIL-MAP-AND-DATA           *
*******************************************************************
*
      COPY   STPDT037.
*
 C531-EXIT.
     EXIT.
*
 C600-SEND-CONTROL-MAP-DATAONLY  SECTION.
```

Fig. 15.4 *Continued.*

```
*****************************************************************
*            SEND CONTROL MAP DATAONLY - SYMBOLIC MAP          *
*            PERFORMED FROM:  C000-PROCESS-CONTROL-MAP         *
*                  SENT FOR INVALID CONDITIONS                 *
*****************************************************************
*
     MOVE UNPROT-FSET  TO  MVC-A-VEND-CD-1
                          MVC-A-VEND-CD-2
                          MVC-A-VEND-CD-3.
*
     MOVE -1   TO  MVC-L-VEND-CD-1.
     MOVE '1'  TO  CA-MAP-CONTROL.
*
     EXEC CICS SEND
               MAP       ('MAPPOVC')
               MAPSET    ('POVMDL1')
               FROM      (VM-CONTROL-MAP)
               DATAONLY
               CURSOR
     END-EXEC.
*
 C600-EXIT.
     EXIT.
*
 D100-RECEIVE-DETAIL-MAP   SECTION.
*****************************************************************
*             PERFORMED FROM:  G000-DELETE-PROCESSING          *
*  ENTER -  PROCESSES TRANSACTION        CLEAR - ENDS SESSION  *
*  PF3 - SETS DISPLAY OF CTL MAP         PF5  - RETURNS TO MENU *
*             ALL OTHER KEYS ARE INVALID                       *
*          STATUS-OF-RECEIVE  =   'G'  =  GOOD RECEIVE         *
*                                 'C'  =  RETURN TO CTL-MAP    *
*                                 'I'  =  INVALID KEY PRESSED  *
*****************************************************************
*
     MOVE LOW-VALUES  TO  VM-DETAIL-MAP.
*
     IF EIBAID  =  DFHENTER
*
         EXEC CICS RECEIVE
                   MAP       ('MAPPOVD')
                   MAPSET    ('POVMDL2')
                   INTO      (VM-DETAIL-MAP)
                   RESP      (WS-RESP)
         END-EXEC
*
```

Fig. 15.4 *Continued.*

```
        IF WS-RESP  =  DFHRESP(NORMAL)    OR
           WS-RESP  =  DFHRESP(MAPFAIL)
             MOVE 'G'  TO  STATUS-OF-RECEIVE
        ELSE
             MOVE 'D100-'  TO  WS-RESP-SECTION
             PERFORM Z999-RESPONSE-ERROR
*
     ELSE
        IF EIBAID  =  DFHCLEAR
             PERFORM C110-END-SESSION
        ELSE
        IF EIBAID   =  DFHPF3
             MOVE 'C'  TO  STATUS-OF-RECEIVE
        ELSE
        IF EIBAID  =  DFHPF5
             PERFORM C120-TRANSFER-XCTL-TO-MENU
        ELSE
             MOVE 'I'         TO  STATUS-OF-RECEIVE
             MOVE 'INVALID KEY PRESSED - PLEASE TRY AGAIN'
                              TO  MVD-D-MESSAGE
             MOVE ASKIP-BRT   TO  MVD-A-MESSAGE.
*
 D100-EXIT.
     EXIT.
*
 D200-SEND-DETAIL-MAP-DATAONLY  SECTION.
 *******************************************************************
 *        SEND DETAIL MAP DATA ONLY - SYMBOLIC MAP                 *
 *     PERFORMED FROM:   G000-DELETE-PROCESSING                    *
 * SENT IF INVALID KEY IS PRESSED ON A RECEIVE OF THE DETAIL MAP   *
 *******************************************************************
 *
     MOVE '2'  TO  CA-MAP-CONTROL.
*
     EXEC CICS SEND
               MAP     ('MAPPOVD')
               MAPSET  ('POVMDL2')
               FROM    (VM-DETAIL-MAP)
               DATAONLY
     END-EXEC.
*
 D200-EXIT.
     EXIT.
*
 E121-POST-JOURNAL-RECORD  SECTION.
```

Fig. 15.4 *Continued.*

```
*********************************************************************
*     POST JOURNAL ENTRY - LINK TO JOURNAL PROGRAM 'JRNLPOST'     *
*        PERFORMED FROM:  F110-READ-VENDOR-FOR-UPDATE             *
*********************************************************************
*
     MOVE 'VM'                   TO   JR-PREFIX.
     MOVE VENDOR-MASTER-RECORD   TO   JR-RECORD-DATA.
     MOVE SPACES                 TO   JR-PASSWORD.
*
     EXEC CICS LINK
               PROGRAM   ('JRNLPOST')
               COMMAREA  (JOURNAL-RECORD)
               LENGTH    (524)
     END-EXEC.
*
 E121-EXIT.
     EXIT.
*
 F110-READ-VENDOR-FOR-UPDATE  SECTION.
*********************************************************************
*   READ VENDOR RECORD FOR UPDATE - POST BEFORE JOURNAL RECORD   *
*           PERFORMED FROM:  G100-DELETE-VENDOR-RECORD           *
*********************************************************************
*
     EXEC CICS READ  UPDATE
               DATASET ('VENDMAST')
               INTO    (VENDOR-MASTER-RECORD)
               RIDFLD  (CA-VENDOR-CODE)
               RESP    (WS-RESP)
     END-EXEC.
*
     IF WS-RESP  =  DFHRESP(NORMAL)
        MOVE 'G'  TO  STATUS-OF-READ
     ELSE
        IF WS-RESP  =  DFHRESP(NOTFND)
           MOVE 'E'  TO  STATUS-OF-READ
        ELSE
           MOVE 'F110-'  TO  WS-RESP-SECTION
           PERFORM Z999-RESPONSE-ERROR.
*
     MOVE 'B'  TO  JR-TYPE.
     PERFORM E121-POST-JOURNAL-RECORD.
*
 F110-EXIT.
     EXIT.
*
```

Fig. 15.4 *Continued.*

```
G000-DELETE-PROCESSING   SECTION.
********************************************************************
*                   PERFORMED FROM:   AA00-MAINLINE               *
*        DETAIL MAP IS SENT IF AN INVALID KEY WAS PRESSED         *
*                 OR DELETE RECORD WAS NOT FOUND                  *
********************************************************************
*
     PERFORM D100-RECEIVE-DETAIL-MAP.
*
     IF GOOD-RECEIVE
         PERFORM G100-DELETE-VENDOR-RECORD
         IF GOOD-DELETE
             PERFORM B100-SEND-CONTROL-MAP-AND-DATA
         ELSE
             PERFORM D200-SEND-DETAIL-MAP-DATAONLY
     ELSE
         IF RETURN-TO-CTL-MAP
             PERFORM B100-SEND-CONTROL-MAP-AND-DATA
         ELSE
             PERFORM D200-SEND-DETAIL-MAP-DATAONLY.
*
 G000-EXIT.
     EXIT.
*
 G100-DELETE-VENDOR-RECORD   SECTION.
********************************************************************
*             PERFORMED FROM:   G000-DELETE-PROCESSING            *
*   RECORD NOT FOUND COULD NOT OCCUR UNLESS RECORD WAS DELETED    *
*   BY ANOTHER TERMINAL SINCE BEING KEYED-IN ON CONTROL SCREEN    *
********************************************************************
*
     MOVE 'E'   TO   STATUS-OF-DELETE.
*
     PERFORM F110-READ-VENDOR-FOR-UPDATE.
*
     IF RECORD-NOT-FOUND
         MOVE 'RECORD TO BE DELETED - NOT FOUND'
                         TO   MVD-D-MESSAGE
         MOVE ASKIP-BRT   TO   MVD-A-MESSAGE
     ELSE
         PERFORM G110-DELETE-VM-RECORD
         MOVE 'RECORD DELETED SUCCESSFULLY'   TO   MVC-D-MESSAGE
         MOVE ASKIP-BRT                       TO   MVC-A-MESSAGE
         MOVE 'G'                             TO   STATUS-OF-DELETE.
*
 G100-EXIT.
```

Fig. 15.4 *Continued.*

```
*
 G110-DELETE-VM-RECORD  SECTION.
*****************************************************************
*       DELETE VENDOR RECORD - POST 'BEFORE' JOURNAL RECORD      *
*              PERFORMED FROM:  G100-DELETE-VENDOR-RECORD         *
*****************************************************************
*
     EXEC CICS DELETE
               DATASET ('VENDMAST')
     END-EXEC.
*
 G110-EXIT.
     EXIT.
*
*
 Z999-RESPONSE-ERROR  SECTION.
*****************************************************************
* INVALID EIBRESP CODE RETURNED DURING EXECUTION OF CICS COMMAND *
*****************************************************************
*
     MOVE WS-RESP  TO  WS-RESP-ERR-CD.
*
     EXEC CICS SEND
               FROM    (WS-RESP-ERROR)
               LENGTH (61)
               ERASE
     END-EXEC.
*
     EXEC CICS RETURN
     END-EXEC.
*
 Z999-EXIT.
     EXIT.
```

16

Temporary Storage and Transient Data

Temporary-storage control, like the use of field attributes, may cause you some difficulty. The use of a single temporary storage record does not seem to pose any special problems, but the employment of multiple queue records in a browse program's paging logic often does. In this chapter, I will first discuss temporary-storage control commands and then the use of single queue records. I will then cover several techniques used for paging logic that employ multiple temporary-storage (TS) queue items. Chapter 17 presents a complete browse program detailing one of the paging methods presented in this chapter.

A TS queue created by one program or task can be used in the same or different program task. TS queues can be created in either main storage or auxiliary storage. Main-storage queues are not used very often, and the browse program in the next chapter uses auxiliary storage, which is the default. TS queues can be used to supplement or replace the COMMAREA in many situations. The COMMAREA uses main storage and, if it is large enough, it may be more efficient to write several smaller TS queue items. These queues are available from the time they are created until they are deleted by a program or by the startup of the CICS system. They do not require that any predefined CICS table entries be made.

Transient data (TD) queues are used to store data that will be accessed by another CICS program in the same region or by a batch program outside of the CICS region. The use of transient data has similarities to that of the use of temporary storage, but there are important differences. Unlike temporary storage queues, transient-data queue records are automatically deleted when they are read and require predefined CICS table entries. These table names are defined in a table named the destination control table (DCT).

Transient-data queues are often used to pass data to automatically triggered tasks. Programs in these tasks read the queue and initiate the updating of files, printing of reports, or the initiation of batch jobs by submitting job control language (JCL) statements to an internal reader. Chapter 20 presents examples that explain some uses of transient data and related commands.

Relating TS Queues to VSAM Files

TS auxiliary queues can be likened to VSAM files. A queue name consists of up to eight programmer-defined characters. Using an eight-character queue name is common practice. These queues can be used by many different programs executing at different terminals. Make a TS queue unique to the terminal at which the task is being executed; otherwise, a program running at another terminal could unknowingly delete your queue. This is generally accomplished by using the EIB field EIBTRMID as the first four positions of the queue name. The next four positions should be characters meaningful to the program or system, such as MAP1, BROW, or PAGE. If you are using only one queue in a program, EIBTRNID may be used for the second four characters of the queue name.

You are responsibile for deleting TS queues when they are no longer needed. TS is a finite resource and can become full if queues no longer needed are not deleted. In addition to the eight-character queue name, these queues have an item number attached to each queue record. It is easier to understand TS queues if you consider the queue name and item number as parts of the queue's key. For instance, if EIBTRMID is TERM and the transaction code is POVB, a queue of three records can be visualized as having keys of TERMPOVB/1, TERMPOVB/2, and TERMPOVB/3.

TS control commands include:

- WRITEQ TS—Writes a new or additional TS queue record

- WRITEQ TS REWRITE—Updates a TS queue record

- READQ TS—Reads a TS queue record previously created

- DELETEQ TS—Deletes a TS queue no longer needed

Required Working-Storage Fields

Prior to using TS queues, you must define several fields in working storage: the queue name, the data portion of the queue, the length of the queue, and an item number. Length and item can be hard-coded if they are not variable. You may encounter some programs that define the data portion of the queue in the linkage section. The names used in the command descriptions are:

```
01   TS-QUEUE
       05   TS-TERMID          PIC  X(4).
       05   TS-QUEUE-NAME      PIC  X(4).

01   TS-DATA.
       05   TS-FIELD-1          . . .
       05   TS-FIELD-2          . . .
             . . .
01   TS-LENGTH                 PIC  S9999   COMP   VALUE  ZEROES.
01   TS-ITEM                   PIC  S9999   COMP   VALUE  ZEROES.
```

You must move the terminal identifier EIBTRMID into TS-TERMID, and the transaction code EIBTRNID, or a programmer-defined suffix, into TS-QUEUE-NAME. Queue length, TS-LENGTH, can be defined as a constant or can have length moved to it prior to executing a TS command. Item number, TS-ITEM, can be a constant or can have a value moved to it, added to it, or subtracted from it. Both TS-LENGTH and TS-ITEM must be defined as halfword binary values. For example:

```
MOVE EIBTRMID   TO   TS-TERMID.
MOVE EIBTRNID   TO   TS-QUEUE-NAME.
MOVE 1          TO   TS-ITEM.
MOVE 100        TO   TS-LENGTH.
```

Write a TS Queue

You must create or write a TS queue before it can be accessed. TS queue WRITE command format is:

```
EXEC CICS WRITEQ TS
          QUEUE   (TS-QUEUE)
          FROM    (TS-DATA)
          LENGTH  (TS-LENGTH)
          ITEM    (TS-ITEM)
          RESP    (data-area)
END-EXEC.
```

The letters TS following the WRITEQ command are optional, but are customarily included. The queue name is TS-QUEUE, and the data written is in the working-storage or linkage section data-area TS-DATA. Working-storage fields TS-LENGTH and TS-ITEM, defined as binary halfwords, are set prior to the write. Variable or fixed-length records may be written to the queue; specify the appropriate length in TS-LENGTH. The system assigns a sequential item number starting from 1 when you write a queue. I have found that fewer problems occur when the item is set by the program prior to the write. All examples move a value to the working-storage field used to hold the value of ITEM, prior to issuing a write.

- Conditions Raised—You need not normally check for any conditions after writing a TS queue.

Rewrite a TS Queue

TS queues are updated by including a REWRITE option. The format of the TS queue REWRITE option is similar to that of the WRITEQ TS command with the REWRITE option added as follows:

```
EXEC CICS WRITEQ TS
          REWRITE
          QUEUE   (TS-QUEUE)
          FROM    (TS-DATA)
          LENGTH (TS-LENGTH)
          ITEM    (TS-ITEM)
          RESP    (data-area)
END-EXEC.
```

The queue name is TS-QUEUE, and the data rewritten is located in the data-area, TS-DATA. Working-storage fields TS-LENGTH and TS-ITEM, defined in working storage as binary halfwords, are set prior to the write. A TS record to be changed must be read prior to issuing a REWRITE.

- Conditions Raised—normally, you need not check for any conditions after rewriting a queue. Conditions that might occur during testing include: QIDERR (queue not found) and ITEMERR (the queue exists, but the item specified was not found).

Read a TS Queue

The READQ TS command format is similar to that of the write queue. READQ TS and INTO replaces WRITEQ TS and the FROM option. A previously written queue is read by setting the item number to the proper value before reading the queue. READQ TS command format is:

```
EXEC CICS READQ TS
          QUEUE   (TS-QUEUE)
          [INTO   (TS-DATA) |
          SET     (ptr-ref)    |
          SET     (ADDRESS OF struc)]
          LENGTH (TS-LENGTH)
          ITEM    (TS-ITEM)
          RESP    (data-area)
END-EXEC.
```

You can omit ITEM, in which case, the next TS queue record is retrieved. Always include ITEM on all applicable TS commands, since there is less chance of errors occurring when a program directly controls item number. TS queue records can be read either sequentially or randomly by specifying the appropriate ITEM number. They can be read in reverse sequence by decreasing ITEM. TS-LENGTH must be set to the maximum possible length expected if processing variable-length queue records; it will contain the length of the record retrieved following the read. The data area should be large enough to contain the largest anticipated record if processing variable length records.

- Conditions Raised—Normally, you need not check for any conditions after reading a TS queue. Conditions that can occur during testing include QIDERR and ITEMERR.

Delete a TS Queue

The TS delete queue command format requires only the queue name. The entire queue must be deleted; it is not possible to delete individual items. A queue is generally deleted upon initial entry into a program. An ABEND of a prior task might have occurred before the queue was deleted by the prior task. DELETEQ TS command format is:

```
EXEC CICS DELETEQ TS
          QUEUE  (TS-QUEUE)
          RESP   (data-area)
END-EXEC.
```

- Conditions Raised—It is normally advisable to check for the QIDERR condition after executing the DELETEQ TS command. QIDERR occurs because programs using queues often delete the queue, if it exists, at the beginning of a program and should delete it prior to exiting the program, if it is no longer required. I prefer to handle the QIDERR by testing the RESP data-area; some programs you must maintain may provide for this condition by issuing the IGNORE CONDITION command. If the program attempts to delete the queue and the queue does not exist, no ABEND occurs if the condition has been ignored.

Using Single Queue Records

The use of a single queue record, which functions as a scratchpad, is rather simple. One program writes a TS queue record and that record can be read and rewritten by other programs. The queue can be deleted by the program creating the queue or by one of the programs accessing the queue. A single queue might be used to hold keys of records passed from program to program. When many programs in a system are interrelated, it sometimes simplifies a system if a TS queue is used. Passing record keys from program to program or from task to task in the COMMAREA in a multiprogram system can sometimes become complicated if different-size COMMAREAs are used. Many installations define a general use copybook for COMMAREA, which has a user-redefinable area at its end.

TS Paging Logic Techniques

You may be wondering how you would send previously displayed screens when using the file control browse commands described in chapter 11. TS queues are often employed for paging logic (scrolling) in browse programs. Paging refers to the sequential scrolling forward or backward through a list of sequential records, such as a vendor code and name list. A selection is often made from this list and passed to another program. Chapter 17 details one technique for performing this logic.

Paging done using temporary storage is usually controlled in a program by item number and *externally* by the use of PF keys. Using PF8 for forward scrolling and PF7 for backward paging is customary. You can include program logic to start a browse at the first or last map written to the queue. Include logic in all paging routines to prevent scrolling beyond the limits of the item numbers that have been created.

Your data processing installation may have standard scrolling routines already defined that you can incorporate into your programs. Many different approaches may be taken to paging logic depending on the situation and file being accessed. Most of the techniques employing temporary storage and used to write paging logic routines fall into one of the following categories:

- Write the entire symbolic map out to temporary storage and retrieve records as necessary.

- Write only significant map data to temporary storage. The items can be retrieved as needed and the symbolic map formatted with significant data saved.

- Write only record keys to temporary storage. This method requires rereading records when paging backward.

- Read all records before displaying any maps.

Write the entire symbolic map to temporary storage

As each map displays during a browse function, the symbolic map writes out to a TS queue and the item number increments by one. Displaying the prior map requires decreasing the item number by 1 and reading the queue containing the last symbolic map displayed. The queue record is read into the symbolic map's working-storage area, and the map displays. Each time the item number is incremented, its highest value must be saved. This is done so that when backward paging is performed, followed by forward paging, the program will know when to stop paging forward or to start creating additional TS records. You must employ logic to prevent decreasing the item number below 1 when paging backward.

Write only significant map data to temporary storage

This technique is similar to writing the entire symbolic map to temporary storage, but only significant map data is saved in working storage and written to a queue. When a program pages backward or forward, it reconstructs the symbolic map from the data saved in the queue record. This method has the advantage of creating smaller queues, but it requires more program code. Develop your techniques in accordance with company standards or, if none exist, establish standards for your installation.

Write only record keys to temporary storage

The key of the first or last record displayed on each map can be saved in a TS queue. As the user scrolls backward or forward, the program can reread records starting with keys equal to or greater than the saved keys. Each map can be reformatted as it was the first time the map was displayed. This method requires the least amount of temporary storage and is the technique used for the browse program in chapter 17. An advantage of this method is that because records are reread when backward scrolling takes place, any file maintenance changes reflect in the display. A disadvantage is that records do have to be reread when paging takes place in order to format the map.

Read all records before displaying any maps

This is perhaps the simplest scrolling method to work with. All maps to be displayed as part of a browse are written to temporary storage before any map is displayed. When all the maps for a given browse have been written to the queue, the program starts the display from the first map written. You can use forward and backward scrolling. This method differs from the first scrolling method discussed in that the former writes maps to temporary storage only when they are initially displayed, whereas this method writes all maps to temporary storage before any map is displayed. The drawback to using this method for long browses is that many more records must be read and their maps saved even if they did not need to be displayed.

Paging Logic Techniques without Using Temporary Storage

Paging logic can be accomplished without using TS queues. Two methods are sometimes employed. The first is to save the first and last key displayed on a map in the COMMAREA. Then, depending on the AID key pressed, issue a READNEXT or READPREV command. This logic can get complicated. For instance, when paging backward, the READPREV command is executed and a map is formatted from bottom to top. If 15 items are displayed per page and you page backward and only 10 records are read, the first five lines of the screen's multiple data contains spaces and must be adjusted.

The second method is to use COMMAREA to store the code of the first or last item on each page. These codes can be indexed through and records reread in order to affect paging logic. This is a good method if key size is small and you can limit the number of pages to be browsed.

TS Random Access Methods

As mentioned previously, you can enhance your understanding of TS queue if you can relate queues to VSAM files that have item number as a key. If the terminal at which a program is being executed has an ID of TERM and the TRANSID is POVB, you can conceptualize map key and symbolic map data saved as shown in Table 16.1.

When a program sends the first map, it writes out a TS queue with a *key* of TEMPPOVB/1 and data consisting of the first or last record key displayed on the map. The program increments item number as the program pages forward by adding one to the working-storage item field. It creates queue records with *keys* of TEMPPOVB/2, TEMPPOVB/3, etc. An alternate approach is to save the entire symbolic map in temporary storage and use it to reconstruct the map as paging takes place.

Backward scrolling is accomplished by subtracting 1 from item number each time the program scrolls backward. Item number must be defined in the working-storage COMMAREA when scrolling, since it changes with for-

TABLE 16.1   Map Key and Symbolic Map Data Saved.

Key Queue Name	Item	First or Last Key	or	Symbolic Map Data
TERMPOVB	1	Map 1 key		Map 1 data
"	2	" 2 "		" 2 "
"	3	" 3 "		" 3 "

ward or backward paging. Also save the item number of the last map displayed in COMMAREA. You can write routines to skip to the first or last record displayed, after scrolling forward or backward several pages.

Some Uses of TS Queues

A single TS queue is often used as a scratchpad to hold the contents of a record read with the intent to update it in a succeeding transaction or program. In pseudoconversational programming, a record is often read in one transaction and displayed on the screen. The record's data may then be changed, and the record reread for update by another transaction.

A user at a different terminal may have altered the record you were preparing to update before your changes were completed. When your program reads the record for update, it can read the TS queue containing the contents of the record as originally read. If the data of the record just read is different from the record saved in TS, an indicative message can display on the terminal. The user's changes are lost in this case and must be reentered. This logic can be performed more efficiently by using the COMMAREA when record size is small.

I found the use of a TS queue valuable in a case where a database file was loaded in ascending date sequence and the user wanted a display in descending date order. This database did not permit backward reading through the use of a command such as READPREV. I simulated the use of STARTBR and READPREV commands by employing a TS queue. The technique required reading each of the required records in ascending date sequence and writing a TS queue ITEM for each record. The records were then accessed in descending date sequence by reading the TS queue items in reverse order by subtracting 1 from ITEM number as each queue item was retrieved. The TS queue was read in reverse order until ITEM was decreased to zero. This use of a TS queue worked well because the number of data records was small and the transaction was not used frequently.

This technique is inefficient if there are numerous records and the display is a high-use transaction. It is inefficient to read, write, and then reread each TS queue record. You are, in effect, sorting a segment of the file into a different sequence. The use of a SORT is not permitted in an online system. It is important when you create online files that their records be loaded in the sequence corresponding to the order in which records will most commonly be read. Consider the use of alternate indexes if the same file is commonly accessed in different sequences.

Temporary storage is sometimes used to pass security data from a controlling program to other programs in a system. For instance, a single TS queue record can be created when the first program in the system is entered. The queue can be built by reading appropriate files so that it contained a list of permissible functions available to the signed on user. This list can be passed in the TS queue, which can be read and acted on by other programs within the system.

Often, several screens of data need to be entered and edited before any updating is performed. TS is often used to hold and redisplay data until it has all been entered and edited. Updating is performed when all entered data has been successfully edited.

Transient Data (TD) Queues

Use transient-data queues to pass data from one task to another task that reads and processes the data. Data can only be read sequentially from a TD queue; there is no random access or associated item number like there is with TS queues. Transient data cannot be changed once it has been written to a TD queue.

There are two types of transient data, extrapartition transient data and intrapartition transient data. Data written to an intrapartition transient-data queue can be used to trigger the initiation of another task by automatic task initiation (ATI). Transient data queues cannot be defined dynamically as can temporary-storage queues. They must be defined in a table named the destination control table (DCT).

Destination Control Table (DCT)

The destination control table contains entries that initiate a transaction when a predefined number of records are written to a transient-data queue. The trigger level is a numeric entry in the DCT indicating how many records must be written to the TD queue before a transaction defined in the DCT is initiated. The DCT name, up to four characters in length, is used by transient-data commands to direct data to the appropriate TD queue.

Automatic Transaction Initiation (ATI)

A transaction starts automatically when the trigger level defined in the DCT is reached. A program in the initiated task generally reads all the records in the queue and performs the required function using the data obtained from the queue. A record in a TD queue is automatically deleted from the queue as soon as it is read. New tasks are initiated each time a trigger level is reached.

Extrapartition Destination Data

Extrapartition TD queues are generally used to pass data to sequential files that reside outside of the CICS region. Data files can be written to a TD queue to be processed and printed by a batch program. Extrapartition TD queues cannot be deleted. They are not as commonly used as intrapartition TD queues.

Intrapartition Destination Data

Intrapartition destination data TD queues are generally used to pass data that is read, processed, and printed by another task. Data may be passed to a TD queue with the intent to use that data to update files in the initiated task. TD queues may also be used to submit job control language (JCL) to a system's internal reader, which reads the JCL and initiates a batch job. Chapter 20 presents an example of this use of transient data.

TD Queue Commands

The three types of CICS commands used to process TD queues are: WRITEQ TD, READQ TD, and DELETEQ TD. The *TD* is required to distinguish these commands from TS commands; TS is the default. DELETEQ TD cannot be used with extrapartition data; otherwise, the commands are the same for both extrapartition data and intrapartition data.

Write a TD Queue

The CICS command used to write a transient data queue record is WRITEQ TD. WRITEQ TD has the following format:

```
EXEC CICS WRITEQ TD
          QUEUE    (name)
          FROM     (data-area)
          LENGTH   (data-value)
END-EXEC.
```

The QUEUE option specifies the name of the queue, up to four characters in length, which must be defined in the DCT. The FROM option specifies the name of the input data area, while LENGTH, which is defined as a binary halfword (PIC S9999 COMP), holds the length of the output record. CICS ENQ and DEQ commands discussed in chapter 20 are generally used when writing TD queues in order to ensure that records from other transactions are not interspersed. This is a problem if we are writing print records or JCL to a transient data queue.

READ a TD Queue

The READQ TD command provides for the retrieval of transient data queue records written by a WRITEQ TD command. You can use the INTO or SET options to direct the queue's record into either a working-storage or linkage section input area. The condition QZERO indicates that a transient data queue is empty and must be handled. You must specify the LENGTH option's data-value as a halfword binary value; set it to the length of the largest record to be read. The actual length of the record read is returned in the LENGTH field's data value. This length is equal to the value of the size of the record written to the queue. READQ TD has the following format:

```
EXEC CICS READQ TD
          QUEUE   (name)
          [INTO   (data-area)   |
          SET     (ptr-ref)   |
          SET     (ADDRESS OF struc) ]
          LENGTH  (data-value)
END-EXEC.
```

Delete a TD Queue

The DELETEQ TD command is used to delete all records from an intra-partition transient data queue. You cannot use it to delete an extrapartition TD queue. DELETEQ TD has the following format:

```
EXEC CICS DELETEQ TD
          QUEUE (name)
END-EXEC.
```

17

The Browse Program

Chapter 16 discussed several paging techniques. This chapter employs, for the browse program, the technique of writing only a record's key to temporary storage as a map displays. This example covers most of the functions you are required to perform in a browse program. If you understand this technique, you will find it easy to follow the logic of other programs that use temporary storage for their paging routines.

Only one map (see Fig. 2.9) is used for the browse program. The user can key in the TRANSID POVB and press ENTER to display the browse map. The browse can also be invoked by a transfer of control from another program. The user has the option of returning to the vendor file maintenance submenu (see Fig. 6.3) or ending the session. The screen displays up to 15 vendor file records from which the user can make a selection and pass the selected vendor code to an invoking program. The user can page forward if the required vendor is not displayed and can page backward in order to view a previously displayed screen. Most browse programs that use TS queues do not permit backward paging beyond the vendor used as a starting point for the browse.

The user can reset the browse starting position during any point of the display by entering a new code on the screen and pressing a designated PF key. When the browse starting point is reset, the user can scroll forward and then backward from that point. Reset the browse after displaying a map and finding that the desired record is far from the record shown on the screen. The RESET BROWSE option encourages a user to limit the scope of a

browse. This is desirable because a browse function may involve considerable file I/O.

BMS Browse Map

Figure 17.1 contains the BMS map corresponding to the browse map shown
in Fig. 2.9. Define all browse map field attributes as ASKIP, except for the
SELECTION and RESET VENDOR CODE fields. Define the SELECTION
field attribute as IC, NUM, which makes the field UNPROT and inserts the
cursor at this field when the map is sent. The RESET VENDOR CODE field
attribute is set to UNPROT. The DFHMDF macro labeled MCOCCUR shows
how the OCCURS clause can be used to generate 15 lines of map data, each
of which contains 79 characters plus an attribute. The generated symbolic
map is read into the program data area VM-BROWSE-MAP defined in the
browse program's source code.

Fig. 17.1 Vendor file browse BMS map.

```
          PRINT NOGEN
POVMBR1   DFHMSD TYPE=MAP,                                          X
                 TIOAPFX=YES,                                       X
                 CTRL=(FRSET,FREEKB),                               X
                 TERM=3270,                                         X
                 LANG=COBOL,                                        X
                 MODE=INOUT
*
MAPPOVC   DFHMDI SIZE=(24,80),                                      X
                 COLUMN=01,                                         X
                 LINE=01
*
MCDATE    DFHMDF POS=(01,01),                                       X
                 LENGTH=08,                                         X
                 ATTRB=ASKIP
*
          DFHMDF POS=(01,27),                                       X
                 LENGTH=25,                                         X
                 ATTRB=ASKIP,                                       X
                 INITIAL='ABC MANUFACTURING COMPANY'
*
          DFHMDF POS=(01,72),                                       X
                 LENGTH=07,                                         X
                 ATTRB=ASKIP,                                       X
                 INITIAL='POVMBR1'
*
MCTIME    DFHMDF POS=(02,01),                                       X
                 LENGTH=08,                                         X
```

Fig. 17.1 *Continued.*

```
                ATTRB=ASKIP
*
        DFHMDF POS=(02,30),                                        X
               LENGTH=18,                                          X
               ATTRB=ASKIP,                                        X
               INITIAL='VENDOR FILE BROWSE'
*
        DFHMDF POS=(03,03),                                        X
               LENGTH=21,                                          X
               ATTRB=ASKIP,                                        X
               INITIAL='VENDOR CD VENDOR NAME'
*
        DFHMDF POS=(03,39),                                        X
               LENGTH=06,                                          X
               ATTRB=ASKIP,                                        X
               INITIAL='STREET'
*
        DFHMDF POS=(03,60),                                        X
               LENGTH=12,                                          X
               ATTRB=ASKIP,                                        X
               INITIAL='CITY / STATE'
*
MCOCCUR DFHMDF POS=(04,01),                                        X
               LENGTH=79,                                          X
               ATTRB=ASKIP,                                        X
               OCCURS=0015
*
MCSELEC DFHMDF POS=(19,01),                                        X
               LENGTH=02,                                          X
               ATTRB=(UNPROT,NUM,IC),                              X
               PICIN='99'
*
        DFHMDF POS=(19,04),                                        X
               LENGTH=11,                                          X
               ATTRB=ASKIP,                                        X
               INITIAL=': SELECTION'
*
        DFHMDF POS=(20,06),                                        X
               LENGTH=18,                                          X
               ATTRB=ASKIP,                                        X
               INITIAL='RESET VENDOR CODE:'
*
MCRVCOD DFHMDF POS=(20,25),                                        X
               LENGTH=06,                                          X
               ATTRB=(UNPROT)
*
```

Fig. 17.1 *Continued.*

```
         DFHMDF POS=(20,32),                                        X
               LENGTH=01,                                           X
               ATTRB=(ASKIP,DRK)
*
         DFHMDF POS=(21,01),                                        X
               LENGTH=51,                                           X
               ATTRB=ASKIP,                                         X
               INITIAL='1. FWD - PF8     4. KEY IN SELECTION   -X
               PF6'
*
         DFHMDF POS=(22,01),                                        X
               LENGTH=51,                                           X
               ATTRB=ASKIP,                                         X
               INITIAL='2. BWD - PF7     5. KEY IN RESET VENDOR-X
               PF9'
*
         DFHMDF POS=(23,01),                                        X
               LENGTH=53,                                           X
               ATTRB=ASKIP,                                         X
               INITIAL='3. MENU - PF5    6. END OF SESSION     -X
               CLEAR'
*
MAPMESG  DFHMDF POS=(24,01),                                        X
               LENGTH=79,                                           X
               ATTRB=ASKIP
*
         DFHMSD TYPE=FINAL
               END
```

User-Friendly Symbolic Maps

The user-friendly symbolic map, VM-BROWSE-MAP, is unique to the vendor browse and is hard-coded in the program.

Browse Program Source Code

Figure 17.2 shows the browse program's source code. The program's initial entry logic is shown following the main processing logic, which is executed much more frequently than initial entry in a browse program. This technique is often employed in online programming to minimize paging requirements.

Procedure division

AA00-MAINLINE. If this program is started by a TRANSID, the program moves low-values to WS-COMMAREA and starts its browse at the beginning of the file. This is done to keep the program as simple as possible. If EIB-CALEN is greater than 0, then this program was either started by another program or is returning to itself in the pseudoconversational mode. The EIB field EIBTRNID contains the transaction identifier of the current task. For instance, if this program is started by the inquiry program, EIBTRNID equals POVI. When this program issues a RETURN command with a TRANSID, a new task is started and EIBTRNID equals POVB. Note that the length of COMMAREA returned by this section is 19 because the COMMAREA contains additional fields that are used for paging logic. Inquiry and maintenance programs that start this program pass an eight-character COMMAREA.

B000-PROCESS-MAP. This section employs the CICS HANDLE AID command. EIBAID can be tested as with previous RECEIVE MAP commands, but I want to illustrate how HANDLE AID functions. HANDLE AID is invoked upon an execution of a RECEIVE MAP command. Control passes to section B100-PAGE-FORWARD if PF8 is pressed. Pressing PF7 transfers control to section B200-PAGE-BACKWARD, etc. ANYKEY transfers control to B000-INVALID-KEY for any key not specified; it does not include the ENTER key. In this example, if ENTER is pressed, control passes to the statement following the RECEIVE MAP command, paragraph B000-INVALID-KEY. You can program the enter key to pass control to B500-RESET-KEY by adding ENTER (B500-RESET-KEY) to the HANDLE AID command.

Fig. 17.2 Vendor file browse program source code.

```
        IDENTIFICATION DIVISION.
        PROGRAM-ID. POVMBROW.
****************************************************************
*              PURCHASING SYSTEM - VENDOR FILE BROWSE         *
*        - STARTED BY PURCHASING SYSTEM MAINTENANCE PROGRAMS   *
*              OR DIRECTLY BY ENTERING  TRANSID 'POVB'         *
*        PF1 - PAGE FORWARD          PF6 - RETURN WITH SELECTION *
*        PF2 - PAGE BACKWARD         PF7 - RESET BROWSE KEY     *
****************************************************************
 ENVIRONMENT DIVISION.
 DATA DIVISION.
*
 WORKING-STORAGE  SECTION.
*
```

Fig. 17.2 *Continued.*

```
01  WS-PROGRAM-FIELDS.
    05  FILLER      PIC X(22)        VALUE 'POVMBROW - START OF WS'.
    05  WS-CRT-MESSAGE    PIC X(17)    VALUE 'SESSION COMPLETED'.
    05  SUB              PIC S9999    COMP    VALUE ZEROES
    05  WS-SELECTION     PIC 99               VALUE ZEROES.
    05  WS-XCTL-PROGRAM  PIC X(8)             VALUE SPACES.
    05  WS-RESP          PIC S9(8)    VALUE +0     COMP.


01  WS-RESP-ERROR.
    05  FILLER               PIC X(39)    VALUE
        'PROGRAM POVMBROW: ERROR EIBRESP CODE = '.
    05  WS-RESP-ERR-CD    PIC 99          VALUE ZEROES.
    05  FILLER            PIC X(15)    VALUE
        '  IN SECTION '.
    05  WS-RESP-SECTION    PIC X(5)    VALUE SPACES.
*
01  WS-DISPLAY-DATA.
    05  WS-SELECT                PIC 99.
    05  FILLER                   PIC X.
    05  WS-VM-KEY                PIC X(8).
    05  FILLER                   PIC X.
    05  WS-VENDOR-NAME           PIC X(25).
    05  FILLER                   PIC X.
    05  WS-STREET-ADDRESS        PIC X(20).
    05  FILLER                   PIC X.
    05  WS-CITY-STATE            PIC X(20).
*
01  TEMPORARY-STORAGE-FIELDS.
    05  TS-QUEUE.
        10  TS-EIBTRMID          PIC X(4).
        10  TS-QUEUE-NAME        PIC X(4).
    05  TS-LENGTH                PIC S9999        COMP  VALUE +6.
    05  TS-RECORD.
        10  TS-VENDOR-CD         PIC X(6).
    05  TS-SUB                   PIC S9999        COMP  VALUE ZEROES.
*
01  WS-COMMAREA.
    05  CA-FUNCTION-CODE         PIC X.
        88  CA-INQUIRY                   VALUE 'I'.
        88  CA-ADDITION                  VALUE 'A'.
        88  CA-CHANGE                    VALUE 'C'.
        88  CA-DELETE                    VALUE 'D'.
        88  CA-BROWSE                    VALUE 'B'.
    05  CA-MAP-CONTROL           PIC X.
    05  CA-VENDOR-CODE.
        10  CA-VEND-1            PIC X.
        10  CA-VEND-2            PIC X(4).
        10  CA-VEND-3            PIC X.
    05  CA-LAST-KEY              PIC X(6).
    05  CA-TS-ITEM               PIC S9999        COMP.
    05  CA-TS-MAXIMUM            PIC S9999        COMP.
    05  CA-TS-EOF-SWITCH         PIC X.
```

Fig. 17.2 *Continued.*

```
 01  VM-BROWSE-MAP.
     05   FILLER              PIC X(12).
*
     05   MVC-L-DATE          PIC S9(4)    COMP.
     05   MVC-A-DATE          PIC X.
     05   MVC-D-DATE          PIC X(8).
*
     05   MVC-L-TIME          PIC S9(4)    COMP.
     05   MVC-A-TIME          PIC X.
     05   MVC-D-TIME          PIC X(8).
*
     05   MVC-OCCURS   OCCURS   15 TIMES.
          10   MVC-L-OCCURS   PIC S9(4)    COMP.
          10   MVC-A-OCCURS   PIC X.
          10   MVC-D-OCCURS   PIC X(79).
*
     05   MVC-L-SELECTION     PIC S9(4)    COMP.
     05   MVC-A-SELECTION     PIC X.
     05   MVC-D-SELECTION     PIC 99.
*
     05   MVC-L-RESET-CODE    PIC S9(4)    COMP.
     05   MVC-A-RESET-CODE    PIC X.
     05   MVC-D-RESET-CODE    PIC X(6).
*
     05   MVC-L-MESSAGE       PIC S9(4)    COMP.
     05   MVC-A-MESSAGE       PIC X.
     05   MVC-D-MESSAGE       PIC X(79).
*
*01  VENDOR-MASTER-RECORD
                             COPY     VENDMAST.
*01  WS-STATUS-FIELDS
                             COPY     STWSSTAT.
*01  WS-DATE-AND-TIME
                             COPY     STWSDTTM.
*01  ATTRIBUTE-LIST
                             COPY     STWSATTR.
*01  DFHAID
                             COPY     DFHAID.
*
 01  END-OF-WORKING-STORAGE  PIC X(15)    VALUE 'END WS POVMBROW'.
*
*
 LINKAGE SECTION.
*
 01  DFHCOMMAREA             PIC X(19).
*
 01  BLL-CELLS.
     05   FILLER             PIC S9(8)    COMP.
     05   BLL-CWA-ADDRESS    PIC S9(8)    COMP.
*
*01  CWA-DATA
               COPY     STLNKCWA.
```

Fig. 17.2 *Continued.*

```
PROCEDURE DIVISION.
*********************************************************************
*     PROGRAM STRUCTURE IS:                                         *
*        AA00-MAINLINE                                              *
*           B000-PROCESS-MAP                                        *
*              B100-PAGE-FORWARD                                    *
*                 B110-SEND-MAP-DATAONLY                            *
*                    B111-RESET-OCCURS-ATTRIBUTES                   *
*                 B120-RETURN-TO-CICS                               *
*                 B130-READ-TS                                      *
*                 B140-START-BROWSE                                 *
*                 B150-BROWSE-PROCESSING                            *
*                    B151-FORMAT-OCCURS                             *
*                    B152-FORMAT-MAP                                *
*                    B153-WRITE-TS-RECORD                           *
*                 B110-SEND-MAP-DATAONLY                            *
*                    B111-RESET-OCCURS-ATTRIBUTES                   *
*              B200-PAGE-BACKWARD                                   *
*                 B110-SEND-MAP-DATAONLY                            *
*                     B111-RESET-OCCURS-ATTRIBUTES                  *
*                 B120-RETURN-TO-CICS                               *
*                 B130-READ-TS                                      *
*                 B140-START-BROWSE                                 *
*                 B150-BROWSE-PROCESSING                            *
*                    B151-FORMAT-OCCURS                             *
*                    B152-FORMAT-MAP                                *
*                    B153-WRITE-TS-RECORD                           *
*              B300-TRANSFER-XCTL-TO-MENU                           *
*                 B310-INITIALIZE-AND-DELETEQ                       *
*              B400-RETURN-WITH-SELECTION                           *
*                 B310-INITIALIZE-AND-DELETEQ                       *
*                 B410-XCTL-TO-INVOKING-PROGRAM                     *
*                 B110-SEND-MAP-DATAONLY                            *
*                     B111-RESET-OCCURS-ATTRIBUTES                  *
*                 B120-RETURN-TO-CICS                               *
*              B500-RESET-KEY                                       *
*                 B310-INITIALIZE-AND-DELETEQ                       *
*                 B140-START-BROWSE                                 *
*                 B150-BROWSE-PROCESSING                            *
*                    B151-FORMAT-OCCURS                             *
*                    B152-FORMAT-MAP                                *
*                    B153-WRITE-TS-RECORD                           *
*                 B110-SEND-MAP-DATAONLY                            *
*                     B111-RESET-OCCURS-ATTRIBUTES                  *
*                 B120-RETURN-TO-CICS                               *
*              B600-END-SESSION                                     *
*                 B310-INITIALIZE-AND-DELETEQ                       *
*                                                                   *
*        C000-INITIAL-ENTRY                                         *
*              B310-INITIALIZE-AND-DELETEQ                          *
*              B140-START-BROWSE                                    *
*              B150-BROWSE-PROCESSING                               *
```

Fig. 17.2 *Continued.*

```
*                   B151-FORMAT-OCCURS                         *
*                   B152-FORMAT-MAP                            *
*                   B153-WRITE-TS-RECORD                       *
*            C100-SEND-MAP-AND-DATA                            *
*              C110-GET-DATE-AND-TIME                          *
*            B111-RESET-OCCURS-ATTRIBUTES                      *
*****************************************************************
AA00-MAINLINE   SECTION.
*     SERVICE RELOAD BLL-CELLS.
      IF EIBCALEN  =  0
          MOVE LOW-VALUES   TO  WS-COMMAREA
          PERFORM C000-INITIAL-ENTRY
      ELSE
          MOVE DFHCOMMAREA  TO  WS-COMMAREA
          IF EIBTRNID  =  'POVB'
             PERFORM B000-PROCESS-MAP
      ELSE
             PERFORM C000-INITIAL-ENTRY.
*
      EXEC CICS RETURN
              TRANSID  ('POVB')
              COMMAREA (WS-COMMAREA)
              LENGTH   (19)
      END-EXEC.
*
*
B000-PROCESS-MAP   SECTION.
*****************************************************************
*                 PERFORMED FROM: AA00-MAINLINE                *
*****************************************************************
*
      MOVE LOW-VALUES   TO  VM-BROWSE-MAP.
*
      EXEC CICS HANDLE AID
              PF8              (B100-PAGE-FORWARD)
              PF7              (B200-PAGE-BACKWARD)
              PF5              (B300-TRANSFER-XCTL-TO-MENU)
              PF6              (B400-RETURN-WITH-SELECTION)
              PF9              (B500-RESET-KEY)
              CLEAR            (B600-END-SESSION)
              ANYKEY           (B000-INVALID-KEY)
      END-EXEC.
*
      EXEC CICS IGNORE CONDITION
              MAPFAIL
      END-EXEC.
*
      EXEC CICS RECEIVE
              MAP              ('MAPPOVC')
              MAPSET           ('POVMBR1')
              INTO             (VM-BROWSE-MAP)
      END-EXEC.
```

Fig. 17.2 *Continued.*

```
*
*   ENTER IS AN INVALID KEY
*
 B000-INVALID-KEY.
     MOVE 'I'            TO   STATUS-OF-RECEIVE.
     MOVE 'INVALID KEY PRESSED - PLEASE TRY AGAIN'
                         TO   MVC-D-MESSAGE.
     MOVE ASKIP-BRT      TO   MVC-A-MESSAGE.
     MOVE -1             TO   MVC-L-SELECTION.
     PERFORM B110-SEND-MAP-DATAONLY.
*
 B000-EXIT.
     EXIT.
*
 B100-PAGE-FORWARD   SECTION.
 ****************************************************************
 *          INVOKED BY HANDLE AID FROM:   B000-PROCESS-MAP      *
 ****************************************************************
*
     ADD 1   TO   CA-TS-ITEM.
*
     IF CA-TS-ITEM  IS GREATER THAN  CA-TS-MAXIMUM
         IF CA-LAST-KEY  =  HIGH-VALUES
             SUBTRACT 1  FROM  CA-TS-ITEM
             MOVE 'CURRENT PAGE IS LAST PAGE'
                            TO   MVC-D-MESSAGE
             MOVE ASKIP-BRT      TO   MVC-A-MESSAGE
             MOVE -1             TO   MVC-L-SELECTION
             PERFORM B110-SEND-MAP-DATAONLY
             PERFORM B120-RETURN-TO-CICS
         ELSE
             MOVE CA-LAST-KEY   TO   CA-VENDOR-CODE
*
 ****************************************************************
 * CA-LAST-KEY CONTAINS THE KEY OF THE LAST VENDOR DISPLAYED   *
 * ON THE PREVIOUS PAGE.  THE START BROWSE WILL, AS THE LOGIC  *
 * IS WRITTEN, DISPLAY THIS ITEM AGAIN AT THE TOP OF THE NEXT  *
 * PAGE.  YOU CAN GET AROUND THIS IN ONE OF TWO WAYS:          *
 *    1) IF YOUR KEY IS NUMERIC, ADD 1 TO CA-VENDOR-CODE       *
 *    2) ISSUE AN ADDITIONAL READNEXT AFTER THE STARTBR        *
 ****************************************************************
*
     ELSE
         PERFORM B130-READ-TS
         MOVE TS-VENDOR-CD  TO   CA-VENDOR-CODE.
*
     PERFORM B140-START-BROWSE.
     IF GOOD-STARTBR
         PERFORM B150-BROWSE-PROCESSING
         MOVE -1  TO   MVC-L-SELECTION
     ELSE
         MOVE 'START BROWSE KEY BEYOND END OF FILE'
```

Fig. 17.2 *Continued.*

```
                        TO   MVC-D-MESSAGE
          MOVE ASKIP-BRT  TO   MVC-A-MESSAGE
          MOVE -1         TO   MVC-L-RESET-CODE.
*
    PERFORM B110-SEND-MAP-DATAONLY.
    PERFORM B120-RETURN-TO-CICS.
*
 B100-EXIT.
    EXIT.
*
 B110-SEND-MAP-DATAONLY  SECTION.
*
**********************************************************************
*                PERFORMED FROM:  B000-PROCESS-MAP                   *
*                                 B100-PAGE-FORWARD                  *
*                                 B200-PAGE-BACKWARD                 *
*                                 B400-RETURN-WITH-SELECTION         *
*                                 B500-RESET-KEY                     *
**********************************************************************
*
    PERFORM B111-RESET-OCCURS-ATTRIBUTES
            VARYING SUB  FROM  1 BY 1  UNTIL  SUB  =  16.
*
    MOVE UNPROT-NUM-FSET  TO  MVC-A-SELECTION.
    MOVE UNPROT-FSET      TO  MVC-A-RESET-CODE.
*
    EXEC CICS SEND
            MAP     ('MAPPOVC')
            MAPSET  ('POVMBR1')
            FROM    (VM-BROWSE-MAP)
            DATAONLY
            CURSOR
    END-EXEC.
*
 B110-EXIT.
    EXIT.
*
 B111-RESET-OCCURS-ATTRIBUTES  SECTION.
**********************************************************************
*                PERFORMED FROM:  B110-SEND-MAP-DATAONLY            *
*                                 C100-SEND-MAP-AND-DATA            *
**********************************************************************
*
    MOVE ASKIP-FSET  TO  MVC-A-OCCURS (SUB).
*
 B111-EXIT.
    EXIT.
*
 B120-RETURN-TO-CICS  SECTION.
**********************************************************************
*                PERFORMED FROM:  B100-PAGE-FORWARD                 *
*                                 B200-PAGE-BACKWARD                *
```

Fig. 17.2 *Continued.*

```
*                                      B400-RETURN-WITH-SELECTION      *
*                                      B500-RESET-KEY                  *
***********************************************************************
*
     EXEC CICS RETURN
             TRANSID  ('POVB')
             COMMAREA (WS-COMMAREA)
             LENGTH   (19)
     END-EXEC.
*
 B120-EXIT.
     EXIT.
*
 B130-READ-TS  SECTION.
***********************************************************************
*               PERFORMED FROM:  B100-PAGE-FORWARD                    *
*                                B200-PAGE-BACKWARD                   *
***********************************************************************
*
     MOVE EIBTRMID  TO  TS-EIBTRMID.
     MOVE 'POVB'    TO  TS-QUEUE-NAME.
*
     EXEC CICS READQ TS
             QUEUE  (TS-QUEUE)
             INTO   (TS-RECORD)
             LENGTH (TS-LENGTH)
             ITEM   (CA-TS-ITEM)
     END-EXEC.
*
 B130-EXIT.
     EXIT.
*
 B140-START-BROWSE  SECTION.

***********************************************************************
*            PERFORMED FROM:  B100-PAGE-FORWARD                       *
*                             B200-PAGE-BACKWARD                      *
*                             B500-RESET-KEY                          *
*                             C000-INITIAL-ENTRY                      *
***********************************************************************
*
     EXEC CICS STARTBR
             DATASET ('VENDMAST')
             RIDFLD  (CA-VENDOR-CODE)
             GTEQ
             RESP    (WS-RESP)
     END-EXEC.
*
     IF WS-RESP  =  DFHRESP(NORMAL)
         MOVE 'G' TO  STATUS-OF-BROWSE
     ELSE
         IF WS-RESP  =  DFHRESP(NOTFND)
```

Fig. 17.2 *Continued.*

```
             MOVE 'E'   TO   STATUS-OF-BROWSE
         ELSE
             MOVE 'B140-'  TO  WS-RESP-SECTION
             PERFORM Z999-RESPONSE-ERROR.
*
 B140-EXIT.
     EXIT.
*
*
 B150-BROWSE-PROCESSING   SECTION.
*********************************************************************
*           PERFORMED FROM:   B100-PAGE-FORWARD                     *
*                             B200-PAGE-BACKWARD                    *
*                             B500-RESET-KEY                        *
*                             C000-INITIAL-ENTRY                    *
*********************************************************************
*
     MOVE LOW-VALUES   TO   VM-BROWSE-MAP.
*
     PERFORM B151-FORMAT-OCCURS
            VARYING SUB FROM 1 BY 1   UNTIL   SUB   GREATER   15.
*
     PERFORM B152-FORMAT-MAP   UNTIL   TS-SUB   GREATER   14
                              OR    STATUS-OF-READ  =   'F'.
*
 B150-ENDBR.
     EXEC CICS ENDBR
              DATASET ('VENDMAST')
     END-EXEC.
*
     IF END-OF-FILE
         MOVE HIGH-VALUES   TO   CA-LAST-KEY
         MOVE 'CURRENT PAGE IS LAST PAGE'
                           TO   MVC-D-MESSAGE
         MOVE ASKIP-BRT    TO   MVC-A-MESSAGE
     ELSE
         MOVE ASKIP-DRK     TO   MVC-A-MESSAGE.
     IF CA-TS-EOF-SWITCH  =   'E'
         NEXT SENTENCE
     ELSE
         IF CA-TS-ITEM   IS GREATER THAN   CA-TS-MAXIMUM
             PERFORM B153-WRITE-TS-RECORD.
*
 B150-EXIT.
     EXIT.
*
 B151-FORMAT-OCCURS   SECTION.
*
*********************************************************************
*           PERFORMED FROM:  B150-BROWSE-PROCESSING                 *
*********************************************************************
*
```

Fig. 17.2 *Continued.*

```
     MOVE SPACES   TO  MVC-D-OCCURS (SUB).
*
 B151-EXIT.
     EXIT.
*
 B152-FORMAT-MAP  SECTION.
**********************************************************************
*              PERFORMED FROM:  B150-BROWSE-PROCESSING              *
**********************************************************************
*
     EXEC CICS READNEXT
               DATASET ('VENDMAST')
               INTO    (VENDOR-MASTER-RECORD)
               RIDFLD  (CA-VENDOR-CODE)
               RESP    (WS-RESP)
     END-EXEC.
*
     IF WS-RESP  =  DFHRESP(NORMAL)
         MOVE 'G'  TO  STATUS-OF-READ
     ELSE
         IF WS-RESP  =  DFHRESP(ENDFILE)
             MOVE 'F'  TO  STATUS-OF-READ
             GO TO  B152-EXIT
         ELSE
             MOVE 'B152-'  TO  WS-RESP-SECTION
             PERFORM Z999-RESPONSE-ERROR.
*
     ADD 1  TO  TS-SUB.
*
     IF TS-SUB  =  1
         MOVE CA-VENDOR-CODE  TO  TS-VENDOR-CD.
*
     IF CA-TS-ITEM  IS GREATER THAN  CA-TS-MAXIMUM
         MOVE CA-VENDOR-CODE  TO  CA-LAST-KEY.
*
     MOVE SPACES             TO  WS-DISPLAY-DATA.
     MOVE TS-SUB             TO  WS-SELECT.
*
     MOVE CA-VEND-1          TO  WS-VENDOR-CD-1.
     MOVE CA-VEND-2          TO  WS-VENDOR-CD-2.
     MOVE CA-VEND-3          TO  WS-VENDOR-CD-3.
     MOVE WS-VENDOR-CODE     TO  WS-VM-KEY.
*
     MOVE VM-VENDOR-NAME     TO  WS-VENDOR-NAME.
     MOVE VM-STREET-ADDRESS  TO  WS-STREET-ADDRESS.
     MOVE VM-CITY-STATE      TO  WS-CITY-STATE.
*
     MOVE WS-DISPLAY-DATA    TO  MVC-D-OCCURS (TS-SUB).
*
 B152-EXIT.
     EXIT.
*
 B153-WRITE-TS-RECORD  SECTION.
```

Fig. 17.2 *Continued.*

```
*********************************************************************
*              PERFORMED FROM:  B150-BROWSE-PROCESSING             *
*********************************************************************
*
     IF END-OF-FILE
         MOVE 'E'  TO  CA-TS-EOF-SWITCH.
*
     ADD 1  TO  CA-TS-MAXIMUM.
*
     MOVE EIBTRMID  TO  TS-EIBTRMID.
     MOVE 'POVB'    TO  TS-QUEUE-NAME.
*
     EXEC CICS WRITEQ TS
               QUEUE  (TS-QUEUE)
               FROM   (TS-RECORD)
               LENGTH (TS-LENGTH)
               ITEM   (CA-TS-ITEM)
     END-EXEC.
*
 B153-EXIT.
     EXIT.
*
 B200-PAGE-BACKWARD  SECTION.
*********************************************************************
*        INVOKED BY HANDLE AID FROM:  B000-PROCESS-MAP             *
*********************************************************************
*
     SUBTRACT 1  FROM  CA-TS-ITEM.
*
     IF CA-TS-ITEM  IS LESS THAN  1
          ADD 1  TO  CA-TS-ITEM
          MOVE 'CURRENT PAGE IS FIRST PAGE TO BE DISPLAYED'
                        TO  MVC-D-MESSAGE
          MOVE ASKIP-BRT  TO  MVC-A-MESSAGE
          MOVE -1         TO  MVC-L-SELECTION
          PERFORM B110-SEND-MAP-DATAONLY
          PERFORM B120-RETURN-TO-CICS.

     PERFORM B130-READ-TS.
     MOVE TS-VENDOR-CD  TO  CA-VENDOR-CODE.
     PERFORM B140-START-BROWSE.
     IF GOOD-STARTBR
         PERFORM B150-BROWSE-PROCESSING
         MOVE -1  TO  MVC-L-SELECTION
     ELSE
         MOVE 'START BROWSE KEY BEYOND END OF FILE'
                        TO  MVC-D-MESSAGE
        MOVE ASKIP-BRT  TO  MVC-A-MESSAGE
        MOVE -1         TO  MVC-L-RESET-CODE.
*
     PERFORM B110-SEND-MAP-DATAONLY.
     PERFORM B120-RETURN-TO-CICS.
*
```

Fig. 17.2 *Continued.*

```
 B200-EXIT.
     EXIT.
*
 B300-TRANSFER-XCTL-TO-MENU  SECTION.
**********************************************************************
*               PERFORMED FROM:  B000-PROCESS-MAP               *
**********************************************************************
*
     PERFORM B310-INITIALIZE-AND-DELETEQ.
*
     EXEC CICS XCTL
               PROGRAM ('POVMAINT')
     END-EXEC.
*
 B300-EXIT.
     EXIT.
*
 B310-INITIALIZE-AND-DELETEQ  SECTION.
*
**********************************************************************
*         PERFORMED FROM:  B300-TRANSFER-XCTL-TO-MENU          *
*                          B400-RETURN-WITH-SELECTION          *
*                          B500-RESET-KEY                      *
*                          B600-END-SESSION                    *
*                          C000-INITIAL-ENTRY                  *
**********************************************************************
*
     MOVE 1           TO  CA-TS-ITEM.
     MOVE ZEROES      TO  CA-TS-MAXIMUM.
     MOVE LOW-VALUES  TO  CA-LAST-KEY.
     MOVE SPACES      TO  CA-TS-EOF-SWITCH.
*
     EXEC CICS IGNORE CONDITION
             QIDERR
     END-EXEC.
*
     MOVE EIBTRMID  TO  TS-EIBTRMID.
     MOVE 'POVB'    TO  TS-QUEUE-NAME.
*
     EXEC CICS DELETEQ TS
             QUEUE (TS-QUEUE)
     END-EXEC.
*
 B310-EXIT.
     EXIT.
*
 B400-RETURN-WITH-SELECTION  SECTION.
**********************************************************************
*         INVOKED BY HANDLE AID FROM:  B000-PROCESS-MAP         *
**********************************************************************
*
     IF (MVC-D-SELECTION  IS GREATER THAN  0)   AND
```

Fig. 17.2 *Continued.*

```
          (MVC-D-SELECTION  IS LESS THAN    16)
          MOVE MVC-D-SELECTION  TO  WS-SELECTION
          MOVE MVC-D-OCCURS (WS-SELECTION)  TO  WS-DISPLAY-DATA
          IF WS-SELECT  =  WS-SELECTION
              PERFORM B310-INITIALIZE-AND-DELETEQ
              MOVE WS-VM-KEY        TO  WS-VENDOR-CODE
              MOVE WS-VENDOR-CD-1  TO  CA-VEND-1
              MOVE WS-VENDOR-CD-2  TO  CA-VEND-2
              MOVE WS-VENDOR-CD-3  TO  CA-VEND-3
              PERFORM B410-XCTL-TO-INVOKING-PROGRAM.
*
      MOVE 'INVALID SELECTION - PLEASE RE-ENTER SELECTION'
                     TO  MVC-D-MESSAGE.
      MOVE ASKIP-BRT  TO  MVC-A-MESSAGE.
*
      MOVE -1         TO  MVC-L-SELECTION.
*
      PERFORM B110-SEND-MAP-DATAONLY.
      PERFORM B120-RETURN-TO-CICS.
*
 B400-EXIT.
     EXIT.
*
 B410-XCTL-TO-INVOKING-PROGRAM  SECTION.
 *******************************************************************
 *          PERFORMED FROM:  B400-RETURN-WITH-SELECTION           *
 *******************************************************************
 *
      IF CA-ADDITION       MOVE 'POVMADDN'  TO  WS-XCTL-PROGRAM
      ELSE  IF CA-CHANGE   MOVE 'POVMCHGE'  TO  WS-XCTL-PROGRAM
      ELSE  IF CA-DELETE   MOVE 'POVMDLET'  TO  WS-XCTL-PROGRAM
      ELSE                 MOVE 'POVMINQY'  TO  WS-XCTL-PROGRAM.
*
      MOVE 'B'  TO  CA-FUNCTION-CODE.
*
      EXEC CICS XCTL
              PROGRAM  (WS-XCTL-PROGRAM)
              COMMAREA (WS-COMMAREA)
              LENGTH   (8)
      END-EXEC.
*
 B410-EXIT.
     EXIT.
*
 B500-RESET-KEY  SECTION.
 *******************************************************************
 *       INVOKED BY HANDLE AID FROM:  B000-PROCESS-MAP            *
 *******************************************************************
 *
      MOVE MVC-D-RESET-CODE   TO  CA-VENDOR-CODE.
      MOVE SPACES             TO  MVC-D-RESET-CODE.
*
```

Fig. 17.2 *Continued.*

```
    PERFORM B310-INITIALIZE-AND-DELETEQ.
    PERFORM B140-START-BROWSE.
    IF GOOD-STARTBR
        PERFORM B150-BROWSE-PROCESSING
        MOVE -1  TO  MVC-L-SELECTION
    ELSE
        MOVE 'START BROWSE KEY IS BEYOND END OF FILE - PLEASE RE-
            'ENTER KEY'    TO  MVC-D-MESSAGE
    MOVE ASKIP-BRT  TO  MVC-A-MESSAGE
    MOVE -1          TO  MVC-L-RESET-CODE.
*
    PERFORM B110-SEND-MAP-DATAONLY.
    PERFORM B120-RETURN-TO-CICS.
*
 B500-EXIT.
    EXIT.
*
 B600-END-SESSION  SECTION.
********************************************************************
*              INVOKED BY :  B000-PROCESS-MAP                     *
********************************************************************
*
    PERFORM B310-INITIALIZE-AND-DELETEQ.
*
    EXEC CICS SEND
              FROM   (WS-CRT-MESSAGE)
              LENGTH (17)
              ERASE
    END-EXEC.
*
    EXEC CICS RETURN
    END-EXEC.
*
 B600-EXIT.
    EXIT.
*
 C000-INITIAL-ENTRY  SECTION.
********************************************************************
*              PERFORMED FROM:  AA00-MAINLINE                     *
********************************************************************
*
    MOVE LOW-VALUES  TO  VM-BROWSE-MAP.
    PERFORM B310-INITIALIZE-AND-DELETEQ.
    PERFORM B140-START-BROWSE.
    IF GOOD-STARTBR
        PERFORM B150-BROWSE-PROCESSING
    ELSE
        MOVE 'START BROWSE KEY BEYOND END OF FILE'
                        TO  MVC-D-MESSAGE
        MOVE ASKIP-BRT  TO  MVC-A-MESSAGE.
    PERFORM C100-SEND-MAP-AND-DATA.
```

Fig. 17.2 *Continued.*

```
*
 C000-EXIT.
     EXIT.
*
 C100-SEND-MAP-AND-DATA   SECTION.
*****************************************************************
*             PERFORMED FROM:  C000-INITIAL-ENTRY              *
*****************************************************************
*
*    PERFORM C110-GET-DATE-AND-TIME.
     PERFORM B111-RESET-OCCURS-ATTRIBUTES
           VARYING SUB   FROM  1 BY 1  UNTIL   SUB  =  16.
*
     MOVE WS-CURRENT-DATE   TO   MVC-D-DATE.
     MOVE WS-MAP-TIME       TO   MVC-D-TIME.
*
     MOVE -1                TO   MVC-L-SELECTION.
     MOVE UNPROT-NUM-FSET   TO   MVC-A-SELECTION.
     MOVE UNPROT-FSET       TO   MVC-A-RESET-CODE.
*
     EXEC CICS SEND
               MAP     ('MAPPOVC')
               MAPSET ('POVMBR1')
               FROM    (VM-BROWSE-MAP)
               ERASE
               CURSOR
     END-EXEC.
*
 C100-EXIT.
     EXIT.
*
 C110-GET-DATE-AND-TIME   SECTION.
*****************************************************************
*             PERFORMED FROM:  C100-SEND-MAP-AND-DATA          *
*****************************************************************
*
     COPY   STPDDTTM.
*
 C110-EXIT.
     EXIT.
*
*
 Z999-RESPONSE-ERROR   SECTION.
*****************************************************************
* INVALID EIBRESP CODE RETURNED DURING EXECUTION OF CICS COMMAND *
*****************************************************************
*
     MOVE WS-RESP   TO   WS-RESP-ERR-CD.
*
     EXEC CICS SEND
               FROM   (WS-RESP-ERROR)
               LENGTH (61)
```

Fig. 17.2 *Continued.*

```
             ERASE
      END-EXEC.
*
      EXEC CICS RETURN
      END-EXEC.
*
 Z999-EXIT.
      EXIT.
```

B100-PAGE-FORWARD.   You can accomplish forward paging by adding 1 to the COMMAREA field CA-TS-ITEM. If CA-TS-ITEM is greater than CA-TS-MAXIMUM, the following logic is executed:

1. If CA-LAST-KEY = HIGH-VALUES, this indicates that the end of the file has been reached on a previous entry into the program; if so, an appropriate message displays.

2. If end of file has not been reached, then the CA-LAST-KEY, the last key read during a previous entry into the program, is moved to CA-VENDOR-CODE to initialize the browse starting key. As pointed out in the program comments, CA-LAST-KEY contains the key of the last vendor displayed on the previous page. The STARTBR command starts the browse with the last record from the previous page displayed at the top of the new page. This can be prevented by:

    ■ Adding 1 to the key, if it is numeric.
    ■ Issuing an additional READNEXT command after the STARTBR command, if the key is not numeric.

If CA-TS-ITEM is equal to or less than CA-TS-MAXIMUM, the program has paged backward and is now paging forward. CA-TS-ITEM is used to read the TS queue. Then the vendor record key obtained, TS-VENDOR-CD, moves to CA-VENDOR-CODE to initialize the browse starting point.

B110-SEND-MAP-DATAONLY.   Prior to the SEND MAP command, all OC-CURS attributes are set by B111-RESET-OCCURS-ATTRIBUTES to ASKIP, FSET. This results in the data displayed in the 15 occurrence fields returning to the program when the RECEIVE MAP command executes. This is necessary if a selection is entered on the screen and PF6 is pressed. FSET moves to the attribute of other enterable fields to ensure that they return to the program on a receive. When data is entered correctly and an incorrect PF key is pressed, an indicative message is sent to the screen. The map contains FRSET; therefore, all FSET attributes on the screen are turned off unless the attribute byte in the symbolic map contains FSET. On a subsequent

RECEIVE MAP command, only fields keyed in immediately prior to the receive return to the program, unless they have been FSET.

B120-RETURN-TO-CICS. This section returns control to CICS with a COMM-AREA containing several fields needed for the paging routines. The new fields are discussed as encountered.

B130-READ-TS. This section sets the TS queue name and reads the record corresponding to the specified item number. The queue name in this program contains eight characters and consists of the four-character terminal ID and the four-character transaction code POVB. Do not substitute the EIB field EIBTRNID for the constant POVB, because if this program is started by another program, EIBTRNID does not equal POVB upon initial entry. If your program contains more than one TS queue, you must always use unique names for the last four positions of queue name.

B140-START-BROWSE. If CA-VENDOR-CODE is greater than the last key on the file, then the NOTFND condition returns in WS-RESP because the RESP option is included on the STARTBR command. This results in an E returning in STATUS-OF-BROWSE. STARTBR sets the starting position in the file at the vendor master file (VENDMAST) vendor code that is greater than or equal to (GTEQ) the code in CA-VENDOR-CODE.

B150-BROWSE-PROCESSING. Initialize the OCCURS fields on the symbolic map to spaces by performing B151-FORMAT-OCCURS. This is necessary when the program is near the end of the file because low-values in a map field are not transmitted on a receive or send of a map. If the last page displayed contains only 5 vendors, the data from the last 10 vendors of the previous page is present at the bottom of the screen. A send containing low-values in the occurrence fields does not erase the last 10 occurrences. Moving spaces to the occurrence fields prior to the send does erase the unwanted information from the screen because spaces are transmitted.

If the end of file is reached in the routine B152-FORMAT-MAP, control passes to B150-ENDBR and STATUS-OF-READ will contain an F, which signals END-OF-FILE. After a browse is complete, terminating the browse by issuing the ENDBR command is good practice. If CA-TS-EOF-SWITCH equals E, this indicates that the end of a file had been reached on a previous entry into the program and the final TS queue has been written. If CA-TS-ITEM is greater than CA-TS-MAXIMUM, the program is paging forward and displaying data for the first time; therefore, a queue record must be written. If CA-TS-ITEM is not greater than CA-TS-MAXIMUM, the program is paging forward after having performed backward paging and the queue record key has already been written to temporary storage.

B152-FORMAT-MAP. The READNEXT command is executed 15 times or until the end of file is reached. The first vendor code of each map is saved in the TS field TS-VENDOR-CD. The first time a new screen is formatted, the last key on the screen is saved in CA-LAST-KEY. This key is used in the page-forward routine. The occurrence fields are formatted and moved to the map.

B153-WRITE-TS-RECORD. This section sets the queue name and writes a TS queue containing the key of the last record displayed on the map. The queue record is written *from* the TS-RECORD in working storage. CA-TS-MAXIMUM increments each time a TS queue record is written. It is used as an upper limit when the program pages backward and then forward again. CA-TS-EOF-SWITCH contains an E when the end of file has been reached. This is a signal that the final TS queue record has been written.

B200-PAGE-BACKWARD. Backward paging is accomplished by subtracting 1 from CA-TS-ITEM. If the result is not less than the first item written to temporary storage, the appropriate queue is retrieved and its data, TS-VENDOR-CD, is used to start the browse.

B300-TRANSFER-XCTL-TO-MENU. This section transfers control back to the submenu program POVMAINT (see map in Fig. 6.3). Deleting TS queues no longer required before exiting a program is good practice.

B310-INITIALIZE-AND-DELETEQ. This section initializes WS-COMMAREA fields required for paging logic and deletes the TS queue. The entire queue must be deleted; individual items of a queue cannot be removed. This program allows the browse starting point to be reset; therefore, you might have to reinitialize certain fields. CA-TS-ITEM is used by paging logic to keep track of the last page displayed. It is added to or subtracted from in forward and backward paging routines. CA-TS-MAXIMUM holds the item number of the last map written to temporary storage. CA-LAST-KEY holds the key of the last browse record read. CA-TS-EOF-SWITCH signals that the end of file has been reached on a READNEXT command.

The IGNORE CONDITION command previously discussed also directs the program to ignore the QIDERR condition if it occurs. The QIDERR condition occurs when a queue to be deleted does not exist. If the program does not provide for this condition, the task ABENDs if the condition occurred. You also can use the HANDLE CONDITION command or RESP option in this situation as shown in Fig. 17.3.

This queue should not normally exist when the program is first entered but might be present if a previous execution of the program had

```
EXEC CICS HANDLE CONDITION
          QIDERR (B310-EXIT)
END-EXEC.

          or

EXEC CICS DELETEQ TS
          QUEUE (TS-QUEUE)
          RESP  (WS-RESP)
END-EXEC.

IF WS-RESP  =  DFHRESP (QIDERR)    OR
   WS-RESP  =  DFHRESP (NORMAL)
     NEXT SENTENCE
ELSE
     MOVE 'B310-' TO WS-RESP-SECTION
     PERFORM Z999-RESPONSE-ERROR.
```

Fig. 17.3 Using HANDLE CONDITION or RESP option to test for an IGNORE condition.

ABENDed. Application programs using TS queues should always delete the queue when it is no longer required because a queue consumes system resources.

B400-RETURN-WITH-SELECTION. This section provides the facility to return a selected code to an invoking program in routine B410-XCTL-TO-IN-VOKING-PROGRAM. The range of the selected vendor is validated. If the selection is within the allowable range, 1 through 15, the map selection is used as a subscript to move the appropriate map occurrence to WS-DIS-PLAY-DATA. The map received returns only FSET fields. For simplicity of understanding, the entire line MVC-D-OCCURS was FSET in routine B111-RESET-OCCURS-ATTRIBUTES.

In practice, employ techniques to minimize the transmission of map data. You might save the occurs selection number and vendor code in the COMM-AREA or temporary storage. At a minimum, break the occurs line into its individual fields and FSET only selection number and vendor code. The WS-DISPLAY-DATA field WS-SELECT is compared to WS-SELECTION. The map selection entry can be in the range of 1 through 15, but the last map displayed might have fewer than 15 entries. Once a valid selection is verified, the TS queue is deleted. The vendor code is then moved to WS-COM-MAREA subfields and a perform issued to transfer control to the appropriate program.

B410-XCTL-TO-INVOKING-PROGRAM. This section assumes that another program transferred control to this program and passed a COM-

MAREA function code for the inquiry or maintenance function. The appropriate program name moves to the field WS-XCTL-PROGRAM; a B moves to CA-FUNCTION-CODE and control transfers to the designated program. Section AA00-MAINLINE of the invoking inquiry or maintenance program contains the following logic to accept the vendor code being transferred as shown in Fig. 17.4.

B500-RESET-KEY.   The browse starting key resets when the user enters a key into the RESET VENDOR CODE field and presses PF9. A start browse is performed and, if successful, the map is formatted and displayed. If the RESET key is beyond the end of the file, the cursor positions at the start of the RESET field and an appropriate message is displayed.

B600-END-SESSION.   Delete the TS queue before returning control to CICS.

C000-INITIAL-ENTRY.   This section deletes the TS queue and initializes related fields. The STARTBR command in routine B140-START-BROWSE sets the starting point at the beginning of the vendor file if this program is started by the menu program discussed in chapter 9; EIBCALEN equals zero upon initial entry into this program and CA-VENDOR-CODE is set to low-values in section AA00-MAINLINE. CA-VENDOR-CODE is a subfield of WS-COMMAREA. B150-BROWSE-PROCESSING formats the screen with the first 15 vendors in the file. If an inquiry or maintenance program had passed a vendor code to this program in COMMAREA, then the first vendor displayed is equal to or greater than that code.

```
IF EIBCALEN = 0
    PERFORM B000-INITIAL-ENTRY
ELSE
    MOVE DFHCOMMAREA TO WS-COMMAREA
    IF CA-BROWSE
        MOVE SPACE        TO  CA-FUNCTION-CODE
        MOVE LOW-VALUES   TO  VM-CONTROL-MAP
        PERFORM C400-VERIFY-VENDOR-FILE-STATUS
        IF GOOD-VERIFY
            PERFORM C500-SEND-DETAIL-MAP-AND-DATA
        ELSE
            PERFORM B100-SEND-CONTROL-MAP-AND-DATA
    ELSE
        IF CA-RECEIVE-CTL-MAP
            PERFORM C000-PROCESS-CONTROL-MAP
        ELSE
            PERFORM . . .
```

Fig. 17.4 Section AA00-MAINLINE logic.

18

CICS Debugging and Testing

Debugging and testing CICS programs is easier in an online environment than it is for batch systems. Debugging refers to the process of removing obvious errors such as ABENDs from a program, while testing refers to providing that a program functions as specified. Many interactive aids exist that make it easy for the CICS programmer to determine and correct the cause of program errors. Some of the aids available include execution diagnostic facility (EDF), interactive testing tools, CICS ABEND determination aids, and CICS dumps.

A programmer familiar with some of these tools can usually diagnose and correct online program problems faster than can be done in a batch environment. Testing may be easier and faster in an online environment, but it must be more thorough than in a batch system. Batch program errors often occur without a user being aware that a problem ever existed. Online program errors may be visible to users at many different locations across the country and can trigger concerned phone calls to data center representatives.

Overtesting a system and its programs, even if it means a delay in implementation, is better than rushing a system into production and correcting errors as they occur.

The best designed and tested systems contain some oversights and errors, but it is important to minimize their occurrence. The credibility and reputation of a data processing installation is not enhanced when there are numerous ABENDs while a user is working with an online system in a production environment.

Execution Diagnostic Facility

EDF is sometimes the only tool you will have to debug and test a CICS program. Use it only to test command-level CICS programs. The execution of CICS programs is intercepted every time a CICS command is encountered and at other points during the execution of the program. Each command displays before execution, and most display after execution is complete. When the commands are displayed, you have the ability to make changes to commands and conditions, display and alter working storage, browse temporary storage queues, display the EIB, and bypass the display of undesired CICS commands. During execution of the program, you can force the program to be ABENDed, with or without a CICS dump. You can terminate EDF after the desired point in the program execution has been reached. You can bring the last map displayed back to the screen at each point at which the program stops to display a command. When a program ABEND occurs, you can use EDF to determine and temporarily correct the error condition.

EDF initiation

EDF is run as a CICS transaction and can be initiated on the terminal being used by entering a TRANSID of CEDF on a cleared screen and pressing ENTER. EDF can be invoked on a different terminal by clearing the screen and entering the ID of the other terminal, after keying in CEDF plus a space (i.e., CEDF T023). When EDF is run on a single terminal, program maps display interspersed between the display of EDF screens. When two terminals are used to run EDF, one screen displays a program's map while a second terminal will display and monitor EDF screens. EDF is most often on one terminal, and I will present a typical EDF session as it would be run using this approach. If you run EDF on two adjacent terminals, the technique used is basically the same.

You can invoke EDF for the browse program discussed in the last chapter as follows:

1. Clear the screen.

2. Key in CEDF and press ENTER.

3. THIS TERMINAL: EDF MODE ON displays.

4. Clear the screen.

5. Key in the TRANSID POVB and press ENTER.

6. The program initiation screen shown in Fig. 18.1 displays.

```
TRANSACTION: POVB   PROGRAM: POVMBROW   TASK NUMBER 0000402   DISPLAY:   00
STATUS:   PROGRAM INITIATION

     EIBTIME     = 112215
     EIBDATE     = 99023
     EIBTRNID    = 'POVB'
     EIBTASKN    = 402
     EIBTRMID    = 'T022'

     EIBCPOSN    = 4
     EIBCALEN    = 0
     EIBAID      = X'7D'                              AT X'0014477B'
     EIBFN       = X'0000'                            AT X'0014477C'
     EIBRCODE    = X'000000000000'                    AT X'0014477E'
     EIBDS       = '........'
+    EIBREQID    = '........'




ENTER:   CONTINUE
PF1 : UNDEFINED            PF2 : SWITCH HEX/CHAR   PF3 : END EDF SESSION
PF4 : SUPPRESS DISPLAYS    PF5 : WORKING STORAGE   PF6 : USER DISPLAY
PF7 : SCROLL BACK          PF8 : SCROLL FORWARD    PF9 : STOP CONDITIONS
PF10: PREVIOUS DISPLAY     PF11: UNDEFINED         PF12: UNDEFINED
```

Fig. 18.1 EDF program initiation screen.

Program initiation screen

The program initiation screen shown in Fig. 18.1 displays the EIB as it exists upon initial entry into the program. Line 1 of the screen is basically the same for all EDF displays and contains:

- TRANSACTION: POVB—This is the TRANSID associated with the task. For this screen, it is the TRANSID entered to initiate the browse program. If the browse is invoked from the inquiry program, the TRANSID of the inquiry program (POVI) displays on this line until the program executes a return with a TRANSID of POVB. Look at the displayed EIB fields and note that the EIB field EIBTRNID contains the same TRANSID displayed on line 1.

- PROGRAM: POVMBROW—This is the program name associated with the browse program.

- TASK NUMBER 0000402—This is a sequential task number assigned by the system. This task number remains the same until the program executes a return. A return terminates the current task, and, if the return contains a TRANSID, a new task is initiated and assigned the next available sequential number. Note that the EIB field EIBTASKN contains this same task number.

■ DISPLAY: 00—This reflects the current screen being displayed. As succeeding screens display, you can view previous displays. The number displayed next to DISPLAY decrements by one for each prior screen displayed, i.e., –01, –02, etc.

Line 2 contains the status of the EDF screen displayed. The status of this first screen is PROGRAM INITIATION. The status changes as different EDF screens display.

Line 3 for this display is blank, but displays the COMMAREA, if one existed.

The remaining EIB fields commonly referenced are:

■ EIBTIME and EIBDATE—These contain the time and date at which the transaction was initiated.

■ EIBTRMID—The terminal at which the transaction is running.

■ EIBCPOSN—The position of the cursor. We initiated the transaction by entering a four-position TRANSID; therefore, the cursor ends up in screen position 4.

■ EIBCALEN—The COMMAREA length. This length is always equal to zero when a transaction is initiated by keying a TRANSID on the screen and pressing ENTER. If a program is invoked by another program that passes a COMMAREA or if it is returned with a TRANSID and a COMMAREA, then EIBCALEN equals the length of that COMMAREA.

■ EIBAID—This contains the hexadecimal code associated with the AID key that was last pressed. X'7D' is the code associated with the ENTER key. See appendix A.2 for a list of the decimal values associated with the AID keys.

The PF keys at the bottom of the screen change for some EDF screens, but a given function is always associated with the same PF keys. I will discuss the more important PF keys in succeeding EDF screen examples. ENTER: CONTINUE displays, above the PF key instructions. EDF progresses if you press the ENTER key. Keep pressing ENTER until you come to the EDF screen display in Fig. 18.2. Since EDF stops at every CICS command, a few intervening screens display for the ASSIGN and ADDRESS commands contained in the date and time routine shown in Appendix B for copy library member STPDDTTM.

ABOUT-TO-EXECUTE command screen

EDF displays a screen prior to the execution of a CICS command. This is illustrated by the highlighted status field on line 2 of Fig. 18.2. The highlighted CICS command about to be executed is shown on line 3. The command EXEC CICS SEND is followed on succeeding lines by its options

```
TRANSACTION: POVB   PROGRAM: POVMBROW   TASK NUMBER 0000402   DISPLAY:  00
STATUS:  ABOUT TO EXECUTE COMMAND
EXEC CICS SEND MAP
 MAP('MAPPOVC')
 FROM('..............01/23/99...11.22.15............................)
 MAPSET('POVMBR1')
 TERMINAL
 ERASE




 OFFSET:X'00132C'     LINE:00268          EIBFN=X'1804'


ENTER:   CONTINUE
PF1 : UNDEFINED          PF2 : SWITCH HEX/CHAR    PF3 : UNDEFINED
PF4 : SUPPRESS DISPLAYS  PF5 : WORKING STORAGE    PF6 : USER DISPLAY
PF7 : SCROLL BACK        PF8 : SCROLL FORWARD     PF9 : STOP CONDITIONS
PF10: PREVIOUS DISPLAY   PF11: UNDEFINED          PF12: ABEND USER TASK
```

Fig. 18.2 EDF about-to-execute command screen.

and arguments. EDF sometimes displays a default option, such as TERMI-NAL, which was not coded in the program's CICS command. You can over-type any EDF display at which the cursor stops when you press the TAB key. You can negate a command by overtyping the command function with either NOP or NOOP. You can alter the arguments for options such as MAP, MAPSET, and FROM by overtyping the existing data. You can overtype in character format or can press PF2 to switch to a hexadecimal display and make the change in hex. If an argument displays a period, it is best to switch to hex if a change must be made to the field.

At the bottom of the screen above the instructions, two or three fields might display:

- OFFSET: X'00132C'—This is the program CLIST offset and may be used to locate the CICS command about to execute.

- LINE: 0268—This is the line number corresponding to the translator printout of the CICS program. LINE only displays if the program was translated using the DEBUG option. The DEBUG option generates larger program load modules because the translator line numbers must be saved to be displayed.

- EIBFN = X'1804'—This EIB function code is updated when a CICS command has been executed. X'1804' represents the SEND MAP command.

Program map display screen

Press the ENTER key to continue the EDF session. The next screen displayed is the program map being sent. It is similar to the screen shown in Fig. 1.11. You can enter data on this display of the map or you can wait until the next display of the same map. Data entered on this map is remembered and need not be entered again on the next display of the map.

Command execution complete screen

A command execution complete screen similar to that shown in Fig. 18.3 is displayed at the completion of most CICS commands. ABEND, RETURN, and XCTL do not display a command execution complete screen. The EDF map displays two new fields: the response field and EIBRESP. The response field shows RESPONSE: NORMAL. Response is usually NORMAL unless a response condition has occurred, in which case, the invoked condition will be displayed in the response field. You can use the response field to test various conditions by overtyping the contents of the response field. A program then follows the logic path that would have occurred if the condition had actually happened. The EIB field EIBRESP contains the response code corresponding to the invoked condition, and is equal to zero on a normal re-

```
TRANSACTION: POVB    PROGRAM: POVMBROW    TASK NUMBER 0000402    DISPLAY:   00
STATUS:   COMMAND EXECUTION COMPLETE
EXEC CICS SEND MAP
  MAP('MAPPOVC')
  FROM('..............01/23/99...11.22.15...........................  ...)
  MAPSET('POVMBR1')
  TERMINAL
  ERASE




  OFFSET:X'00132C'    LINE:00268        EIBFN=X'1804'
  RESPONSE: NORMAL                      EIBRESP=0

ENTER:  CONTINUE
PF1 : UNDEFINED            PF2 : SWITCH HEX/CHAR    PF3 : END EDF SESSION
PF4 : SUPPRESS DISPLAYS    PF5 : WORKING STORAGE    PF6 : USER DISPLAY
PF7 : SCROLL BACK          PF8 : SCROLL FORWARD     PF9 : STOP CONDITIONS
PF10: PREVIOUS DISPLAY     PF11: UNDEFINED          PF12: ABEND USER TASK
```

Fig. 18.3 EDF command execution complete screen.

```
TRANSACTION: POVB    PROGRAM: POVMBROW    TASK NUMBER 0000402   DISPLAY:   00
ADDRESS: 0010060C                          WORKING STORAGE
00100600    000000                                  D7D6E5D4   ............POVM
00100610    000004   C2D9D6E6 E2C5E2E2 C9D6D540 C3D6D4D7   BROWSESSION COMP
00100620    000014   D3C5E3C5 C4000000 00404040 40404040   LETED...........
00100630    000024   40000000 00000000 00000000 00000000   ................
00100640    000034   00000000 00000000 00000000 00000000   ................
00100650    000044   00000000 00000000 00000000 00000000   ................
00100660    000054   00000000 00000000 00000000 00000000   ................
00100670    000064   00000000 00000000 00000000 00000000   ................
00100680    000074   00000000 00000000 00000000 00000000   ................
00100690    000084   00000000 00000000 00000000 00000000   ................
001006A0    000094   00000000 00000000 00000000 00000000   ................
001006B0    0000A4   00000000 00000000 00000000 00000000   ................
001006C0    0000B4   00000000 00000000 00000000 00000000   ................
001006D0    0000C4   00000000 00000000 00000000 00000000   ................
001006E0    0000D4   00000000 00000000 00000000 00000000   ................
001006F0    0000E4   00000000 00000000 00000000 00000000   ................


ENTER:   CURRENT DISPLAY
PF1 : UNDEFINED              PF2 : BROWSE TEMP STORAGE   PF3 : UNDEFINED
PF4 : EIB DISPLAY            PF5 : WORKING STORAGE       PF6 : USER DISPLAY
PF7 : SCROLL BACK HALF       PF8 : SCROLL FORWARD HALF   PF9 : UNDEFINED
PF10: SCROLL BACK FULL       PF11: SCROLL FORWARD FULL   PF12: REMEMBER DISPLAY
```

Fig. 18.4 EDF working-storage screen.

turn. A program can examine this code by including the RESP option on CICS commands. You can end the EDF session at any screen that displays the instruction PF3: END EDF SESSION.

Working-storage display screen

A working-storage screen similar to Fig. 18.4 displays if you press the PF5 keys while Fig. 18.3 displays. The working-storage screen displays the highlighted starting address of main storage, followed on succeeding lines by a column of main-storage address, working-storage offsets, four columns of hexadecimal data, and the corresponding 16 bytes of data in character format. Any data in the program's working storage can be changed by overtyping either the hexadecimal data or the character data and pressing the ENTER key. Working storage may be scrolled through in a forward or backward direction depending on the PF key used. The programmer-defined working-storage literal END WS PROGNAME signals the end of working storage. Press PF2 to invoke the CEBR screen. Press PF4 to display the EIB from the working-storage screen. Press PF6: USER DISPLAY to redisplay the user map last displayed. Normally, up to the last 10 CICS command screens are saved for possible redisplay. The working-

```
CEBR (from EDF) TS QUEUE  CEBRT022 RECORD      1 OF    0    COL   1 OF    0
ENTER COMMAND ===>
        *********************  TOP OF QUEUE  ********************************
        *********************  BOTTOM OF QUEUE  *****************************




TEMPORARY STORAGE QUEUE CEBRT022              IS EMPTY
PF1 : HELP                 PF2 : SWITCH HEX/CHAR     PF3 : RETURN TO EDF
PF4 : VIEW TOP             PF5 : VIEW BOTTOM         PF6 : REPEAT LAST FIND
PF7 : SCROLL BACK HALF     PF8 : SCROLL FORWARD HALF PF9 : UNDEFINED
PF10: SCROLL BACK FULL     PF11: SCROLL FORWARD FULL PF12: UNDEFINED
```

Fig. 18.5 CEBR browse temporary storage screen.

storage screen or any EDF display that has PF12 : REMEMBER DISPLAY, allows you to press this key to save the current screen for future display. You can overtype the highlighted main-storage address at the top of the screen with the address of any area of main storage that is in the region or partition. Only the program's working storage can be altered; other main storage is display only. Press the ENTER key to get out of the working-storage display and to return to the current display, Fig. 18.3, for this example.

CEBR screen

The CEBR screen shown in Fig. 18.5 can be accessed from the working-storage screen discussed above by pressing PF2 while on that screen. CEBR is used to browse temporary storage queues. Line 1 of the CEBR screen initially displays the default queue name CEBRT022, which consists of CEBR plus the four-character terminal name T022. This queue name can be overtyped with the desired queue name; for our browse program we would type T022POVB. The queue name can also be entered on the command line by entering the command QUEUE followed by the queue name:

```
ENTER COMMAND ===> QUEUE T022POVB.
```

Line 1 also indicates the current item and the total number of items in the queue. This is shown by `RECORD`   × OF   y, where x is the current item and y is the last item in the queue.

Line 1 also indicates the current column displayed and the total number of characters in the queue as *COL* × *OF* *y* where x represents the current column displayed and y the number of the last character in the queue.

CEBR Commands.   Additional commands may be entered on the command line in a fashion similar to the QUEUE command discussed above. Some of these commands are:

- TOP—Displays the first page of the queue. PF4 performs this same function.
- BOTTOM—Displays the last page of the queue. PF5 also displays the bottom page.
- LINE—Sets the line number entered following this command to the second line of the displayed queue. PF7 and PF8 can also be used to scroll backward or forward.
- COLUMN—Shifts the displayed queue to start at the column number that is entered following this command. PF10 and PF11 can be used to shift the displayed screen left or right.
- PURGE—Erases the queue.
- FIND—Searches forward to find the string entered following this command. The item in the queue containing the string displays as the second line on the page. The search argument is preceded by a delimiter, such as a slash (/). Any character not included in the string can be used as a delimiter. The same delimiter must immediately follow any string that contains a blank. PF6 enables you to repeat the last find executed. Some examples of the FIND command are:

```
FIND /JOHN
FIND /JOHN SMITH/
FIND '01/23/99
FIND '/99 A'
```

Other PF keys display a help screen, switch from character to *hex*, or return to the working storage display in EDF. You can also invoke CEBR from a screen outside of EDF by entering CEBR on a cleared screen. The commands and function keys are similar to those just described.

RETURN EDF screen

Press ENTER to continue and the EDF display moves to Fig. 18.6, the return screen. The return EDF screen only displays an about-to-execute

```
TRANSACTION: POVB   PROGRAM: POVMBROW   TASK NUMBER 0000402   DISPLAY:  00
STATUS:  ABOUT TO EXECUTE COMMAND
EXEC CICS RETURN
 TRANSID('POVB')
 COMMAREA(' 1..........')
 LENGTH(12)




 OFFSET:X'0012C4'     LINE:00231          EIBFN=X'0E08'

ENTER:  CONTINUE
PF1 : UNDEFINED          PF2 : SWITCH HEX/CHAR    PF3 : UNDEFINED
PF4 : SUPPRESS DISPLAYS  PF5 : WORKING STORAGE    PF6 : USER DISPLAY
PF7 : SCROLL BACK        PF8 : SCROLL FORWARD     PF9 : STOP CONDITIONS
PF10: PREVIOUS DISPLAY   PF11: UNDEFINED          PF12: ABEND USER TASK
```

Fig. 18.6 Return EDF screen.

screen. As mentioned previously, there is no command execution complete
screen for RETURN, ABEND, and XCTL commands. The arguments of
TRANSID and COMMAREA can be overtyped if this assists in testing.

Program termination screen

The program termination screen shown in Fig. 18.7 displays when you
press ENTER while the return screen displays.

Task termination screen

The task termination screen shown in Fig. 18.8 displays next when you
press the ENTER key. You have the option at this point to continue or to
end the EDF session. Overtype the NO next to REPLY with YES to continue
the EDF session or just press the ENTER key with NO displayed to end the
session. The browse screen shown in Fig. 1.11 redisplays whether or not the
session is continued and a new task initiates when you press an AID key.

Program initiation redisplayed

The program initiation screen shown in Fig. 18.9 displays if you overtyped
YES on the task termination screen in Fig. 18.8 and pressed ENTER to continue the EDF session. This program initiation screen is similar to the

```
TRANSACTION: POVB    PROGRAM: POVMBROW    TASK NUMBER 0000402    DISPLAY;  00
STATUS:   PROGRAM TERMINATION




















ENTER:  CONTINUE
PF1 : UNDEFINED          PF2 : SWITCH HEX/CHAR    PF3 : END EDF SESSION
PF4 : SUPPRESS DISPLAYS  PF5 : WORKING STORAGE    PF6 : USER DISPLAY
PF7 : SCROLL BACK        PF8 : SCROLL FORWARD     PF9 : STOP CONDITIONS
PF10: PREVIOUS DISPLAY   PF11: UNDEFINED          PF12: ABEND USER TASK
```

Fig. 18.7 EDF program termination screen

```
TRANSACTION: POVB    PROGRAM: POVMBROW    TASK NUMBER 0000402    DISPLAY:  00
STATUS:   TASK TERMINATION



















TO CONTINUE EDF SESSION REPLY YES                            REPLY: NO
ENTER:  CONTINUE
PF1 : UNDEFINED          PF2 : SWITCH HEX/CHAR    PF3 : END EDF SESSION
PF4 : SUPPRESS DISPLAYS  PF5 : WORKING STORAGE    PF6 : USER DISPLAY
PF7 : SCROLL BACK        PF8 : SCROLL FORWARD     PF9 : STOP CONDITIONS
PF10: PREVIOUS DISPLAY   PF11: UNDEFINED          PF12: UNDEFINED
```

Fig. 18.8 EDF task termination screen.

```
TRANSACTION: POVB    PROGRAM: POVMBROW    TASK NUMBER 0000416    DISPLAY:   00
STATUS:  PROGRAM INITIATION
    COMMAREA        = ' 1.........'
    EIBTIME         = 112327
    EIBDATE         = 99023
    EIBTRNID        = 'POVB'
    EIBTASKN        = 416
    EIBTRMID        = 'T022'

    EIBCPOSN        = 1441
    EIBCALEN        = 19
    EIBAID          = X'7D'                              AT X'0014477B'
    EIBFN           = X'0000'                            AT X'0014477C'
    EIBRCODE        = X'000000000000'                    AT X'0014477E'
    EIBDS           = '........'
+   EIBREQID        = '........'



ENTER:   CONTINUE
PF1 : UNDEFINED           PF2 : SWITCH HEX/CHAR    PF3 : END EDF SESSION
PF4 : SUPPRESS DISPLAYS   PF5 : WORKING STORAGE    PF6 : USER DISPLAY
PF7 : SCROLL BACK         PF8 : SCROLL FORWARD     PF9 : STOP CONDITIONS
PF10: PREVIOUS DISPLAY    PF11: UNDEFINED          PF12: UNDEFINED
```

Fig. 18.9 EDF succeeding entry program initiation screen.

screen displayed in Fig. 18.1; however, I want to point out a few significant changes. Note that the task number at the top of the screen and in EIB-TASKN has changed from 402 to 416. The COMMAREA now displays on line 3, and its length is shown in the COMMAREA length field EIBCALEN. The cursor position (EIBCPOSN) reflects the position of the cursor on the screen before an AID key is pressed.

EDF stop conditions screen

The display on condition screen shown in Fig. 18.10 displays if you press PF9 on any EDF screen that lists PF9 : STOP CONDITIONS. This screen allows you to suppress the display of EDF screens you do not want to view in order to stop only at specified commands or upon encountering specific conditions. You can suppress displays of the EDF screens presented in the sample EDF session until the return screen displays. Just enter RETURN next to EXEC CICS in Fig. 18.10 and press the PF4 key as indicated in the instructions to suppress displays and continue processing. This screen allows you to enter a handle condition at which you wish to stop, next to CICS EXCEPTIONAL CONDITION. You can enter conditions such as NOTFND and PGMIDERR next to this field identifier and press PF4 until one of the indicated conditions is encountered. You can continue pressing PF4 to suppress displays on any EDF screen that contains the PF4 : SUPPRESS DISPLAYS instruction.

You can stop at specific line numbers if the program is translated with the DEBUG option that generated line numbers. The line number is the translator listing line number and must contain six digits. It is the line number at which a command starts. You can also enter the program offset corresponding to the command.

Generally, this screen is used to bypass the display of undesired EDF screens by entering a command beyond those you wish to suppress. For instance, in a browse program you press the ENTER key numerous times to get past a series of READNEXT commands in an EDF session. You can find the command following the READNEXT command in your program and set a stop condition to suppress all displays until that command is reached.

Program ABEND display

A screen similar to that shown in Fig. 18.11 displays when an ABEND occurs. A common program ABEND is the ASRA, a four-character code displayed on the screen, denoting that a program data exception has occurred. This is generally the result of nonnumeric data being present in a numeric field used in a program calculation. Normally, an ASRA occurs between two CICS commands and determining which instruction caused the ABEND is difficult. One of two CICS commands is sometimes included in a test version of a program to determine where the ASRA occurred: ASKTIME and/or

```
TRANSACTION: POVB   PROGRAM: POVMBROW   TASK NUMBER 0000416   DISPLAY:  00
DISPLAY ON CONDITION:-

      COMMAND:              EXEC CICS
      OFFSET:                    X'......'
      LINE NUMBER:               ........
      CICS EXCEPTIONAL CONDITION:
      ANY CICS ERROR CONDITION         YES
      TRANSACTION ABEND                YES
      NORMAL TASK TERMINATION          YES
      ABNORMAL TASK TERMINATION        YES




ENTER:   CURRENT DISPLAY
PF1 : UNDEFINED          PF2 : UNDEFINED          PF3 : UNDEFINED
PF4 : SUPPRESS DISPLAYS  PF5 : WORKING STORAGE    PF6 : USER DISPLAY
PF7 : UNDEFINED          PF8 : UNDEFINED          PF9 : UNDEFINED
PF10: UNDEFINED          PF11: UNDEFINED          PF12: REMEMBER DISPLAY
```

Fig. 18.10 EDF stop conditions screen.

```
TRANSACTION: POVB    PROGRAM: POVMBROW    TASK NUMBER 0000416    DISPLAY:  00
STATUS:  PROGRAM INITIATION

   EIBTIME      = 112745
   EIBDATE      = 99023
   EIBTRNID     = 'POVB'
   EIBTASKN     = 416
   EIBTRMID     = 'T022'

   EIBCPOSN     = 1441
   EIBCALEN     = 19
   EIBAID       = X'7D'                             AT X'0014477B'
   EIBFN        = X'0000'                           AT X'0014477C'
   EIBRCODE     = X'000000000000'                   AT X'0014477E'
   EIBDS        = '........'
+  EIBREQID     = '........'
                                     INTERRUPT: DATA EXCEPTION
  ABEND :    ASRA                     PSW: X'087C0008D013292A'

ENTER:   CONTINUE
PF1 : UNDEFINED            PF2 : SWITCH HEX/CHAR     PF3 : END EDF SESSION
PF4 : SUPPRESS DISPLAYS    PF5 : WORKING STORAGE     PF6 : USER DISPLAY
PF7 : SCROLL BACK          PF8 : SCROLL FORWARD      PF9 : STOP CONDITIONS
PF10: PREVIOUS DISPLAY     PF11: UNDEFINED           PF12: UNDEFINED
```

Fig. 18.11 EDF ABEND screen.

ENTER. Remember to remove such commands and any test data placed in working storage from a program before compiling its production version. The ASKTIME command was discussed in Chapter 10. The format of the ENTER command is:

```
EXEC CICS ENTER
          TRACEID (nnn)
END-EXEC.
```

This command results in an entry to a CICS trace table and will not affect the execution of your program, but it can help you to narrow in on a program ASRA. The TRACEID entry (nnn) can be any number between 000 and 199, and is displayed when EDF stops at the ENTER command.

The ASKTIME and ENTER commands can be placed between other CICS commands and, unless suppressed, display on an EDF screen as other CICS commands do. If several ASKTIME commands are placed in a program, you must keep track of which one is being executed. This may be done manually or by placing an indicative field at the beginning of working storage to signal which ASKTIME command is being executed. You can then press PF5 to display working storage and visually check this field. The ENTER command has an advantage over ASKTIME in that you can assign a sequence number to TRACEID that displays on the EDF screen and enables you to determine which of multiple commands is being executed. You can also move suspected data fields to the beginning of working storage to make them easier to find and examine when working storage is displayed.

ABEND a CICS task

A CICS task can be ABENDed from any screen displaying PF12 : ABEND USER TASK. Pressing PF12 prompts you to ENTER ABEND CODE AND REQUEST ABEND AGAIN. You can ABEND the task with or without a dump. If a dump is desired, you enter the desired ABEND code you want to show up on the dump next to REPLY :, which displays. If no dump is needed, just enter NO and press PF12 again to ABEND the task.

Interactive Testing Tools

There are excellent interactive testing tools available that can significantly decrease the time required to test and debug CICS programs. EDF has limitations that are overcome by some of the interactive testing tools. Debugging tools I have worked with do not require you to modify your program in order to stop between CICS commands. Your program can be stopped at any section or paragraph name or at various statement numbers. You can display and change most EIB and working-storage fields by reference to their symbolic names. The point at which a program is to be stopped can be altered at various break points as the execution of a program progresses and the flow of a program's logic can be altered. I use EDF along with these tools and find that they complement one another. I use EDF to trace the basic flow of a program and resort to an interactive testing tool in order to diagnose more difficult problems.

CICS Dumps

CICS dumps are sometimes used in order to determine the cause of an ABEND that occurs in a production environment. CICS dumps are similar to batch dumps and their discussion is beyond the scope of this book.

CICS ABEND Determination Aids

There are CICS ABEND determination aids that, when available, practically eliminate the need for CICS dumps. Aids that I have worked with allow you to display online a menu listing all ABENDS that have occurred in the test and production system. You can select the ABEND that occurred in your program and display the information and data unique to it. There is no need to wait until a dump is printed and then search through a series of dumps to find the one that is yours. The information is displayed in a user-friendly fashion and it is easy for you to determine the cause of the ABEND. The online ABEND determination aid is much easier to work with and master than is the dump reading.

CICS Testing Techniques

Although it is always desirable to have files defined before testing begins, occasionally there may be a time lag between the times when a program is written and when the needed files are available. I recommend testing programs as soon as possible after they are written. Programs often contain numerous details that can be forgotten with the passing of time. If no test data is available, create some in the test version of your program. Instead of performing a section that reads a file, perform a special section written for testing that moves constant data to the fields of the required record layout. When the required file becomes available, remove the test data from your program. The program may later encounter some errors when the live file's data is used, but you will have eliminated most other errors and the program flow should be running smoothly.

19

Color and Reverse-Video Attribute Extensions

The use of color attributes and reverse video in CICS applications should eventually become commonplace due to the widespread availability of color monitors. The use of these attributes is similar to the use of attributes described in chapters 6 and 7. Essentially all that is required to use these features is to include an additional entry in the DFHMSD macro and one or two extra entries in the DFHMDF macro when defining the BMS map.

The generated symbolic map includes four additional single-character fields. Handled in a fashion similar to other attributes, these fields must be provided for when creating user-friendly symbolic maps. They are automatically included by screen generators. Figure 19.1 shows a BMS map that defines some of the fields of the screen shown in Fig. 6.3 with color attributes. Asterisks have been inserted in column 1, between macros, to increase readability. The map is used in this chapter to demonstrate the use of the color and highlighting features of CICS.

Extended Attributes

The use of extended attributes requires supporting entries on the DFHMSD and DFHMDF macros of the BMS map. The DFHMSD entry defines whether extended attributes are supported, while the DFHMDF entries define attributes such as color and reverse-video for individual fields.

Fig. 19.1   Color BMS map attribute usage.

```
          PRINT NOGEN
POVMNT1   DFHMSD TYPE=MAP,                                          X
                 TIOAPFX=YES,                                       X
                 CTRL=(FREEKB,FRSET),                               X
                 TERM=3270,                                         X
                 LANG=COBOL,                                        X
                 EXTATT=YES,                                        X
                 MODE=INOUT
*
MAPPOVM   DFHMDI SIZE=(24,80),                                      X
                 COLUMN=01,                                         X
                 LINE=01
*
          DFHMDF POS=(01,27),                                       X
                 LENGTH=25,                                         X
                 ATTRB=ASKIP,                                       X
                 COLOR=YELLOW,                                      X
                 INITIAL='ABC MANUFACTURING COMPANY'
*
          DFHMDF POS=(01,72),                                       X
                 LENGTH=07,                                         X
                 ATTRB=ASKIP,                                       X
                 COLOR=TURQUOISE,                                   X
                 INITIAL='POVMNT1'
*
          DFHMDF POS=(02,23),                                       X
                 LENGTH=32,                                         X
                 ATTRB=ASKIP,                                       X
                 COLOR=YELLOW,                                      X
                 HILIGHT=REVERSE,                                   X
                 INITIAL='VENDOR FILE MAINTENANCE SUB-MENU'
                    .
                    .
                    .


          DFHMDF POS=(11,23),                                       X
                 LENGTH=10,                                         X
                 ATTRB=ASKIP,                                       X
                 COLOR=GREEN,                                       X
                 HILIGHT=REVERSE,                                   X
                 INITIAL='SELECTION: '
*
MSELECT   DFHMDF POS=(11,34),                                       X
                 LENGTH=01,                                         X
                 COLOR=RED,                                         X
                 HILIGHT=REVERSE,                                   X
                 ATTRB=(UNPROT,IC),                                 X
```

Fig. 19.1 *Continued.*

```
                   INITIAL=' '
*
          DFHMDF POS=(11,36),                                    X
                 LENGTH=01,                                      X
                 ATTRB=PROT

          DFHMDF POS=(16,25),                                    X
                 LENGTH=30,                                      X
                 ATTRB=ASKIP,                                    X
                 COLOR=TURQUOISE,                                X
                 INITIAL='KEY IN SELECTION   -PRESS ENTER'
*
          DFHMDF POS=(18,25),                                    X
                 LENGTH=30,                                      X
                 ATTRB=ASKIP,                                    X
                 COLOR=TURQUOISE,                                X
                 INITIAL='END OF SESSION     -PRESS CLEAR'
*
MAPMESG DFHMDF POS=(24,01),                                      X
                 LENGTH=79,                                      X
                 COLOR=GREEN,                                    X
                 ATTRB=ASKIP
*
          DFHMSD TYPE=FINAL
                 END
```

EXTATT operand and parameters

The following excerpt from Fig. 19.1 shows the format of the DFHMSD macro that supports extended attributes:

```
POVMNT1  DFHMSD TYPE=MAP,            X
                TIOAPFX=YES,         X
                CTRL=(FREEKB,FRSET), X
                TERM=3270,           X
                LANG=COBOL,          X
                EXTATT=YES,          X
                MODE=INOUT
```

Note that this macro is similar to the other DFHMSD macros that were defined and used in prior BMS maps. The only additional entry, EX-TATT=YES, is required to support extended attributes. The permissible parameters for the EXTATT operand and their meanings are as follows:

```
                   ┌─ NO
         EXTATT= ──┤  YES
                   └  MAPONLY
```

- NO—This parameter, which is the default, indicates that the BMS map does *not* use extended attributes.

- YES—The inclusion of this parameter indicates that extended attributes are to be used with the BMS map and that supporting entries are to be generated as part of the symbolic map.

- MAPONLY—This parameter is used to indicate that extended attributes will be used by the physical map but not by the symbolic map. The symbolic map entries that support extended attributes will *not* be generated. A SEND MAP, which includes the physical map, displays the terminal's default colors.

The COLOR operand

The following DFHMDF entry, taken from Fig. 19.1, is typical of those supporting color attributes:

```
DFHMDF POS=(01,27),                          X
       LENGTH=25,                            X
       ATTRB=ASKIP,                          X
       COLOR=YELLOW,                         X
       INITIAL='ABC MANUFACTURING COMPANY'
```

This macro is similar to other DFHMDF macros that were defined and used in prior BMS maps. The only new entry, COLOR=YELLOW, is included to indicate that the value ABC MANUFACTURING COMPANY is to be displayed in yellow. Colors used in examples in this chapter are for illustration of their use only; they are not recommended combinations. The permissible parameters for the COLOR operand are shown in Fig. 19.2.

The HILIGHT operand

Figure 19.3 shows the DFHMDF entries, taken from Fig. 19.1, that are typical of those supporting HILIGHT attributes.

The only new entry used is the HILIGHT operand, which indicates that the lines are to be displayed in reverse-video. The entry for Line 11, column 23, shows how to display a field that contains an initial value in reverse video. Reverse video indicates that the foreground and background colors

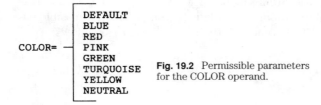

Fig. 19.2 Permissible parameters for the COLOR operand.

```
         DFHMDF POS=(11,23),                         X
                LENGTH=10,                           X
                ATTRB=ASKIP,                         X
                COLOR=GREEN,                         X
                HILIGHT=REVERSE,                     X
                INITIAL='SELECTION:'

MSELECT  DFHMDF POS=(11,34),                         X
                LENGTH=01,                           X
                COLOR=RED,                           X
                HILIGHT=REVERSE,                     X
                ATTRB=(UNPROT,IC),                   X
                INITIAL=' '
```

Fig. 19.3 DFHMDF entries typical of those supporting HILIGHT attributes.

are to be reversed on the screen. For example, a light color that is normally displayed on a dark background will be displayed as a dark color on a light background. The SELECTION: literal displays as dark letters on a green background. The initial selection entry field in line 11, column 34, displays as spaces in a red reverse video field.

The permissible parameters for the HILIGHT operand depend on the terminal used. The possible entries are:

```
                       ┌─ OFF
                       │  BLINK
HIGHLIGHT= ───────────│  REVERSE
                       │  UNDERLINE
                       └─
```

- OFF—This parameter is the default; it indicates that highlighting is *not* used.

- BLINK—BLINK indicates that a field is to be alternately displayed and not displayed. This blinking effect causes irritation to many viewers, and its use is generally not recommended.

- REVERSE—This parameter is included to indicate that the foreground and background colors of a field are to be reversed.

- UNDERLINE—A field for which this parameter is indicated will be displayed with underscore characters.

Extended Attribute Symbolic Maps

Symbolic map entries are generated for all BMS map DFHMDF macros that contain a label. For example, the BMS map in Fig. 19.1, contains two labels MSELECT and MAPMESG. Two symbolic map entries are generated for this map. The symbolic map entry for the MAPMESG field is similar to that shown in Fig. 19.4.

```
01  MAPPOVMI.
    . . .
    02  FILLER                      PIC X(12).
    02  MAPMESGL                    PIC S9(4) COMP.
    02  MAPMESGF                    PIC X.
    02  FILLER REDEFINES MAPMESGF.
        03  MAPMESGA                PIC X.
    02  FILLER                      PIC X(4).
    02  MAPMESGI                    PIC X(79).

01  MAPPOVMO REDEFINES MAPPOVMI.
    . . .
    02  FILLER                      PIC X(12).
    02  FILLER                      PIC X(3).
    02  MAPMESGC                    PIC X.
    02  MAPMESGP                    PIC X.
    02  MAPMESGH                    PIC X.
    02  MAPMESGV                    PIC X.
    02  MAPMESGO                    PIC X(79).
```

Fig. 19.4 Sample symbolic map entry for the MAPMESG field.

This symbolic map contains four new output map entry *types* not present in previously discussed symbolic maps. The entries are MAPMESGC, MAPMESGP, MAPMESGH, and MAPMESGV. Note the suffixes C, P, H, and V used for these entries. Four additional entries containing these suffixes are generated for each BMS map DFHMDF field containing a label. The fields are always generated in the indicated sequence and must be provided for if you create your own more-readable symbolic maps. The field suffixes are defined as follows:

```
C = Color
P = Program Symbol
H = Highlight
V = Validation
```

The only entries from the above list discussed in this text are the color and highlight attributes. The color and highlight characteristics of a field may be altered in the symbolic map prior to issuing a SEND MAP command containing the symbolic map. The character used to modify the color and highlight attributes may be taken from the DFHBMSCA copy member, or you can add entries to the standard attribute list copy member, STWSATTR, defined in Appendix B. Figure 19.5 shows the DFHBMSCA entries.

The color entries in DFHBMSCA are easy to understand and work with, but if you wish to employ your own labels, I suggest the names shown in Fig. 19.6 to expand the copy member STWSATTR.

You can change the color of the message field from green (the BMS-map-defined color) to yellow, and the highlighting from reverse video to normal display, by executing the following moves prior to issuing a SEND MAP command containing the symbolic map:

```
MOVE DFHYELLO    TO  MAPMESGC.
MOVE DFHDFHI     TO  MAPMESGH.
```

or

```
MOVE YELLOW       TO  MAPMESGC.
MOVE HLT-DEFAULT  TO  MAPMESGH.
```

```
05  DFHDFCOL    PIC X    VALUE ' '.
05  DFHBLUE     PIC X    VALUE '1'.
05  DFHRED      PIC X    VALUE '2'.
05  DFHPINK     PIC X    VALUE '3'.
05  DFHGREEN    PIC X    VALUE '4'.
05  DFHTURQ     PIC X    VALUE '5'.
05  DFHYELLO    PIC X    VALUE '6'.
05  DFHNEUTR    PIC X    VALUE '7'.

05  DFHDFHI     PIC X    VALUE ' '.
05  DFHBLINK    PIC X    VALUE '1'.
05  DFHREVRS    PIC X    VALUE '2'.
05  DFHUNDLN    PIC X    VALUE '4'.
```

Fig. 19.5 DFHBMSCA entries.

```
05  COL-DEFAULT     PIC X    VALUE ' '.
05  BLUE            PIC X    VALUE '1'.
05  RED             PIC X    VALUE '2'.
05  PINK            PIC X    VALUE '3'.
05  GREEN           PIC X    VALUE '4'.
05  TURQUOISE       PIC X    VALUE '5'.
05  YELLOW          PIC X    VALUE '6'.
05  NEUTRAL         PIC X    VALUE '7'.

05  HLT-DEFAULT     PIC X    VALUE ' '.
05  BLINK           PIC X    VALUE '1'.
05  REVERSE-VIDEO   PIC X    VALUE '2'.
05  UNDERLINE       PIC X    VALUE '4'
```

Fig. 19.6 Suggested names.

20

Additional CICS Commands and Techniques

This chapter is an introduction to additional CICS commands that you may encounter, and techniques that you should find helpful, though you can design and write most CICS applications and programs using only the CICS commands discussed up to this point. These additional commands and techniques are the START command, the internal reader, fast-path processing, and program stacking.

The numeric editing of input data seems not to have any general industrywide standard. Most data processing installations have standards that apply to their companies, and many have standard modules commonly used for editing. These modules may take the form of copy members or linked-to programs or may just be copied from one program to another. This chapter also discusses numeric editing considerations and includes a copy member routine that should satisfy most of your editing requirements.

CICS Commands

ABEND

You can use ABEND to abort a program and release a task's main storage when an error is detected, rather than have CICS perform the termination. The specification of ABCODE results in a dump with the display of the specified code when the program is terminated. ABCODE's abend code, which may be up to four characters, can be either defined in working storage or may be hard-coded by enclosing the code in quotes. The CANCEL option cancels any exits established by a HANDLE ABEND command. The ABEND command has the following format:

```
EXEC CICS ABEND
        [ABCODE (name)]
        [CANCEL]
END-EXEC.
```

BIF DEEDIT

Use this CICS built-in function to remove unwanted characters from an input field; it is most often used for numeric editing. You can use BIF DEEDIT to remove special characters, such as commas, decimals, and plus and minus signs, keyed into an input field. The resulting field is right-justified, and its high-order positions are zero-filled. BIF DEEDIT has the following format:

```
EXEC CICS BIF DEEDIT
        FIELD   (data-area)
        LENGTH  (data-value)
END-EXEC.
```

The following examples and comments should help to clarify the use of BIF DEEDIT. The length of the input field is eleven (11). See Table 20.1.

TABLE 20.1 Example of BIFDEEDIT Execution Results.

Data-area		Comments
Before	After	
121,201.00	00012120100	Commas and decimals are removed
200	00000000200	High order positions are zero-filled
2.00	00000000200	Note that 'after' field is same as above
555-55-5555	00555555555	Special characters removed
$9,876.54	00000987654	Same as above
12/25/99	00000122599	Same as above
123.45–	00000012345	Non Low-order '–' is stripped
123.45–	0000001234N	Low-order '–' results in signed lo-order
–123.45	00000012345	High-order sign is stripped
+123.45	00000012345	Same as above
123.45+	00000012345	Low-order + is removed/ignored
12345	00000012345	Non Low-order sign is stripped
1234M	0000001234M	Low-order letter/sign remains
123.45CR	00000012345	Non Low-order 'CR' is stripped
123.45CR	0000001234N	Low-order 'CR' results in minus sign
123.45DR	0000001234R	'DR' treated as are other letters
123 456 789	00000000123	Characters following a space are ignored
1A2B3C4D5EF	0000012345F	All but low-order letters are removed
123_____	00000000123	Underline characters are removed

BIF DEEDIT appears to be a very powerful editing tool, but in practice, its use is limited. As seen in the preceding examples, 2.00 and 200 both translate into 200. If decimal places are to be entered into a field, they must always be entered even if the decimal field is all zeroes. For example, if a field has two decimal places, then 200 must be entered as 200.00. Also invalid characters are removed without notification of incorrect entry. For example, a field entered as 1,23,456,789,,0 would not be detected as being erroneous; the commas would just be removed. The numeric editing commonly required is discussed later in this chapter under "Numeric Editing."

DELAY

The DELAY command creates a pause in the processing of a task. It can suspend the processing of the task for an indicated interval of time or until a specified time. You can use it to create a short delay if a resource to be enqueued is not currently available, before reissuing the ENQ command. DELAY has the following format:

```
EXEC CICS DELAY
         [INTERVAL  (hhmmss)    |
          TIME      (hhmmss)]
END-EXEC.
```

DEQ

The DEQ command releases a resource enqueued by the ENQ command. The resource must be specified in the same manner as it was by the preceding ENQ command. The LENGTH option should be coded only if the resource is a character string. If no preceding ENQ command is issued for the resource to be dequeued, the DEQ command is ignored. CICS automatically releases any enqueued resources not dequeued when the task ends. The DEQ command has the following format:

```
EXEC CICS DEQ
         RESOURCE (data-area)
         [LENGTH   (data-value)]
END-EXEC.
```

ENQ

The ENQ command reserves exclusive use of a resource required by a program or task. Its function is similar to that of exclusive control when a program issues a read for update command. This command is generally used by programs that write data to a device such as the internal reader or to a printer. You do not want your JCL or report to be interspersed with those of other users. Coordinate the use of the ENQ command in accordance with standards set by an installation. The enqueue system works only if all programs within a system enqueue on common resources in an identical fashion. Specify the resource to be enqueued in the same manner as it will be in a succeeding DEQ command. Always release a resource as soon as it is no longer needed by issuing a DEQ command to make the resource available to other tasks. A resource is automatically released by CICS when a task ends if the DEQ command has not been issued. Code the LENGTH option, specified as a binary halfword with a value of 1 through 255, only if the resource is a character string. The ENQBUSY condition is raised if a resource is not available when the ENQ command is issued. Your program can act on this condition or permit the program to wait until the resource becomes available. The ENQ command has the following format:

```
EXEC CICS ENQ
          RESOURCE (data-area)
          LENGTH   (data-value)
END-EXEC.
```

Some examples of ENQ are:

```
EXEC CICS ENQ
          RESOURCE (WS-IRDR)
END-EXEC.
```

            or

```
EXEC CICS ENQ
          RESOURCE ('IRDR')
          [LENGTH   (4)   |
          LENGTH   (WS-LEN-4)]
END-EXEC.
```

FREEMAIN

The FREEMAIN command releases storage acquired by the GETMAIN command. CICS releases acquired storage automatically when a task ends if the FREEMAIN is not issued. The DATA option reference is to the linkage section data-area pointed to by a BLL pointer or referenced using the VS COBOL II ADDRESS special register. The FREEMAIN command has the following format:

```
EXEC CICS FREEMAIN
          DATA (data-area)
END-EXEC.
```

GETMAIN

The GETMAIN command acquires main storage for use in the linkage section when the locate mode, rather than the move mode, of processing is used. Acquiring storage for output type operations is necessary only when storage is not automatically acquired by an input operation. For instance, if a write command is not preceded by a read command, then storage must be acquired.

Read commands that use the SET option acquire their own storage. GET-MAIN uses the SET option to establish addressability using BLL pointers discussed in chapter 10, or the VS COBOL II ADDRESS special register discussed in chapter 25. LENGTH must have its data value specified as a halfword binary value when the value is defined in working storage. The storage acquired can be initialized to a given value, such as low-values or spaces, by defining a 1-byte data-value in working storage and including the INITIMG option. GET-MAIN is efficient to use if your program contains a large output record that is not formatted and written on every execution of a transaction. Do not needlessly tie up main storage. The GETMAIN command has the following format:

```
EXEC CICS GETMAIN
        [SET     (ptr-ref)   |
         SET     (ADDRESS OF struc)]
         LENGTH  (data-value)
        [INITIMG (data-value)]
END-EXEC.
```

HANDLE ABEND

The HANDLE ABEND command directs control to a program, section, or paragraph if an abend occurs. This command is generally placed at the beginning of the procedure division and functions similarly to a GO TO statement. The abend program or routine can contain logic for any desired abend processing. The PROGRAM option designates the program to receive control if an abend occurs, while the LABEL option directs control to the specified section or paragraph name. The CANCEL option deactivates a HANDLE ABEND command, while RESET reactivates the condition. HANDLE ABEND has the following format:

```
EXEC CICS HANDLE ABEND
        [PROGRAM (name)
        [LABEL   (section/paragraph)]
        [CANCEL  |
         RESET]
END-EXEC.
```

POP HANDLE

The POP HANDLE command restores the status of conditions suspended by the issuance of a PUSH HANDLE command. The PUSH HANDLE and POP HANDLE commands are used generally in subprograms or standard subroutines that issue HANDLE CONDITION, HANDLE AID, HANDLE ABEND, and IGNORE commands of their own. The POP HANDLE command has the following format:

```
EXEC CICS POP HANDLE
END-EXEC.
```

PUSH HANDLE

The PUSH HANDLE command is generally used at the beginning of a subprogram or subroutine to suspend all active conditions. You can restore these conditions to their status prior to entering the subprogram or subroutine by issuing the POP HANDLE command before exiting. Use the PUSH HANDLE and POP HANDLE commands in subprograms or standard subroutines issuing HANDLE CONDITION, HANDLE AID, HANDLE ABEND, and IGNORE commands of their own. The PUSH HANDLE command has the following format:

```
EXEC CICS PUSH HANDLE
END-EXEC.
```

RETRIEVE

Data passed to a program initiated by issuing a START command can be accessed in the started program by issuing the RETRIEVE command. Optional data is retrieved into the field specified by the INTO or SET option. The LENGTH option's data-area, a halfword binary value, specifies the maximum expected size of the passed data. It contains the actual length of the retrieved data after the RETRIEVE command is executed. You issue multiple START commands from different tasks to start the same transaction at the same time. In this case, you may issue multiple RETRIEVE commands to retrieve all of the passed data. When using the RETRIEVE command, test ENDDATA and NOTFND conditions if data is passed. The RETRIEVE command has the following format:

```
EXEC CICS RETRIEVE
          [INTO  (data-area   |
           SET   (ptr-ref)    |
           SET   (ADDRESS OF struc)]
           LENGTH (data-area)
END-EXEC.
```

SEND CONTROL

The SEND CONTROL command sends control options, such as FREEKB, CURSOR, and ERASE, without sending a map or text to the terminal. You can also use the SEND MAP or SEND TEXT commands to send control options to the screen. SEND CONTROL has the following format:

```
EXEC CICS SEND CONTROL
          [FREEKB
          [CURSOR    (data-value)]
          [ERASE]
END-EXEC.
```

START

The START command initiates another task while the current task continues. Program control returns to the instruction immediately following the START command. The started task can execute simultaneously with the starting task and returns control to CICS when it has completed. The TRANSID option specifies the name of the transaction code used to initiate a new program. Data may optionally be passed to the initiated program by including the FROM and LENGTH options. The LENGTH's data area must be specified as a halfword binary value. You can access passed data in the started program by issuing the RETRIEVE command. You may optionally include the INTERVAL or TIME options to start a task at some time in the future; if these options are omitted, the task is started immediately. For example, a task can be started immediately, at one-hour intervals, or at eight o'clock. You can specify TERMID to associate the started task with a given terminal. The START command has the following format:

```
EXEC CICS START
          TRANSID   (name)
          [FROM     (data-area)]
          [LENGTH   (data-value)]
          [INTERVAL (hhmmss) |
           TIME     (hhmmss)]
          [TERMID   (name)]
END-EXEC.
```

SUSPEND

The SUSPEND command suspends a long running task so that other waiting tasks of a higher priority can execute. Control returns to the statement following the SUSPEND command, which has the following format:

```
EXEC CICS SUSPEND
END-EXEC.
```

SYNCPOINT

The SYNCPOINT command commits updates for logical units of work in long-running tasks. Including the ROLLBACK option results in all database changes made since the initiation of the task, or since the execution of any SYNCPOINT commands, being backed out. SYNCPOINT has the following format:

```
EXEC CICS SYNCPOINT
          [ROLLBACK]
END-EXEC.
```

Practical Applications and Techniques

Some examples of commands presented in this and in preceding chapters should clarify their practical use. Job control language (JCL) statements were submitted to the internal reader, in some of the earlier releases of CICS, by using the transient data command discussed in chapter 16. The ENQ and DEQ commands presented in this chapter were used with this technique to ensure that data from other tasks was not interspersed with JCL data. The discussion includes the internal reader because you might find its use in some of the older versions of CICS that you have to maintain. Current versions of CICS provide a job entry subsystem (JES) spooling facility you should use in place of the internal reader described in this section. This spooling facility is the responsibility of your systems programming group, who can direct you in its use.

Submitting JCL to the internal reader

Check with your systems programming department to determine what type of job submission facility is available at your installation before using this technique. The use of the internal reader to submit JCL may cause problems in a JES3 global-local environment that result in the CICS region being hung. Using the internal reader might restrict some installations from using certain functions contained in the latter releases of CICS.

A CICS application program can build JCL statements and submit them to the system's internal reader. The internal reader is a buffer read by the system and used to initiate a batch job. This JCL can invoke a standard procedure (proc) to run a batch job. You can establish a table to route reports to a designated printer based on the userid of the person logged on to the system. This default printer can be displayed as an unprotected field on the screen to enable the user to route a report to an alternate printer. Screen-entered record keys can be passed as PARM data to the proc invoked by the submitted JCL. You can obtain the userid for a JOB card by executing the CICS ASSIGN command and including the USERID option.

The program steps required to submit a job to the internal reader (IRDR) are the following:

1. Use the ENQ command to enqueue on the resource IRDR or any resource designated by your installation. This command gives your program exclusive control of the IRDR resource until you release control by executing a DEQ command. Remember that all programs within a system that write to a common resource must enqueue on the same resource. A program that does not enqueue can obtain concurrent access to the resource while it is enqueued by another program. This can lead to the intertwining of output data.

```
M100-SUBMIT-JCL   SECTION.

    EXEC CICS ENQ
              RESOURCE ('IRDR')
              LENGTH    (4)
              RESP      (WS-RESP)
    END-EXEC.

    . . .

    PERFORM N100-WRITE-TDQ
              VARYING SUB FROM 1 BY 1
                UNTIL SUB  >  END-OF-JCL-SUB.

    EXEC CICS DEQ
              RESOURCE ('IRDR')
              LENGTH    (4)
    END-EXEC.

M100-EXIT.
    EXIT.


N100-WRITE-TDQ   SECTION.

    MOVE WS-JCL-STATEMENT (SUB)  TO  TD-DATA-AREA.

    EXEC CICS WRITEQ TD
              QUEUE   ('IRDR')
              FROM    (TD-DATA-AREA)
              LENGTH  (80)
    END-EXEC.

N100-EXIT.
    EXIT.
```

Fig. 20.1 Sample code to write to Internal Reader.

2. Write the eighty-character JCL statements that you want to invoke a proc to the transient data queue named IRDR or to an installation-defined indirect TD queue. A proc is initiated to minimize the number of JCL statements written to the internal reader. The last JCL statement written to the internal reader must contain /*EOF in columns one through five. The /*EOF delimits the job and signals that it is eligible for immediate processing.

3. Issue the DEQ command to release control of the IRDR to make it accessible to other tasks, when all JCL has been written (Fig. 20.1).

Include RESP option on the ENQ command and test it for ENQBUSY condition. You can display an indicative message, such as:

```
JOB SUBMIT FACILITY BUSY - PLEASE TRY AGAIN
```

if the resource has been enqueued by another task. If you omit the RESP option from the ENQ command, the task waits for the resource to become available.

The JCL would have been built in working storage as eighty-character records prior to performing M100-SUBMIT-JCL. These eighty-character fields are redefined by the programmer-defined subscripted field named WS-JCL-STATEMENT. END-OF-JCL-SUB contains the value of the total number of JCL statements. The JCL is written, one statement at a time, to the transient data queue. The internal reader submits the JCL for execution.

Using the START command

A practical use of the START command that I encountered was the result of a requirement to verify if data written to a TD queue was processing in a timely fashion. All transactions in the system wrote file update transactions to a TD queue. The queue was read and processed by the task initiated when the DCT trigger level was reached. Occasionally, the transaction to be initiated became disabled and the file updates were not processed. A control file was updated with a signal as the result of a dummy TD queue record written at predetermined time intervals. A program the system commonly used tested the signal in the control file and displayed an indicative message if the file was not updated during the designated time interval. For example:

Program A.   Program A automatically initiates when CICS is brought up in the morning. If it is earlier than 8:00, the program issues a START command with the TIME option to restart the program again at 8:00 and return control to CICS. At 8:00, and once each hour, the program restarts through the use of the INTERVAL option. The dummy TD queue record is then written and the program returns to CICS. Program A is executed hourly until CICS is brought down. The pertinent code required to accomplish this is as shown in Fig. 20.2.

Program B.   Program B employs the START command in a similar fashion to initiate itself hourly, on the half-hour. This program reads a control file and checks the time stored in this file by Program C. If the time check indicates that Program C has not been run within the last half-hour, a signal in the control file is set to *ON*.

Program C.   Program C initiates when the trigger level in the DCT is reached. This program reads the TD queue written by various programs in the system and by Program A, which writes a dummy record to the queue on an hourly basis. The read of the dummy record results in an update to the control file with the signal in the control record set to *OFF*. If the transaction or program is disabled, this program does not execute and the signal in the control file record remains *ON*.

Program D.   Program D examines the signal set in the control file by programs B and C. If the signal is *ON*, an indicative message is sent to the user indicating that Program C has not been run since the time stored in

```
        EXEC CICS ASKTIME
                  ABSTIME (WS-ABSTIME)
        END-EXEC.

        EXEC CICS FORMATTIME
                  ABSTIME (WS-ABSTIME)
                  TIME    (WS-HHMMSS)
        END-EXEC.

* IF IT IS NOT 8:00 YET, RESTART THIS PROGRAM AT 8:00

        IF WS-HHMMSS  <  080000
           EXEC CICS START
                     TRANSID ('TRNA')
                     TIME    (080000)
           END-EXEC

           EXEC CICS RETURN
           END-EXEC.

* RESTART THIS TRANSACTION HOURLY

        EXEC CICS START
                  TRANSID  ('TRNA')
                  INTERVAL (010000)
        END-EXEC.

         .  .  .

* WRITE DUMMY RECORD TO TD QUEUE

        EXEC CICS WRITEQ TD
                  QUEUE ('UPDF')
                  FROM  (TD-DATA-AREA)
                  LENGTH (WS-TD-REC-LEN)
        END-EXEC.

         .  .  .
```

Fig. 20.2   Code required to execute program A hourly.

the control record. The user is instructed to notify data processing to take appropriate action.

Fast path processing

Users of a system quickly become familiar with programs in the system. They sometimes request the ability to transfer from one program to any other program in the system. This is called *fast path processing*. This technique is not related to IMS database fast path processing. If a system of programs is small, you can probably store their transaction identifiers and program names in the COMMAREA. For larger systems, you may employ a file the transaction identifier can key, and which contains the program name as a data element. You can also store the TRANSID and program name pairs in a main or auxiliary temporary storage queue. Typically, the user enters the TRANSID on the screen and presses a designated PF key to transfer control to the target program. Depending on the system's requirements, you may pass common data to other programs in the system.

Program stacking

Some systems require the return to previously executed programs, in the sequence in which they were executed. The name of the program just executed and previously executed programs can be stored in a program stack. Programs can be reexecuted in sequence and removed from the stack as control is returned to each program in the chain. The program stack can be stored in the COMMAREA and passed to all programs within a system. Coding for this type of processing is easier if the system initiation menu or a control program initializes the program stack.

Numeric editing

The introduction to this chapter mentioned that the numeric editing of input data seems not to have any general industrywide standard. Users often want to have the ability to enter data into a field in its edited format and expect the system to notify them of any input format errors. Most data processing installations have standards that apply to their departments, and many have standard modules commonly used for editing. These modules may take the form of copy members, called programs, linked-to programs, or may just be copied from one program to another. This section discusses numeric editing considerations and includes a copy member module that should satisfy most of your editing requirements. This module was written for ease of understanding and modification and should be easy enough to follow and customize for your own unique data-entry requirements. Other data-entry techniques were discussed in chapter 2 and were illustrated in Fig. 2.4. Some programs enter whole numbers and decimal digits into two separate map fields. This technique is awkward in that it requires tabbing to the decimal portion of a numeric field when the whole number portion is not completely filled with data.

As mentioned earlier, BIF DEEDIT has limited uses since it basically removes nonnumeric data, right justifies, and zero-fills high-order positions. The following examples and comments show how data edited using the module in this section appear on the screen after being edited. The edit mask used for the examples is ---------9.99, although any valid numeric edit mask could be used. Constrast the first part of this example with corresponding data edited by BIF DEEDIT in the example presented earlier in this chapter.

The examples shown in Table 20.2 illustrate some of the requirements of a good numeric edit module.

TABLE 20.2 Example of Good Numeric Edit Module Execution Results.

Screen before	Screen after	Comments
121,201.00	121201.00	Commas are removed
200	200.00	Field is decimal aligned
2.00	2.00	This field is different than that above

Screen before	Screen after	Comments
555-55-5555	555-55-5555	Error - imbedded/excess signs
$9,876.54	$9,876.54	Error - dollar sign not permitted
12/25/99	12/25/99	Error - slash (/) not permitted
123.45–	–123.45	Sign can be entered in high- or lo-order position of field
–123.45	–123.45	High-order sign is OK
+123.45	123.45	High-order + is removed/ignored
123.45+	123.45	Lo-order + is removed/ignored
1234M	1234M	Error - alpha is invalid
123.45CR	123.45CR	Error - alpha is invalid
123.45DR	123.45DR	Same as above
123 456 789	123 456 789	Error - imbedded characters are invalid
1A2B3C4D5EF	1A2B3C4D5EF	Error - alpha is invalid
123_____	123	Underline characters are removed
10.+	10.00	Sign can immediately precede or follow a decimal point
–.10	–0.10	Same as above
10. –	10.–	Error - no imbedded spaces before a sign
– .10	–.10	Error - no imbedded spaces after a sign
–10.2–	–10.2–	Error - only one sign is permitted
10–23	10–23	Error - no imbedded sign is allowed
10 23	10 23	Error - no imbedded spaces are permitted
1234,567	1234567	Valid -routine allows any number of digits *before* first comma
1,23345,678	1,2345,678	Error - 3 digits must follow every comma
123.45,6	123.45,6	Error - comma cannot occur after a decimal is entered
,123.56	,123.56	Error - cannot have a leading comma
123.456.789	123.456.789	Error - only one decimal point permitted
123_456_789	123_456_789	Error - only trailing underline allowed
		Error - no digits or decimal number
0	0.00	Zeroes will be returned if zeroes, spaces, or low-values are passed

The features of the edit module in this chapter can be summarized as follows:

1. Only specified characters are permitted. The copy module in this chapter allows the entry of only the digits 0 through 9, one sign, one decimal, commas, and underline characters. All other characters are flagged as errors.

2. Only one optional leading or trailing plus (+) or minus (–) sign is permitted; *plus* is the default entry.

3. No imbedded blanks are permitted; this includes blanks immediately following a leading sign or preceding a trailing sign.

4. Only one optional decimal point followed by up to 6 decimal digits is permitted. Excess decimal digits are flagged as errors. The number of decimal places specified can vary from field to field.

5. Up to 12 whole number digits separated by commas in appropriate groups of three are permitted. Any number of digits can precede the first comma. Excess whole number digits are flagged as errors, as is improper comma usage. Commas need not be entered; however, if they are used, they must be followed by three digits.

```
MOVE mapfldI   TO   WS-NUMEDT-INPUT.
MOVE nn        TO   WS-NUMEDT-DIGITS.
MOVE d         TO   WS-NUMEDT-DECIMALS.

PERFORM Z99Y-NUMERIC-EDIT.
IF NUMEDT-STATUS = SPACES
     MOVE WS-NUMEDT-OUTPUT  TO   xx
     MOVE WS-NUMEDT-OUTPUT  TO   edit field
     MOVE edit field        TO   mapfldO
ELSE
     PERFORM bad edit logic.
```

```
Where: mapfldI        = map input field to be edited.  Define
                        in map as PIC X(map field size)
       nn             = maximum number of whole numbers
                        permitted.   00 is the minimum, 12 is
                        maximum.  This can be adjusted for
                        each field
       d              = maximum number of decimal digits
                        permitted.   0 is the minimum, 6 is
                        maximum.  This can be adjusted for
                        each field
       xx             = working storage, COMMAREA, file,
                        linkage section field, etc.
       edit field     = the edit mask that is used to define
                        the map output display field
       mapfldO        = map output field, either edited or
                        original field if errors.  The map's
                        output field can be defined with an
                        edit mask, but the input field must
                        be defined as X's.
  bad edit logic - can perform routines that will:
                        highlight an erroneous field and
                        position the cursor at the field, set
                        an error indicator switch, display
                        the error message stored in
                        NUMED-MESSAGE, etc.
```

Fig. 20.3   How to invoke the Edit module.

6. All error conditions are recorded by moving a two-character status code to a working-storage status field named NUMED-STATUS. The program can test this code and display an appropriate error message. This routine moves a descriptive message to the working storage field NUMED-MESSAGE if errors are detected.

7. Trailing underline characters are removed, while any other underline characters result in an input field being detected as being invalid.

8. The routine can be customized during program execution for designated characters. Moving low-values to any of the fields NUMED-COMMA, NUMED-DECIMAL, NUMED-MINUS, NUMED-PLUS, and/or NUMED-UNDERLINE prior to performing the routine Z99Y-NUMERIC-EDIT results in those fields being treated as invalid input. Each field is restored to its initial value by the routine before the routine is exited.

9. The edit module should be easy to use. The module in this chapter requires the inclusion of one copy member in the working storage section (STWSNUME) and one in the procedure division (STPDNUME). The routine is invoked as shown in Fig. 20.3.

Figure 20.4 shows numeric edit's WORKING-STORAGE SECTION copy member (STWSNUME). Figure 20.5 shows numeric edit's PROCEDURE DIVISION copy member (STPDNUME). This routine contains numerous comments enabling you to modify the edit module if necessary; they should also make it easier for you to understand the module.

Fig. 20.4 Working-storage copy member (STWSNUME) for numeric editing.

```
***********************************************************************
*    'STWSNUME'   WORKING STORAGE FOR NUMERIC EDIT ROUTINE          *
*  COPY 'STPDNUME' INTO PROCEDURE DIVISION FOR NUMERIC EDIT         *
***********************************************************************
*
 01  NUMED-FIELDS.
     05  NUMED-INPUT.
         10  NUMED-IN          PIC X     OCCURS 24 TIMES.
*
     05  NUMEDOUT.
         10  NUMED-OUTPUT      PIC S9(12)V9(6)   VALUE ZEROES.
*
     05  NUMED-MESSAGE         PIC X(79)         VALUE SPACES.
     05  NUMED-DIGITS          PIC 99            VALUE ZEROES.
     05  NUMED-DECIMALS        PIC 9             VALUE ZEROES.
     05  NUMED-DIGIT-COUNT     PIC 99            VALUE ZEROES.
     05  NUMED-DEC-NUM-COUNT   PIC 9             VALUE ZEROES.
     05  NUMED-DEC-PT- COUNT   PIC 9             VALUE ZEROES.
     05  NUMED-SIGN-COUNT      PIC 9             VALUE ZEROES.
     05  NUMED-NUM-AFTER-COMMA-COUNT    PIC 99  VALUE ZEROES.
     05  NUMED-NUM-AFTER-COMMA-SWITCH   PIC X   VALUE 'N'.
     05  NUMED-NEG-SIGN                  PIC X   VALUE 'N'.
*
 01  NUMED-BUILD.
     05  NUMED-B-DIGITS.
         10  NUMED-B-DIG       PIC X     OCCURS 12 TIMES.
     05  NUMED-B-DECIMALS.
         10  NUMED-B-DEC       PIC X     OCCURS  6 TIMES.
*
* THE FOLLOWING CAN BE DEACTIVATED BY MOVING LOW-VALUES TO FIELD
* IMMEDIATELY PRIOR TO EACH PERFORM OF Z99Y-NUMERIC-EDIT.  THE
* ROUTINE RESTORES FIELDS TO THEIR INITIAL STATUS PRIOR TO EXITING
*
 01  NUMED-CUSTOMIZE.
     05  NUMED-COMMA          PIC X             VALUE ','.
     05  NUMED-DECIMAL        PIC X             VALUE '.'.
     05  NUMED-MINUS          PIC X             VALUE '-'.
     05  NUMED-PLUS           PIC X             VALUE '+'.
     05  NUMED-UNDERLINE      PIC X             VALUE '_'.
*
 01  NUMED-SUBSCRIPTS.
```

Fig. 20.4 *Continued.*

```
     05  NES1                    PIC S9(4)   COMP   VALUE ZEROES.
     05  NES2                    PIC S9(4)   COMP   VALUE ZEROES.
     05  NESBEG                  PIC S9(4)   COMP   VALUE ZEROES.
     05  NESEND                  PIC S9(4)   COMP   VALUE ZEROES.
     05  NESDEC                  PIC S9(4)   COMP   VALUE ZEROES.
*
     05  NUMED-STATUS            PIC XX             VALUE SPACES.
         88  NUMED-GOOD-EDIT                        VALUE ' '.
         88  INVALID-DIGIT-DEC-PASSED               VALUE 'IP'.
         88  EXCESS-SIGNS                           VALUE 'ES'.
         88  EXCESS-DECIMAL-POINTS                  VALUE 'EP'.
         88  EXCESS-WHOLE-NUMBERS                   VALUE 'EN'.
         88  EXCESS-DECIMAL-DIGITS                  VALUE 'ED'.
         88  INVALID-CHAR-INCL-IMBED-BLANKS         VALUE 'IC'.
         88  INVALID-FORMAT                         VALUE 'IF'.
         88  COMMA-AFTER-DECIMAL                    VALUE 'CD'.
         88  NO-DIGITS-ENTERED                      VALUE 'ND'.
         88  NOT-3-DIGITS-AFTER-COMMA               VALUE 'N3'.
```

Fig. 20.5 Procedure division copy member (STPDNUME) for numeric editing.

```
Z99Y-NUMERIC-EDIT   SECTION.
*
*********************************************************************
*     'STPDNUME'  NUMERIC EDIT ROUTINE   PROCEDURE DIVISION       *
*                                                                 *
*  GOOD EDIT:    SPACES ARE RETURNED IN NUMED-STATUS              *
*                OUTPUT IS  RETURNED IN NUMED-OUTPUT              *
*  INPUT ERROR: 2CHAR ERROR CODE IS RETURNED IN NUMED-STATUS     *
*                ZEROES ARE RETURNED IN NUMED-OUTPUT             *
*                ERROR MESSAGE IS RETURNED IN NUMED-MESSAGE      *
*********************************************************************
*
     MOVE SPACES  TO  NUMED-STATUS.
     MOVE ZEROES  TO  NUMED-OUTPUT.
     MOVE ZEROES  TO  NUMED-BUILD.
     MOVE ZEROES  TO  NUMED-DEC-PT-COUNT.
     MOVE ZEROES  TO  NUMED-SIGN-COUNT.
     MOVE ZEROES  TO  NUMED-DIGIT-COUNT.
     MOVE ZEROES  TO  NUMED-DEC-NUM-COUNT.
     MOVE 3       TO  NUMED-NUM-AFTER-COMMA-COUNT.
     MOVE 'N'     TO  NUMED-NUM-AFTER-COMMA-SWITCH.
     MOVE 'N'     TO  NUMED-NEG-SIGN.
     MOVE SPACES  TO  NUMED-MESSAGE.
*
* PASSED DIGIT AND DECIMAL COUNT REQUIREMENTS:
```

Fig. 20.5 *Continued.*

```
*    1) MUST BE NUMERIC
*    2) DIGITS CANNOT EXCEED 12
*    3) DECIMALS CANNOT EXCEED 6
*    4) BOTH CANNOT BE ZEROES
*
     IF (NUMED-DIGITS     IS  NUMERIC   AND
         NUMED-DIGITS     IS LESS THAN  13)
       AND
        (NUMED-DECIMALS  IS  NUMERIC   AND
         NUMED-DECIMALS  IS LESS THAN   7)
           NEXT SENTENCE
     ELSE
         MOVE 'IP'  TO  NUMED-STATUS
         GO TO  Z99Y-RESTORE-NUMED-FIELDS.
*
     IF NUMED-DIGITS    =  0    AND
        NUMED-DECIMALS  =  0
         MOVE 'IP'  TO  NUMED-STATUS
         GO TO  Z99Y-RESTORE-NUMED-FIELDS.
*
* ZEROES WILL BE RETURNED IN NUMED-OUTPUT IF SPACES,
* LOW-VALUES, OR ZEROES ARE PASSED IN NUMED-INPUT
*
     IF NUMED-INPUT  =  SPACES  OR  LOW-VALUES  OR  ZEROES
         GO TO  Z99Y-RESTORE-NUMED-FIELDS.
*
     MOVE ZEROES  TO  NESBEG.
     PERFORM Z99Y-FIND-1ST-SIGNIF-CHAR
             VARYING NES1    FROM 1 BY 1
                UNTIL NESBEG  IS GREATER THAN  ZEROES.
*
     GO TO  Z99Y-LOCATE-END-OF-FIELD.
*
   Z99Y-FIND-1ST-SIGNIF-CHAR.
     IF NUMED-IN (NES1)  NOT =  SPACE
         MOVE NES1  TO  NESBEG.
*
   Z99Y-LOCATE-END-OF-FIELD.

     MOVE ZEROES  TO  NESEND.
     PERFORM Z99Y-FIND-LAST-SIGNIF-CHAR
             VARYING NES1    FROM  24 BY  -1
                UNTIL NESEND  IS GREATER THAN  ZEROES
                   OR NES1    IS EQUAL TO      ZEROES.
*
*  NES1 WOULD ONLY = 0 IF THE ONLY CHARACTERS IN A FIELD
*  WERE UNDERLINE CHARACTERS
*
```

Fig. 20.5 *Continued.*

```
    IF NESEND  =  0
        MOVE 'ND'  TO  NUMED-STATUS
        GO TO  Z99Y-RESTORE-NUMED-FIELDS
    ELSE
        GO TO  Z99Y-INITIATE-EDITING.
*
 Z99Y-FIND-LASTSIGNIF-CHAR.
*
* TRAILING UNDERLINE CHARACTERS ARE ELIMINATED
*    OTHERS WILL BE FLAGGED AS ERRORS DURING EDITING
*
    IF NUMED-IN (NES1)  =  NUMED-UNDERLINE
        MOVE SPACE  TO  NUMED-IN (NES1).
*
    IF NUMED-IN (NES1)  NOT =  SPACE
        MOVE NES1  TO  NESEND.
*
 Z99Y-INITIATE-EDITING.
    MOVE ZEROES  TO  NESDEC.
    PERFORM Z99Z-EDIT-PASS
            VARYING NES1  FROM NESBEG  BY  1
                UNTIL NES1  IS GREATER THAN  NESEND
                    OR NUMED-STATUS  IS NOT =  SPACES.
*
    IF NUMED-STATUS  IS NOT =  SPACES
        GO TO  Z99Y-RESTORE-NUMED-FIELDS.
*
* AT THIS POINT NUMED-DEC-PT-COUNT = 0 OR 1 AND NO ERRORS HAVE
*    BEEN FOUND IN INPUT DATA
*
    IF NUMED-DEC-PT-COUNT  =  1
        MOVE ZEROES  TO  NES2
        PERFORM Z99Y-NE-SET-DECIMALS
                VARYING NES1  FROM  NESDEC  BY  1
                    UNTIL NES1  IS GREATER THAN  NESEND
    ELSE
        MOVE NESEND  TO  NESDEC.
*
    GO TO  Z99Y-FORMAT-WHOLE-NUMBER.
*
 Z99Y-NE-SET-DECIMALS.
*
* STARTING AT DECIMAL POINT, STORE ALL DECIMAL DIGITS UNTIL
*    THE END OF THE FIELD IS ENCOUNTERED
*
    IF NUMED-IN (NES1)  IS NUMERIC
        ADD 1                     TO  NES2
```

Fig. 20.5 *Continued.*

```
             MOVE NUMED-IN (NES1)  TO  NUMED-B-DEC (NES2).
*
  Z99Y-FORMAT-WHOLE-NUMBER.
*
     MOVE 12  TO  NES2.
     PERFORM Z99Y-NE-SET-WHOLE-NUMBER
              VARYING NES1  FROM  NESDEC  BY  -1
               UNTIL NES1  IS EQUAL TO  0
               OR NES2  IS EQUAL TO  0.
*
     GO TO  Z99Y-MOVE-BUILT-NUM-TO-OUTPUT.
*
  Z99Y-NE-SET-WHOLE-NUMBER.
*
* STORE ALL WHOLE NUMBER DIGITS FROM RIGHT TO LEFT OF WHOLE
*   NUMBER PORTION OF THE FIELD.  DECIMAL AND COMMAS, IF ANY,
*   ARE BYPASSED.
*
     IF NUMED-IN (NES1)  IS NUMERIC
         MOVE NUMED-IN (NES1)  TO  NUMED-B-DIG (NES2)
         SUBTRACT 1         FROM  NES2.
*
  Z99Y-MOVE-BUILT-NUM-TO-OUTPUT.
     MOVE NUMED-BUILD  TO  NUMED-OUT.
*
     IF NUMED-NEG-SIGN  =  'Y'
         MULTIPLY -1  BY  NUMED-OUTPUT.
*
  Z99Y-RESTORE-NUMED-FIELDS.
*
* RESTORE FIELDS THAT MAY HAVE BEEN NEGATED BY BEING SET TO
*   LOW-VALUES BEFORE PERFORMING Z99Y-NUMERIC-EDIT
*
     MOVE ','  TO  NUMED-COMMA.
     MOVE '.'  TO  NUMED-DECIMAL.
     MOVE '-'  TO  NUMED-MINUS.
     MOVE '+'  TO  NUMED-PLUS.
     MOVE '_'  TO  NUMED-UNDERLINE.

     IF NUMED-STATUS  =  SPACES
         MOVE SPACES                    TO  NUMED-MESSAGE
     ELSE
     IF NUMED-STATUS  =  'IP'
         MOVE 'INVALID NUMBER OF DIGITS OR DECIMALS PASSED'
                                   TO  NUMED-MESSAGE
     ELSE
     IF NUMED-STATUS  =  'ES'
```

Fig. 20.5 *Continued.*

```
    MOVE 'EXCESS SIGNS'              TO NUMED-MESSAGE
ELSE
IF NUMED-STATUS  =  'EP'
    MOVE 'EXCESS DECIMAL POINTS'  TO  NUMED-MESSAGE
ELSE
IF NUMED-STATUS  =  'EN'
    MOVE 'EXCESS WHOLE NUMBERS'  TO  NUMED-MESSAGE
ELSE
IF NUMED-STATUS  =  'ED'
    MOVE 'EXCESS DECIMAL DIGITS'  TO  NUMED-MESSAGE
ELSE
IF NUMED-STATUS  =  'IC'
    MOVE 'INVALID CHARACTER'      TO  NUMED-MESSAGE
ELSE
IF NUMED-STATUS  =  'IF'
    MOVE 'INVALID FORMAT'         TO  NUMED-MESSAGE
ELSE
IF NUMED-STATUS  =  'CD'
    MOVE 'COMMA AFTER DECIMAL'    TO  NUMED-MESSAGE
ELSE
IF NUMED-STATUS  =  'ND'
    MOVE 'NO DIGITS ENTERED'      TO  NUMED-MESSAGE
ELSE
IF NUMED-STATUS  =  'N3'
    MOVE 'NOT 3 DIGITS FOLLOWING A COMMA'
             TO  NUMED-MESSAGE
ELSE
        MOVE 'UNSPECIFIED ERROR'       TO  NUMED-MESSAGE.
*
 Z99Y-EXIT.
    EXIT.
*
*
 Z99Z-EDIT-PASS  SECTION.
*****************************************************************
*              PERFORMED FROM:  Z99Y-NUMERIC-EDIT              *
*****************************************************************
*
* THE ONLY VALID CHARACTERS ARE: THE DIGITS 0 THROUGH 9,
*    A SINGLE SIGN (- OR +), COMMAS, OR A SINGLE DECIMAL POINT
*    IMBEDDED SPACES ARE NOT PERMITTED
* ANY 'VALID' CHARACTERS MAY BE DEACTIVATED BY MOVING LOW-VALUES
*    TO THE CHARACTER'S WORKING STORAGE FIELD BEFORE PERFORMING
*    Z99Y-NUMERIC-EDIT.  FIELDS ARE RESET AT END OF ROUTINE.
*
    IF  NUMED-IN (NES1)  IS NUMERIC
      OR
```

Fig. 20.5 *Continued.*

```
         (NUMED-IN (NES1)    =     NUMED-DECIMAL   OR   NUMED-COMMA
                           OR   NUMED-MINUS     OR   NUMED-PLUS)
           NEXT SENTENCE
     ELSE
           MOVE 'IC'  TO  NUMED-STATUS
           GO TO   Z99Z-EXIT.
*
* MAY BE A MAXIMUM OF 1 SIGN THAT, IF PRESENT, MUST BE AT THE
*   START OR END OF A FIELD.
*
     IF NUMED-IN (NES1)  =  '-'  OR  '+'
         ADD 1  TO  NUMED-SIGN-COUNT
         IF NUMED-SIGN-COUNT  IS GREATER THAN  1
             MOVE 'ES'  TO  NUMED-STATUS
             GO TO  Z99Z-EXIT
         ELSE
             IF NES1  =  NESBEG  OR  NESEND
                 NEXT SENTENCE
             ELSE
             MOVE 'IF'  TO  NUMED-STATUS
             GO TO  Z99Z-EXIT.
*
* SET NEGATIVE SIGN INDICATOR
*
     IF NUMED-IN (NES1)  =  '-'
         MOVE 'Y'  TO  NUMED-NEG-SIGN.
*
* SAVE LOCATION OF DECIMAL POINT, IF ANY, IN NESDEC
*   MAY BE A MAXIMUM OF 1 DECIMAL POINT
*
     IF NUMED-IN (NES1)  =  '.'
         MOVE NES1  TO  NESDEC
         ADD 1      TO  NUMED-DEC-PT-COUNT
         IF NUMED-DEC-PT-COUNT  IS GREATER THAN  1
             MOVE 'EP'  TO  NUMED-STATUS
             GO TO  Z99Z-EXIT.
*
* TEST THAT COUNT OF WHOLE NUMBERS IN INPUT FIELD DOES NOT EXCEED
*   THE MAXIMUM NUMBER OF DIGITS PASSED TO THE ROUTINE
* NESDEC = ZERO UNTIL A DECIMAL POINT HAS BEEN ENCOUNTERED
*
     IF NESDEC  =  0
     IF NUMED-IN (NES1)  IS NUMERIC
         ADD 1  TO  NUMED-DIGIT-COUNT
         IF NUMED-DIGIT-COUNT  >  NUMED-DIGITS
             MOVE 'EN'  TO  NUMED-STATUS
             GO TO  Z99Z-EXIT.
```

Fig. 20.5 *Continued* .

```
*
* NESDEC IS GREATER THAN ZERO WHEN A DECIMAL POINT HAS BEEN
*   ENCOUNTERED AND ITS POSITION SAVED IN NESDEC
* COMMA MUST NOT FOLLOW DECIMAL POINT
* TEST THAT COUNT OF DECIMAL POS. IN INPUT FIELD DOES NOT EXCEED
*   THE MAXIMUM NUMBER OF DIGITS PASSED TO THE ROUTINE
*
      IF NESDEC  IS GREATER THAN  0
         IF NUMED-IN (NES1) = ','
            MOVE 'CD' TO  NUMED-STATUS
            GO TO  Z99Z-EXIT
         ELSE
            IF NUMED-IN (NES1) IS NUMERIC
               ADD 1 TO  NUMED-DEC-NUM-COUNT
               IF NUMED-DEC-NUM-COUNT >  NUMED-DECIMALS
                  MOVE 'ED' TO  NUMED-STATUS
                  GO TO  Z99Z-EXIT.
*
* CHECK THAT AT LEAST ONE WHOLE NUMBER OR ONE DECIMAL DIGIT
*   WAS ENTERED
*
      IF NES1  =  NESEND
         IF NUMED-DIGIT-COUNT    IS GREATER THAN  0
           OR
            NUMED-DEC-NUM-COUNT  IS GREATER THAN  0
            NEXT SENTENCE
         ELSE
            MOVE 'ND' TO  NUMED-STATUS
            GO TO  Z99Z-EXIT.
*
*
* CHECK FOR TWO CONSECUTIVE NON-NUMERIC CHARACTERS
*   ONLY VALID COMBINATIONS OF TWO NON-NUMERIC CHARACTERS
*   ARE: +.   -.   .+   .-
*
      IF NES1  NOT =  NESEND
         MOVE NES1 TO  NES2
         ADD 1     TO  NES2
         IF NUMED-IN (NES1)     IS  NUMERIC
            NEXT SENTENCE
         ELSE
            IF NUMED-IN (NES2) IS  NUMERIC
               NEXT SENTENCE
            ELSE
               IF ((NUMED-IN (NES1)  =  '-'  OR  '+')   AND
                   NES1  =  NESBEG                       AND
                   NUMED-IN (NES2)  =  '.')
```

Fig. 20.5 *Continued.*

```
                    OR
                    ((NUMED-IN (NES2)   =   '-'   OR   '+')      AND
                     NES2  =  NESEND                             AND
                     NUMED-IN (NES1)   =   '.')
                      NEXT SENTENCE
                ELSE
                    MOVE 'IF'  TO  NUMED-STATUS
                    GO TO  Z99Z-EXIT.
*
* ANY NUMBER OF HIGH ORDER DIGITS MAY PRECEDE THE 'FIRST' COMMA.
* LEADING COMMAS ARE FLAGGED AS ERRORS.
* IF NUMED-NUM-AFTER-COMMA-COUNT IS GREATER THAN 0 WHEN A COMMA,
*   DECIMAL, OR THE END OF INPUT DATA IS REACHED, THEN
*   LESS THAN 3 DIGITS FOLLOWED A COMMA
*
    IF NUMED-IN (NES1)   =   ','
        IF NUMED-DIGIT-COUNT  =  0
            MOVE 'IF'  TO  NUMED-STATUS
            GO TO  Z99Z-EXIT.
*
* EXACTLY 3 DIGITS MUST FOLLOW AN OPTIONAL COMMA.
* NUMED-NUM-AFTER-COMMA-COUNT IS INITIALLY SET TO 3
*
    IF NUMED-IN (NES1)   =   ','
        IF NUMED-NUM-AFTER-COMMA-COUNT   =   3
            MOVE 'Y'   TO  NUMED-NUM-AFTER-COMMA-SWITCH
            MOVE ZERO  TO  NUMED-NUM-AFTER-COMMA-COUNT
        ELSE
            MOVE 'N3'  TO  NUMED-STATUS
            GO TO  Z99Z-EXIT.
*
* COUNT DIGITS FOLLOWING A COMMA
*
    IF NUMED-IN (NES1)   IS NUMERIC
        IF NUMED-NUM-AFTER-COMMA-SWITCH   =   'Y'
            ADD 1  TO  NUMED-NUM-AFTER-COMMA-COUNT.
*
    IF NES1  =  NESDEC  OR  NESEND
        IF NUMED-NUM-AFTER-COMMA-SWITCH    =   'Y'
            IF NUMED-NUM-AFTER-COMMA-COUNT   =   3
                MOVE 'N'   TO  NUMED-NUM-AFTER-COMMA-SWITCH
            ELSE
                MOVE 'N3'  TO  NUMED-STATUS
                GO TO  Z99Z-EXIT.
*
Z99Z-EXIT.
    EXIT.
```

21

Using SQL to Access DB2 Data

Accessing DB2 data using SQL in a CICS environment is easy. This chapter familiarizes you with the basic coding techniques required to perform common database functions. Inquiry, insert, update, delete, and browse are explained through the use of examples. You are given the code required to convert programs presented in previous chapters from VSAM to SQL for these functions.

Required working storage and procedure division entries discussed in this chapter include host variables, host structures, SQL communications area (SQLCA) with its SQLCODE, declaring a table, and declaring a cursor. SQL procedure division statements discussed include SELECT, INSERT, UPDATE, DELETE, OPEN CURSOR, FETCH, and CLOSE CURSOR. In addition, this chapter explains the WHENEVER statement, indicator variables, variable-length character columns, the DB2 declarations generator DCLGEN, and program preparation.

You'll find it easier to understand this chapter if you are already familiar with SQL/DB2 concepts, but you should be able to follow the examples without having this background. Covering all the DB2/SQL options that can be used in a CICS program is difficult in an introduction, but this chapter gives you a good background for more advanced study.

DB2 Database Structure

A DB2 database consists of simple tables which are linked together by common keys that represent a column in each table. Entries in the database consist of rows which are equivalent to VSAM records, and columns that represent data fields. The examples in this chapter use a table named VEN-DOR that is identical in format to the vendor master file used in programs discussed in prior chapters. Data retrieved from the VENDOR table is moved to the vendor master record for compatibility of label reference with previously presented programs. Figure 21.1 shows the VENDOR table format used for examples in this chapter.

SQL Command Format

SQL statements may be embedded within a CICS program. The SQL command format is similar to that of CICS commands. All SQL commands used in a program begin with EXEC SQL and end with END-EXEC. Do not start the EXEC SQL before column twelve, and put both EXEC and SQL on the same line. Place SQL statements between the EXEC SQL and the END-EXEC. The embedded SQL statement, consisting of parts referred to as clauses, is similar to that of SQL statements used outside of a program. The following SELECT statement contains FROM, INTO, and WHERE clauses:

```
EXEC SQL
      SELECT  NAME
      FROM    VENDOR
      INTO    :HV-NAME
      WHERE   VCODE   =   HV-VCODE
END-EXEC.
```

Declaring a Table

Declare a table by using the SQL DECLARE TABLE statement. This statement lists the columns made available to a program as well as their data format. Figure 21.2 shows working storage entries used for examples in this chapter. For simplicity, all fields in the VENDOR table are required entries (NOT NULL) consisting of character data (CHAR) and decimal data (DECIMAL). Note that the first decimal digit consists of the integer plus any decimals; therefore, PIC S9(7)v99 is defined as DECIMAL(9, 2). NULL indicates that a column can have no data. Spaces and zeroes are not the same as NULL. You can use the declare table statement to limit retrieval access to selected columns by defining only required columns. The group level 01 HV-VENDOR defined in Fig. 21.2 consists of the COBOL, programmer-defined entries that correspond to the declare table statement's columns. The declare cursor statement is discussed later in this chapter when the browse program is converted to SQL access.

VENDOR

VCODE	NAME	ADDR	CITY	STATE	ZIP	ATTNOF	PHONE	CONTACT	DLRSCOMTD

Fig. 21.1 Vendor table format used for examples in this chapter.

Fig. 21.2 Working storage used in chapter's examples.

```
WORKING-STORAGE   SECTION.
*
*******************************************************************
*     DB2/SQL WORKING STORAGE ENTRIES FOR ALL EXAMPLES           *
*******************************************************************
*
*******************************************************************
*                      DECLARE TABLES                            *
* USED TO CONVERT THE FOLLOWING PROGRAMS TO DB2/SQL:             *
*         POVMINQY, POVMADDN, POVMCHGE, POVMDLET                 *
*         NOT USED BY POVMBROW - BROWSE PROGRAM                  *
*******************************************************************
*
     EXEC SQL DECLARE VENDOR TABLE
              (VCODE        CHAR(06)   NOT NULL,
               NAME         CHAR(25)   NOT NULL,
               ADDR         CHAR(20)   NOT NULL,
               CITY         CHAR(18)   NOT NULL,
               STATE        CHAR(02)   NOT NULL,
               ZIP          CHAR(05)   NOT NULL,
               ATTNOF       CHAR(20)   NOT NULL,
               PHONE        CHAR(10)   NOT NULL,
               CONTACT      CHAR(25)   NOT NULL,
               DLRSCOMTD  DECIMAL(9,2) NOT NULL)
     END-EXEC.



*******************************************************************
*                     DECLARE CURSOR                             *
*        ONLY USED BY BROWSE PROGRAM POVMBROW                    *
*******************************************************************
*
     EXEC SQL DECLARE VM-CURSOR  CURSOR FOR
          SELECT VCODE, NAME,     ADDR,    CITY,
                 STATE, ZIP,      ATTNOF,
                 PHONE, CONTACT, DLRSCOMTD
          FROM    VENDOR
          WHERE   VCODE  >=  :HV-VENDOR-CODE
          ORDER BY VCODE
     END-EXEC.
*
*******************************************************************
*                 INCLUDE HOST VARIABLES                         *
*******************************************************************
 01  HV-VENDOR-CODE      PIC X(6).
```

Fig. 21.2 *Continued.*

```
01  HV-VENDOR.
    05  HV-VCODE        PIC X(06).
    05  HV-NAME         PIC X(25).
    05  HV-ADDR         PIC X(20).
    05  HV-CITY         PIC X(18).
    05  HV-STATE        PIC X(02).
    05  HV-ZIP          PIC X(05).
    05  HV-ATTNOF       PIC X(20).
    05  HV-PHONE        PIC X(10).
    05  HV-CONTACT      PIC X(25).
    05  HV-DLRSCOMTD    PIC S9(7)V99    COMP-3.
*
***********************************************************************
*                       INCLUDE SQLCA                                 *
***********************************************************************
*
    EXEC SQL
        INCLUDE SQLCA
    END-EXEC.
*
***********************************************************************
*           SQL ERROR MESSAGE FIELDS                                  *
***********************************************************************
*
01  WS-SQL-ERROR-MESSAGE.
    05  FILLER                    PIC X(22)    VALUE
        'SQL ERROR - PROGRAM = '.
    05  WS-SQL-ERROR-PROGRAM      PIC X(8).
    05  FILLER                    PIC X(12)    VALUE
        'PARAGRAPH = '.
    05  WS-SQL-ERROR-PARAGRAPH    PIC X(5).
    05  FILLER                    PIC X(10)    VALUE
        'SQLCODE = '.
    05  WS-SQLCODE                PIC 999-.


01  WS-SQL-ERR-LENGTH             PIC S9999    VALUE +60   COMP.
```

Host Variables

Host variables are working storage data elements holding variable input and output data. They are the medium for passing data to and retrieving data used by SQL statements. Use level 01 or 77 entries for host variables not used within a host structure. Use host variables to hold data fields that may represent columns of the database or other variable data. HV-VENDOR-CODE in Fig. 21.2 is an example of a host variable. Precede host variables with a colon in SQL statements, but omit the colon when referring to host variables outside the SQL statement.

Host Structure

A host structure is a set of host variables having a maximum of two levels, 01 through 48, with an additional 49 level permitted if variable-length-character columns are defined. Use the host structure to access all of a table's data whereas a host variable must be defined for each column retrieved. Precede the structure name by a colon in an SQL statement, but omit the colon before the structure name outside the SQL statement. HV-VENDOR in Fig. 21.2 is an example of a host structure. HV- is a programmer-chosen prefix, while the suffix, though it need not be, is the same as the names in the DECLARE TABLE statement.

SQL Communications Area (SQLCA)

The SQL communications area is defined in working storage that DB2 uses to communicate with a program. Use an INCLUDE SQLCA statement to include it within an SQL statement as shown in Fig. 21.2. The first three fields of SQLCA are:

```
01  SQLCA.
    05  SQLCAID          PIC X(8).
    05  SQLCABC          PIC S9(9)    COMP.
    05  SQLCODE          PIC S9(9)    COMP.
        . . .
```

SQL Error Messages

The SQLCA field used extensively by examples in this chapter is SQL-CODE. This code returns the status of the SQL statement just executed. Its function is similar to a VSAM status return code or an EIBRESP code. Some of the more common SQLCODE return codes are:

0	SQL statement successfully executed
100	not found condition on SQL table retrieval request
-803	duplicate record condition on an insert request into a table that has a unique index

Convert Inquiry Program to SQL

The inquiry program presented in chapter 12 could be quickly converted to an SQL inquiry against a DB2 database. Accomplish this by:

- Including the code in Fig. 21.2 in the working storage section.
- Replacing section C410-READ-VENDOR-FILE with the code in Fig. 21.3.
- Adding a new section Z999-SQL-RETURN-CODE-ERROR shown in Fig. 21.4.

The SELECT statement

In Fig. 21.3, CA-VENDOR-CODE is moved into the host variable field HV-VENDOR-CODE, which is referenced in the SELECT statement. This state-

```
C410-READ-VENDOR-FILE  SECTION.
******************************************************************
*     PERFORMED FROM:  C400-VERIFY-VENDOR-FILE-STATUS            *
******************************************************************
*
     MOVE CA-VENDOR-CODE  TO  HV-VENDOR-CODE.
*
     EXEC SQL
         SELECT VCODE,       NAME,        ADDR,        CITY,
                STATE,       ZIP,         ATTNOF,
                PHONE,       CONTACT,     DLRSCOMTD
           INTO  :HV-VCODE,  :HV-NAME,    :HV-ADDR,   :HV-CITY,
                 :HV-STATE,  :HV-ZIP,     :HV-ATTNOF,
                 :HV-PHONE,  :HV-CONTACT, :HV-DLRSCOMTD
           FROM   VENDOR
           WHERE  VCODE  =  :HV-VENDOR-CODE
     END-EXEC.

     IF SQLCODE  =  0
         MOVE HV-VENDOR  TO  VENDOR-MASTER-RECORD
         MOVE 'G'  TO  STATUS-OF-READ
     ELSE
         IF SQLCODE  =  100
             MOVE 'E'  TO  STATUS-OF-READ
         ELSE
             MOVE 'POVMINQY'  TO  WS-SQL-ERROR-PROGRAM
             MOVE 'C410-'     TO  WS-SQL-ERROR-PARAGRAPH
             MOVE SQLCODE     TO  WS-SQLCODE
             PERFORM Z999-SQL-RETURN-CODE-ERROR.
*
C410-EXIT.
     EXIT.
```

Fig. 21.3 SELECT data into host variables.

```
Z999-SQL-RETURN-CODE-ERROR   SECTION.
********************************************************************
*        DISPLAY SQL ERROR MESSAGE AND RETURN TO CICS             *
********************************************************************
*
* THIS SECTION IS SIMPLIFIED.   YOUR INSTALLATION MIGHT CALL AN
* ERROR PROCESSING PROGRAM AND ABEND THE TASK TO BACKOUT UPDATES.
*
        EXEC CICS SEND
                  FROM    (WS-SQL-ERROR-MESSAGE)
                  LENGTH  (WS-SQL-ERR-LENGTH)
                  ERASE
        END-EXEC.
*
        EXEC CICS RETURN
        END-EXEC.
*
  Z999-EXIT.
        EXIT.
```

Fig. 21.4 SQL error return code routine.

ment accesses the single table row that matches the code moved to HV-VEN-
DOR-CODE. The individual columns of the VENDOR table are retrieved into
their respective host variables. For instance, VCODE into HV-VCODE, NAME
into HV-NAME etc. If a row is not found for the requested vendor, then an
SQLCODE of 100 is returned. Retrieving more than one row for a column
that is defined as a primary key is not possible. Any other SQLCODE signals
a serious error and the program prepares an appropriate error message and
performs Z999-SQL-RETURN-CODE-ERROR. You must declare a cursor in
cases where it is permissible to retrieve more than one row on a SELECT
statement. Declaring a cursor is explained later in this chapter. The SELECT
in Fig. 21.3 can retrieve data into a host structure instead of the equivalent
host variables by replacing the SELECT statement with the following:

```
EXEC SQL
        SELECT VCODE, NAME,     ADDR,     CITY,
               STATE, ZIP,      ATTNOF,
               PHONE, CONTACT, DLRSCOMTD
        INTO   :HV-VENDOR
        FROM   VENDOR
        WHERE  VCODE  =   :HV-VENDOR-CODE
END-EXEC.
```

Note that in Fig. 21.3 and in the above SELECT statement, retrieving
VCODE normally is not necessary since this code is known and because it
is equal to the host variable :HV-VENDOR-CODE. If you remove VCODE
from the SELECT, you must remove HV-VCODE from the host structure,

HV-VENDOR. For simplicity and compatibility with VENDOR-MASTER-RECORD, I've left it in the SELECTs.

You could code the previous example SELECT * as follows, because all fields are being retrieved:

```
EXEC SQL
     SELECT *
     INTO   :HV-VENDOR
     FROM   VENDOR
     WHERE  VCODE  =  :HV-VENDOR-CODE
END-EXEC.
```

This, however, is not recommended since columns in the table may be added, or their size changed, without the corresponding changes being made to the host variables in the host structure.

Convert Addition Program to SQL

You can convert the addition program presented in chapter 13 to an SQL insert against a DB2 database. You can accomplish this by:

- Including the code in Fig. 21.2 in the working storage section.

- Replacing section C410-READ-VENDOR-FILE with the code in Fig. 21.3.

- Replacing section E120-WRITE-VENDOR-RECORD with the code in Fig. 21.5.

- Adding a new section Z999-SQL-RETURN-CODE-ERROR shown in Fig. 21.4.

- Moving the program name 'POVMADDN' to WS-SQL-ERROR-PROGRAM in C410-READ-VENDOR-FILE if an error occurs.

The INSERT statement

In Fig. 21.5, VENDOR-MASTER-RECORD is moved into the host structure HV-VENDOR, and its subfields are referenced as host variables in the VALUES clause of the INSERT statement. This statement inserts a single table row containing the data in the columns referenced by the host variables. If the row to be inserted already exists, an error code of −803 is returned in SQLCODE only if the table has a unique index. Duplicates are permissible if a unique index has not been defined for a table. Any other SQLCODE signals a serious error and the program prepares an appropriate error message and performs Z999-SQL-RETURN-CODE-ERROR.

```
E120-WRITE-VENDOR-RECORD   SECTION.
**********************************************************************
*        WRITE VENDOR RECORD - PERFORM JOURNAL POSTING              *
*           PERFORMED FROM:  E100-ADD-VENDOR-RECORD                 *
**********************************************************************
*
     MOVE VENDOR-MASTER-RECORD  TO  HV-VENDOR.
*
     EXEC SQL
         INSERT INTO   VENDOR
                   (VCODE,      NAME,        ADDR,       CITY,
                    STATE,      ZIP,         ATTNOF,
                    PHONE,      CONTACT,     DLRSCOMTD)
             VALUES (:HV-VCODE, :HV-NAME,  :HV-ADDR,  :HV-CITY,
                    :HV-STATE, :HV-ZIP,    :HV-ATTNOF,
                    :HV-PHONE, :HV-CONTACT, :HV-DLRSCOMTD)
     END-EXEC.

     IF SQLCODE  =  0
        MOVE 'G'  TO  STATUS-OF-WRITE
     ELSE
        IF SQLCODE  =  803
           MOVE 'E'  TO  STATUS-OF-WRITE
        ELSE
           MOVE 'POVMADDN'  TO  WS-SQL-ERROR-PROGRAM
           MOVE 'E120-'     TO  WS-SQL-ERROR-PARAGRAPH
           MOVE SQLCODE     TO  WS-SQLCODE
           PERFORM Z999-SQL-RETURN-CODE-ERROR.
*
     MOVE 'A'  TO  JR-TYPE.
     PERFORM E121-POST-JOURNAL-RECORD.
*
E120-EXIT.
     EXIT.
```

Fig. 21.5 Insert data from host variables.

Convert Change Program to SQL

You can convert the change program presented in chapter 14 to SQL changes against a DB2 database. You can accomplish this by (note that there is no read for update by a SELECT statement.)

- Including the code in Fig. 21.2 in the working storage section.
- Replacing section C410-READ-VENDOR-FILE with the code in Fig. 21.3.

- Replacing part of section F110-READ-VENDOR-FOR-UPDATE with code similar to that in Fig. 21.3.
- Replacing section F120-REWRITE-VENDOR-RECORD with the code in Fig. 21.6.
- Adding a new section Z999-SQL-RETURN-CODE-ERROR shown in Fig. 21.4.
- Moving the program name 'POVMCHGE' to WS-SQL-ERROR-PROGRAM in C410-READ-VENDOR-FILE if an error occurs.

The UPDATE statement

In Fig. 21.6, VENDOR-MASTER-RECORD is moved into the host structure HV-VENDOR, and its subfields are referenced as host variables in the SET clause of the UPDATE statement. This statement replaces all the VENDOR columns specified in the SET clause with data contained in their corresponding host variables. Note that VCODE, the rows' unique primary key, is not replaced. Any SQLCODE other than zero indicates a serious error and the program prepares an appropriate error message and performs Z999-SQL-RETURN-CODE-ERROR. An SQLCODE of 100 indicates a not found condition, but should not occur, because the row was retrieved in section F110-READ-VENDOR-FOR-UPDATE prior to the update.

Convert Delete Program to SQL

You can convert the delete program presented in chapter 15 to an SQL delete against a DB2. You can accomplish this by (note that there is no read for update by a SELECT statement):

- Including the code in Fig. 21.2 in the working storage section.
- Replacing section C410-READ-VENDOR-FILE with the code in Fig. 21.3.
- Replacing part of section F110-READ-VENDOR-FOR-UPDATE with code similar to that in Fig. 21.3.
- Replacing section G110-DELETE-VM-RECORD with the code in Fig. 21.7.
- Adding a new section Z999-SQL-RETURN-CODE-ERROR shown in Fig. 21.4.
- Moving the program name 'POVMDLET' to WS-SQL-ERROR-PROGRAM in C410-READ-VENDOR-FILE if an error occurs.

The DELETE statement

In Fig. 21.7, CA-VENDOR-CODE is moved into the host variable HV-VENDOR-CODE prior to issuing the DELETE statement. This statement deletes the entire row that has its VCODE equal to HV-VENDOR-CODE. Any SQLCODE other than zero indicates a serious error and the program prepares an appropriate error message and performs Z999-SQL-RETURN-CODE-ERROR. An SQLCODE of 100 indicates a not found condition, but should not occur, because the row was retrieved in section F110-READ-VENDOR-FOR-UPDATE prior to the delete.

Convert Browse Program to SQL

You can convert the browse program presented in chapter 17 to SQL functions against a DB2 database. This could be accomplished by

- Including the code in Fig. 21.2 in the working storage section.
- Replacing section B140-START-BROWSE with the code in Fig. 21.8.

```
F120-REWRITE-VENDOR-RECORD  SECTION.
*********************************************************************
*      REWRITE VENDOR RECORD - POST 'AFTER' JOURNAL RECORD      *
*         PERFORMED FROM:  F100-CHANGE-VENDOR-RECORD            *
*********************************************************************
*
     MOVE CA-VENDOR-CODE        TO  HV-VENDOR-CODE.
     MOVE VENDOR-MASTER-RECORD  TO  HV-VENDOR.
*
     EXEC SQL
         UPDATE VENDOR
            SET NAME    = :HV-NAME,
                ADDR    = :HV-ADDR,     CITY      = :HV-CITY,
                STATE   = :HV-STATE,    ZIP       = :HV-ZIP,
                ATTNOF  = :HV-ATTNOF,   PHONE     = :HV-PHONE,
                CONTACT = :HV-CONTACT,  DLRSCOMTD = :HV-DLRSCOMTD
          WHERE VCODE = :HV-VENDOR-CODE
     END-EXEC.
*
     IF SQLCODE  NOT =  0
         MOVE 'POVMCHGE'  TO  WS-SQL-ERROR-PROGRAM
         MOVE 'F120-'     TO  WS-SQL-ERROR-PARAGRAPH
         MOVE SQLCODE     TO  WS-SQLCODE
         PERFORM Z999-SQL-RETURN-CODE-ERROR.
*
     MOVE 'A'  TO  JR-TYPE.
     PERFORM E121-POST-JOURNAL-RECORD.
*
 F120-EXIT.
     EXIT.
```

Fig. 21.6 Update all the columns of a row.

```
G110-DELETE-VM-RECORD   SECTION.
***********************************************************************
*    DELETE VENDOR RECORD - POST 'BEFORE' JOURNAL RECORD         *
*         PERFORMED FROM:  G100-DELETE-VENDOR-RECORD             *
***********************************************************************
*
     MOVE CA-VENDOR-CODE   TO   HV-VENDOR-CODE.
*
     EXEC SQL DELETE
          FROM VENDOR
          WHERE VCODE   =   :HV-VENDOR-CODE
     END-EXEC.
*
     IF SQLCODE   NOT =   0
        MOVE 'POVMDLET'   TO   WS-SQL-ERROR-PROGRAM
        MOVE 'G110-'      TO   WS-SQL-ERROR-PARAGRAPH
        MOVE SQLCODE      TO   WS-SQLCODE
        PERFORM Z999-SQL-RETURN-CODE-ERROR.
*
 G110-EXIT.
     EXIT.
```

Fig. 21.7 Delete an entire row.

- Replacing parts of sections B150-BROWSE-PROCESSING and B152-FORMAT-MAP.
- Adding a new section Z999-SQL-RETURN-CODE-ERROR shown in Fig. 21.4.

The required program code is covered later in the chapter.

Declaring a cursor

The working storage defined in Fig. 21.2 shows the code required to declare a cursor for the browse program. The cursor, VM-CURSOR, is a pointer to rows made available, in accordance with the declare cursor statement, when the cursor is opened. Conceptually, when a declare cursor statement is opened, as many rows as meet the WHERE condition specified (VCODE >= :HV-VENDOR-CODE) are retrieved and a sequential file created. This file is referred to as the *results table*. When the cursor is opened, VM-CURSOR points to the first record in the results table. The FETCH command, discussed later in this chapter, retrieves each row sequentially from the results table until it runs out of data, at which time, the cursor is closed.

Opening a cursor

In Fig. 21.8, CA-VENDOR-CODE is moved into the host variable HV-VEN-DOR-CODE prior to opening the cursor. The host variable is referenced by the declare cursor statement in working storage (Fig. 21.2). SQLCODE is set to zero if at least one qualifying row is available when the cursor is opened. A code of 100 indicates that no rows were available. Any other SQLCODE indicates a serious error and the program prepares an appropriate error message and performs Z999-SQL-RETURN-CODE-ERROR.

Closing a cursor

The close of a cursor is conceptually similar to the close of a file. You can open and close a cursor as often as necessary in a program. Replace the CICS ENDBR statement in paragraph B150-END-BROWSE of Fig. 17.2 with the following close cursor statement:

```
B150-ENDBR.

    EXEC SQL
        CLOSE VM-CURSOR
    END-EXEC.
```

Multiple cursors

You may define more than one cursor for the same or different tables in a program. You cannot read backward in a results table, but as you read forward using one cursor, a second cursor can be opened and closed as required to access records occurring earlier in the table. This ability to define more than one cursor against a table permits multiple positioning on the same table.

The FETCH statement

The FETCH statement functions similar to a read of a sequential file after the file has been opened. FETCH makes the first 'results table' record available after a cursor is opened. Succeeding FETCHes retrieve records in sequence until the end of the results table is indicated by an SQLCODE of 100. You cannot skip fetching rows in the results table, but you can bypass them by program logic based on appropriate conditions after they have been retrieved by a FETCH statement. You can close a cursor prior to reaching the end of the results table. Figure 21.9 demonstrates the use of the FETCH statement to retrieve results table columns into the host variables defined in Fig. 21.2.

```
B140-START-BROWSE    SECTION.
*****************************************************************
*            PERFORMED FROM:   B100-PAGE-FORWARD               *
*                              B200-PAGE-BACKWARD              *
*                              B500-RESET-KEY                  *
*                              C000-INITIAL-ENTRY              *
*****************************************************************
*
     MOVE CA-VENDOR-CODE   TO   HV-VENDOR-CODE.
*
     EXEC SQL
          OPEN VM-CURSOR
     END-EXEC.
*
     IF SQLCODE  =  0
        MOVE 'G'  TO   STATUS-OF-BROWSE
     ELSE
        IF SQLCODE  =  100
           MOVE 'E'  TO   STATUS-OF-BROWSE
        ELSE
           MOVE 'POVMBROW'   TO   WS-SQL-ERROR-PROGRAM
           MOVE 'B140-'      TO   WS-SQL-ERROR-PARAGRAPH
           MOVE SQLCODE      TO   WS-SQLCODE
           PERFORM Z999-SQL-RETURN-CODE-ERROR.
*
 B140-EXIT.
     EXIT.
```

Fig. 21.8 Opening a cursor.

The WHENEVER statement

Examples presented in this chapter tested SQLCODE for a return code after the execution of SQL statements to determine status. This is the recommended way to test the status of SQL execution. You might, however, encounter the WHENEVER statement in programs you have to maintain. This statement functions similar to the CICS handle condition commands. You must define it before the execution of an SQL statement and remains in effect until another WHENEVER is executed. The format of WHENEVER is:

```
EXEC SQL
     WHENEVER NOT FOUND
        GO TO  ... /
        CONTINUE
END-EXEC.
```

The conditions you are most likely to use with WHENEVER are:

- NOT FOUND—Equivalent to testing SQLCODE for 100.
- SQLERROR—Equivalent to testing SQLCODE for < 0.
- SQLWARNING—Equivalent to testing SQLCODE for a positive value other than 100.

The actions you can take are:

- CONTINUE—Ignore the condition and continue program execution.
- GO TO ...—GO TO a designated paragraph or section.

```
B152-FORMAT-MAP   SECTION.
*************************************************************
*          PERFORMED FROM:  B150-BROWSE-PROCESSING          *
*************************************************************
*
     EXEC SQL FETCH VM-CURSOR
          INTO  :HV-VCODE, :HV-NAME,     :HV-ADDR,  :HV-CITY,
                :HV-STATE, :HV-ZIP,       :HV-ATTNOF,
                :HV-PHONE, :HV-CONTACT, :HV-DLRSCOMTD
     END-EXEC.
*
     IF SQLCODE  =  0
         MOVE 'G'        TO   STATUS-OF-READ
         MOVE HV-VENDOR  TO   VENDOR-MASTER-RECORD
     ELSE
         IF SQLCODE  =  100
             MOVE 'F'  TO   STATUS-OF-READ
             GO TO  B152-EXIT
         ELSE
             MOVE 'POVMBROW'  TO   WS-SQL-ERROR-PROGRAM
             MOVE 'B152-'     TO   WS-SQL-ERROR-PARAGRAPH
             MOVE SQLCODE     TO   WS-SQLCODE
             PERFORM Z999-SQL-RETURN-CODE-ERROR.
*
     ADD 1  TO   TSUB.
               .
               .
               .

 B152-EXIT.
     EXIT.
```

Fig. 21.9 Partial replacement logic for B152-FORMAT-MAP.

Indicator Variables

The examples in this chapter have referred to the VENDOR table, which had all CHAR and DECIMAL columns defined as NOT NULL for simplicity and compatibility with the VENDOR-MASTER-RECORD. Use indicator variables to determine if a value in a specified field contains a NULL value, or to place a NULL value in a given field. An error occurs if an indicator variable is not defined for a column to be retrieved that contains a NULL value. The following working storage entry declares the miscellaneous codes table, MISCCODES:

```
EXEC SQL DECLARE MISCCODES TABLE
         (MCODE          CHAR(06)   NOT NULL,
          DESCR1         CHAR(25)   NOT NULL,
          DESCR2         CHAR(25),
          DESCR3         CHAR(25))
END-EXEC.
```

The key MCODE and description DESCR1 are defined as NOT NULL and cannot contain null values. DESCR2 and DESCR3 do not specify NOT NULL and may therefore contain a null value. An error results if DESCR2 or DESCR3 contains a null value and a retrieve is attempted without defining an indicator variable. You may define the host variables and the associated indicator variable in working storage as:

```
01   HV-MCODE                PIC X(6).
01   HV-DESCR1               PIC X(25).

01   HV-DESCR2               PIC X(25).
01   IND-VAR-2      COMP     PIC S9(4).

01   HV-DESCR3               PIC X(25).
01   IND-VAR-3      COMP     PIC S9(4).
```

You must define the indicator variables IND-VAR-2 and IND-VAR-3 as halfword binary fields. You must test if a null value is present in the columns DESCR2 and DESCR3, because null values are not retrieved. If you define an indicator variable, a negative value is placed in IND-VAR-2 and/or IND-VAR-3 if a null value is present. The value in the host variable is unchanged if a null value is present in the column. You can test for a null value as shown in Fig. 21.10.

Indicator variables are used on the EXEC SQL statement immediately following the host variable and are preceded by a colon with no embedded space. The indicator variables IND-VAR-2 and IND-VAR-3 are tested for a negative value that indicates that columns DESCR2 and/or DESCR3 contained a null value. Since no data is returned into HV-DESCR2 or HV-DE-SCR3 if their corresponding columns contain a null value, spaces are moved to the map if nulls are present. An error results if an indicator variable is not

```
EXEC SQL
     SELECT DESCR1, DESCR2, DESCR3
     INTO     :HV-DESCR1,  :HV-DESCR2:IND-VAR-2,
                           :HV-DESCR3:IND-VAR-3
     FROM    MISCCODES
     WHERE   MCODE   =   :HV-MCODE
END-EXEC.

IF SQLCODE   =   100
   PERFORM B230-NOTFOUND
ELSE
   IF SQLCODE   NOT =   0
      PERFORM Z999-SQL-RETURN-CODE-ERROR.

MOVE HV-MCODE    TO   MAP-MCODE.
MOVE HV-DESCR1   TO   MAP-DESCR1.

IF IND-VAR-2   IS NEGATIVE
   MOVE SPACES   TO   MAP-DESCR2
ELSE
   MOVE HV-DESCR2   TO   MAP-DESCR2.

IF IND-VAR-3   IS NEGATIVE
   MOVE SPACES   TO   MAP-DESCR3
ELSE
   MOVE HV-DESCR3   TO   MAP-DESCR3.
```

Fig. 21.10   Testing for a null value.

included next to HV-DESCR2 and HV-DESCR3 on the SELECT statement and the table contains a null value for one of these fields.

Setting NULL Values in a Column

You can use indicator variables also to set columns to null values on INSERT and UPDATE statements. Move –1 to the indicator variable prior to executing the insert or update if the column is to be set to nulls. If the host variable contains valid data, then move zero to the indicator variable prior to executing the insert or update. Figure 21.11 shows how to insert null values into DESCR2 and DESCR3, then how to update a row using the contents of the host variables HV-DESCR2 and HV-DESCR3.

Using Indicator Variables in Host Structures

Indicator variables are used in a host structure in a similar fashion to their use with host variables. You can define the host variable HV-MCODE and the host structure for the previously discussed host variables as:

```
01   HV-MCODE                      PIC X(6).

01   HV-MISCCODES.
     05   HV-DESCR1                PIC X(25).
     05   HV-DESCR2                PIC X(25).
     05   HV-DESCR3                PIC X(25).

01   MISC-INDICATORS,
     05   IND-VAR   OCCURS 3   COMP   PIC S9(4).
```

```
. . .
MOVE -1  TO  IND-VAR-2.
MOVE -1  TO  IND-VAR-3.

EXEC SQL
    INSERT INTO MISCCODES
           (MCODE, DESCR1, DESCR2, DESCR3)
    VALUES (:HV-MCODE,  :HV-DESCR1,
            :HV-DESCR2:IND-VAR-2,
            :HV-DESCR3:IND-VAR-3)
    WHERE  MCODE  =  :HV-MCODE
END-EXEC.

IF SQLCODE  =  0
    . . .


. . .
MOVE 0  TO  IND-VAR-2.
MOVE 0  TO  IND-VAR-3.

EXEC SQL
    UPDATE MISCCODES
       SET DESCR1  =  :HV-DESCR1,
           DESCR2  =  :HV-DESCR2:IND-VAR-2,
           DESCR3  =  :HV-DESCR3:IND-VAR-3
    WHERE  MCODE  =  :HV-MCODE
END-EXEC.

IF SQLCODE  =  0
    . . .
```

Fig. 21.11 How to insert null values and update a row.

The host structure HV-MISCCODES is followed by a set of three indicator variable items. Each item refers to its corresponding item in the host structure. For example, IND-VAR(1) is associated with HV-DESCR1, IND-VAR(2) with HV-DESCR2, and IND-VAR(3) with HV-DESCR3. An SQL statement refers to the host structure preceded by a colon, which must be immediately followed by IND-VAR preceded by a colon. Figure 21.12 shows a SELECT statement illustrating the technique.

Note that IND-VAR(1) was not tested for a negative value, because in the DECLARE TABLE statement for the MISCCODES table, its corresponding column DESCR1 was defined as NOT NULL. Since DESCR1 cannot be null, its corresponding indicator value IND-VAR(1) is always zero.

Variable Character Columns

If you defined the description columns in the MISCCODES table as VARCHAR(25) instead as CHAR(25), define the host structure HV-MISCCODES as shown in Fig. 21.13.

Each group level, HV-DESCR1, HV-DESCR2, and HV-DESCR3 consists of a length and data element that must be defined with a 49 level. The L suffix items represent the length of the variable length character data, while the D suffixed items represent the actual character data. The data fields of the host structure only contain as many characters as are represented by the length of the field after a retrieval of data. Therefore, moving spaces to the host structure variable length data fields before data is retrieved is a good programming practice. The length moved to the L suffixed fields determines the length of the character data inserted or replaced if the host variables are used with the INSERT or UPDATE statements.

Using DCLGEN to Declare Tables

Program examples in this book refer to the DECLARE VENDOR TABLE in Fig. 21.1. Depending on your installation standards, you may declare tables and generate host structures using the DB2 declarations generator, DCLGEN. This facility permits parameters to pass to the generator to create a dataset that you can include in your program when it is precompiled. DCLGEN creates a table declaration, and a host structure that has the same names as the columns in the defined table. You must previously define the table, because information is extracted from the DB2 catalog to build the define table and host structure entries. The advantage of using DCLGEN and including its generated dataset is that coding time and table transcription errors can be reduced. If the DCLGEN stored the vendor table in a member called DECVENDOR, the following INCLUDE statement is placed in working storage:

```
EXEC SQL
     INCLUDE DECVENDOR
END-EXEC.


EXEC SQL
     SELECT DESCR1, DESCR2, DESCR3
     INTO   :HV-MISCCODES:IND-VAR
     FROM   MISCCODES
     WHERE  MCODE  =  :HV-MCODE
END-EXEC.

IF SQLCODE  =  100
   PERFORM B230-NOTFOUND
ELSE
   IF SQLCODE  NOT =  0
      PERFORM Z999-SQL-RETURN-CODE-ERROR.

MOVE HV-MCODE    TO   MAP-MCODE.
MOVE HV-DESCR1   TO   MAP-DESCR1.

IF IND-VAR(2)  IS NEGATIVE
   MOVE SPACES   TO   MAP-DESCR2
ELSE
   MOVE HV-DESCR2  TO  MAP-DESCR2.

IF IND-VAR(3)  IS NEGATIVE
   MOVE SPACES   TO   MAP-DESCR3
ELSE
   MOVE HV-DESCR3   TO   MAP-DESCR3.
```

Fig. 21.12 Using an SQL statement that contains a host structure.

```
01  HV-MCODE                        PIC X(6).

01  HV-MISCCODES.
    05  HV-DESCR1.
        49  HV-DESCR1-L    COMP    PIC S9(4).
        49  HV-DESCR1-D            PIC X(25).
    05  HV-DESCR2.
        49  HV-DESCR2-L    COMP    PIC S9(4).
        49  HV-DESCR2-D            PIC X(25).
    05  HV-DESCR3.
        49  HV-DESCR3-L    COMP    PIC S9(4).
        49  HV-DESCR3-D            PIC X(25).

01  MISC-INDICATORS,
    05  IND-VAR   OCCURS 3  COMP    PIC S9(4).
```

Fig. 21.13 How to define the host structure HVMISC-CODES when using variable-character columns.

Program Preparation

A coded program must go through a series of steps before it is ready to be executed. You must perform the usual CICS command translation and pre-compile the program to translate embedded SQL statements to a form recognized by the compiler. The precompiler also performs syntax checking of embedded SQL statements and creates a data base request module called the DBRM. This module contains SQL statement and table information passed to a step called the BIND step. The program can then be compiled and link edited. Before the program can be executed, it must be passed through the BIND step. This step validates table and column names, checks authorization to access the requested data, and determines the most efficient access paths to the requested table data. The program is now ready for testing.

Using IMS-DL/I
Calls With CICS

This chapter explains IMS (Information Management System) using DL/I (Data Language I) calls in a CICS environment. It should be easy to understand if you have worked with DL/I in a batch environment, because DL/I commands are used in a similar fashion in both batch and CICS applications. Those of you not familiar with DL/I should be able to follow the material presented because only basic DL/I functions are used and explained.

IMS Database Structure

IMS is a hierarchical database consisting of segments that can be thought of as records of different types within a file. The vendor file used in previous examples in this text can be a database in an IMS environment. Databases consist of one or more segment types. A segment at a lower level is dependent on a segment at a higher level, which is referred to as its *parent*, while the lower level segment is called a *child* of the parent. The VENDOR segment is the parent of the purchase order segments (POORDER), while POORDER segments are children of the parent.

This example contains two segment types. There may be many segment occurrences of each segment type. Numerous vendors are in the database, and each vendor may have many open purchase orders. The simplified examples in this chapter use only the segment named VENDOR, which is identical in format to the vendor master file used in programs discussed in earlier chapters.

Data Base Description (DBD)

Databases are defined by a data base description (DBD) control block used to name the database, its segments, and other fields in the segment, such as its sequence fields (keys). A DBD defines the physical structure of a database. For examples in this chapter, the DBD name is VENDDBD, the segment name VENDOR, and the sequence field is named VENDKEY. DBDs are generally defined and assembled by a database administrator before they can be used by an application program.

DL/I Calls

Database functions are performed by passing parameters to a DL/I call embedded within a CICS program. Depending on the type of call, some or all of the following parameters pass to the DL/I interface module named CBLTDLI: function code, program communication block (PCB) mask, input output area, and segment search arguments (SSAs). For example:

```
CALL 'CBLTDLI' USING  function code
                      PCB mask
                      I/O Area
                      SSA.
```

Program Specification Block (PSB)

A program specification block (PSB) defines which databases a program can access. It defines the segments available to the program by including a program communication block (PCB) for each database. A PCB defines permissible functions for each segment and the logical structure of segments in the defined database. For simplicity, all program examples in this chapter use a PSB named VENDPSB containing a single PCB called VENDPCB that defines the vendor database (VENDDBD). All functions are permitted: get, insert, replace, and delete. In practice, your installation probably has a separate PSB for each program. For instance, a PSB can limit the permissible functions of an inquiry program to only a *Get* function.

Program Communication Block Mask

The program communication block is coded in the linkage section and defined as a PCB mask. The mask defined in Fig. 22.1 is named PCB-VENDOR; it defines several PCB fields. The examples in this chapter refer only to the status code (PCB-STATUS-VEND). Check the status code after each call to DL/I. A PCB mask is one of the parameters passed to and returned by calls to CBLTDLI. Figure 22.1 shows additional working storage and linkage section entries used by examples in this chapter.

Fig. 22.1 Entries used in chapter's examples.

```
WORKING-STORAGE  SECTION.
*
**********************************************************************
*     DL/I WORKING STORAGE AND LINKAGE SECTION ENTRIES FOR ALL      *
*     EXAMPLES USED TO CONVERT THE FOLLOWING PROGRAMS TO DL/I:      *
*     POVMINQY, POVMADDN, POVMCHGE, POVMDLET, AND POVMBROW          *
**********************************************************************
*
**********************************************************************
*                SEGMENT SEARCH ARGUMENT (SSA)                      *
**********************************************************************
*
 01  SSA-VENDOR-Q.
     05  SSA-VEND-SEG-NAME-Q    PIC X(8)    VALUE 'VENDOR  '.
     05  SSA-VEND-LP            PIC X       VALUE '('.
     05  SSA-VEND-NAME          PIC X(8)    VALUE 'VENDKEY'.
     05  SSA-VEND-OP            PIC XX      VALUE SPACES.
     05  SSA-VEND-KEY           PIC X(6)    VALUE SPACES.
     05  SSA-VEND-RP            PIC X       VALUE ')'.
*
 01  SSA-VENDOR-U.
     05  SSA-VEND-SEG-NAME-U    PIC X(8)    VALUE 'VENDOR  '.
     05  FILLER                 PIC X       VALUE SPACE.
*
**********************************************************************
*                DL/I MISCELLANEOUS FIELDS                          *
**********************************************************************
*
 01  DLI-FUNCTION               PIC X(4)    VALUE SPACES.
 01  WS-PSB-NAME                PIC X(8)    VALUE 'VENDPSB'.
*
**********************************************************************
*                DL/I ERROR MESSAGE FIELDS                          *
**********************************************************************
*
 01  WS-DLI-ERROR-MESSAGE.
     05  FILLER                 PIC X(23)   VALUE
         'DL/I ERROR - PROGRAM = '.
     05  WS-DLI-ERROR-PROGRAM   PIC X(8).
     05  FILLER                 PIC X(7)    VALUE
         'PARA = '.
     05  WS-DLI-ERROR-PARAGRAPH PIC X(5).
     05  FILLER                 PIC X(18)   VALUE
         'DLI RETURN CODE = '.
     05  WS-DLI-STATUS          PIC XX      VALUE SPACES.
     05  FILLER                 PIC X(11)   VALUE ' UIBFCTR = '.
     05  WS-DLI-UIBFCTR         PIC X       VALUE SPACE.
 01  WS-DLI-ERR-LENGTH          PIC S9999   VALUE 75   COMP.
*
**********************************************************************
*   REPLACEMENT FIELDS FOR LINKAGE SECTION - INCLUDES PCB MASK      *
**********************************************************************
*
```

Fig. 22.1 *Continued.*

```
 LINKAGE SECTION.
*
 01  DFHCOMMAREA                         PIC X(8).

 01  BLL-CELLS.
     05  FILLER                          PIC S9(8)    COMP.
     05  BLL-CWA-ADDRESS                 PIC S9(8)    COMP.
     05  BLL-T037-STATE-TABLE-ADDRESS    PIC S9(8)    COMP.
     05  BLL-UIB-PTR                     PIC S9(8)    COMP.
     05  BLL-PCB-LIST-PTR                PIC S9(8)    COMP.
     05  BLL-PCB-VEND-PTR                PIC S9(8)    COMP.
*01  CWA-DATA
                     COPY STLNKCWA.
*01  T037-STATE-CODE-TABLE
                     COPY T037STAT.
*01  USER-INTERFACE-BLOCK
                     COPY DLIUIB.
 01  PCB-ADDRESS-LIST.
     05  PCB-VEND-PTR                    PIC S9(8)    COMP.

 01  PCB-VENDOR.
     05  PCB-DBD-VEND                    PIC X(8).
     05  PCB-LEVEL-VEND                  PIC XX.
     05  PCB-STATUS-VEND                 PIC XX.
     05  PCB-PROC-OPT-VEND               PIC X(4).
     05  FILLER                          PIC X(4).
     05  PCB-SEG-NAME-VEND               PIC X(8).
     05  PCB-KEY-LEN-VEND                PIC S9(5)    COMP.
     05  PCB-SEN-SEGS-VEND               PIC S9(5)    COMP.
     05  PCB-KEY-FB-VEND                 PIC X(6).
```

Function Code

Function code is a four-character code defining the request to be performed against the IMS database. The function code area used to hold the requested function codes in this chapter is a programmer-defined field named DLI-FUNCTION. There are many DL/I function codes; the ones referred to in this chapter are:

- DLET—delete segments that have been read and held for update. All children, and segments dependent on those children, are also deleted when a parent is deleted.

- GHU—get a segment and hold it for update for the key specified in the SSA (defined later in this chapter). A segment is held until it is updated, deleted, or another DL/I call is issued using the same PCB.

- GN—get the next segment in the database. The segment retrieved depends upon current position in the database, contents of the SSA, and the parameters passed to the call.

- GU—get a unique segment for the key specified in the SSA with no update intended, and establish position in the database.
- ISRT—insert a segment into a database.
- REPL—update a segment that has been read and held for update.

I/O Area

DL/I retrieves segments into this area, and when inserts or replacements are made, DL/I obtains required data from this area. The input/output area used for all examples in this chapter is the VENDOR-MASTER-RECORD area used in previous chapters.

Segment Search Argument (SSA)

A segment search argument (SSA) is a programmer-defined area in working storage that is used as a parameter to a DL/I call. It contains information that indicates to the call, which segments are to be retrieved. Two basic types of SSA's are used by examples in this chapter: a qualified SSA named SSA-VENDOR-Q, and an unqualified SSA named SSA-VENDOR-U. Figure 22.2 shows SSA's defined in Fig. 22.1.

Qualified SSA

Use a qualified SSA to read a specific segment; it is employed as a key to retrieve a requested segment. The qualified SSA-VENDOR-Q can be visualized as shown in Fig. 22.3. The fields of SSA-VENDOR-Q are:

- SSA-VEND-SEG-NAME-Q—an eight-character segment name, defined in the DBD, that is to be retrieved; in this chapter, it is always the VENDOR segment.
- SSA-VEND-LP—the left parenthesis defines this as a qualified SSA. Unqualified SSA's have space in the ninth position.
- SSA-VEND-NAME—holds the eight-character name of a key that must be defined in the DBD.
- SSA-VEND-OP—a two-character relational operator that defines the type of search to be made. For instance, equal to (EQ or '= '), greater than or equal to (GE, '=>' or '>=').
- SSA-VEND-KEY—the *value* of the key to be searched for is moved to this field prior to issuing a DL/I call.
- SSA-VEND-RP—terminating right parenthesis of the qualified SSA.

```
01  SSA-VENDOR-Q.
    05  SSA-VEND-SEG-NAME-Q    PIC X(8)    VALUE 'VENDOR  '.
    05  SSA-VEND-LP            PIC X       VALUE '('.
    05  SSA-VEND-NAME          PIC X(8)    VALUE 'VENDKEY'.
    05  SSA-VEND-OP            PIC XX      VALUE SPACES.
    05  SSA-VEND-KEY           PIC X(6)    VALUE SPACES.
    05  SSA-VEND-RP            PIC X       VALUE ')'.
*
01  SSA-VENDOR-U.
    05  SSA-VEND-SEG-NAME-U    PIC X(8)    VALUE 'VENDOR  '.
    05  FILLER                 PIC X       VALUE SPACE.
```

Fig. 22.2 SSAs defined in Fig. 22.1.

Segment Name	LP	Key Name	Rel Op	Key Value	RP
VENDORbb	(	VENDKEYb	=b	value	)

Fig. 22.3 The qualified SSA-VENDOR-Q.

Unqualified SSA

The unqualified SSA is named SSA-VENDOR-U. It defines the segment to be retrieved by an unqualified DL/I call. For example, if the VENDOR database contains several segment types, only the VENDOR segments are retrieved by including SSA-VENDOR-U on a GN call to DL/I. SSA-VEND-SEG-NAM-U holds the name of the specific segment (in this case VENDOR) to be retrieved. The space in position nine defines this as an unqualified SSA.

PCB Returned Status Codes

After each call, a status code is returned in the PCB mask in the linkage section. Its function is similar to a VSAM status return code or an EIBRESP code. Codes that may be encountered in the examples in this chapter are:

Spaces	Call was executed successfully.
GB	End of database encountered during get next processing.
GE	Not found condition on segment retrieval.
II	Duplicate segment already exists in the database during an insert request.

User Interface Block (UIB)

The user interface block is defined in the linkage section by the copy member DLIUIB. The fields most often referred to in the DLIUIB copy member are:

```
01  DLIUIB.
    02  UIBPCBAL          PIC S9(8)    COMP.
    02  UIBRCODE.
        03  UIBFCTR       PIC X.
        . . .
```

The field UIBPCBAL is a pointer to an address list used to establish addressability to one or more PCB's used by a program. The required technique is part of the coding used with a PSB scheduling call. Test the field UIBFCTR after each DL/I call for LOW-VALUES; any other value indicates a serious error and must be provided for by the application program:

```
CALL 'CBLTDLI' USING  . . .

IF UIBFCTR  NOT =  LOW-VALUES
    PERFORM error routine.
```

PSB Scheduling Call

CICS programs require the scheduling of a PSB to establish addressability to the UIB and PCB(s) the program uses. A PSB scheduling call is coded as follows:

```
MOVE 'PCB ' TO  DLI-FUNCTION.

CALL 'CBLTDLI'  USING  DLI-FUNCTION
                       WS-PSB-NAME
                       BLL-UIB-PTR.
```

The literal PCB is required to be moved to DLI-FUNCTION. WS-PSB-NAME is an eight-character working storage field holding the name of the PSB to be scheduled. The linkage section's BLL-CELLS field BLL-UIB-PTR, defined in Fig. 22.1, establishes addressability to DLIUIB. The DLIUIB field UIBPCBAL is then moved to the BLL-CELLS field BLL-PCB-LIST-PTR to establish addressability to PCB-ADDRESS-LIST. The PCB address list contains one or more PCB addresses used to establish addressability to the PCB(s) used in program calls. Programs in this chapter use VENDPSB, which includes only one PCB, VENDPCB. Figure 22.4 illustrates the basic scheduling call and related coding.

Figure 22.5 defines the complete code used to schedule the PSB for all examples in this chapter.

PSB Termination Call

A program may issue a termination (TERM) call when it has completed processing the databases associated with the PSB. This results in the termination of the scheduled PSB, applies any database changes, and frees system

```
01  BLL-CELLS.
    05  FILLER              PIC S9(8)    COMP.
    05  BLL-UIB-PTR         PIC S9(8)    COMP.
    05  BLL-PCB-LIST-PTR    PIC S9(8)    COMP.
    05  BLL-PCB-VEND-PTR    PIC S9(8)    COMP.

01  DLIUIB.
    02  UIBPCBAL            PIC S9(8)    COMP.
    02  . . .

01  PCB-ADDRESS-LIST.
    05  PCB-VEND-PTR        PIC S9(8)    COMP.

01  PCB-VENDOR.
    . . .
```

```
MOVE 'PCB ' TO  DLI-FUNCTION.

CALL 'CBLTDLI'  USING  DLI-FUNCTION
                       WS-PSB-NAME
                       BLL-UIB-PTR.

MOVE UIBPCBAL       TO  BLL-PCB-LIST-PTR.
MOVE PCB-VEND-PTR   TO  BLL-PCB-VEND-PTR.
```

Fig. 22.4 The basic scheduling call and related coding.

resources. A PSB is automatically released when a task ends. Programs in this chapter do not issue a termination call. The format of a termination call is:

```
MOVE 'TERM' TO  DLI-FUNCTION.

CALL 'CBLTDLI'  USING  DLI-FUNCTION.
```

Code Common to All Programs

All programs in this chapter converted from VSAM to DL/I contain the following:

- The code in Fig. 22.1 included in the working storage and linkage sections.

- The PSB scheduling call defined in Fig. 22.5, section A100-SCHEDULE-PSB, performed at the beginning of AA00-MAINLINE. Each program moves its program name to WS-DLI-ERROR-PROGRAM in section A100-SCHEDULE-PSB.

- The error routine Z999-DLI-STATUS-CODE-ERROR, defined in Fig. 22.6 is included in each program.

Convert Inquiry Program to DL/I Calls

You can convert the inquiry program in chapter 12 from VSAM to DL/I by replacing section C410-READ-VENDOR-FILE with code in Fig. 22.7, as well as including the common code described above.

The GU function

In Fig. 22.7, 'GU' is moved to the DL/I function code field DLI-FUNCTION, the relational operator '=' is moved to the SSA field SSA-VEND-OP, and CA-VENDOR-CODE is moved into the SSA key field SSA-VEND-KEY. The call to CBLTDLI returns the segment that exactly matches the key moved to SSA-VEND-KEY into VENDOR-MASTER-RECORD. A segment found condition is indicated by a PCB-STATUS-VEND of spaces. If a segment is not found for the requested vendor, then a status code of GE is returned.

Any other status code signals a serious error and the program prepares an appropriate error message and performs Z999-DLI-STATUS-CODE-ERROR. A successful GU call establishes position in the database. The first segment in the database is returned if a GU call that has no SSA is executed.

```
 A100-SCHEDULE-PSB  SECTION.
 ****************************************************************
 *                 PERFORMED FROM:  AA00-MAINLINE              *
 ****************************************************************
 *
       MOVE 'PCB ' TO  DLI-FUNCTION.
 *
       CALL 'CBLTDLI' USING  DLI-FUNCTION
                             WS-PSB-NAME
                             BLL-UIB-PTR.
 *
       SERVICE RELOAD  DLIUIB.

       IF UIBFCTR  NOT = LOW-VALUES
           MOVE 'progname'  TO  WS-DLI-ERROR-PROGRAM
           MOVE 'A100-'     TO  WS-DLI-ERROR-PARAGRAPH
           MOVE UIBFCTR     TO  WS-DLI-STATUS
           PERFORM Z999-DLI-STATUS-CODE-ERROR.

       MOVE UIBPCBAL  TO  BLL-PCB-LIST-PTR.
 *     SERVICE RELOAD  PCB-ADDRESS-LIST.

       MOVE PCB-VEND-PTR  TO  BLL-PCB-VEND-PTR.
 *     SERVICE RELOAD  PCB-VENDOR.
 *
 A100-EXIT.
       EXIT.
```

Fig. 22.5 Schedule the PSB.

```
Z999-DLI-STATUS-CODE-ERROR   SECTION.
*******************************************************************
*           DISPLAY DLI ERROR MESSAGE AND RETURN TO CICS          *
*******************************************************************
*
* THIS SECTION IS SIMPLIFIED.  YOUR INSTALLATION MIGHT CALL AN
* ERROR PROCESSING PROGRAM AND ABEND THE TASK TO BACKOUT UPDATES.
*
     EXEC CICS SEND
               FROM   (WS-DLI-ERROR-MESSAGE)
               LENGTH (WS-DLI-ERR-LENGTH)
               ERASE
     END-EXEC.
*
     EXEC CICS RETURN
     END-EXEC.
*
 Z999-EXIT.
     EXIT.
```

Fig. 22.6 DL/I return code error routine.

Convert Addition Program to DL/I

You can convert the addition program presented in chapter 13 to DL/I. This can be accomplished by:

- Replacing section C410-READ-VENDOR-FILE with the code in Fig. 22.7.
- Replacing section E120-WRITE-VENDOR-RECORD with the code in Fig. 22.8.
- Moving the program name 'POVMADDN' to WS-DLI-ERROR-PROGRAM in C410-READ-VENDOR-FILE if an error occurs.

The ISRT function

In Fig. 22.8, VENDOR-MASTER-RECORD contains the segment data that is to be added to the VENDOR database. The value ISRT is moved to the function code field DLI-FUNCTION. Note that an unqualified SSA, SSA-VENDOR-U, is required in the insert call. The key is retrieved from VENDOR-MASTER-RECORD on this insert. Successful execution of this function returns a status code of spaces and adds a single VENDOR segment containing the data in VENDOR-MASTER-RECORD.

If the segment to be inserted already exists, a status code of II is returned in PCB-STATUS-VEND. Any other return code signals a serious error and the program prepares an appropriate error message and performs Z999-DLI-STATUS-CODE-ERROR.

Convert Change Program to DL/I

You can convert the change program presented in chapter 14 to make changes against a DL/I database. You can accomplish this by:

- Replacing section C410-READ-VENDOR-FILE with the code in Fig. 22.7.

- Replacing part of section F110-READ-VENDOR-FOR-UPDATE with code similar to that in Fig. 22.7 while substituting GHU for function code GU.

- Replacing section F120-REWRITE-VENDOR-RECORD with the code in Fig. 22.9.

- Moving the program name 'POVMCHGE' to WS-DLI-ERROR-PROGRAM in C410-READ-VENDOR-FILE if an error occurs.

```
C410-READ-VENDOR-FILE   SECTION.
*************************************************************************
*         PERFORMED FROM:  C400-VERIFY-VENDOR-FILE-STATUS        *
*************************************************************************
*
     MOVE 'GU'              TO   DLI-FUNCTION.
     MOVE '='               TO   SSA-VEND-OP.
     MOVE CA-VENDOR-CODE    TO   SSA-VEND-KEY.
*
     CALL 'CBLTDLI' USING   DLI-FUNCTION
                            PCB-VENDOR
                            VENDOR-MASTER-RECORD
                            SSA-VENDOR-Q.

     IF UIBFCTR  NOT =  LOW-VALUES
         MOVE 'POVMINQY'  TO  WS-DLI-ERROR-PROGRAM
         MOVE 'C410-'     TO  WS-DLI-ERROR-PARAGRAPH
         MOVE UIBFCTR     TO  WS-DLI-STATUS
         PERFORM Z999-DLI-STATUS-CODE-ERROR.

     IF PCB-STATUS-VEND  =  SPACES
         MOVE 'G' TO  STATUS-OF-READ
     ELSE
         IF PCB-STATUS-VEND  =  'GE'
             MOVE 'E'  TO  STATUS-OF-READ
         ELSE
             MOVE 'POVMINQY'        TO  WS-DLI-ERROR-PROGRAM
             MOVE 'C410-'           TO  WS-DLI-ERROR-PARAGRAPH
             MOVE PCB-STATUS-VEND   TO  WS-DLI-STATUS
             PERFORM Z999-DLI-STATUS-CODE-ERROR.
*
C410-EXIT.
     EXIT.
```

Fig. 22.7 Read an exact key.

```
E120-WRITE-VENDOR-RECORD  SECTION.
*********************************************************************
*          WRITE VENDOR RECORD - PERFORM JOURNAL POSTING           *
*              PERFORMED FROM:  E100-ADD-VENDOR-RECORD             *
*********************************************************************
*
     MOVE 'ISRT'  TO  DLI-FUNCTION.
*
     CALL 'CBLTDLI' USING  DLI-FUNCTION
                           PCB-VENDOR
                           VENDOR-MASTER-RECORD
                           SSA-VENDOR-U.

     IF UIBFCTR  NOT =  LOW-VALUES
         MOVE 'POVMADDN'  TO  WS-DLI-ERROR-PROGRAM
         MOVE 'E120-'     TO  WS-DLI-ERROR-PARAGRAPH
         MOVE UIBFCTR     TO  WS-DLI-STATUS
         PERFORM Z999-DLI-STATUS-CODE-ERROR.

     IF PCB-STATUS-VEND  =  SPACES
         MOVE 'G'  TO  STATUS-OF-WRITE
     ELSE
         IF PCB-STATUS-VEND  =  'II'
             MOVE 'E'  TO  STATUS-OF-WRITE
         ELSE
             MOVE 'POVMADDN'       TO  WS-DLI-ERROR-PROGRAM
             MOVE 'E120-'          TO  WS-DLI-ERROR-PARAGRAPH
             MOVE PCB-STATUS-VEND  TO  WS-DLI-STATUS
             PERFORM Z999-DLI-STATUS-CODE-ERROR.
*
     MOVE 'A'  TO  JR-TYPE.
     PERFORM E121-POST-JOURNAL-RECORD.
*
 E120-EXIT.
     EXIT.
```

Fig. 22.8 Add a record to the DL/I database.

The REPL function

A Get Hold call must be issued before performing a replace function. A GHU functions similarly to a GU, while additionally holding a segment for update. In Fig. 22.9, the value REPL is moved into DLI-FUNCTION before issuing a call to CBLTDLI. The data to be changed must be moved into the appropriate fields of VENDOR-MASTER-RECORD prior to issuing a REPL call. No SSA is required on an REPL call. Execution of this call replaces the segment that has been changed. A DL/I call fails if the key field in the I/O area has been modified. It also fails if another call has been executed using the same PCB against the database after the GHU call was executed. Any return code other than spaces indicates a serious error; the program prepares an appropriate error message and performs Z999-DLI-STATUS-CODE-ERROR.

Convert Delete Program to DL/I

You can convert the delete program presented in chapter 15 to a delete against a DL/I database. You can accomplish this by:

- Replacing section C410-READ-VENDOR-FILE with the code in Fig. 22.7.
- Replacing part of section F110-READ-VENDOR-FOR-UPDATE with code similar to that in Fig. 22.7 while substituting GHU for function code GU.
- Replacing section G110-DELETE-VM-RECORD with the code in Fig. 22.10.
- Moving the program name 'POVMDLET' to WS-DLI-ERROR-PROGRAM in C410-READ-VENDOR-FILE if an error occurs.

The DLET function

In Fig. 22.10, issuing the DLET function deletes the segment read and held for update. No SSA is required with a DLET call.

```
F120-REWRITE-VENDOR-RECORD   SECTION.
**********************************************************************
*        REWRITE VENDOR RECORD - POST 'AFTER' JOURNAL RECORD        *
*              PERFORMED FROM:  F100-CHANGE-VENDOR-RECORD           *
**********************************************************************
*
     MOVE 'REPL'   TO  DLI-FUNCTION.
*
     CALL 'CBLTDLI' USING  DLI-FUNCTION
                           PCB-VENDOR
                           VENDOR-MASTER-RECORD.

     IF UIBFCTR  NOT =  LOW-VALUES
         MOVE 'POVMCHGE'  TO  WS-DLI-ERROR-PROGRAM
         MOVE 'F120-'     TO  WS-DLI-ERROR-PARAGRAPH
         MOVE UIBFCTR     TO  WS-DLI-STATUS
         PERFORM Z999-DLI-STATUS-CODE-ERROR.
*
     IF PCB-STATUS-VEND  NOT =  SPACES
         MOVE 'POVMCHGE'         TO  WS-DLI-ERROR-PROGRAM
         MOVE 'F120-'            TO  WS-DLI-ERROR-PARAGRAPH
         MOVE PCB-STATUS-VEND TO  WS-DLI-STATUS
         PERFORM Z999-DLI-STATUS-CODE-ERROR.
*
     MOVE 'A' TO  JR-TYPE.
     PERFORM E121-POST-JOURNAL-RECORD.
*
 F120-EXIT.
     EXIT.
```

Fig. 22.9 Update a segment in the DL/I database.

```
G110-DELETE-VM-RECORD  SECTION.
*****************************************************************
*       DELETE VENDOR RECORD - POST 'BEFORE' JOURNAL RECORD     *
*            PERFORMED FROM:  G100-DELETE-VENDOR-RECORD         *
*****************************************************************
*
     MOVE 'DLET'  TO  DLI-FUNCTION.
*
     CALL 'CBLTDLI' USING  DLI-FUNCTION
                           PCB-VENDOR
                           VENDOR-MASTER-RECORD.

     IF UIBFCTR  NOT =  LOW-VALUES
         MOVE 'POVMDLET'  TO  WS-DLI-ERROR-PROGRAM
         MOVE 'G110-'     TO  WS-DLI-ERROR-PARAGRAPH
         MOVE UIBFCTR     TO  WS-DLI-STATUS
         PERFORM Z999-DLI-STATUS-CODE-ERROR.
*
     IF PCB-STATUS-VEND  NOT =  SPACES
         MOVE 'POVMDLET'        TO  WS-DLI-ERROR-PROGRAM
         MOVE 'G110-'           TO  WS-DLI-ERROR-PARAGRAPH
         MOVE PCB-STATUS-VEND   TO  WS-DLI-STATUS
         PERFORM Z999-DLI-STATUS-CODE-ERROR.
*
 G110-EXIT.
     EXIT.
```

Fig. 22.10 Delete a segment.

Any return code other than spaces indicates a serious error and the program prepares an appropriate error message, then performs Z999-DLI-STATUS-CODE-ERROR.

Convert Browse Program to DL/I

You can convert the browse program presented in chapter 17 to run against a DL/I database. The required program code is explained later in the chapter. You can accomplish this by:

- Replacing section B140-START-BROWSE with the code in Fig. 22.11.

- Deleting ENDBR command in section B150-BROWSE-PROCESSING and replacing part of B152-FORMAT-MAP with the code in Fig. 22.12.

Set starting position for browse

The GU function was used earlier in the chapter to read a specific segment in the database. Figure 24.11 shows how it is used to set position in the database at the first record equal to or greater than the value moved into SSA-VEND-

KEY prior to executing the GU function. Execution of this function not only sets position in the database, it also reads the qualifying segment.

Any return code other than spaces or GE indicates a serious error and the program prepares an appropriate error message and performs Z999-DLI-STATUS-CODE-ERROR. A return code of GE indicates that the key moved to SSA-VEND-KEY is beyond the end of the VENDOR database.

The Get Next (GN) function

Figure 22.12 illustrates the use of the get next function. After position in the database has been established by execution of a GU function, then

```
B140-START-BROWSE  SECTION.
*****************************************************************
*                PERFORMED FROM:  B100-PAGE-FORWARD          *
*                                 B200-PAGE-BACKWARD         *
*                                 B500-RESET-KEY             *
*                                 C000-INITIAL-ENTRY         *
*****************************************************************
*
      MOVE 'GU'            TO  DLI-FUNCTION.
      MOVE '=>'            TO  SSA-VEND-OP.
      MOVE CA-VENDOR-CODE  TO  SSA-VEND-KEY.
*
      CALL 'CBLTDLI' USING  DLI-FUNCTION
                            PCB-VENDOR
                            VENDOR-MASTER-RECORD
                            SSA-VENDOR-Q.

      IF UIBFCTR  NOT =  LOW-VALUES
          MOVE 'POVMBROW'  TO  WS-DLI-ERROR-PROGRAM
          MOVE 'B140-'     TO  WS-DLI-ERROR-PARAGRAPH
          MOVE UIBFCTR     TO  WS-DLI-STATUS
          PERFORM Z999-DLI-STATUS-CODE-ERROR.
*
      IF PCB-STATUS-VEND  =  SPACES
          MOVE 'G'  TO  STATUS-OF-BROWSE
      ELSE
          IF PCB-STATUS-VEND  =  'GE'
              MOVE 'E'  TO  STATUS-OF-BROWSE
          ELSE
              MOVE 'POVMBROW'       TO  WS-DLI-ERROR-PROGRAM
              MOVE 'B140-'          TO  WS-DLI-ERROR-PARAGRAPH
              MOVE PCB-STATUS-VEND  TO  WS-DLI-STATUS
              PERFORM Z999-DLI-STATUS-CODE-ERROR.
*
  B140-EXIT.
      EXIT.
```

Fig. 22.11 Read browse starting segment.

```
*
  B152-FORMAT-MAP  SECTION.
***********************************************************************
*                PERFORMED FROM:  B150-BROWSE-PROCESSING              *
***********************************************************************
*
      ADD 1  TO  TS-SUB.

      IF TS-SUB  =  1
         GO TO  B152-SETUP-SCREEN.
      MOVE 'GN'  TO  DLI-FUNCTION.
*
      CALL 'CBLTDLI' USING  DLI-FUNCTION
                            PCB-VENDOR
                            VENDOR-MASTER-RECORD
                            SSA-VENDOR-U.

      IF UIBFCTR  NOT =  LOW-VALUES
         MOVE 'POVMBROW'  TO  WS-DLI-ERROR-PROGRAM
         MOVE 'B152-'     TO  WS-DLI-ERROR-PARAGRAPH
         MOVE UIBFCTR     TO  WS-DLI-STATUS
         PERFORM Z999-DLI-STATUS-CODE-ERROR.
*
      IF PCB-STATUS-VEND  =  SPACES
         MOVE 'G'          TO  STATUS-OF-READ
      ELSE
         IF PCB-STATUS-VEND  =  'GB'
            MOVE 'F'  TO  STATUS-OF-READ
            GO TO  B152-EXIT
         ELSE
            MOVE 'POVMBROW'         TO  WS-DLI-ERROR-PROGRAM
            MOVE 'B152-'            TO  WS-DLI-ERROR-PARAGRAPH
            MOVE PCB-STATUS-VEND  TO  WS-DLI-STATUS
            PERFORM Z999-DLI-STATUS-CODE-ERROR.
*
  B152-SETUP-SCREEN.

      IF TS-SUB  =  1
         MOVE-CA-VENDOR-CODE  TO  TS-VENDOR-CODE.
            .
            .
            .
  B152-EXIT.
      EXIT.
```

Fig. 22.12 Partial replacement logic for B152-FORMAT-MAP.

succeeding reads are accomplished by issuing the GN function. Paragraph
B152-FORMAT-MAP is performed by paragraph B150-BROWSE-PRO-
CESSING until fifteen records have been moved to the screen, or the end
of the file has been reached as indicated by a status code of GB. Note that
the add of 1 to TSUB has been relocated to the top of the paragraph in Fig.

22.12. It is used as a first-time indicator because the first time through paragraph B152-FORMAT-MAP, you do not want to execute a GN function since the first record has been read by the GU function in Fig. 22.11.

Any return code other than spaces or GB indicates a serious error and the program prepares an appropriate error message and performs Z999-DLI-STATUS-CODE-ERROR.

Program Preparation

A program containing DL/I calls is prepared similar to other CICS programs; it must go through a series of steps before it is ready to be executed. The usual CICS command translation must be performed. The program can then be compiled and link edited. The program is then ready for testing.

Using EXEC DLI Commands to Access a DL/I Database

This chapter introduces you to the use of EXEC DLI commands to access a DL/I database in a CICS environment. You can use EXEC DLI, a higher level interface than DL/I calls, in place of DL/I calls to access IMS databases through DL/I or DBCTL (database control). A major advantage of using EXEC DLI is the simplicity of coding using EXEC DLI compared to using DL/I calls to perform the same functions. Other benefits of using EXEC DLI are the elimination of SSAs and BLL cells with the resulting removal of the need for DLIUIB and the PCB mask. EXEC DLI can fully exploit a 31-bit environment; in addition, program execution stops at EXEC DLI commands when using EDF for testing.

Coding required to convert programs introduced in previous chapters from VSAM access to EXEC DLI commands is explained for the inquiry, insert, replace, delete, and browse functions, along with required working storage and procedure division entries. Data base structure, data base description (DBD), program specification block (PSB), program communication block (PCB), input/output area, and program status code usage are similar to that explained in chapter 22.

EXEC DLI commands are used in a similar fashion in both batch and online applications. PSB scheduling is one of the major differences between the use of EXEC DLI in CICS and batch programs; it is not required by batch programs. This chapter is easy to understand if you read the last chapter. The simplified examples in this chapter use only the segment named VENDOR, which is identical in format to the vendor master file used in programs discussed in earlier chapters.

EXEC DLI Command Syntax

You can access and update DL/I databases by issuing EXEC DLI commands in a CICS program. Commands begin with EXEC DLI and are terminated by the END-EXEC delimiter. Similar to that of a CICS command the syntax of a command is:

```
EXEC DLI function
        [options and arguments]
END-EXEC.
```

Function Code

Function code is a four-character code defining the request to be performed against the database. The function codes used in this chapter are almost identical to those used with DL/I calls. The EXEC DLI function codes referred to in this chapter are:

- DLET—delete segments that have been read for update. All children, and segments dependent on those children, are also deleted when a parent is deleted.
- GN—get the next segment in the database. The segment retrieved depends upon current position in the database, and the options and arguments included with the command.
- GU—get a unique segment for the key specified in a WHERE option (explained later in the chapter) and establish position in the database.
- ISRT—insert a segment into a database.
- REPL—effect an update to a segment.
- SCHD—schedule a PSB for use by a CICS program.
- TERM—terminate the scheduled PSB.

PSB Scheduling Function

CICS programs that use EXEC DLI commands require the scheduling of a PSB in order to define the PSB, with its associated PCBs, that a program will use. PSB scheduling uses the SCHD function to obtain a PSB for a program as follows:

```
EXEC DLI SCHD PSB(VENDPSB)
END-EXEC.
```

Programs in this chapter use VENDPSB, which includes only one PCB, VENDPCB. Figure 23.1 defines the complete code used to schedule the PSB used for all examples in this chapter.

PSB Termination Function

A program can terminate a PSB using a TERM function when it has completed processing databases associated with the PSB. This results in the termination of the scheduled PSB, applies any database changes, and frees system resources. A PSB is automatically released when a task ends. Programs in this chapter do not terminate the PSB. The format of a termination function is:

```
EXEC DLI TERM
END-EXEC.
```

Options and Arguments

Most EXEC DLI commands used by program examples in this chapter contain common options with their related arguments. For example, the

```
WORKING-STORAGE  SECTION.
*
********************************************************************
* DL/I WORKING STORAGE ENTRIES FOR ALL EXAMPLES USED TO CONVERT  *
* THE FOLLOWING PROGRAMS TO EXEC DLI:                            *
* POVMINQY, POVMADDN, POVMCHGE, POVMDLET, AND POVMBROW           *
********************************************************************
*
********************************************************************
*              DLI ERROR MESSAGE FIELDS                          *
********************************************************************
*
 01  WS-DLI-ERROR-MESSAGE.
     05  FILLER                   PIC X(22)    VALUE
         'DLI ERROR - PROGRAM = '.
     05  WS-DLI-ERROR-PROGRAM     PIC X(8).
     05  FILLER                   PIC X(7)     VALUE
         'PARA = '.
     05  WS-DLI-ERROR-PARAGRAPH   PIC X(5).
     05  FILLER                   PIC X(18)    VALUE
         'DLI STATUS CODE = '.
     05  WS-DLI-STATUS            PIC XX       VALUE SPACES.

 01  WS-DLI-ERR-LENGTH            PIC S9999    VALUE 63    COMP.
```

Fig. 23.1 Entries used in chapter's examples.

SEGMENT option always has VENDOR as its argument. Options and arguments used are:

```
EXEC DLI function  USING PCB(1)
          SEGMENT      (VENDOR)
          INTO/FROM    (VENDOR-MASTER-RECORD)
          SEGLENGTH    (169)
          WHERE        (VENDKEY ro CA-VENDOR-CODE)
          FIELD-LENGTH (6)
END-EXEC.
```

USING PCB option

The USING PCB option specifies which PCB in the scheduled PSB is to be used with an EXEC DLI command. Program examples in this chapter have only one PCB, VENDPCB; therefore, USING PCB is immediately followed by the digit 1 enclosed by a pair of parentheses. The first PCB in the scheduled PSB is assumed if this option is omitted. The digit inside the parentheses indicates the relative position of a PCB within a PSB when there is more than one PCB. For example, USING PCB(2) refers to the second PCB defined in a PSB.

SEGMENT option

Use the SEGMENT option to specify the segment type to be used with an EXEC DLI command. The only segment type used by examples in this chapter is the VENDOR segment. SEGMENT must be specified on GU, ISRT, REPL, and DLET commands; it is optional with GN commands.

INTO and FROM options

Use the INTO and FROM options to define the input or output area to be used with EXEC DLI commands. Segment data is retrieved into this area, and when inserts or replacements are made, DL/I obtains segment data from this area. The input/output area used for all examples in this chapter is the VENDOR-MASTER-RECORD area used in previous chapters.

SEGLENGTH option

Use the SEGLENGTH option to define the length of a segment to be operated upon. The length of the VENDOR segment is 169 bytes, which is the size of the VENDOR-MASTER-RECORD I/O area. You must specify SEGLENGTH for programs not compiled using the VS COBOL II compiler. Segment length defaults to I/O area length if you omit SEGLENGTH when using VS COBOL II. The length of the I/O area used with the INTO or FROM options must be at least as large as the length defined if using the SEGLENGTH option, otherwise storage is overwritten by transferred data.

WHERE option

The WHERE option is very powerful and flexible; use it to specify the occurrence of the segment type you wish to retrieve. All examples in this chapter compare the DBD defined key field VENDKEY against the commarea field CA-VENDOR-CODE. You must use the relational operator (ro) in symbolic form; you cannot use letters in place of symbols as you can with DL/I calls. For example, = (equal to) and => (equal to or greater than) are valid relational operators, while EQ and GE are invalid.

FIELDLENGTH option

The FIELDLENGTH option must be specified on commands containing a WHERE option if you are not using the VS COBOL II compiler. This option refers to the length of the field to the right of a relational operator in a WHERE option. For examples in this chapter, the length of CA-VENDOR-CODE is six (6) characters long.

DL/I Interface Block (DIB)

The DL/I interface block (DIB) consists of fields automatically generated by the translator and placed in a program's working storage. These fields can be examined after the execution of each EXEC DLI command to determine the status of the last command executed. Information contained in DIB fields is similar to that returned in the PCB mask area when using DL/I calls. The only DIB field to which examples in this chapter refer is a two-character alphanumeric status code field named DIBSTAT. It is used in a fashion similar to the status code returned by the execution of a DL/I call.

DIBSTAT status codes

After each call, a status code is returned in the DIB field DIBSTAT. Its function is similar to a VSAM status return code or an EIBRESP code. Status codes used in this chapter are identical to those returned by the execution of DL/I calls in chapter 22. Those codes are:

Spaces	Call was executed successfully.
GB	End of database encountered during get next processing.
GE	Not found condition on segment retrieval.
II	Duplicate segment already exists in the database during an insert request.

Code Common to All Programs

All programs in this chapter converted from VSAM access to the use of EXEC DLI commands contain:

- The code in Fig. 23.1 in the working storage section.
- The PSB scheduling call defined in Fig. 23.2, section A100-SCHEDULE-PSB, performed at the beginning of AA00-MAINLINE. Each program moves its program name to WS-DLI-ERROR-PROGRAM in section A100-SCHEDULE-PSB.
- The error routine Z999-DLI-STATUS-CODE-ERROR, defined in Fig. 23.3, in each program.

Convert Inquiry Program to EXEC DLI

You can convert the inquiry program in chapter 12 from VSAM access to the use of EXEC DLI commands by replacing section C410-READ-VENDOR-FILE with code in Fig. 23.4, as well as including the common code described above.

The GU function

Figure 23.4 illustrates the code required to perform a GU function. The equal (=) relational operator on the WHERE option specifies that the key contained in CA-VENDOR-CODE must be equal to a field defined in the VENDOR segment's DBD named VENDKEY. A matching segment is returned into the I/O area VENDOR-MASTER-RECORD. A segment found condition is indicated by a DIBSTAT return code of spaces.

```
A100-SCHEDULE-PSB   SECTION.
*******************************************************************
*                PERFORMED FROM:  AA00-MAINLINE                   *
*******************************************************************
*
     EXEC DLI SCHD PSB (VENDPSB)
     END-EXEC.
*
     IF DIBSTAT  NOT =  SPACES
         MOVE 'progname'  TO  WS-DLI-ERROR-PROGRAM
         MOVE 'A100-'     TO  WS-DLI-ERROR-PARAGRAPH
         MOVE DIBSTAT     TO  WS-DLI-STATUS
         PERFORM Z999-DLI-STATUS-CODE-ERROR.
*
A100-EXIT.
     EXIT.
```

Fig. 23.2 Schedule the PSB.

```
Z999-DLI-STATUS-CODE-ERROR   SECTION.
******************************************************************
*              DISPLAY DLI ERROR MESSAGE AND RETURN TO CICS      *
******************************************************************
*
* THIS SECTION IS SIMPLIFIED.  YOUR INSTALLATION MIGHT CALL AN
* ERROR PROCESSING PROGRAM AND ABEND THE TASK TO BACKOUT UPDATES.
*
      EXEC CICS SEND
               FROM    (WS-DLI-ERROR-MESSAGE)
               LENGTH (WS-DLI-ERR-LENGTH)
               ERASE
      END-EXEC.
*
      EXEC CICS RETURN
      END-EXEC.
*
 Z999-EXIT.
     EXIT.
```

Fig. 23.3 DL/I return code error routine.

If a segment was not found for the requested vendor, then DIBSTAT contains a status code of GE. Any other status code signals a serious error and the program prepares an appropriate error message and performs Z999-DLI-STATUS-CODE-ERROR. Execution of a successful GU establishes position in the database. Position is established at the first segment in the database if a GU function is executed including a SEGMENT option that specified the VENDOR segment type, but omitted the WHERE option. There is no GHU function when using EXEC DLI commands. Permissible functions that immediately follow a GU, such as REPL and DLET, are determined by the processing options specified when the PCB is defined.

Convert Addition Program to EXEC DLI

You can convert the addition program presented in chapter 13 to use EXEC DLI commands by:

- Replacing section C410-READ-VENDOR-FILE with the code in Fig. 23.4.

- Replacing section E120-WRITE-VENDOR-RECORD with the code in Fig. 23.5.

- Moving the program name 'POVMADDN' to WS-DLI-ERROR-PROGRAM in C410-READ-VENDOR-FILE if an error occurs.

```
C410-READ-VENDOR-FILE  SECTION.
*****************************************************************
*       PERFORMED FROM:  C400-VERIFY-VENDOR-FILE-STATUS        *
*****************************************************************
*
     EXEC DLI GU  USING PCB(1)
                 SEGMENT     (VENDOR)
                 INTO        (VENDOR-MASTER-RECORD)
                 SEGLENGTH   (169)
                 WHERE       (VENDKEY = CA-VENDOR-CODE)
                 FIELDLENGTH (6)
     END-EXEC.

     IF DIBSTAT  =  SPACES
         MOVE 'G'  TO  STATUS-OF-READ
     ELSE
         IF DIBSTAT  =  'GE'
             MOVE 'E'  TO  STATUS-OF-READ
         ELSE
             MOVE 'POVMINQY'  TO  WS-DLI-ERROR-PROGRAM
             MOVE 'C410-'     TO  WS-DLI-ERROR-PARAGRAPH
             MOVE DIBSTAT     TO  WS-DLI-STATUS
             PERFORM Z999-DLI-STATUS-CODE-ERROR.
*
C410-EXIT.
     EXIT.
```

Fig. 23.4 Read an exact key.

The ISRT function

In Fig. 23.5, VENDOR-MASTER-RECORD contains the segment data to be added to the VENDOR database. Note that no WHERE option is specified on the lowest level segment, the segment type to be inserted. The key is retrieved from VENDOR-MASTER-RECORD on this insert. Successful execution of this function returns spaces to DIBSTAT, while adding a single VENDOR segment containing the data in VENDOR-MASTER-RECORD. If the segment to be inserted already exists, a status code of II is returned in DIBSTAT.

Any other return code signals a serious error and the program prepares an appropriate error message and performs Z999-DLI-STATUS-CODE-ERROR.

Convert Change Program to EXEC DLI

The change program presented in chapter 14 can be converted to update segments using EXEC DLI by:

- Replacing section C410-READ-VENDOR-FILE with the code in Fig. 23.4.
- Replacing part of section F110-READ-VENDOR-FOR-UPDATE with code similar to that in Fig. 23.4. There is no coding difference in a read for inquiry purposes versus a read for update when using EXEC DLI.
- Replacing section F120-REWRITE-VENDOR-RECORD with the code in Fig. 23.6.
- Moving the program name 'POVMCHGE' to WS-DLI-ERROR-PROGRAM in C410-READ-VENDOR-FILE if an error occurs.

The REPL function

An EXEC DLI GU must be performed prior to executing a command with an REPL function. There is no GHU function to use with EXEC DLI commands; you must define a segment to be replaced as replace-sensitive in the PCB. In

```
E120-WRITE-VENDOR-RECORD   SECTION.
*******************************************************************
*          WRITE VENDOR RECORD - PERFORM JOURNAL POSTING          *
*          PERFORMED FROM:   E100-ADD-VENDOR-RECORD               *
*******************************************************************
*
    EXEC DLI ISRT   USING PCB(1)
             SEGMENT    (VENDOR)
             FROM       (VENDOR-MASTER-RECORD)
             SEGLENGTH  (169)
    END-EXEC.

    IF DIBSTAT  =  SPACES
        MOVE 'G'  TO   STATUS-OF-WRITE
    ELSE
        IF DIBSTAT  =  'II'
            MOVE 'E'  TO   STATUS-OF-WRITE
        ELSE
            MOVE 'POVMADDN'  TO  WS-DLI-ERROR-PROGRAM
            MOVE 'E120-'     TO  WS-DLI-ERROR-PARAGRAPH
            MOVE DIBSTAT     TO  WS-DLI-STATUS
            PERFORM Z999-DLI-STATUS-CODE-ERROR.
*
    MOVE 'A'  TO   JR-TYPE.
    PERFORM E121-POST-JOURNAL-RECORD.
*
E120-EXIT.
    EXIT.
```

Fig. 23.5 Add a record to the DL/I database.

```
F120-REWRITE-VENDOR-RECORD  SECTION.
***************************************************************
*       REWRITE VENDOR RECORD - POST 'AFTER' JOURNAL RECORD    *
*           PERFORMED FROM:  F100-CHANGE-VENDOR-RECORD         *
***************************************************************
*
      EXEC DLI REPL  USING PCB(1)
              SEGMENT   (VENDOR)
              FROM      (VENDOR-MASTER-RECORD)
              SEGLENGTH (169)
      END-EXEC.
*
      IF DIBSTAT  NOT =  SPACES
          MOVE 'POVMCHGE'  TO  WS-DLI-ERROR-PROGRAM
          MOVE 'F120-'     TO  WS-DLI-ERROR-PARAGRAPH
          MOVE DIBSTAT     TO  WS-DLI-STATUS
          PERFORM Z999-DLI-STATUS-CODE-ERROR.
*
      MOVE 'A'  TO  JR-TYPE.
      PERFORM E121-POST-JOURNAL-RECORD.
*
 F120-EXIT.
      EXIT.
```

Fig. 23.6 Update a segment in the DL/I database.

Fig. 23.6, the value REPL defines this command as a replace function. Move the data to be changed into the appropriate data fields of VENDOR-MAS-TER-RECORD prior to executing the REPL command. Do not use a WHERE option with a REPL function. Execution of this command replaces the VEN-DOR segment with the fields in the I/O area. A REPL function fails if the key field in the I/O area has been modified. It also fails if another EXEC DLI command is executed using the same PCB, after the GU function is executed.

Any return code other than spaces indicates a serious error; the program prepares an appropriate error message and performs Z999-DLI-STATUS-CODE-ERROR.

Convert Delete Program to EXEC DLI

You can convert the delete program presented in chapter 15 to delete segments using the EXEC DLI DLET function by:

■ Replacing section C410-READ-VENDOR-FILE with the code in Fig. 23.4.

■ Replacing part of section F110-READ-VENDOR-FOR-UPDATE with code similar to that in Fig. 23.4. There is no coding difference in a read for inquiry purposes versus a read for delete when using EXEC DLI commands.

- Replacing section G110-DELETE-VM-RECORD with the code in Fig. 23.7.
- Moving the program name 'POVMDLET' to WS-DLI-ERROR-PROGRAM in C410-READ-VENDOR-FILE if an error occurs.

The DLET function

In Fig. 23.7, executing the DLET function deletes the segment read by executing an EXEC DLI command with the GU function. No commands using the same PCB can be issued between the GU and the DLET functions. All children segments dependent on a parent are deleted when the parent is deleted.

Any return code other than spaces indicates a serious error and the program prepares an appropriate error message, then performs Z999-DLI-STA-TUS-CODE-ERROR.

Convert Browse Program to EXEC DLI

You can convert the browse program presented in chapter 17 to EXEC DLI commands. The required program code is explained later in the chapter.

- Replacing section B140-START-BROWSE with the code in Fig. 23.8.
- Deleting ENDBR command in section B150-BROWSE-PROCESSING and replacing part of B152-FORMAT-MAP with the code in Fig. 23.9.

```
G110-DELETE-VM-RECORD   SECTION.
**********************************************************************
*      DELETE VENDOR RECORD - POST 'BEFORE' JOURNAL RECORD         *
*           PERFORMED FROM:  G100-DELETE-VENDOR-RECORD             *
**********************************************************************
*
     MOVE 'DLET'  TO  DLI-FUNCTION.
*
     EXEC DLI DLET  USING PCB(1)
               SEGMENT    (VENDOR)
               FROM       (VENDOR-MASTER-RECORD)
               SEGLENGTH (169)
     END-EXEC.
*
     IF DIBSTAT  NOT =  SPACES
          MOVE 'POVMDLET'  TO  WS-DLI-ERROR-PROGRAM
          MOVE 'G110-'     TO  WS-DLI-ERROR-PARAGRAPH
          MOVE DIBSTAT     TO  WS-DLI-STATUS
          PERFORM Z999-DLI-STATUS-CODE-ERROR.
*
G110-EXIT.
     EXIT.
```

Fig. 23.7 Delete a segment.

```
B140-START-BROWSE   SECTION.
********************************************************************
*             PERFORMED FROM:   B100-PAGE-FORWARD               *
*                               B200-PAGE-BACKWARD              *
*                               B500-RESET-KEY                  *
*                               C000-INITIAL-ENTRY              *
********************************************************************
*
     EXEC DLI GU   USING PCB(1)
                SEGMENT    (VENDOR)
                INTO       (VENDOR-MASTER-RECORD)
                SEGLENGTH  (169)
                WHERE      (VENDKEY => CA-VENDOR-CODE)
                FIELDLENGTH (6)
     END-EXEC.
*
     IF DIBSTAT  =  SPACES
         MOVE 'G'  TO  STATUS-OF-BROWSE
     ELSE
         IF DIBSTAT  =  'GE'
             MOVE 'E'  TO  STATUS-OF-BROWSE
         ELSE
             MOVE 'POVMBROW'  TO  WS-DLI-ERROR-PROGRAM
             MOVE 'B140-'     TO  WS-DLI-ERROR-PARAGRAPH
             MOVE DIBSTAT     TO  WS-DLI-STATUS
             PERFORM Z999-DLI-STATUS-CODE-ERROR.
*
 B140-EXIT.
     EXIT.
```

Fig. 23.8 Read browse starting segment.

Set starting position for Browse

The GU function was used earlier in the chapter to read a specific segment
in the database. Figure 23.8 shows how to use it to set position in the database at the first record equal to or greater than the value in CA-VENDOR-
CODE. Execution of this function not only sets position in the database, it
also reads the qualifying segment.

Any return code other than spaces or GE indicates a serious error and
the program prepares an appropriate error message and performs Z999-
DLI-STATUS-CODE-ERROR. A return code of GE indicates that the key in
CA-VENDOR-CODE is beyond the end of the database.

The Get Next (GN) function

Figure 23.9 illustrates the use of the get next function. After positioning in
the database has been established by execution of a GU function, then suc-

ceeding reads are accomplished by issuing the GN function. Paragraph B152-FORMAT-MAP is performed by paragraph B150-BROWSE-PRO-CESSING until fifteen records have been moved to the screen or the end of the file has been reached as indicated by a status code of GB. Note that the add of 1 to TSUB relocates to the top of the paragraph in Fig. 23.9. Use it as a first-time indicator because the first time through paragraph B152-FOR-MAT-MAP, you do not want to execute a GN function, since the first record has been read by the GU function in Fig. 23.8.

```
*
  B152-FORMAT-MAP  SECTION.
 *******************************************************************
 *               PERFORMED FROM:  B150-BROWSE-PROCESSING          *
 *******************************************************************
 *
      ADD 1  TO  TS-SUB.

      IF TS-SUB  =  1
          GO TO  B152-SETUP-SCREEN.
 *
      EXEC DLI GN  USING PCB(1)
              SEGMENT    (VENDOR)
              INTO       (VENDOR-MASTER-RECORD)
              SEGLENGTH (169)
      END-EXEC.
 *
      IF DIBSTAT  =  SPACES
          MOVE 'G'  TO  STATUS-OF-READ
      ELSE
          IF DIBSTAT  =  'GB'
              MOVE 'F'  TO  STATUS-OF-READ
              GO TO  B152-EXIT
          ELSE
              MOVE 'POVMBROW'  TO  WS-DLI-ERROR-PROGRAM
              MOVE 'B152-'     TO  WS-DLI-ERROR-PARAGRAPH
              MOVE DIBSTAT     TO  WS-DLI-STATUS
              PERFORM Z999-DLI-STATUS-CODE-ERROR.
 *
  B152-SETUP-SCREEN.

      IF TS-SUB  =  1
          MOVE-CA-VENDOR-CODE  TO  TS-VENDOR-CODE.
              .
              .
              .
  B152-EXIT.
      EXIT.
```

Fig. 23.9 Partial replacement logic for B152-FORMAT-MAP.

Any return code other than spaces or GB indicates a serious error and the program prepares an appropriate error message and performs Z999-DLI-STATUS-CODE-ERROR.

Program Preparation

A program containing EXEC DLI commands is prepared similar to other CICS programs; you must take it through a series of steps before you can execute it. Perform the usual CICS command translation, then you can compile and link edit the program, which is now ready for testing.

24

Using CA-DATACOM/DB in a CICS Environment

CA-DATACOM/DB accesses and updates data in a CICS environment by issuing calls for the requested function. This chapter teaches you the basic
coding methods required to perform typical CA-DATACOM/DB functions. If
you have worked with CA-DATACOM/DB in a batch environment, you will
find this chapter very easy to understand; CA-DATACOM/DB commands
are used in a similar fashion in both batch and CICS applications. This chapter presents most of the functions commonly used in a CICS environment;
with a little practice, you will find CA-DATACOM/DB easy to work with.

CA-DATACOM/DB Database Structure

A CA-DATACOM/DB database is similar to DB2 in that it is relational and
consists of simple tables linked together by common keys that represent a
column in each table. Entries in the database consist of rows equivalent to
VSAM records and columns that represent data fields. The examples in this
chapter use a vendor table named VMS that is identical in format to the
vendor master file used in the SQL chapter and in programs discussed in
earlier chapters. CA-DATACOM/DB tables are defined by a three-character
table name defined in a data dictionary. Data retrieved from the VMS table
moves to the vendor master record for compatibility of label reference with
previously presented programs. Figure 24.1 shows the VMS table format
used for examples in this chapter.

VMS

VCODE	NAME	ADDR	CITY	STATE	ZIP	ATTNOF	PHONE	CONTACT	DLRSCOMTD

Fig. 24.1 VMS table used for examples in this chapter.

User Requirements Table (URT)

Define a user requirements table (URT) for each program. It contains an entry for each CA-DATACOM/DB table required by the program. Entries specify whether a table can have additions, be updated, or if it may only be read. CA-DATACOM/CICS services automatically open and close tables for the application program.

CA-DATACOM/DB Call to DBNTRY

You can embed calls to CA-DATACOM/DB within a CICS program and mix CA-DATACOM/DB, SQL, and VSAM statements in the same program. Database functions are performed by issuing a call to the entry point DBN-TRY. Depending on the command, some or all of the following parameters are passed to DBNTRY: user information block (UIB), request area, work area, and element list. Parameters passed to the CA-DATACOM/DB *called* module DBENTRY are:

```
CALL 'DBENTRY' USING  UIB
                      Request-Area
                      [Work-Area]
                      [Element-List].
```

The first two parameters are required for all requests. Figure 24.2 shows working storage entries used for examples in this chapter.

User Information Block (UIB)

The user information block is a 32 byte-area defined in working storage that must be passed for calls to DBNTRY. CA-DATACOM/DB uses it for problem determination, audit analysis, and security checking. No information is required in this area, but I recommend that program name be placed in the first eight bytes to aid in problem determination. The format of the UIB as used in Fig. 24.2 is:

```
01  UIB.
        05  UIB-PROGNAME      PIC X(8)     VALUE 'POVMname'.
        05  FILLER            PIC X(24)    VALUE SPACES.
```

Fig. 24.2 Working-storage used in chapter's examples.

```
WORKING-STORAGE  SECTION.
*
*********************************************************************
*   CA-DATACOM/DB WORKING STORAGE ENTRIES FOR ALL EXAMPLES         *
*   USED TO CONVERT THE FOLLOWING PROGRAMS TO CA-DATACOM/DB:       *
*   POVMINQY, POVMADDN, POVMCHGE, POVMDLET, AND POVMBROW           *
*********************************************************************
*
*********************************************************************
*                   USER INTERFACE BLOCK (UIB)                    *
*********************************************************************
*
 01  UIB.
     05  UIB-PROGNAME            PIC X(8)    VALUE 'POVMname'.
     05  FILLER                  PIC X(24)   VALUE SPACES.


*********************************************************************
*                        REQUEST AREA                             *
*********************************************************************
*
 01  REQUEST-AREA.
     05  RQ-CC                   PIC X(5)    VALUE SPACES.
     05  RQ-TABLE                PIC XXX     VALUE 'VMS'.
     05  RQ-KEY-NAME             PIC X(5)    VALUE 'KVMST'.
     05  RQ-RETURN-CODE          PIC XX      VALUE SPACES.
     05  FILLER                  PIC X(61).
     05  RQ-KEY.
         10  RQ-VENDOR-CODE      PIC X(6)    VALUE SPACES.
         10  RQ-KEY              PIC X(174)  VALUE SPACES.


*
*********************************************************************
*                   CA-DATACOM/DB WORK AREA                       *
*********************************************************************
 01  WORK-AREA.
     05  VMELM-RECORD    PIC X(169).


*
*********************************************************************
*                   CA-DATACOM/DB ELEMENT LIST                    *
*********************************************************************
*
 01  ELEMENT-LIST.
     05  EL-VM           PIC X(5)    VALUE 'VMELM'.
     05  EL-SC-1         PIC X       VALUE SPACE.
     05  FILLER          PIC X(5)    VALUE SPACES.
```

Fig. 24.2 *Continued.*

```
*
*****************************************************************
*              CA-DATACOM/DB ERROR MESSAGE FIELDS               *
*****************************************************************
*
 01  WS-DC-ERROR-MESSAGE.
     05  FILLER                    PIC X(32)    VALUE
         'CA-DATACOM/DB ERROR - PROGRAM = '.
     05  WS-DC-ERROR-PROGRAM       PIC X(8).
     05  FILLER                    PIC X(12)    VALUE
         'PARAGRAPH = '.
     05  WS-DC-ERROR-PARAGRAPH     PIC X(5).
     05  FILLER                    PIC X(17)    VALUE
         'DC RETURN CODE = '.
     05  WS-DC-RETURN-CODE         PIC 999-.

 01  WS-DC-ERR-LENGTH             PIC S9999    VALUE 78    COMP.
```

CA-DATACOM/DB Request Area

Use the request area to pass items such case command code, table name, key name, return code, and record key between a program and CA-DATACOM/DB. Figure 24.2 shows the request area fields referred to in this chapter as subfields to REQUEST-AREA.

```
 01  REQUEST-AREA.
     05  RQ-CC                    PIC X(5)    VALUE SPACES.
     05  RQ-TABLE                 PIC XXX     VALUE 'VMS'.
     05  RQ-KEY-NAME              PIC X(5)    VALUE 'KVMST'.
     05  RQ-RETURN-CODE           PIC XX      VALUE SPACES.
     05  FILLER                   PIC X(61).
     05  RQ-KEY.
         10  RQ-VENDOR-CODE       PIC X(6)    VALUE SPACES.
         10  RQ-KEY               PIC X(174)  VALUE SPACES.
```

Command codes

The command code, RQ-CC, is a five-character field used to pass the request to be performed to CA-DATACOM/DB. There are numerous command codes; this chapter explains those used in the examples presented.

ADDIT   insert a record into a table.

DELET   delete records read for update. Exclusive control is released when this command is executed.

LOCKG   locate or position the database at the first record is equal to or greater than the key passed in the request area. This function is similar to a start browse in that it establishes a starting point for a readnext; no table record is retrieved. A program uses this command to set the position of the database at the beginning by moving low-values, spaces, or zeroes to the key field in the request area before issuing this command.

RDUKX   read a table entry for *update* for the exact key passed in the request area. It obtains exclusive control until the record is upated, deleted or released.

REDKX   read a table entry for the exact key passed in the request area with no update intended.

REDLE   read the located entry. Use this command after a locate command to read the located entry. A table record is skipped if a readnext is issued immediately after a locate command.

REDNX   read the next record in a table. This command generally follows a locate and a REDLE command during browse processing.

UPDAT   this command will update a record that has been read for update. Exclusive control is released after this command has been excuted.

Table name

Table name is a three-character code uniquely identifying a table to CA-DATACOM/DB. All program examples in this chapter use VMS for the table name, as shown in Fig. 24.2 for the field RQ-TABLE.

Key name

Key name is a five-character name of the field identifying the key field to CA-DATACOM/DB. Keys are groupings of one or more fields in the record. A table can have more than one key. Figure 24.2 defines the value of this field as KVMST for the field RQ-KEY-NAME.

Return code

The return code, RQ-RETURN-CODE, contains the status of the request just executed. Its function is similar to a VSAM status return code or an EIBRESP code. Some of the more common return codes are:

Spaces   Request was successfully executed.
10   Duplicate record on an addition request.
14   Not found condition on table retrieval request.
          It also indicates end of file during readnext processing.

Key value

The value of the key used with various command codes is either placed into or retrieved from this field. Figure 24.2 defines this field as RQ-KEY. The maximum length of the key, which can consist of more than one field, is 180 bytes. Working storage immediately following this field is overlaid if the length defined for this field is shorter than the key's actual size. Some commands, such as LOCKG, return a key value into this field. You can access this field, but should never change its contents prior to executing commands that depend on its contents, such as REDLE.

Work Area

This is the input/output area used by CA-DATACOM/DB. Working storage immediately following this area can be overlaid by retrieval commands. This occurs if the size of the area defined is less than the total length of elements defined in the element list, which is explained in the next paragraph. The work area in Fig. 24.2 is named WORK-AREA and contains one data element called VMELM-RECORD. The length of VMELM-RECORD is 169 bytes, which is the size of VENDOR-MASTER-RECORD.

Program examples use this record layout to keep reference of fields common with previous chapters' examples. The work area is:

```
01  WORK-AREA.
    05  VMELM-RECORD    PIC X(169).
```

Element List

The element list details those elements to be accessed, added, or changed. Names in the element list must positionally correspond to those listed in the work area. You can define more than one element for a table. Elements are used to build a record layout composed of fields in the table. Element names are five characters in length and are followed by an optional one-character security code. One element named VMELM is defined for ELEMENT-LIST in Fig. 24.2; it references the corresponding element in the work area field WORK-AREA. No security code is used. The last entry in an element list must be a five-character field set equal to spaces as shown below.

```
01  ELEMENT-LIST.
    05  EL-VM       PIC X(5)    VALUE 'VMELM'.
    05  EL-SC-1     PIC X       VALUE SPACE.
    05  FILLER      PIC X(5)    VALUE SPACES.
```

Convert Inquiry Program to CA-DATACOM/DB

You can easily convert the inquiry program presented in chapter 12 from VSAM to CA-DATACOM/DB access by:

- Including the code in Fig. 24.2 in the working storage section
- Replacing section C410-READ-VENDOR-FILE with the code in Fig. 24.3
- Adding a new section Z999-DC-RETURN-CODE-ERROR—shown in Fig. 24.4

The REDKX command

In Fig. 24.3, 'REDKX' is moved to the request area command code (RQ-CC) and CA-VENDOR-CODE is moved into the request area field RQ-VENDOR-CODE. Both fields are part of the field REQUEST-AREA, which is referenced in the Call statement. This statement accesses the single table row that matches the key moved to CA-VENDOR-CODE. All columns of the VMS table are retrieved into the work area, because the element chosen contains all columns in the record.

```
C410-READ-VENDOR-FILE  SECTION.
****************************************************************
*     PERFORMED FROM:  C400-VERIFY-VENDOR-FILE-STATUS         *
****************************************************************
*
      MOVE 'REDKX'          TO  RQ-CC.
      MOVE CA-VENDOR-CODE   TO  RQ-VENDOR-CODE.
*
      CALL 'DBNTRY'  USING  UIB
                            REQUEST-AREA
                            WORK-AREA
                            ELEMENT-LIST.

      IF RQ-RETURN-CODE  =  SPACES
          MOVE WORK-AREA  TO  VENDOR-MASTER-RECORD
          MOVE 'G'  TO  STATUS-OF-READ
      ELSE
          IF RQ-RETURN-CODE  =  14
              MOVE 'E'  TO  STATUS-OF-READ
          ELSE
              MOVE 'POVMINQY'      TO  WS-DC-ERROR-PROGRAM
              MOVE 'C410-'         TO  WS-DC-ERROR-PARAGRAPH
              MOVE RQ-RETURN-CODE  TO  WS-DC-RETURN-CODE
              PERFORM Z999-DC-RETURN-CODE-ERROR.
*
C410-EXIT.
      EXIT.
```

Fig. 24.3 Read an exact key.

```
Z999-DC-RETURN-CODE-ERROR  SECTION.
****************************************************************
*       DISPLAY DC ERROR MESSAGE AND RETURN TO CICS          *
****************************************************************
*
* THIS SECTION IS SIMPLIFIED.  YOUR INSTALLATION MIGHT CALL AN
* ERROR PROCESSING PROGRAM AND ABEND THE TASK TO BACKOUT UPDATES.
*
     EXEC CICS SEND
               FROM   (WS-DC-ERROR-MESSAGE)
               LENGTH (WS-DC-ERR-LENGTH)
               ERASE
     END-EXEC.
*
     EXEC CICS RETURN
     END-EXEC.
*
 Z999-EXIT.
     EXIT.
```

Fig. 24.4 CA-DATACOM/DB return code error routine.

If a row in the VMS table is not found for the requested vendor, then a return code of 14 is returned. Any other return code signals a serious error and the program prepares an appropriate error message and performs Z999-DC-RETURN-CODE-ERROR.

Convert Addition Program to CA-DATACOM/DB.

You can convert the addition program presented in chapter 13 to use CA-DATACOM/DB by:

- Including the code in Fig. 24.2 in the working storage section.

- Replacing section C410-READ-VENDOR-FILE with the code in Fig. 24.3.

- Replacing section E120-WRITE-VENDOR-RECORD with the code in Fig. 24.5.

- Adding a new section Z999-DC-RETURN-CODE-ERROR shown in Fig. 24.4.

- Moving the program name 'POVMADDN' to WS-DC-ERROR-PROGRAM in C410-READ-VENDOR-FILE if an error occurs.

The ADDIT command

In Fig. 24.5, VENDOR-MASTER-RECORD is moved into the work area, and the value ADDIT is moved to the request area field named RQ-CC. Note that no value needs to be moved to the request area field (RQ-VENDOR-CODE) because keys are automatically retrieved from the work area. This command inserts a single table row that contains the data in the columns referenced in the work area.

If the row to be inserted already exists, an error code of 10 is returned in RQ-RETURN-CODE. Any other return code signals a serious error and the

```
E120-WRITE-VENDOR-RECORD  SECTION.
*********************************************************************
*          WRITE VENDOR RECORD - PERFORM JOURNAL POSTING          *
*          PERFORMED FROM:  E100-ADD-VENDOR-RECORD                *
*********************************************************************
*
     MOVE VENDOR-MASTER-RECORD  TO  WORK-AREA.
*
     MOVE 'ADDIT'               TO  RQ-CC.
*
     CALL 'DBNTRY'  USING  UIB
                           REQUEST-AREA
                           WORK-AREA
                           ELEMENT-LIST.

     IF RQ-RETURN-CODE  =  SPACES
         MOVE 'G'  TO  STATUS-OF-WRITE
     ELSE
         IF RQ-RETURN-CODE  =  10
             MOVE 'E'  TO  STATUS-OF-WRITE
         ELSE
             MOVE 'POVMADDN'       TO  WS-DC-ERROR-PROGRAM
             MOVE 'E120-'          TO  WS-DC-ERROR-PARAGRAPH
             MOVE RQ-RETURN-CODE   TO  WS-DC-RETURN-CODE
             PERFORM Z999-DC-RETURN-CODE-ERROR.
*
     MOVE 'A'  TO  JR-TYPE.
     PERFORM E121-POST-JOURNAL-RECORD.
*
E120-EXIT.
     EXIT.
```

Fig. 24.5 Add a record to the CA-DATACOM/DB database.

program prepares an appropriate error message and performs Z999-DC-RETURN-CODE-ERROR.

Convert Change Program to CA-DATACOM/DB

The change program presented in chapter 14 can be converted to make changes against a CA-DATACOM/DB database by:

- Including the code in Fig. 24.2 in the working storage section.

- Replacing section C410-READ-VENDOR-FILE with the code in Fig. 24.3.

- Replacing part of section F110-READ-VENDOR-FOR-UPDATE with code similar to that in Fig. 24.3 while substituting RDUKX for command code REDKX.

- Replacing section F120-REWRITE-VENDOR-RECORD with the code in Fig. 24.6.

- Adding a new section Z999-DC-RETURN-CODE-ERROR shown in Fig. 24.4.

- Moving the program name 'POVMCHGE' to WS-DC-ERROR-PROGRAM in C410-READ-VENDOR-FILE if an error occurs.

The UPDAT command

In Fig. 24.6, it is necessary to move the VENDOR-MASTER-RECORD to the work area and the value UPDAT into the command code field RQ-CC before issuing a call to DBNTRY. Execution of this statement replaces all the VMS table columns that have been changed.

Any return code other than spaces indicates a serious error and the program prepares an appropriate error message and performs Z999-DC-RETURN-CODE-ERROR.

Convert Delete Program to CA-DATACOM/DB

You can convert the delete program presented in chapter 15 to a delete against a CA-DATACOM/DB database by:

- Including the code in Fig. 24.2 in the working storage section.

- Replacing section C410-READ-VENDOR-FILE with the code in Fig. 24.3.

- Replacing part of section F110-READ-VENDOR-FOR-UPDATE with code similar to that in Fig. 24.3 while substituting RDUKX for command code REDKX.

- Replacing section G110-DELETE-VM-RECORD with the code in Fig. 24.7.
- Adding a new section Z999-DC-RETURN-CODE-ERROR shown in Fig. 24.4.
- Moving the program name 'POVMDLET' to WS-DC-ERROR-PROGRAM in C410-READ-VENDOR-FILE if an error occurs.

The DELET command

In Fig. 24.7, issuing the DELET statement deletes the entire row of the record read for update. Any return code other than spaces indicates a seri-

```
F120-REWRITE-VENDOR-RECORD  SECTION.
********************************************************************
*     REWRITE VENDOR RECORD - POST 'AFTER' JOURNAL RECORD         *
*         PERFORMED FROM:  F100-CHANGE-VENDOR-RECORD              *
********************************************************************
*
      MOVE VENDOR-MASTER-RECORD  TO   WORK-AREA.
*
      MOVE 'UPDAT'               TO   RQ-CC.
*
      CALL 'DBNTRY' USING   UIB
                            REQUEST-AREA
                            WORK-AREA
                            ELEMENT-LIST.
*
      IF RQ-RETURN-CODE  NOT =  SPACES
          MOVE 'POVMCHGE'     TO   WS-DC-ERROR-PROGRAM
          MOVE 'F120-'        TO   WS-DC-ERROR-PARAGRAPH
          MOVE RQ-RETURN-CODE TO   WS-DC-RETURN-CODE
          PERFORM Z999-DC-RETURN-CODE-ERROR.
*
      MOVE 'A'  TO  JR-TYPE.
      PERFORM E121-POST-JOURNAL-RECORD.
*
 F120-EXIT.
      EXIT.
```

Fig. 24.6 Update a table in the CA-DATACOM/DB database.

ous error and the program prepares an appropriate error message and performs Z999-DC-RETURN-CODE-ERROR.

Convert Browse Program to CA-DATACOM/DB

You can convert the browse program presented in chapter 17 to run against a CA-DATACOM/DB database. The required program code explanation follows.

- Including the code in Fig. 24.2 in the working storage section.
- Replacing section B140-START-BROWSE with the code in Fig. 24.8.
- Deleting ENDBR command in section B150-BROWSE-PROCESSING and replacing part of B152-FORMAT-MAP.
- Adding a new section Z999-DC-RETURN-CODE-ERROR shown in Fig. 24.4.

The LOCKG command

As mentioned earlier, the LOCKG command sets position in the database at a desired record. Figure 24.8 shows how to use it to set position in the database at the first record equal to or greater than the value moved into RQ-VENDOR-CODE prior to issuing the LOCKG request. This command does not read a record; it only establishes position.

```
G110-DELETE-VM-RECORD  SECTION.
**************************************************************
*    DELETE VENDOR RECORD - POST 'BEFORE' JOURNAL RECORD    *
*        PERFORMED FROM:  G100-DELETE-VENDOR-RECORD         *
**************************************************************
*
     MOVE 'DELET'  TO  RQ-CC.
*
     CALL 'DBNTRY'  USING  UIB
                          REQUEST-AREA.
*
     IF RQ-RETURN-CODE  NOT =  SPACES
         MOVE 'POVMDLET'      TO  WS-DC-ERROR-PROGRAM
         MOVE 'G110-'         TO  WS-DC-ERROR-PARAGRAPH
         MOVE RQ-RETURN-CODE  TO  WS-DC-RETURN-CODE
         PERFORM Z999-DC-RETURN-CODE-ERROR.
*
 G110-EXIT.
     EXIT.
```

Fig. 24.7 Delete a table entry.

```
B140-START-BROWSE  SECTION.
********************************************************************
*                PERFORMED FROM:  B100-PAGE-FORWARD               *
*                                 B200-PAGE-BACKWARD              *
*                                 B500-RESET-KEY                  *
*                                 C000-INITIAL-ENTRY              *
********************************************************************
*
     MOVE 'LOCKG'          TO  RQ-CC.
     MOVE CA-VENDOR-CODE   TO  RQ-VENDOR-CODE.
*
     CALL 'DBNTRY'  USING  UIB
                           REQUEST-AREA.
*
     IF RQ-RETURN-CODE  =  SPACES
         NEXT SENTENCE
     ELSE
         IF RQ-RETURN-CODE  =  14
             MOVE 'E'  TO  STATUS-OF-BROWSE
             GO TO  B140-EXIT
         ELSE
             MOVE 'POVMBROW'     TO  WS-DC-ERROR-PROGRAM
             MOVE 'B140-'        TO  WS-DC-ERROR-PARAGRAPH
             MOVE RQ-RETURN-CODE TO  WS-DC-RETURN-CODE
             PERFORM Z999-DC-RETURN-CODE-ERROR.

     MOVE 'REDLE'  TO  RQ-CC.
*
     CALL 'DBNTRY'  USING  UIB
                           REQUEST-AREA
                           WORK-AREA
                           ELEMENT-LIST.
*
     IF RQ-RETURN-CODE  =  SPACES
         MOVE WORK-AREA  TO  VENDOR-MASTER-RECORD
         MOVE 'G'  TO  STATUS-OF-BROWSE
     ELSE
         MOVE 'POVMBROW'     TO  WS-DC-ERROR-PROGRAM
         MOVE 'B140-'        TO  WS-DC-ERROR-PARAGRAPH
         MOVE RQ-RETURN-CODE TO  WS-DC-RETURN-CODE
         PERFORM Z999-DC-RETURN-CODE-ERROR.
*
 B140-EXIT.
     EXIT.
```

Fig. 24.8 Locate and read browse starting key.

Any return code other than spaces or 14 indicates a serious error and the program prepares an appropriate error message and performs Z999-DC-RETURN-CODE-ERROR. A return code of 14 indicates that the key moved to RQ-VENDOR-CODE is beyond the end of the table.

The REDLE command

The REDLE command reads the table record located at the position in the CA-DATACOM/DB established by a previous locate command. The REDLE command in Fig. 24.8 reads the record located by the previous LOCKG command.

Any return code other than spaces indicates a serious error and the program prepares an appropriate error message and performs Z999-DC-RETURN-CODE-ERROR.

The REDNX command

Figure 24.9 illustrates the use of the readnext command. After a LOCKG command has established position and the located record has been read by a REDLE command, then succeeding reads are accomplished by issuing REDNX commands. Paragraph B150-BROWSE-PROCESSING performs paragraph B152-FORMAT-MAP until 15 records have been moved to the screen or the end of the file has been reached as indicated by a return code of 14. Note that the add of 1 to TSUB has been relocated to the top of the paragraph in Fig. 24.9. Use it as a first-time indicator, because the first time through paragraph B152-FORMAT-MAP, you do not want to issue a read-next command. Since the first record has been read by the REDLE command in Fig. 24.8.

Any return code other than spaces or 14 indicates a serious error and the program prepares an appropriate error message and performs Z999-DC-RETURN-CODE-ERROR.

Program Preparation

A program that contains CA-DATACOM/DB is prepared like other CICS programs; it must go through a series of steps before it is ready to be executed. Perform the usual CICS command translation, then you can compile and link edit the program, which is now ready for testing.

```
*
 B152-FORMAT-MAP   SECTION.
 *****************************************************************
 *            PERFORMED FROM:  B150-BROWSE-PROCESSING            *
 *****************************************************************
 *
      ADD 1  TO   TS-SUB.

      IF TS-SUB  =  1
         GO TO  B152-SETUP-SCREEN.

      MOVE 'REDNX'          TO  RQ-CC.
 *
      CALL 'DBNTRY'  USING  UIB
                            REQUEST-AREA
                            WORK-AREA
                            ELEMENT-LIST.
 *
      IF RQ-RETURN-CODE  =  SPACES
         MOVE 'G'         TO   STATUS-OF-READ
         MOVE WORK-AREA  TO   VENDOR-MASTER-RECORD
      ELSE
         IF RQ-RETURN-CODE  =  14
            MOVE 'F'  TO   STATUS-OF-READ
            GO TO  B152-EXIT
         ELSE
            MOVE 'POVMBROW'      TO   WS-DC-ERROR-PROGRAM
            MOVE 'B152-'         TO   WS-DC-ERROR-PARAGRAPH
            MOVE RQ-RETURN-CODE  TO   WS-DC-RETURN-CODE
            PERFORM Z999-DC-RETURN-CODE-ERROR.
 *
 B152-SETUP-SCREEN.

      IF TS-SUB  =  1
         MOVE-CA-VENDOR-CODE  TO   TS-VENDOR-CODE.
                 .
                 .
                 .
 B152-EXIT.
      EXIT.
```

Fig. 24.9 Partial replacement logic for B152-FORMAT-MAP.

Chapter

25

Converting CICS Programs to VS COBOL II

25

Converting CICS Programs to VS COBOL II

You can convert CICS programs from OS/VS COBOL to VS COBOL II with minimal changes required if your programs use the move mode of processing and do not use BLL cells. Code input/output areas and maps in working storage when a program uses the move mode of processing. Reference them in the linkage section by a program using the locate mode of processing. Conversion is not difficult, but is more cumbersome if programs use the locate mode. This chapter steps you through the process required to convert programs presented in previous chapters to VS COBOL II. In addition, you'll learn how to schedule a PSB using VS COBOL II and some suggestions for using some of the new VS COBOL II features to improve CICS programming.

Elimination of BLL Cells

Elimination of the need for BLL Cells by VS COBOL II is the most significant change affecting CICS applications programmers. Do not use BLL Cells and the associated SERVICE RELOAD in CICS VS COBOL II programs. The ADDRESS special register and pointer variables provide much simpler access to linkage section data. Also, you need not set additional address pointers to data areas that exceed 4096 bytes, and you can place linkage section fields in any order.

ADDRESS Special Register

ADDRESS special registers hold the address of 01 and 77 level data areas defined in the linkage section. The ADDRESS register is used in place of BLL Cell pointers on CICS commands that use the SET option, such as AD-DRESS, GETMAIN, LOAD, READ, READQ, RECEIVE, or RETRIEVE. Previous chapters showed the syntax of each of these and of other CICS commands; these chapters are referenced as they relate to VS COBOL II. The following examples also based on programs presented in prior chapters should make clear the use of the ADDRESS special register.

LOAD Command using ADDRESS Register

Figure 25.1 demonstrates the use of the ADDRESS special register with the LOAD command. You can use the new code to convert the linked program JRNLPOST, shown in Fig. 10.2, to VS COBOL II. The first part of Fig. 25.1 shows the LOAD command using BLL Cells with OS/VS COBOL. The second part demonstrates the use of the LOAD command with VS COBOL II. BLL Cells and the SERVICE RELOAD have been removed and the SET command uses the ADDRESS special register to set addressability to T053-SEQUENCE-TABLE.

Note that under VS COBOL II, if table size exceeds 4096 bytes, as did the table in Fig. 10.3, you need not add 4096. BLL Cells are no longer required and VS COBOL II sets addressability to the entire table's area. Table reference fields TABLE-1, TABLE-2, and TABLE-3 can be arranged in any sequence as shown in Fig. 25.2, the VS COBOL II version of Fig. 10.3.

CWA Addressing with VS COBOL II

Change the inquiry program in chapter 12, addition program in chapter 13, change program in chapter 14, delete program in chapter 15, and browse program in chapter 17 to VS COBOL II by using the ADDRESS special register. You address the CWA in a similar manner to that used with the LOAD command. When you use a BLL pointer to set addressability to a linkage section field, you must substitute ADDRESS OF for the BLL pointer. ADDRESS OF refers to the 01 level to which the BLL pointer had previously set addressability. You can substitute the code in Fig. 25.3 as appropriate, in the inquiry, addition, change, delete, and browse programs to convert them to VS COBOL II.

The code in Fig. 25.3 is basically all that is required to convert the book's programs so that they can be compiled under VS COBOL II. Some of the VS COBOL II enhancements that will improve the structure and maintenance of your programs are discussed later in the chapter. Use the ADDRESS special register mentioned previously in place of BLL Cell pointers on CICS commands that use the SET option, such as ADDRESS, GETMAIN, LOAD, READ, READQ, RECEIVE, or RETRIEVE.

```
        LOAD Command using BLL Cells and OS/VS COBOL

LINKAGE SECTION.

01  DFHCOMMAREA                  PIC X(524).

01  BLL-CELLS.
    02  FILLER                   PIC S9(8)    COMP.
    02  BLL-SEQ-TABLE-ADDRESS    PIC S9(8)    COMP.

01  T053-SEQUENCE-TABLE.
    05  T053-SEQUENCE-NUMBER     PIC S9(5)    COMP-3.


    EXEC CICS LOAD
              PROGRAM ('T053JRSQ')
              SET     (BLL-SEQ-TABLE-ADDRESS)
    END-EXEC.

*   SERVICE RELOAD T053-SEQUENCE-TABLE.



  LOAD Command using ADDRESS Register and VS COBOL II

LINKAGE SECTION.

01  DFHCOMMAREA                  PIC X(524).

01  T053-SEQUENCE-TABLE.
    05  T053-SEQUENCE-NUMBER     PIC S9(5)    COMP-3.


    EXEC CICS LOAD
              PROGRAM ('T053JRSQ')
              SET     (ADDRESS OF T053-SEQUENCE-TABLE)
    END-EXEC.
```

Fig. 25.1 Coding comparison of OS/VS COBOL to VS COBOL II for LOAD command.

Using Pointer Variables

The only program presented in this text that requires an explanation before you can convert it to VS COBOL II is the DL/I program in chapter 22. The

```
LOAD Command using ADDRESS Register and VS COBOL II

LINKAGE SECTION.

01   DFHCOMMAREA                 PIC X(524).

01   TABLE-3                     PIC X(4000).

01   TABLE-2                     PIC X(9606).

01   TABLE-1                     PIC X(10).


     EXEC CICS LOAD
               PROGRAM ('T002BIGT')
               SET     (ADDRESS OF TABLE-2)
     END-EXEC.


     EXEC CICS LOAD
               PROGRAM ('T003MEDT')
               SET     (ADDRESS OF TABLE-3)
     END-EXEC.

     EXEC CICS LOAD
               PROGRAM ('T001SMAT')
               SET     (ADDRESS OF TABLE-1)
     END-EXEC.
```

Fig. 25.2 Coding comparison of OS/VS COBOL to VS COBOL II for LOAD command with various table sizes.

PSB scheduling call in that program requires the use of pointer variables in order to convert it to VS COBOL II. Pointer variables are used to hold addresses of data areas in the linkage section; they must be defined as USAGE IS POINTER. This generates a fullword used to store an address. ADDRESS OF special registers are implicitly defined as pointer variables. No picture clause is permitted when you use USAGE IS POINTER. Figure 25.4 shows the VS COBOL II linkage section replacement of DL/I areas used by the OS/VS COBOL version shown in Fig. 22.1.

Use the VS COBOL II SET statement to set addresses to the ADDRESS special register of data areas in the linkage section. You can also use the SET statement to set the address of a linkage section data area to a pointer variable. For example:

```
SET  ADDRESS OF PCB-ADDRESS-LIST  TO  UIBPCBAL-REDEF.
```

establishes addressability of the PCB-ADDRESS-LIST to the value stored in the pointer variable UIBPCBAL-REDEF. Data (in this case, addresses) stored in PCB-ADDRESS-LIST is available to the program after execution of the SET statement. The value stored in UIBPCBAL is established by a DL/I module that may have set the pointer variable in a fashion similar to the following:

```
SET  UIBPCBAL-REDEF  TO ADDRESS OF  PCB-ADDRESS-LIST.
```

PCB-ADDRESS in Fig. 25.4 is defined as USAGE IS POINTER and OC-CURS n TIMES. The value of n represents the number of PCB's that can be used by the program. It must be equal to the number of PCB's defined in the

Fig. 25.3 Coding comparison of OS/VS COBOL to VS COBOL II for CICS ADDRESS and LOAD commands.

```
     ADDRESS & LOAD Commands using BLL Cells & OS/VS COBOL

   LINKAGE SECTION.
        .   .   .
   01  BLL-CELLS.
       02  FILLER                          PIC S9(8)   COMP.
       02  BLL-CWA-ADDRESS                 PIC S9(8)   COMP.
       02  BLL-T037-STATE-TABLE-ADDRESS    PIC S9(8)   COMP.

   01  CWA-DATA  . . .

   01  T037-STATE-TABLE  . . .


       EXEC CICS ADDRESS
               CWA (BLL-CWA-ADDRESS)
       END-EXEC.

   *   SERVICE RELOAD CWA-DATA.

       EXEC CICS LOAD
               PROGRAM ('T037LOAD')
               SET     (BLL-T037-STATE-TABLE-ADDRESS)
       END-EXEC.

   *   SERVICE RELOAD T037-STATE-TABLE.
```

Fig. 25.3 *Continued.*

```
ADDRESS & LOAD Commands with ADDRESS Register & VS COBOL II

 LINKAGE SECTION.
        .   .   .
 01  CWA-DATA   .   .   .

 01  T037-STATE-TABLE   .   .   .

        EXEC CICS ADDRESS
                 CWA (ADDRESS OF CWA-DATA)
        END-EXEC.

        EXEC CICS LOAD
                 PROGRAM ('T037LOAD')
                 SET     (ADDRESS OF T037-STATE-TABLE)
        END-EXEC.
```

PSB the program uses. The procedure division of your program can use the appropriate value of n to reference a required PCB in the PSB. The DL/I program in chapter 22 has only one PCB, PCB-VENDOR.

PSB Scheduling

For VS COBOL II, the code in Fig. 25.5 replaces the PSB scheduling shown in Fig. 22.2.

ADDRESS OF DLIUIB replaces BLL-UIB-PTR on the Call statement. The SET statements establish addressability to the data areas PCB-ADDRESS-LIST and PCB-VENDOR. If there is a second PCB named PCB-CUST, its pointer is passed in PCB-ADDRESS-LIST and its addressability is established by:

```
SET  ADDRESS OF PCB-CUST  TO ADDRESS OF  PCB-ADDRESS (2).
```

You now have all the information required to convert a DL/I program to VS COBOL II. The remainder of the sample DL/I program is coded the same as discussed in chapter 22.

Alternate Uses of Pointer Variables with DL/I

Although the method just discussed for PSB scheduling is recommended, you may encounter variations to this technique in DL/I programs you have to maintain. For instance, the code in Fig. 25.6 accomplishes the same objective.

You cannot move a field that contains an address directly to a data area defined as USAGE IS POINTER. A field defined as usage COMP must be established in working storage and be redefined as USAGE IS POINTER to use a DL/I address pointer. If a program has more than one PCB, follow the same pattern as the above example.

```
LINKAGE SECTION.

    .   .   .

01  DLIUIB.
    02  UIBPCBAL              PIC S9(8)    COMP.
    02  FILLER                PIC XX.

01  DLIUIB-REDEF  REDEFINES   DLIUIB.
    02  UIBPCBAL-REDEF        USAGE IS POINTER.
    02  FILLER                PIC XX.

01  PCB-ADDRESS-LIST.
    02  PCB-ADDRESS  USAGE IS POINTER  OCCURS  n TIMES.

01  PCB-VENDOR.
    .   .   .
```

Fig. 25.4 Linkage section for VS COBOL II PSB scheduling.

```
MOVE 'PCB ' TO  DLI-FUNCTION.

CALL 'CBLTDLI'  USING  DLI-FUNCTION
                       WS-PSB-NAME
                       ADDRESS OF DLIUIB.

IF UIBFCTR  NOT =  LOW-VALUES
    .   .   .


SET  ADDRESS OF PCB-ADDRESS-LIST  TO  UIBPCBAL-REDEF.
SET  ADDRESS OF PCB-VENDOR        TO  PCB-ADDRESS (1).
```

Fig. 25.5 PSB scheduling when using VS COBOL II.

```
WORKING-STORAGE  SECTION.
      .   .   .
01  WS-POINTERS.
    05  WS-DLI-ADDRESS              PIC S9(8)   COMP.
    05  WS-DLI-POINTER   REDEFINES  WS-DLI-ADDRESS
                         USAGE IS POINTER.
      .   .   .

LINKAGE SECTION.


      .   .   .

01  DLIUIB.
    02  UIBPCBAL              PIC S9(8)   COMP.
    02  FILLER                PIC XX.


01  PCB-ADDRESS-LIST.
    02  PCB-VEND-PTR          PIC S9(8)   COMP.

01  PCB-VENDOR.
      .   .   .

PROCEDURE DIVISION.
      .   .   .

MOVE 'PCB '  TO  DLI-FUNCTION.

CALL 'CBLTDLI'  USING  DLI-FUNCTION
                       WS-PSB-NAME
                       ADDRESS OF DLIUIB.

IF UIBFCTR  NOT =  LOW-VALUES
     .   .   .



MOVE UIBPCBAL                        TO  WS-DLI-ADDRESS.
SET  ADDRESS OF PCB-ADDRESS-LIST  TO  WS-DLI-POINTER.

MOVE PCB-VEND-PTR          TO  WS-DLI-ADDRESS.
SET  ADDRESS OF PCB-VENDOR  TO  WS-DLI-POINTER.
```

Fig. 25.6 Alternate PSB scheduling when using VS COBOL II.

LENGTH Register and Variable Length Records

When using OS/VS COBOL, you must include the LENGTH option on all commands that specify a FROM or INTO option for the input or output data area of *variable-length* records. This requirement is removed with VS COBOL II, which uses the LENGTH special register to determine length from a specified fixed-size input or output area. The LENGTH option must still be coded if the data area referenced in the FROM or INTO options can contain variable data lengths. The data area named in a LENGTH option returns the actual length of a data record read using an INTO option when reading variable-length records into a common I/O area. You must define the data area named in a LENGTH option as a binary halfword. When writing variable-length records from a comon area, or rewriting record of a different length from that read, you must specify the LENGTH option. I recommend the use of the LENGTH option when you are working with variable-length records, and its elimination for fixed length records.

Cobol Call Statements

VS COBOL II permits *call* statements to access subprograms containing CICS commands. You must issue a *static* call to a subprogram link-edited with the calling program. This can result in large programs, because the subprogram becomes part of the load module. CICS LINKed-to programs, unlike called subprograms, are separate modules that can be shared with other programs. Called subprograms should be visualized as being at the same logical level as the calling program, while a linked-to program is at the next lower logical level. A set of one or more called subprograms link-edited together, plus the calling CICS program, is referred to as a *run unit*. The first entry into a called subprogram finds working storage fields in their initial state. Subsequent calls to the same subprogram, within the same task and at the same logical level, find working storage in its last used state. Contrast this to a CICS program initiated by a LINK or XCTL command, which always finds working storage in its initial state. Control may be returned from a subprogram to a calling program by issuing a GOBACK or EXIT PROGRAM statement.

In general, the use of LINK is preferable to program Call statements because a linked program can be maintained separately from the program issuing the LINK. The program issuing the LINK need only be recompiled if new parameters are passed to, or received from, the linked-to program. A change to a program containing a static call always requires the program is-suing the call to be recompiled.

RETURN-CODE usage

The RETURN-CODE special register can be set in a subprogram and exam-ined upon return by a calling program. This register has the implicit defini-tion of a binary halfword. I recommend moving zeroes to RETURN-CODE upon successful completion of a called subprogram. You must not issue any CICS commands in a called subprogram after a value is moved to RETURN-CODE. Likewise, examine the contents of RETURN-CODE upon returning to the calling program, prior to issuing any CICS commands, because CICS commands change the contents of the RETURN-CODE special register.

Call program statement

A calling program must pass DFHEIBLK and DFHCOMMAREA to a called subprogram, if the subprogram contains CICS commands. The format of the *call* statement is:

```
CALL 'subprog' USING  DFHEIBLK  DFHCOMMAREA  PARM-LIST.
```

The procedure division header in the subprogram is coded as:

```
PROCEDURE DIVISION  USING   PARM-LIST.
```

The translator automatically inserts DFHEIBLK and DFHCOMMAREA be-tween USING and PARM-LIST.

Miscellaneous Features and Considerations

VS COBOL II is beneficial in developing programs that are easier to code and maintain, but remember to keep it straightforward and simple when us-ing its new features. Restructure your code if you cannot explain it to an-other programmer.

New features

The following features, although not limited to CICS programs, are those you may wish to incorporate in your online programs:

- EVALUATE statement—can clarify programming if used in its simplest form. When employed in a confusing manner, it can cause extreme main-tenance problems equivalent in difficulty of understanding to that of us-ing cumbersome nested IFs.

- Explicit scope terminators—can be an asset in improving program readability and in reducing maintenance. The END-IF, and END-PERFORM, when used with the in-line PERFORM statement, should be beneficial.

- INITIALIZE statement—is helpful in initializing designated working storage fields.

Considerations

VS COBOL II supports the use of the following statements: INSPECT, STOP RUN, STRING, and UNSTRING. STOP RUN ends a task normally and returns control to CICS; it functions like the CICS RETURN command. I recommend that you *never* use STOP RUN in place of RETURN.

Set all working storage fields to an initial value of spaces, zeroes, low values, etc. This is good programming practice and eliminates the chance of moving characters to a map that cannot be transmitted to the screen. It also limits the chance of passing bad data to another program.

You cannot use CURRENT-TIME and TIME-OF-DAY. Obtain equivalent information by using the CICS FORMATTIME command. Comment out the REMARKS paragraph used by OS/VS COBOL, since it is not supported by VS COBOL II.

For a complete set of differences between OS/VS COBOL and VS COBOL II, refer to IBM's VS COBOL II Application Programming Language Reference manual.

Execute Interface Block Fields

This appendix consists of the most commonly used execute interface block (EIB) fields, a description of these fields, and the attention identifier fields (DFHAID). DFHAID fields can be copied into working storage, and a program can compare the appropriate field against the EIB field EIBAID in order to determine which AID key was pressed.

Execute Interface Block (EIB)

The execute interface block (EIB) is a CICS control block included in a program's linkage section when the program is translated and compiled. An application program should not alter fields in the EIB. The most commonly used EIB fields are shown in Fig. A.1.

The following is a description of EIB Fields:

EIBTIME   Time that the task was initiated. This field can be updated by the ASKTIME command.

EIBDATE   Date the task was started. This field can also be updated by the ASKTIME command.

EIBTRNID   Transaction Identifier (TRANSID) of the task.

EIBTASKN   Contains the task number assigned by CICS.

EIBTRMID   Terminal Identifier at which task was initiated.

EIBCPOSN   Position of the cursor on the screen immediately before a Receive Map command was executed.

EIBCALEN   Length of the communications area passed to a program as determined by the LENGTH option of the previous program that passed a COMMAREA. This length can be zero if the program was started by entering a TRANSID or if no COMMAREA was passed.

EIBAID   Attention Identifier—contents are determined by the AID key pressed.

EIBRESP   Response code returned when a CICS command is executed indicating the condition that occurred. Appendix C contains a list of response codes.

EXECUTE INTERFACE BLOCK (EIB)

The execute interface block (EIB) is a CICS control block that is included in a program's linkage section when the program is translated and compiled. An application program should not alter fields in the EIB. The most commonly used EIB fields are:

```
01  DFHEIBLK.
*                        Time in 0HHMMSS Format
    02  EIBTIME          PIC S9(7)    COMP-3.
*
*                        Date in 00YYDDD Format
    02  EIBDATE          PIC S9(7)    COMP-3.
*
*                        Transaction Identifier
    02  EIBTRNID         PIC X(4).
*
*                        Task Number
    02  EIBTASKN         PIC S9(7)    COMP-3.
*
*                        Terminal Identifier
    02  EIBTRMID         PIC X(4).
*
*                        Cursor Position
    02  EIBCPOSN         PIC S9(4)    COMP.
*
*                        COMMAREA Length
    02  EIBCALEN         PIC S9(4)    COMP.
*
*                        Attention Identifier
    02  EIBAID           PIC X.
*
*                        Response Code
    02  EIBRESP          PIC S9(8)    COMP.
```

Fig. A.1 The most commonly used EIB fields.

Attention Identifier Fields (DFHAID)

A DFHAID field can be compared against the EIB field EIBAID to determine which AID key was pressed by a terminal operator. The most commonly used DFHAID fields are shown in Fig. A.2.

ATTENTION IDENTIFIER FIELDS (DFHAID)

A DFHAID field can be compared against the EIB field EIBAID, in order to determine which AID key was pressed by a terminal operator. The most commonly used DFHAID fields include the following:

```
01  DFHAID.
    02  DFHENTER      PIC X    VALUE QUOTE.
    02  DFHCLEAR      PIC X    VALUE ' '.
    02  DFHPA1        PIC X    VALUE '('.
    02  DFHPA2        PIC X    VALUE ' '.
    02  DFHPA3        PIC X    VALUE ','.
    02  DFHPF1        PIC X    VALUE '1'.
    02  DFHPF2        PIC X    VALUE '2'.
    02  DFHPF3        PIC X    VALUE '3'.
    02  DFHPF4        PIC X    VALUE '4'.
    02  DFHPF5        PIC X    VALUE '5'.
    02  DFHPF6        PIC X    VALUE '6'.
    02  DFHPF7        PIC X    VALUE '7'.
    02  DFHPF8        PIC X    VALUE '8'.
    02  DFHPF9        PIC X    VALUE '9'.
    02  DFHPF10       PIC X    VALUE ' '.
    02  DFHPF11       PIC X    VALUE '='.
    02  DFHPF12       PIC X    VALUE ' '.
    02  DFHPF13       PIC X    VALUE 'A'.
    02  DFHPF14       PIC X    VALUE 'B'.
    02  DFHPF15       PIC X    VALUE 'C'.
    02  DFHPF16       PIC X    VALUE 'D'.
    02  DFHPF17       PIC X    VALUE 'E'.
    02  DFHPF18       PIC X    VALUE 'F'.
    02  DFHPF19       PIC X    VALUE 'G'.
    02  DFHPF20       PIC X    VALUE 'H'.
    02  DFHPF21       PIC X    VALUE 'I'.
    02  DFHPF22       PIC X    VALUE ' '.
    02  DFHPF23       PIC X    VALUE ' '.
    02  DFHPF24       PIC X    VALUE ' '.
```

Fig. A.2 The most commonly used DFHAID fields.

Copy Library

Copy library members common to more than one text program is covered here. Developing copy library members for any data items or routines expected to be used in more than one program or system is good practice. Note the consistency of prefix usage among most data-item copy members. Similar prefixes associate data items with a particular library member.

Copy Library

The copy library entries are arranged alphabetically for ease of locating as follows:

```
************************************************************
*      'JRNLRECD'      JOURNAL RECORD      524 BYTES LONG   *
*    MANY PROGRAMS FORMAT A 'BEFORE' AND 'AFTER' RECORD WHEN *
*    MAINTENANCE IS PERFORMED AGAINST THE FOLLOWING FILES:  *
*           VENDOR-MASTER-FILE      ITEM-MASTER-FILE        *
*                PURCHASE-ORDER-MASTER-FILE                 *
************************************************************
*
 01  JOURNAL-RECORD.
     05  JR-KEY.
         10   JR-EIBDATE            PIC S9(7)    COMP-3.
         10   JR-EIBTIME            PIC S9(7)    COMP-3.
         10   JR-SEQUENCE-NUMBER    PIC S9(5)    COMP-3.
     05  JR-TYPE                    PIC X.
         88   JR-BEFORE-IMAGE                        VALUE 'B'.
         88   JR-AFTER-IMAGE                         VALUE 'A'.
     05  JR-PREFIX                  PIC XX.
         88   JR-VENDOR-MASTER                       VALUE 'VM'.
         88   JR-PURCHASE-ORDER-MASTER               VALUE 'PO'.
         88   JR-ITEM-MASTER                         VALUE 'IM'.
     05  JR-EIBTRMID                PIC X(4).
     05  JR-PASSWORD                PIC X(6).
     05  JR-RECORD-DATA             PIC X(500).
```

Fig. B.1 Journal record.

Fig. B.2 'MAPVDTL1' vendor inquiry and delete detail—symbolic map.

```
************************************************************
*      'MAPVDTL1'    VENDOR INQUIRY & DELETE DETAIL - SYMBOLIC MAP   *
************************************************************
*
 01  VM-DETAIL-MAP.
     05  FILLER                     PIC X(12).
*
     05  MVD-L-DATE                 PIC S9(4)    COMP.
     05  MVD-A-DATE                 PIC X.
     05  MVD-D-DATE                 PIC X(8).
*
     05  MVD-L-TIME                 PIC S9(4)    COMP.
     05  MVD-A-TIME                 PIC X.
     05  MVD-D-TIME                 PIC X(8).
*
     05  MVD-L-VENDOR-CODE          PIC S9(4)    COMP.
     05  MVD-A-VENDOR-CODE          PIC X.
     05  MVD-D-VENDOR-CODE          PIC X(8).
*
     05  MVD-L-VENDOR-NAME          PIC S9(4)    COMP.
     05  MVD-A-VENDOR-NAME          PIC X.
     05  MVD-D-VENDOR-NAME          PIC X(25).
*
     05  MVD-L-PHONE-AREA-CD        PIC S9(4)    COMP.
     05  MVD-A-PHONE-AREA-CD        PIC X.
     05  MVD-D-PHONE-AREA-CD        PIC XXX.
*
     05  MVD-L-PHONE-1              PIC S9(4)    COMP.
     05  MVD-A-PHONE-1              PIC X.
     05  MVD-D-PHONE-1              PIC XXX.
*
     05  MVD-L-PHONE-2              PIC S9(4)    COMP.
     05  MVD-A-PHONE-2              PIC X.
     05  MVD-D-PHONE-2              PIC X(4).
*
     05  MVD-L-CONTACT              PIC S9(4)    COMP.
     05  MVD-A-CONTACT              PIC X.
```

Fig. B.2 *Continued.*

```
      05   MVD-D-CONTACT            PIC X(25).
 *
      05   MVD-L-STREET             PIC S9(4)    COMP.
      05   MVD-A-STREET             PIC X.
      05   MVD-D-STREET             PIC X(20).
 *
      05   MVD-L-DLRS-COMMITTED     PIC S9(4)    COMP.
      05   MVD-A-DLRS-COMMITTED     PIC X.
      05   MVD-D-DLRS-COMMITTED     PIC $$,$$$,$$$.99CR.
 *
      05   MVD-L-CITY               PIC S9(4)    COMP.
      05   MVD-A-CITY               PIC X.
      05   MVD-D-CITY               PIC X(18).
 *
      05   MVD-L-STATE-CODE         PIC S9(4)    COMP.
      05   MVD-A-STATE-CODE         PIC X.
      05   MVD-D-STATE-CODE         PIC XX.
 *
      05   MVD-L-STATE-NAME         PIC S9(4)    COMP.
      05   MVD-A-STATE-NAME         PIC X.
      05   MVD-D-STATE-NAME         PIC X(14).
 *
      05   MVD-L-ZIP-CODE           PIC S9(4)    COMP.
      05   MVD-A-ZIP-CODE           PIC X.
      05   MVD-D-ZIP-CODE           PIC X(5).
 *
      05   MVD-L-ATTENTION-OF       PIC S9(4)    COMP.
      05   MVD-A-ATTENTION-OF       PIC X.
      05   MVD-D-ATTENTION-OF       PIC X(20).
 *
      05   MVD-L-MESSAGE            PIC S9(4)    COMP.
      05   MVD-A-MESSAGE            PIC X.
      05   MVD-D-MESSAGE            PIC X(79).
```

Fig. B.3 'MAPVDTL2' vendor add and change detail symbolic map.

```
 **************************************************************
 *       'MAPVDTL2'   VENDOR ADD & CHANGE DETAIL - SYMBOLIC MAP      *
 **************************************************************
 *
 01   VM-DETAIL-MAP.
      05   FILLER                   PIC X(12).
 *
      05   MVD-L-DATE               PIC S9(4)    COMP.
      05   MVD-A-DATE               PIC X.
      05   MVD-D-DATE               PIC X(8).
 *
      05   MVD-L-TIME               PIC S9(4)    COMP.
      05   MVD-A-TIME               PIC X.
      05   MVD-D-TIME               PIC X(8).
 *
      05   MVD-L-VENDOR-CODE        PIC S9(4)    COMP.
      05   MVD-A-VENDOR-CODE        PIC X.
      05   MVD-D-VENDOR-CODE        PIC X(8).
 *
      05   MVD-C-L-VENDOR-NAME      PIC S9(4)    COMP.
      05   MVD-C-A-VENDOR-NAME      PIC X.
      05   MVD-C-D-VENDOR-NAME      PIC X(5).
 *
      05   MVD-L-VENDOR-NAME        PIC S9(4)    COMP.
      05   MVD-A-VENDOR-NAME        PIC X.
      05   MVD-D-VENDOR-NAME        PIC X(25).
 *
```

Fig. B.3 *Continued.*

```
        05   MVD-C-L-PHONE            PIC S9(4)    COMP.
        05   MVD-C-A-PHONE            PIC X.
        05   MVD-C-D-PHONE            PIC X(6).
*
        05   MVD-L-PHONE-AREA-CD      PIC S9(4)    COMP.
        05   MVD-A-PHONE-AREA-CD      PIC X.
        05   MVD-D-PHONE-AREA-CD      PIC XXX.
*
        05   MVD-L-PHONE-1            PIC S9(4)    COMP.
        05   MVD-A-PHONE-1            PIC X.
        05   MVD-D-PHONE-1            PIC XXX.
*
        05   MVD-L-PHONE-2            PIC S9(4)    COMP.
        05   MVD-A-PHONE-2            PIC X.
        05   MVD-D-PHONE-2            PIC X(4).
*
        05   MVD-L-CONTACT            PIC S9(4)    COMP.
        05   MVD-A-CONTACT            PIC X.
        05   MVD-D-CONTACT            PIC X(25).
*
        05   MVD-C-L-STREET           PIC S9(4)    COMP.
        05   MVD-C-A-STREET           PIC X.
        05   MVD-C-D-STREET           PIC X(17).
*
        05   MVD-L-STREET             PIC S9(4)    COMP.
        05   MVD-A-STREET             PIC X.
        05   MVD-D-STREET             PIC X(20).
*
        05   MVD-C-L-CITY             PIC S9(4)    COMP.
        05   MVD-C-A-CITY             PIC X.
        05   MVD-C-D-CITY             PIC X(5).
*
        05   MVD-L-CITY               PIC S9(4)    COMP.
        05   MVD-A-CITY               PIC X.
        05   MVD-D-CITY               PIC X(18).
*
        05   MVD-C-L-STATE            PIC S9(4)    COMP.
        05   MVD-C-A-STATE            PIC X.
        05   MVD-C-D-STATE            PIC X(6).
*
        05   MVD-L-STATE-CODE         PIC S9(4)    COMP.
        05   MVD-A-STATE-CODE         PIC X.
        05   MVD-D-STATE-CODE         PIC XX.
*
        05   MVD-L-STATE-NAME         PIC S9(4)    COMP.
        05   MVD-A-STATE-NAME         PIC X.
        05   MVD-D-STATE-NAME         PIC X(14).
*
        05   MVD-C-L-ZIP-CODE         PIC S9(4)    COMP.
        05   MVD-C-A-ZIP-CODE         PIC X.
        05   MVD-C-D-ZIP-CODE         PIC X(4).
*
        05   MVD-L-ZIP-CODE           PIC S9(4)    COMP.
        05   MVD-A-ZIP-CODE           PIC X.
        05   MVD-D-ZIP-CODE           PIC X(5).
*
        05   MVD-L-ATTENTION-OF       PIC S9(4)    COMP.
        05   MVD-A-ATTENTION-OF       PIC X.
        05   MVD-D-ATTENTION-OF       PIC X(20).
*
        05   MVD-L-MESSAGE            PIC S9(4)    COMP.
        05   MVD-A-MESSAGE            PIC X.
        05   MVD-D-MESSAGE            PIC X(79).
```

```
************************************************************
*    'MAPVMCTL'    VENDOR MAINTENANCE CONTROL - SYMBOLIC MAP    *
************************************************************
*
01  VM-CONTROL-MAP.
    05  FILLER              PIC X(12).
*
    05  MVC-L-DATE          PIC S9(4)    COMP.
    05  MVC-A-DATE          PIC X.
    05  MVC-D-DATE          PIC X(8).
*
    05  MVC-L-TIME          PIC S9(4)    COMP.
    05  MVC-A-TIME          PIC X.
    05  MVC-D-TIME          PIC X(8).
*
    05  MVC-L-VEND-CD-1     PIC S9(4)    COMP.
    05  MVC-A-VEND-CD-1     PIC X.
    05  MVC-D-VEND-CD-1     PIC X.
*
    05  MVC-L-VEND-CD-2     PIC S9(4)    COMP.
    05  MVC-A-VEND-CD-2     PIC X.
    05  MVC-D-VEND-CD-2     PIC X(4).
*
    05  MVC-L-VEND-CD-3     PIC S9(4)    COMP.
    05  MVC-A-VEND-CD-3     PIC X.
    05  MVC-D-VEND-CD-3     PIC X.
*
    05  MVC-L-MESSAGE       PIC S9(4)    COMP.
    05  MVC-A-MESSAGE       PIC X.
    05  MVC-D-MESSAGE       PIC X(79).
```

Fig. B.4 'MAPVMCTL' vendor maintenance control—symbolic map.

```
************************************************************
*    'POWSVMCA'    PURCHASING SYSTEM - VENDOR COMMAREA    *
************************************************************
*
01  WS-COMMAREA.
    05  CA-FUNCTION-CODE    PIC X           VALUE SPACE.
        88  CA-INQUIRY                      VALUE 'I'.
        88  CA-ADDITION                     VALUE 'A'.
        88  CA-CHANGE                       VALUE 'C'.
        88  CA-DELETE                       VALUE 'D'.
        88  CA-BROWSE                       VALUE 'B'.
*
    05  CA-MAP-CONTROL      PIC X           VALUE SPACE.
        88  CA-RECEIVE-CTL-MAP              VALUE '1'.
        88  CA-RECEIVE-DTL-MAP              VALUE '2'.
*
    05  CA-VENDOR-CODE.
        10  CA-VEND-1       PIC X           VALUE LOW-VALUES.
        10  CA-VEND-2       PIC X(4)        VALUE LOW-VALUES.
        10  CA-VEND-3       PIC X           VALUE LOW-VALUES.
```

Fig. B.5 'POWSVMCA' purchasing system—vendor COMMAREA.

```
****************************************************************
*  'STLNKCWA'  - COMMON WORK AREA (CWA)  - LINKAGE SECTION ENTRY *
*       GENERALLY USED WITH:  'STWSDTTM' AND 'STPDDTTM' COPIES    *
****************************************************************
*
 01  CWA-DATA.
     05  CWA-CURRENT-DATE        PIC X(8).
*        MM/DD/YY
     05  CWA-ALPHA-DATA          PIC X(18).
*        E.G.  SEPTEMBER 10, 1985
     05  CWA-DATE-MMDDYY         PIC X(6).
     05  CWA-DATE-YYMMDD         PIC X(6).
     05  CWA-COMPANY-NAME        PIC X(25).
```

Fig. B.6 'STLNKCWA'—common work area (CWA).

```
****************************************************************
*         'STPDDTTM'  - COMMON DATE/TIME FORMATTING ROUTINE     *
*  RETRIEVE CURRENT DATE FROM CWA - FORMAT EIBTIME TO 'HH.MM.SS' *
*  COPY 'STWSDTTM' INTO WORKING STORAGE FOR REQUIRED WS- FIELDS  *
*  COPY 'STLNKCWA' INTO LINKAGE SECTION UNDER BLL-CELLS          *
*                DEFINE:  BLL-CWA-ADDRESS                        *
****************************************************************
*
        EXEC CICS ASSIGN
                CWALENG (WS-CWA-LENGTH)
        END-EXEC.
*
        IF WS-CWA-LENGTH  IS GREATER THAN  ZERO
            EXEC CICS ADDRESS
                    CWA (BLL-CWA-ADDRESS)
            END-EXEC
*
*           SERVICE RELOAD CWA-DATA
*
            MOVE CWA-CURRENT-DATE  TO  WS-CURRENT-DATE
        ELSE
            MOVE 'ERRORCWA'         TO  WS-CURRENT-DATE.
*
* FORMAT TIME TO 'HH.MM.SS'
        MOVE EIBTIME     TO   WS-EIB-TIME.
        MOVE WS-EIB-HH   TO   WS-MAP-HH.
        MOVE WS-EIB-MM   TO   WS-MAP-MM.
        MOVE WS-EIB-SS   TO   WS-MAP-SS.
```

Fig. B.7 'STPDDTTM'—common date/time formatting routine.

Fig. B.8 'STPDT034' load and search state code table.

```
****************************************************************
*         'STPDT037'      LOAD AND SEARCH STATE CODE TABLE      *
*      GOOD HIT:    STATE NAME IS RETURNED IN WS-STATE-NAME     *
*                   WS-STATE-SEARCH-STATUS = 'G'                *
*      NOT FOUND: ALL  '*'  ARE RETURNED IN WS-STATE-NAME       *
*                   WS-STATE-SEARCH-STATUS = 'E'                *
*   COPY 'STWST037' INTO WORKING STORAGE FOR REQUIRED FIELDS    *
*   COPY 'T037STAT' INTO LINKAGE SECTION FOR STATE TABLE        *
*                DEFINE:  BLL-T037-STATE-TABLE-ADDRESS          *
****************************************************************
*
        EXEC CICS LOAD
                PROGRAM ('T037LOAD')
                SET     (BLL-T037-STATE-TABLE-ADDRESS)
        END-EXEC.
```

Fig. B.8 *Continued.*

```
*
*      SERVICE RELOAD T037-STATE-TABLE.
*
       SET T037-INDEX  TO  1.
       SEARCH T037-STATE-ENTRIES
           AT END
               MOVE 'E'      TO  WS-STATE-SEARCH-STATUS
               MOVE ALL '*'  TO  WS-STATE-NAME
           WHEN
               WS-STATE-CODE  =  T037-STATE-CODE (T037-INDEX)
               MOVE 'G'      TO  WS-STATE-SEARCH-STATUS
               MOVE T037-STATE-NAME (T037-INDEX)  TO  WS-STATE-NAME.
*
       EXEC CICS RELEASE
               PROGRAM ('T037LOAD')
       END-EXEC.



**************************************************************
* 'STWSATTR'   STANDARD ATTRIBUTE LIST USED BY THIS INSTALLATION *
**************************************************************
*
 01  ATTRIBUTE-LIST.
     05  UNPROT-NORM            PIC X      VALUE SPACE.
     05  UNPROT-FSET            PIC X      VALUE 'A'.
     05  UNPROT-BRT             PIC X      VALUE 'H'.
     05  UNPROT-BRT-FSET        PIC X      VALUE 'I'.
     05  UNPROT-DRK             PIC X      VALUE '<'.
     05  UNPROT-DRK-FSET        PIC X      VALUE '('.
     05  UNPROT-NUM             PIC X      VALUE '&'.
     05  UNPROT-NUM-FSET        PIC X      VALUE 'J'.
     05  UNPROT-BRT-NUM         PIC X      VALUE 'Q'.
     05  UNPROT-BRT-NUM-FSET    PIC X      VALUE 'R'.
     05  UNPROT-DRK-NUM         PIC X      VALUE '*'.
     05  UNPROT-DRK-NUM-FSET    PIC X      VALUE ')'.
     05  ASKIP-NORM             PIC X      VALUE '0'.
     05  ASKIP-FSET             PIC X      VALUE '1'.
     05  ASKIP-BRT              PIC X      VALUE '8'.
     05  ASKIP-BRT-FSET         PIC X      VALUE '9'.
     05  ASKIP-DRK              PIC X      VALUE '@'.
     05  ASKIP-DRK-FSET         PIC X      VALUE QUOTE.
```

Fig. B.9 'STWSATTR' standard attribute list used by this installation.

Fig. B.10 'STWSDTTM' working storage for date/time editing.

```
**************************************************************
*      'STWSDTTM'  WORKING STORAGE FOR:  DATE/TIME EDITING      *
*    DATE IS RETRIEVED FROM THE CWA AND TIME FROM EIBTIME       *
* COPY 'STPDDTTM' INTO PROCEDURE DIVISION FOR FORMATTING LOGIC  *
* COPY 'STLNKCWA' INTO LINKAGE SECTION FOR CWA AREA             *
**************************************************************
*
 01  WS-DATE-AND-TIME.
     05  WS-CURRENT-DATE        PIC X(8)          VALUE SPACES.
*
     05  WS-MAP-TIME.
         10  WS-MAP-HH          PIC XX            VALUE 'HH'.
         10  FILLER             PIC X             VALUE '.'.
         10  WS-MAP-MM          PIC XX            VALUE 'MM'.
         10  FILLER             PIC X             VALUE '.'.
         10  WS-MAP-SS          PIC XX            VALUE 'SS'.
*
```

Fig. B.10 *Continued.*

```
      05  WS-EIB-TIME              PIC 9(6)            VALUE ZEROES.
      05 FILLER    REDEFINES   WS-EIB-TIME.
          10   WS-EIB-HH            PIC XX.
          10   WS-EIB-MM            PIC XX.
          10   WS-EIB-SS            PIC XX.
*
  01  WS-CWA-LENGTH              PIC S9(4)    COMP    VALUE ZEROES.



********************************************************************
*       'STWSSTAT'   COMMON PROGRAM STATUS FIELDS              *
********************************************************************
*
  01  WS-STATUS-FIELDS.
      05   STATUS-OF-RECEIVE       PIC X               VALUE SPACE.
          88   GOOD-RECEIVE                            VALUE 'G'.
          88   RETURN-TO-CTL-MAP                       VALUE 'C'.
          88   INVALID-KEY-PRESSED                     VALUE 'I'.
          88   MAPFAIL-ON-RECEIVE                      VALUE 'M'.
*
      05   STATUS-OF-SELECTION     PIC X               VALUE SPACE.
          88   VALID-SELECTION                         VALUE 'G'.
          88   INVALID-SELECTION                       VALUE 'E'.
*
      05   STATUS-OF-FORMAT        PIC X               VALUE SPACE.
          88   VALID-FORMAT                            VALUE 'G'.
          88   INVALID-FORMAT                          VALUE 'E'.
*
      05   STATUS-OF-READ          PIC X               VALUE SPACE.
          88   RECORD-RETRIEVED                        VALUE 'G'.
          88   RECORD-NOT-FOUND                        VALUE 'E'.
          88   END-OF-FILE                             VALUE 'F'.
*
      05   STATUS-OF-VERIFY        PIC X               VALUE SPACE.
          88   GOOD-VERIFY                             VALUE 'G'.
          88   VERIFY-ERROR                            VALUE 'E'.
*
      05   STATUS-OF-DELETE        PIC X               VALUE SPACE.
          88   GOOD-DELETE                             VALUE 'G'.
          88   RECORD-NOT-DELETED                      VALUE 'E'.
*
      05   STATUS-OF-CHANGE        PIC X               VALUE SPACE.
          88   GOOD-CHANGE                             VALUE 'G'.
          88   RECORD-NOT-CHANGED                      VALUE 'E'.
*
      05   STATUS-OF-EDIT          PIC X               VALUE SPACE.
          88   GOOD-EDIT                               VALUE 'G'.
          88   ERROR-ON-EDIT                           VALUE 'E'.
*
      05   STATUS-OF-WRITE         PIC X               VALUE SPACE.
          88   GOOD-WRITE                              VALUE 'G'.
          88   DUPLICATE-RECORD                        VALUE 'E'.
*
      05   STATUS-OF-ADD           PIC X               VALUE SPACE.
          88   GOOD-ADD                                VALUE 'G'.
          88   RECORD-NOT-ADDED                        VALUE 'E'.
*
      05   STATUS-OF-BROWSE        PIC X               VALUE SPACE.
          88   GOOD-STARTBR                            VALUE 'G'.
          88   BROWSE-NOTFND                           VALUE 'E'.
```

Fig. B.11 'STWSSAT' common program status fields.

```
**********************************************************************
*       'STWST037'   STATE CODE AND NAME WORKING STORAGE ENTRIES     *
*       COPY 'T037STAT' INTO LINKAGE SECTION FOR STATE TABLE         *
*       COPY 'STPDT037' INTO PROCEDURE DIVISION FOR SEARCH LOGIC     *
**********************************************************************
*
 01  WS-STATE-CODE-SEARCH-ENTRIES.
     05  WS-STATE-CODE           PIC XX.
     05  WS-STATE-NAME           PIC X(14).
     05  WS-STATE-SEARCH-STATUS  PIC X           VALUE SPACE.
         88  STATE-FOUND                         VALUE 'G'.
         88  STATE-NOT-FOUND                     VALUE 'E'.
```

Fig. B.12 'STWST037' state code and name working storage entries.

```
**********************************************************************
* 'T037STAT' - STATE CODE AND NAME TABLE - LINKAGE SECTION ENTRY *
* COPY 'STWST037' INTO WORKING STORAGE FOR REQUIRED WS- FIELDS   *
* COPY 'STPDT037' INTO PROCEDURE DIVISION FOR SEARCH LOGIC       *
**********************************************************************
*
 01  T037-STATE-TABLE.
     05  T037-STATE-ENTRIES
         OCCURS 50 TIMES
         INDEXED BY   T037-INDEX.
         10  T037-STATE-CODE     PIC XX.
         10  T037-STATE-NAME     PIC X(14).
```

Fig. B.13 'TO37STAT' state code name table.

Fig. B.14 'VENDMAST' vendor master record.

```
**********************************************************************
*       'VENDMAST'   VENDOR MASTER RECORD   -   169 BYTES LONG       *
**********************************************************************
*
 01  VENDOR-MASTER-RECORD.
     05  VM-VENDOR-CODE.
         10  VM-VEND-CD-1        PIC X.
         10  VM-VEND-CD-2        PIC X(4).
         10  VM-VEND-CD-3        PIC X.
     05  VM-VENDOR-NAME          PIC X(25).
     05  VM-STREET-ADDRESS       PIC X(20).
     05  VM-CITY-STATE-ZIP.
         10  VM-CITY-STATE.
             15  VM-CITY         PIC X(18).
             15  VM-STATE        PIC XX.
         10  VM-ZIP-CODE         PIC X(5).
     05  VM-TO-ATTN-OF           PIC X(20).
     05  VM-PHONE-NO.
         10  VM-AREA-CD          PIC XXX.
         10  VM-PHONE-1-3        PIC XXX.
         10  VM-PHONE-4-7        PIC X(4).
     05  VM-CONTACT              PIC X(25).
     05  VM-DOLLARS-COMMITTED    PIC S9(7)V99    COMP-3.
     05  FILLER                  PIC X(33).
*
**********************************************************************
*       WORKING STORAGE FIELDS USED FOR EDITING OF VENDOR CODE      *
**********************************************************************
*
```

Fig. B.14 *Continued.*

```
01  WS-VENDOR-CODE.
    05  WS-VENDOR-CD-1        PIC X           VALUE SPACE.
    05  FILLER               PIC X           VALUE '-'.
    05  WS-VENDOR-CD-2        PIC X(4)        VALUE SPACES.
    05  FILLER               PIC X           VALUE '-'.
    05  WS-VENDOR-CD-3        PIC X           VALUE SPACE.
```

Response code (EIBRESP) Values

This appendix consists of a list of response code (EIBRESP) fields. EIBRESP, an EIB field, is returned to a programmer-defined field when the RESP option is included on a CICS command as described in chapter 5. The response code is returned in a full-word binary field, such as WS-RESP, and can be tested following execution of the command. The response code indicates the condition that was returned when a CICS command was executed. The RESP option practically eliminates the need to use HANDLE CONDITION commands. Response codes function similarly to status codes, which are used with batch VSAM statements. Figure C.1 shows an example.

```
01  WS-RESP          PIC S9(8)    COMP    VALUE ZEROES.

    . . .

    EXEC CICS . . .
              . . .
              RESP (WS-RESP)
    END-EXEC.

    IF WS-RESP  =  DFHRESP (NORMAL)
        NEXT SENTENCE
    ELSE
        IF WS-RESP  =  DFHRESP (response)
          . . .
        ELSE
           PERFORM error processing.
```

Fig. C.1 RESP option example.

Condition	Value	Condition	Value
NORMAL	00	QBUSY	25
NOTFND	13	ITEMERR	26
DUPREC	14	PGMIDERR	27
INVREQ	16	ENDDATA	29
NOSPACE	18	MAPFAIL	36
NOTOPEN	19	QIDERR	44
ENDFILE	20	ENQBUSY	55
LENGERR	22	DISABLED	84
QZERO	23		

Fig. C.2 The most common response conditions and their
related values.

Bibliography

Computer Associates Publications (Check with Computer Associates for latest version, release, and order number because they change periodically.) CA-DATACOM/DB Programming Guide and Reference, and CA-DATACOM/DB SQL Programming Guide and Reference.

International Business Machines Corporation Publications. (Check with IBM for latest version, release, and order number because they change periodically.) CICS/ESA Application Programmer's Reference, CICS/ESA Application Programming Guide, CICS Application Programming Primer VS COBOL II, IBM DATABASE2 Application Programming Guide for CICS/OS/VS Users, IBM DATABASE2 Introduction to SQL, IBM DATABASE2 Reference, IBM DATABASE2 SQL Learner's Guide, VS COBOL II Application Programming: Language Reference, IMS/ESA Version 3 Application Programming: Design Guide, IMS/ESA Version 3 Application Programming: DL/I Calls, and IMS/ESA Version 3 Application Programming: EXEC DLI Commands

Jatich, Alida M. 1991. *CICS Command Level Programming*. New York: Wiley.

Le Bert, Joseph J. 1989. *CICS for Microcomputers*. New York, NY: McGraw-Hill.

_____. 1986. *CICS Made Easy*. New York, NY: McGraw-Hill.

Lowe, Doug. 1987. *The CICS Programmer's Desk Reference*. Fresno, CA: Mike Murach & Associates.

Prince, Ann. 1988. *VS COBOL II: A Guide for Programmers & Managers*. Fresno, CA: Mike Murach & Associates.

Ranade, Jay and Hirday Ranade. 1986. *VSAM Concepts, Programming, and Design*. New York, NY: Macmillan Publishing Company.

Wipfler, Arlene. 1987. *CICS Application Development and Programming*. New York, NY: Macmillan Publishing Company.

Index

ABOUT THE AUTHOR

Joseph LeBert has more than 25 years of programming, analysis, and design experience in data processing. He has published two books with McGraw-Hill, *CICS Made Easy* and *CICS for Microcomputers*. He is also the author of *Advanced Interactive COBOL for Micros* (Prentice-Hall, 1988). He has played a major role in the development, programming, and maintenance of online and batch systems at many major corporations. He resides in Ridgewood, New Jersey.